Psychoanalytic Knowledge

Psychoanalytic Knowledge

Edited by

Man Cheung Chung
Principal Lecturer in Psychology, The University of Plymouth, UK

and

Colin Feltham
Reader in Counselling, Sheffield Hallam University, UK

palgrave
macmillan

First published 2003 by
PALGRAVE MACMILLAN
Houndmills, Basingstoke, Hampshire RG21 6XS and
175 Fifth Avenue, New York, N.Y. 10010
Companies and representatives throughout the world

PALGRAVE MACMILLAN is the global academic imprint of the Palgrave Macmillan division of St. Martin's Press, LLC and of Palgrave Macmillan Ltd. Macmillan® is a registered trademark in the United States, United Kingdom and other countries. Palgrave is a registered trademark in the European Union and other countries.

ISBN 0–333–97391–7 hardback

This book is printed on paper suitable for recycling and made from fully managed and sustained forest sources.

A catalogue record for this book is available from the British Library.

Library of Congress Cataloging-in-Publication Data

Psychoanalytic knowledge / edited by Man Cheung Chung & Colin Feltham.
p. cm.
Includes bibliographical references and index.
ISBN 0–333–97391–7
1. Psychoanalysis. 2. Freud, Sigmund, 1856–1939 I. Chung, Man Cheung, 1962– II. Feltham, Colin, 1950–

BF173.P7763 2003
150.19′6—dc21

2003051969

10 9 8 7 6 5 4 3 2 1
12 11 10 09 08 07 06 05 04 03

Printed and bound in Great Britain by
Antony Rowe Ltd, Chippenham and Eastbourne

On behalf of the contributors, the editors would like to pay tribute to Professor İlham Dilman, who sadly passed away in January 2003, during the compilation of this book. His important contribution to this book, and indeed to the academic community as a whole, has been invaluable and will be remembered for years to come.

Contents

Acknowledgements ix

Notes on the Contributors x

1. Examining the Nature of Psychoanalytic Knowledge 1
   Man Cheung Chung
2. Kant and Freud 20
   Andrew Brook
3. Psychoanalysis as Philosophy, Psychoanalysis as Worldview 40
   C. Fred Alford
4. 'Some Unimaginable Substratum': A Contemporary Introduction to Freud's Philosophy of Mind 54
   David Livingstone Smith
5. Freud and the Neurological Unconscious 76
   Grant Gillett
6. The Etiology of Emotion and Ossification of Self: You Can't Change People because People Don't Change 96
   Michael P. Levine
7. The Illusion of a Future 120
   W. D. Hart
8. Emotion, Evolution and Conflict 132
   James Hopkins
9. Freud, Object Relations, Agency and the Self 157
   Tamas Pataki
10. Autonomy and the Problem of Suffering: Tragedy and Transcendence in Psychoanalytic Discourse 181
    Suzanne R. Kirschner
11. The Self in Psychoanalysis: Heinz Kohut and Narcissism – a Critique 199
    İlham Dilman
12. Challenges to Psychoanalytic Methodology 219
    Malcolm Macmillan

Name Index 239

Subject Index 244

Acknowledgements

We are grateful to Wilhelm Fink Verlag for granting us permission to reprint in this book Suzanne R. Kirschner's chapter 'Autonomy and the Problem of Suffering: Tragedy and Transcendence in Psychoanalytic Discourse', which was previously published in a book titled *Die Autonome Person: Eine Europaische Erfindung?*, eds. Klaus Peter Kopping, Michael Welker and Reiner Wiehl (Wilhelm Fink, 2002).

Notes on the Contributors

C. Fred Alford is Professor of Government and Distinguished Scholar-Teacher at the University of Maryland, College Park. He is author of a dozen books on moral psychology, including *Melanie Klein and Critical Social Theory* (Yale, 1989). His most recent book is *Levinas, the Frankfurt School, and Psychoanalysis* (Wesleyan University Press and Continuum Books, 2002).

Andrew Brook is Professor of Philosophy and Director of the Institute of Interdisciplinary Studies at Carleton University, Ottawa. He is past-president of the Canadian Philosophical Association. He is author, co-author or editor of six books and has about 60 publications in all. He is a licensed psychoanalyst, one expression of a very long-standing interest in making philosophical ideas and methods relevant in practice life.

Man Cheung Chung is a Principal Lecturer in the Department of Psychology at the University of Plymouth. His research interests include history and philosophy of psychology and health/clinical psychology. He has published some 100 articles and chapters in the foregoing areas as well as on other diverse topics. In addition to the present book, he is also editing volumes pertaining to phenomenology, schizophrenia and reasoning.

İlham Dilman was, until recently, a Professor Emeritus of Philosophy at the University of Wales, Swansea. He published 19 books and over 70 papers and articles on a wide range of philosophical topics, including psychoanalysis. His works on Freud include *Freud and Human Nature* (1983), *Freud and the Mind* (1984) and *Freud, Insight and Change* (1988). Shortly after the completion of his chapter for the present book, Professor Dilman passed away unexpectedly in January 2003.

Grant Gillett is a Professor of Medical Ethics at the University of Otago in Dunedin, New Zealand. He is also a practising neurosurgeon. His main philosophical work is in the philosophy of mind and psychiatry, though he also writes on topics in bioethics. His most recent books are *The Mind and Its Discontents* (1999) and he has co-authored *Medical Ethics* (2001) and *Consciousness and Intentionality* (2001). He is interested in postmodern and traditional analytic approaches to bioethics, mind and language, and psychiatry.

W. D. Hart took his PhD from Harvard University in philosophy in 1969. He has taught at the University of Michigan, University College London, the University of New Mexico and the University of Illinois at Chicago, where he has been chair of the philosophy department since 1994. He began his work in logic and philosophy of mathematics, but this spread into metaphysics and epistemology, and since about 1970 has included an interest in Freud and psychoanalysis. He published *The Engines of the Soul* in 1988, edited an anthology on philosophy of mathematics that came out in 1996, and has published about 40 papers.

James Hopkins is Reader in Philosophy at King's College London. He has published a number of articles on the epistemology of psychoanalysis and edited two collections of essays: *Philosophical Essays on Freud*, with Richard Wollheim (Cambridge University Press, 1982) and *Psychoanalysis, Mind and Art*, with Anthony Savile (Blackwell, 1992).

Suzanne R. Kirschner is Associate Professor of Psychology at the College of the Holy Cross in Worcester, Massachusetts. She has published a number of articles on the philosophy, history and anthropology of psychology and psychoanalysis, as well as a book, *The Religious and Romantic Origins of Psychoanalysis: Individuation and Integration in Post-Freudian Theory* (Cambridge University Press, 1996). Recent publications include an ethnographic study of clinicians' reactions to managed mental health care ('Managing Managed Care: Habitus, Hysteresis and the End(s) of Psychotherapy', with W. Lachicotte), and the entry on 'Post-Modern Psychology' in the *Oxford Encyclopedia of Psychology*. She is currently working on a project in which she contrasts psychoanalytic and biobehavioural understandings of personality and 'normality', and explores the social and cultural implications of the rise of contemporary temperament theory in psychology.

Michael P. Levine is Professor of Philosophy at the University of Western Australia and Weismann Distinguished Professor at Baruch College, City University of New York. Recent publications include *Pantheism* (1994); *The Analytic Freud: Philosophy and Psychoanalysis* (ed., 2000); *Integrity and Fragile Self* (with Damian Cox and Marguerite La Caze, 2003); *Racism in Mind* (ed. with Tamas Pataki, 2003).

Malcolm Macmillan has worked in the University of Melbourne and Monash University. He is now an Adjunct-Professor in the School of Psychology at Deakin University. His *Freud Evaluated: The Completed Arc* earned him a Monash DSc in 1992. He is a Fellow of the Australian and American Psychological Societies and has been president of the former. In addition to his work on Freud, he has also published widely in areas such as brain localisation and injury and intellectual disability.

Tamas Pataki is Honorary Senior Fellow in the Department of Philosophy, University of Melbourne, where he also currently lectures, and Honorary Fellow, Deakin University. He has taught in universities in Australia and Hungary and has published articles on the philosophy of mind, psychoanalysis, moral philosophy and aesthetics as well as many popular pieces and reviews. He has a long-standing interest in psychoanalysis and psychiatry. His forthcoming book, co-edited with Michael Levine, is *Racism in Mind* (Cornell, 2003).

David Livingstone Smith is Director of the New England Institute for Cognitive Science and Evolutionary Psychology, and visiting associate professor of philosophy at the University of New England. His publications include *Freud's Philosophy of the Unconscious* (Kluwer, 1999), *Approaching Psychoanalysis* (Karnac, 1999), *Psychoanalysis in Focus* (Sage, 2003) as well as numerous papers in scientific and philosophical journals. He is currently researching the evolutionary psychology of deception, self-deception and unconscious perception; the epistemological implications of unconscious knowledge; and the evolutionary psychology of incest. His forthcoming book, *Natural Born Liars: Evolution, Deception and the Unconscious*, is published by St. Martin's Press.

1
Examining the Nature of Psychoanalytic Knowledge

Man Cheung Chung

This book is concerned with the nature of psychoanalytic knowledge. Why is a new book on this topic justified? The answer is partly reflected by Neu's remark:

> Freud's influence continues to be enormous and pervasive. He gave us a new and powerful way to think about and investigate human thought, action and interaction. He made sense of ranges of experience generally neglected or misunderstood. And while one might wish to reject or argue with some of Freud's particular interpretations and theories, his writings and his insights are too compelling to simply turn away. There is still much to be learned from Freud. (Neu, 1991, p. 1)

Indeed, due to Freud's enormous and pervasive influence[1] on many aspects of our cultures, our ways of thinking, writings and insights, it would be foolish to claim that there is nothing more we can learn from him. Hence, the present book.

To embark on a project which aims to explore the nature of psychoanalytic knowledge is a difficult task. One reason for such difficulty is the absence of any *one psychoanalysis* of the kind that Freud insisted on, when he was constructing psychoanalytic knowledge. That is, Freud believed that he was the only person or authority who could *validate* and *justify* contributions which claimed to be part of psychoanalysis. Over the past few decades, however, psychoanalytic knowledge has grown so substantially that, if Freud were alive, he probably would have been shocked by and possibly distraught at the increasingly diverse ways in which we now understand, discuss and debate psychoanalysis. Today, the view that there is only one psychoanalysis or one type of psychoanalytic knowledge is scarcely held, as Schwartz remarked:

> I think we no longer have to treat Freud as a father but can treat him as a colleague, as the first theorist of the analytic hour. I think we are now

> mature enough to begin to look for ways to engage each other's metaphors and to handle all the difficult and threatening feelings that must inevitably accompany a search for deeper understanding of ourselves, of our place in the world and of our capacity for change.
>
> (Schwartz, 1996, p. 63)

One way to ease the difficulty of this task is to confine ourselves to a particular approach and to concentrate on selected topics which bear relevance to psychoanalytic knowledge. The approach we take is philosophical in nature. We align ourselves with the idea that psychoanalysis is intimately related to philosophy. As Cavell suggests, 'psychoanalytic theory might better be read as philosophy, illuminating as it does conceptual issues about the nature of mind and thought' (Cavell, 1988, p. 859). Primarily, we aim to explore the nature of psychoanalytic knowledge in the light of contemporary philosophical views or critiques of a diversity of topics relevant to it. These topics are the philosophy of mind, the notion of changing oneself, religion, interdisciplinary links with psychoanalytic knowledge, post-Freudian psychoanalytic knowledge, and challenges to psychoanalytic methodology. The diversity in the topics that we cover, of course, reveals the profound nature of psychoanalytic knowledge. We set the scene for our chosen path of philosophical exploration by our opening chapter which demonstrates one example of the influence of philosophy on the formation of psychoanalytic knowledge, followed by another chapter investigating the general relationship between philosophy and psychoanalysis.

1. Scene-setting: the influence of philosophy on the formation of psychoanalytic knowledge and seeing psychoanalysis as philosophy

Various attempts have been made to demonstrate the influence of philosophical ideas on the formation of psychoanalytic knowledge. Brentano (Wallace, 1983), Schopenhauer (Young and Brook, 1994) and Nietzsche (Gedo and Wolf, 1976; Fancher, 1977; Wallace, 1983) are among the philosophers who have played a part in the formation of psychoanalytic concepts. Freud was also thought to have drawn heavily in his epistemology and his philosophy of mind on the Cartesian/Lockean tradition (Nasser, 1994). Parallels have also been made between Freud and Socrates and Plato (Lear, 1998). A recent claim holds that the birth of psychoanalysis as a plausible way of understanding the working of the human mind has a methodological origin in the early Greek concept of techne (Vassalli, 2001).

To extend this approach, Andrew Brook, in Chapter 2, examines the influence of Kantian philosophical ideas on the formation of psychoanalytic knowledge. According to Brook, Freud seldom mentioned that Kant's model of the mind was antecedent to some of his own ideologies. This could be because Kant's model was very much taken for granted among German-speaking intellectuals at the time as being largely correct. Thus, Freud may well have thought that there was no reason to conceptualise psychic life in any other way. Brook argues that Freud believed in two kinds of theory of the psyche. One is concerned with the nature and management of its contents; the other with the structure and function of its subsystems in which the Kantian influences are found. These influences mainly rest in Freud's model of the subsystems of the psychic, in particular, the structural model of Id, Ego and Super-Ego. Also, Brook argues that there are close parallels between Kant's Understanding and Freud's Ego, Kant's Moral Reason and Freud's Super-Ego, and Kant's Inner Sense and Freud's Id. One can also find Kantian influences in Freud's theory of the relation of consciousness and language, the demarcation of the unconscious, his theory of the ego and drives as systems and of what, in them, cannot become conscious. Also, the way in which Freud saw the unconscious (its timelessness, and so on) is paralleled in Kant's doctrine of the unknowability of the noumenal, of things as they really are.

While Brook thus demonstrates the influence of philosophy on the formation of psychoanalytic knowledge, Fred Alford, in Chapter 3, glances at the general relationship between philosophy and psychoanalysis by asking the question: What if we considered psychoanalytic theory as though it were a philosophy? To do so, Alford argues, would only work for such psychoanalytic thinkers as Freud, Klein and Lacan. Alford goes on to portray the kinds of philosophical stories that they tell us. These stories move from Athens to Jerusalem to postmodernism: from faith in reason (Freud), to an account of salvation through reparation (Klein), and finally to an account that expresses serious misgivings about humanism in all its guises (Lacan). Through these stories, Alford argues, the philosophical implications of psychoanalytic knowledge are clear. He concludes by saying that psychoanalysis is a worldview, that is, a comprehensive account of humanity's nature and place in the universe.

2. Psychoanalytic knowledge: philosophy of mind

Having set the scene, we now turn our attention to the primary aim of the book, and examine the nature of psychoanalytic knowledge in terms of contemporary philosophical views on relevant topics. Since one of the main functions of psychoanalysis is to investigate mental life, it is thus natural that one of the main topics which is relevant to psychoanalytic knowledge and which concerns contemporary philosophers and psychologists is the philosophy of mind. Freud's understanding of the mind is profound, and is, according to some recent claims, associated intimately with what we now call cognitive science and neuroscience (for example, see Bilder and LeFever, 1998). This association, some scholars predict, will only become stronger in the future development of psychoanalytic knowledge (Brakel, 1997). Investigation of this association can be seen as a good opportunity for psychoanalysis to reclaim its scientific status (Moraitis, 2000), given the recent challenges to the latter (see later discussion). However, no one would underestimate the difficulties ahead in developing psychoanalytic knowledge as a joint venture between psychoanalysis and cognitive/neuroscience. Why? One simple reason is that psychoanalysis and neuroscience essentially have separate objects of study, and as such, different methods of investigation. Thus, the knowledge that they generate will probably be quite different in essence (Solms, 2000, p. 180).

If Freud were alive, he would not have been too surprised on discovering a relationship between psychoanalysis and cognitive/neuroscience. This is because as part of his attempt to construct psychoanalytic knowledge back in the 1890s, Freud in fact recognised and sought to investigate this relationship. When Freud was at the University of Vienna, he studied many of the subjects that now constitute neuroscience and this undoubtedly influenced his psychoanalytic thinking. His published works on neuroscience included, for example, work on aphasia (Freud, 1891). During his investigation into aphasia, he became intrigued by the profound relationship between body and mind, partly due to reading the works of John Hughlings Jackson, a British neuroscientist and a mind–body dualist. However, Freud later relinquished the doctrine of dualism,[2] pursuing the doctrine of materialism in its stead. Freud's approach to materialism was very much influenced by his teachers, in particular, Ernst Brücke.

Prior to his self-analysis of 1897, Freud set out on a very ambitious project which aimed to discover the foundations of a complete interdisciplinary neuroscience of the mind, in *Project for a Scientific Psychology* (1895). The Project hoped to describe a functional model of the nervous system and to explain psychic phenomena in terms of it. His investigative methods were mainly based on his own imagination and speculation. However, he never fulfilled his ambition. The Project was never published, being abandoned in 1896 or 1897. The failure to see it through to completion was probably due to the limited knowledge of the brain, evolutionary biology and indeed neuroscience at the time. As part of his self-analysis of 1897, Freud shifted his focus from neuroscience to psychological phenomena (that is, metapsychology), in particular, the notion of the unconscious. He no longer wanted to explain psychological phenomena in a neurological manner (Bernfeld, 1944; Jones, 1953; Strachey, 1955). Is this true? Some scholars have argued that Freud in fact never really relinquished the neuroscientific model characterised in the Project, and as such, never stopped looking at psychological phenomena in a neurological manner. Freud's metapsychology was arguably composed of earlier neurological concepts, hidden behind psychological terminology (Amacher, 1965; Brook, 1998; Holt, 1965). The debate continues. In developing psychoanalytic knowledge, Freud is now considered to have taken an approach characterised metaphysically by materialism, neurologically by reductionism (for example, Bernfeld, 1944; Jones, 1953; Amacher, 1965; Solomon, 1974), methodologically by interactionalism-dualism (for example, Kanzer, 1973; Silverstein, 1989; Silverstein and Silverstein, 1990), and characterised by parallelism (for example, Jones, 1953; Marx, 1967), a token-identity approach or a dual-aspect monism (Flanagan, 1986).

The above sets a very rough background for the next two chapters, both concerned with the philosophy of mind. David Smith, in Chapter 4, examines Freud's approach to the mind–body problem, the nature of consciousness, unconscious cognition and the status of folk-psychology, all issues which concern contemporary philosophers and cognitive scientists. Smith provides a description of Freud's attitude towards philosophy, the main philosophical influences on his thought and how Freud's philosophical thoughts cohere with some of the best contemporary work in cognitive science. Along with other colleagues, Smith has claimed elsewhere that Freud was in fact a pioneer of cognitive science and that a connectionist model of mind (a topic in cognitive science) was proposed in Freud's Project (Erdelyi, 1985; Kitcher, 1992; Smith, 1999). Essentially, Smith, in this chapter, argues that Freud was an eliminativist, who wished to replace folk-psychological 'desire-belief' with a neuroscientific language.

Set against this intimate relationship between psychoanalysis and cognitive/neuroscience, the topic of the philosophy of mind is continued by Grant Gillett, who, in Chapter 5, conceptualises the notion of psychoanalytic knowledge as that which aims to explore the aspect of our mental life which causes us to act, not according to our own choice, approval or understanding. Gillett argues that this human phenomenon results from states and events which hide themselves deep beneath the surface of our consciousness. These states and events are driven by forces which originate either in our primitive nature or in the ontogenetic effects of upbringing. According to Gillett, Freud believed that our mind is a layer of consciousness lying over a deep unconscious which follows the laws and principles associated with the understanding of neurobiology of his time. To explore the nature of the unconscious in the light of contemporary thoughts on the philosophy of mind suggests fruitful conceptual links between what is being uncovered in psychoanalysis and the relation between consciousness and the states and events of interest to cognitive neuroscience.

3. Psychoanalytic knowledge: changing oneself?

Some people come to psychoanalysis because they have been distressed by particular problems or because they have been experiencing a sense of extreme unhappiness or emptiness for a long time. So, by coming to psychoanalysis, they are hoping or perhaps expecting to have certain aspects of themselves changed, which should enable them to feel happier about living with themselves and carrying on with their lives. But is changing ourselves possible? In examining the nature of psychoanalytic knowledge, Michael Levine, in Chapter 6, is concerned with the topic of changing or not changing oneself. According to Levine, psychoanalysis can explain and reaffirm certain aspects of our lives that surprise and challenge us, aspects which are, in hindsight, obvious to us. Psychoanalytic theory accounts for this characteristic of psychoanalytic knowledge. According to Levine, psychoanalysis is also a great equaliser. Not only does it show that there is continuum in us from the normal, relatively unproblematic neurotic to the abnormal, debilitating neurotic; it also shows how so much of what is termed the human condition is rooted in our psychological selves. Here is an example. Among our cherished beliefs are the beliefs that in fundamental ways relating to character and emotion (i) we are capable of change, and, more narcissistically, (ii) that we are capable of changing others. In this chapter, Levine is not arguing that we cannot and do not change in various ways. Nor is he arguing that we may not be instrumental in changing ourselves or others. What intrigues him, especially in relation to character, of which emotion is an important part, is why fundamental aspects of us do *not* change, or change very little. It is part of the perennial question of whether character is destiny. In relation to emotion, it turns out that the possibility of change and the manipulation of our emotional repertoire is far more significant than whether or not emotions are rational. Seeing why emotional change is problematic tells us a great deal about our lives. Indeed, much of what we expect or hope to find out in regard to the question of the rationality of emotions can be better discovered by looking at the possibility of emotional change. Questions about the rationality of emotion are linked closely to hypotheses about the etiology of emotion. There are closer links, however, between considerations of etiology and views about the ability to change emotionally.

4. Psychoanalytic knowledge: religion

Freud was intrigued by religious and spiritual phenomena and mythology throughout his life. Thus, the topic of religion plays a significant part in psychoanalytic knowledge. Freud believed that religion[3] was a disguise for some of the psychological phenomena that he wanted to uncover in his works. Freud's psychoanalytic knowledge of religion has been captured in his works *Totem and Taboo* (1912), *The Future of an Illusion* (1927), *Civilization and Its Discontents* (1930) and *Moses and Monotheism* (1939). To Freud, religious thoughts and behaviours were forms of obsessive-compulsive neuroses (for example, being obsessive with ritual procedures and details, feelings of guilt from not engaging in religious acts, feeling a need to protect ourselves from external danger or misfortune). According to Freud, people depend on religion because they are weak, crave dependence and long helplessly for the father of infantile need which they project onto a protective and omnipotent Holy Father. By depending on this Holy Father, we survive all the uncertainties, hostilities, misery, pain and chaos of the world. However, we cannot simply be passive and wait for blessing from the Holy Father. We need to please Him and earn His salvation by submitting to and following preordained divine laws and commandments. In so doing, we are promised an eternal afterlife and other blessings. Believing in and anticipating these blessings makes us fear our own death less and helps us cope better with life's difficulties. Of course, if we do not follow the laws and commandments, but violate them, we will be afraid that the Father will punish us. Thus, we grow up with fear, along with helplessness and dependence.

To Freud, all of the above are illusions and wish-fulfilments. These wishes are forms of mass delusion that believers of most religions share. To Freud, the conflict between what our own instincts demand and what our civilised life demands is immense and cannot be underestimated. According to Freud, aggression originates from the death instinct and searching for happiness is driven by the instinct to gain pleasure and avoid pain. The reality of our civilised life, however, often prevents us from having our needs satisfied. Consequently, we feel the need to dwell on illusions in which we can fulfil our needs. In Chapter 7, W. D. Hart argues that we are bound to fear death and to know that it is inevitable. This is ripe soil for wishful thinking, and hence religion. Hart traces views about religion and immortality, and then his own views about our knowledge and fear of death. Hart's critique of Freud's views on the knowledge and fear of death aims to make us less sanguine than Freud about the withering away of religion. We live, says Hart, in an age of the revenge of the id.

5. Psychoanalytic knowledge and interdisciplinary links

As Neu's quote at the beginning of this introduction states, psychoanalytic knowledge is pervasive. James Hopkins, in Chapter 8, in part seeks to illuminate this pervasive nature of psychoanalytic knowledge. Hopkins aims to show how psychoanalytic knowledge is relevant to and linked with different disciplines. According to Hopkins, if psychoanalytic findings constitute knowledge, then they should fuse with those of other disciplines. He discusses certain aspects of this fusion for evolutionary theory, social psychology, developmental psychology and neuroscience. In so doing, he argues that the theory of parental investment and recent works on affective neuroscience indicate that we should expect human emotional life to show particular continuities and discontinuities, which psychoanalysis, attachment theory and developmental psychology converge in specifying. These can be seen to include the development of in-group cohesion and out-group aggression, and hence the pattern of good *us* versus bad *them*, which underlies much human conflict. This division is produced by the psychoanalytic mechanisms of identification and projection, as these operate from early infancy, and prior to the infant's awareness of itself and others as unique and lasting beings.

6. Post-Freudian psychoanalytic knowledge

Earlier, we said that if Freud were alive, he might have been shocked, even distraught, by the increasingly diverse ways in which we now conceptualise psychoanalytic knowledge. In examining the nature of such knowledge, the following three chapters are concerned with the topic of post-Freudian psychoanalytic knowledge, characterised mainly by object-relations theory and self-psychology theory, and convey philosophical views and critiques pertinent to them.

Object-relations theory is a term coined by Fairbairn and important contributors to it include Balint, Winnicott, Guntrip, Sutherland, Bollas, Ogden, D. Scharff and J. Scharff. These theorists distinguish themselves from orthodox Freudians partly by not focusing on Freud's drive model. Infants, Freud insisted, are driven by instincts (for example, hunger, thirst and pleasure) and are unable to relate to others. They can only establish relationships with others at a later stage. In other words, satisfying their needs is primary, and developing relationships with others, secondary. On the contrary, object-relation theorists see the development of relationships with others as primary. To them, infants are driven by their desire to attach themselves to an object and develop relationships with others at an early stage of development rather than by their need to fulfil instinctual gratification. Thus, object-relation theorists put a great deal of emphasis on the dyadic relationship between mothers and infants. Our conscious and unconscious interpretations of these relationships set the basis for developing later relationships with others.

The word 'object' in object-relations theory does not mean a person. Rather, it means an internal mental structure which was formed throughout early development and through experiences with significant others (usually with the mother initially, but significant others such as the father will also become internalised at a later stage). According to object-relations theorists, to create internal mental objects for oneself requires a process called introjection, followed by another process called splitting. The reason for the splitting process is that the infant finds certain normal feelings (for example, anger) intolerable. Consequently, it has to split off, and repress, this part of itself. This repressed part of the infant can lead to projective identification, essentially a defence mechanism, which leads the infant to project its repressed part (say, anger) onto another person (say, the mother) and subsequently to identify with it there. The infant then finds itself in the paranoid-schizoid position (beginning in the first six months of the infant's life) in which it cannot distinguish the mother from the self. Some infants then move on to the depressive position (beginning when the child is eight months old), a higher level of development. At this stage, the child can take back the bad feeling (say, anger) from the mother and separate it from her. The child can then see the mother as a separate object capable of both good and bad feelings. The child can also see its own good and bad feelings. When it grows older, it will be able to feel empathy for others and will not be overwhelmed by neuroticism. To enable children to reach this higher level of development, however, mothers need to accept the child's projected feelings, or at least most of them, at the early stage of their development. Some children, however, fail to take back their projected feelings, resulting in continued splitting and preoccupation with the paranoid-schizoid position. Such development is often associated with borderline personality.

One implication from this brief explication of object-relations theory is the idea that the mind is partitive, or divided, with dissociated mental contents and activities. This partitive understanding of mind is the focus of Tamas Pataki's contribution in Chapter 9. But the idea that our mind is partitive does not originate from object-relations theorists. Since antiquity, according to Pataki, philosophers have been concerned with various partitive conceptions of the mind, some of them *strongly* partitive in the sense, roughly, that the mind or self is conceived to be divided into independent centres of agency. These conceptions of divided or dissociated mental contents and activities have been thought to be means to understand some problematic forms of mental conflict and incoherence of belief, especially those of the so-called paradoxes of irrationality, weakness of the will (akrasia) and self-deception. Pataki argues that the Freudian conception of mind is both coherent and strongly partitive, against those who have argued that it is either incoherent or non-partitive in the strong sense. Pataki links Freud's structural (partitive) theory of mind to his revolutionary work on internalised object relations. Pataki wants to argue that one of the most important achievements of Freud was his realising the importance of object-relations, of their role in the development of the self and their implications for psychoanalytic knowledge. However, this achievement is often undervalued. Taking a lead from Freud, Pataki argues that conflict of desire and incoherence of belief are not the only phenomena which press towards strongly partitive conceptions of mind. For Pataki, certain kinds of internalised object relations, in general those involving non-conflictual and non-irrational narcissistic attitudes, can develop and consolidate into what are arguably independent agencies or self-like parts. He then suggests that this development, derived as it is from our unswerving need of secure object relations, governs our ability to express a range of reflexive attitudes, including wish-fulfilment, self-deception and akrasia.

To continue the topic of post-Freudian psychoanalytic knowledge, we move on to Suzanne R. Kirschner's paper in Chapter 10 in which she explores Anglo-American post-Freudian psychoanalytic conceptions of autonomy and their development. Kirschner's primary aim is to explore some culturally constituted assumptions which are apparent in the depictions of autonomy found in the writings of ego psychology, object-relations theory and self-psychology. She focuses on four facets of psychoanalytic autonomy: self-assertion, self-reliance, rationality and authenticity. She then explores several themes embedded in the psychoanalytic narrative of autonomy. In psychoanalysis, autonomy is depicted as the crucial *telos* of a movement that is at once tragic, necessary and fortuitous. This conceptualisation of autonomy and its vicissitudes resembles romantic literary and philosophical depictions of the mind's progress. Both romantic and psychoanalytic treatments of the human condition may be viewed as what William James called *complete* spiritual or cultural systems, for they preserve and integrate tragic and dangerous elements in their depictions of the self's development. Kirschner thus extols a sophistication and a depth of psychoanalytic theory that are lacking in many other psychological theories.

To end our examination of post-Freudian psychoanalytic knowledge, İlham Dilman, in Chapter 11, focuses on self-psychology and provides a critique of Heinz Kohut. Kohut was born in Vienna in 1913. When he was young, he was separated from his father but was close to his mother. As an adolescent, to ensure that his intellect was stimulated, Kohut's family hired tutors with whom he discussed the philosophical ideas of, for example, Plato and Kant.[4] When he was 19, he became interested in psychotherapy (August Aichhorn, who was well known in the area of juvenile delinquency, was Kohut's first analyst) and enrolled at the University of Vienna. Kohut finished his medical training at the University of Vienna in 1938 when he was about 25. He then resolved to become a follower of Freud, whom he never met. He went to England for internship, a year after Freud fled Vienna for England in 1938, and subsequently, in 1940, to the United States. Kohut arrived in Chicago where he was given an internship, a subsequent residency (where he worked with Thomas Szasz) and later an assistant professorship in neurology and psychiatry in 1944. He was then 31. In 1949, he finished his training in psychoanalysis at the Institute for Psychoanalysis in Chicago and became a member of staff there.

However, after 25 years of involvement in the American psychoanalytic community, Kohut began to relinquish many of Freud's ideas. For example, and in brief (İlham Dilman provides a detailed discussion of Heinz Kohut's ideologies), instead of focusing on sexual instincts, Kohut focused on the importance of achieving a cohesive and integrated self. Kohut's theory originated from his work with clients who suffered from narcissistic personality disorder. He felt that orthodox Freudian psychoanalysis was not helpful with such clients. Consequently, he felt the need to start observing and gathering new clinical data with clients in contemporary clinical settings. Only then could he generate new theories and treatment methods. Kohut later realised that these clients could in fact benefit from any empathy, acceptance and indeed positive regard that therapists shared with them. So, he focused on empathy and even claimed that empathy could be used as a scientific method of examining complex mental states.

According to Kohut, these clients' pathological narcissism was thought to be associated with the fact that their parents had failed to accept them fully and show them empathy when they were young. Consequently, they never developed positive self-regard or healthy narcissism. In order to develop a cohesive and integrated self, Kohut believed that children need to feel admired, praised and accepted. At the same time, they need to be able to idealise their parents. As a result of this idealisation, they can develop goals and aims in life. However, gradually, they learn that what they have idealised might not be correct. They then learn to assess themselves and their parents more realistically and subsequently replace earlier idealisations with new assessments. Parents' failure to accept and respond appropriately to their children will affect their ability to develop positive self-worth. It follows that acceptance and appropriate response will enable children to develop positive self-worth. People with positive self-worth will depend less on others, and have self-esteem and self-confidence. They will also be ambitious and have specific goals which they set out to fulfil by developing appropriate skills.

To open his chapter, Dilman describes in detail some fundamental ideas of self-psychology. Self-psychology places much emphasis on the development of the self from infancy onwards and on its failures, which Kohut calls 'disorders of the self' and also 'narcissistic disorders' (among these 'low self-esteem' and, at an extreme, 'a haunting sense of worthlessness'). The question for Dilman is: why does Kohut call such disorders narcissistic? The reason, he argues, is that the preoccupations of a person who is unable to be himself are preoccupations with himself. Kohut believed that narcissism is originally a primitive concern that a person has for himself and that, provided it is treated in the right way, it is a help and not a hindrance in the development of a person. Dilman takes issue with this and argues that self-love cannot take a mature form because it is inherently egocentric. He also takes issue with Kohut's conception of self-esteem as an expression of self-love. Dilman argues that self-esteem is a mode of being in which a person has personal dignity. It involves being on good terms with oneself and, as such, is opposite to narcissism. To find it, a person has to be able to renounce his narcissism.

7. Challenges to psychoanalytic methodology

To end our examination of the nature of psychoanalytic knowledge, one has to draw attention to the fact that the validity of psychoanalytic knowledge has been criticised severely in recent years (for example, Grünbaum, 1984; Macmillan, 1997). In such a short introduction, of course, I can rehearse neither the criticisms made, nor the responses. By way of example, one of the issues debated among scholars pertains to the question: can Freudian theory be tested? and hence, how much of what Freud postulated was true? Popper (1963) argued that Freudian theory is, in principle, untestable. This means that we cannot determine the truth or otherwise of what Freud said. For Popper, the reason why psychoanalytic hypotheses cannot be falsified empirically is that psychoanalysis aims to discover hidden or latent psychological states. Hence, it is not a scientific theory. Thus, to Popper, contrary to what Freud (1940) believed, psychoanalysis is not a discipline within the domain of natural science, but a pseudoscience. Taking a positivist approach, Nagel (1959) was concerned with the logical structure and empirical content of psychoanalytic theory as well as the general nature of the tests used to support the theory. He, in the end, echoed Popper's general thesis that psychoanalytic hypotheses were simply too vague to be empirically verified. Popper later picked up on another of Nagel's criticisms – that psychoanalytic theory is of a nature that cannot be refuted by facts.

Contrary to Popper and Nagel, however, Grünbaum (1984) argues that psychoanalytic theory is in principle falsifiable,[5] but not in the clinical setting. This is because the data in the clinical setting tend to be so contaminated by suggestion, false assumption about the nature of evidence and poor logic that to verify them is impossible. The only way forward is to rely on sufficient non-clinical experimental data which might support psychoanalytic theory.[6] This is how we test the validity of psychoanalytic theory. This does not mean that Grünbaum has accepted the validity of psychoanalytic theory. Quite the contrary, he finally found conclusive empirical evidence (as far as he was concerned) which led him to reject psychoanalytic theory. Echoing the general critiques of psychoanalytic knowledge, Erwin (1985) claimed that Freud's important therapeutic and theoretical claims are unfounded and false. In his 'final accounting' of psychoanalysis, Erwin (1996) concluded: there is no evidence that long-term psychoanalysis is generally more effective in producing therapeutic benefits than a credible or inexpensive placebo. He then goes on to say: 'As the century ends, a century that some have called "the century of Freud", the evidence supports the following verdicts. Has the effectiveness of Freud's theory been established? No. How much of his theory has been confirmed? Virtually none of it. These verdicts are likely to be final' (Erwin, 1996, p. 296). However, Erwin is not saying that examinations and discussions of Freudian theory will likely disappear in the near future. There are many issues which are not yet resolved and Freudian theory may play, in Erwin's words, 'a useful heuristic role in guiding experiments' (Erwin, 1996, p. 293).

Looking at the whole issue of the validity of the Freudian theory from a different angle, Cioffi (1998) argues for new criteria for deciding the nature of a pseudoscience. One of his claims relates to his *deceptive procedures* criterion of the pseudo-sciences. That is, 'to claim that an enterprise is pseudoscientific is to claim that it involves the habitual and wilful employment of methodologically deceptive procedures (in a sense of wilful which encompasses refined self-deception)' (Cioffi, 1998, p. 116). In that sense, Cioffi argues, Freud was being deceitful in that he was hiding contradictory evidence to his theories. One would imagine Masson (1984) to be sympathetic to such a charge.

To add to this critique of psychoanalytic knowledge, Malcolm Macmillan, in the final chapter (Chapter 12), asks what psychoanalytic knowledge is knowledge *of*. He argues that it cannot be therapeutic knowledge, not only because Freud did not value psychoanalysis as a therapy, but also because nothing shows psychoanalytic therapy to be more effective than its competitors, and especially because what changes it does bring about are not due to any psychoanalytic process. Nor does it constitute a general psychology giving us knowledge about the sources and development of human behaviour, because psychoanalysis is not one, but a multitude of theories, few of which harmonise with Freud's original. If psychological theories picture what is actually the case about people, how do we decide from which analytic theory to draw intellectual sustenance? Macmillan argues that the lack of a clear answer to the question of what psychoanalytic knowledge is knowledge of results from fundamental defects in the technique of free association for gathering data and in the procedures for interpreting them. The impressions that contemporary schools of psychoanalysis give of what is meant by free association and interpretation are a far cry from the objective enough, trustworthy impression given by Freud. Among schools of psychoanalysis, many factors surrounding the gathering and the interpreting of data are questionable, as are their bases for making rational choice, from school to school. Until such issues are clarified, Macmillan maintains, psychoanalytic knowledge can only be said to be knowledge about those who engage in the clinical craft and theory of psychoanalysis.

Despite the above critiques of psychoanalytic knowledge, many scholars will not be deterred. There are always those who are sympathetic to Freudian theory and try to meet such criticisms and challenges. Grünbaum's criticism provoked much reaction and prompted many debates (for example, Meissner, 1990; Lothane, 2001). Edelson (1988), for example, challenged Grünbaum's work and argued that Freudian theory can indeed be tested and verified in a clinical setting by means of single subject experimental designs. But still Erwin (1997) argued that Edelson's argument did not do damage to Grünbaum's main conclusion that 'insofar as the evidence for the psychoanalytic corpus is now held to derive from the productions of patients in analysis, this warrant is remarkably weak' (Grünbaum, 1984, p. 278). Farrell (1981) also made an important attempt to assess the scientific standing of Freudian theory and has addressed some of the testability issues that philosophers such as Popper (1963) and Nagel (1959), as well as psychologists such as Eysenck and Wilson (1973) and Rachman (1971), found difficult. In the end, he seems to have arrived at some favourable conclusions about psychoanalysis which, however, Erwin (1984) found neither convincing nor justified.

For all the critiques surrounding Freud's so-called scientific approach and the validity of his findings, some scholars have no problem claiming that he was a great scientist. For example, Gedo said: 'One way to summarize his [Freud's] life's work is simply to state that he invented a new scientific discipline that has steadily grown for over a hundred years and in every part of the developed world – an intellectual and organizational feat of some magnitude' (Gedo, 2001, p. 105). And added:

> through the development of a novel observational method, Freud discovered a universe of fresh data that for the first time permitted proper appreciation of the role of childhood experience in structuring mental dispositions of crucial import for adult adaptation, gave rightful emphasis to the dominant role of unconscious mental processes as well as of primary process thinking, and highlighted the essential part played by the automatic repetition of old behavioral patterns in health and disease. These contributions alone would justify Freud's reputation as one of the foremost scientists of the past century. (Gedo, 2001, p. 112)

Some scholars, on the other hand, see no point in deepening the debate on the scientific validity of psychoanalysis. Fonagy stated:

> I see no reason why psychoanalysts should care if psychoanalysis is a science. I can see how they might benefit were this to be the case, but I cannot see that any amount of playing with categories, demarcations and boundaries of science would make it so. The questions which should concern us are about the nature of mental life, the process of cure, the efficacy of analysis as therapy. Naturally these entail critical methodological issues concerning which procedures might be most likely to yield pertinent data. . . . I do not think we know enough about what psychoanalysis is to make a meaningful attempt to link it to an, in any case, ill-defined and heterogenous category of enterprises which we currently call scientific. For some of us psychoanalysis is principally a clinical matter with some generalizations concerning technique and theory. I would prefer to see it as a body of knowledge which is applied to a currently somewhat constrained set of psychotherapeutic situations . . .
> (Fonagy, 1996, p. 116)

Roazen concurred:

> As far as I am concerned it is still too early, or too late, to approach Freud's work as pure science. . . . There are so many other matters to come to

> terms with that I am uninterested in looking at him through only the lenses of scientific methodology. He was struggling with the most intimate aspects of human loves and hates. And his greatness surely lies in his heroic attempt to try to say something noteworthy about the nature of human emotions. I think there is still a great deal more to be recounted and absorbed before we begin to judge the validity of Freud's work as seen from the dispassionate and detached perspective of 'modern science'. Freud was torn between being an artist and a scientist. . . . For me, the strength of Freud's approach lies in his willingness to bring a profoundly humanistic bent to bear on empirical problems. Psychoanalysis will continue to attract interest because it has entered the ancient debate about how we ought to live. (Roazen, 1992, p. 304)

While some scholars would probably argue that such quotations amount to a fudge, or a way to circumvent serious issues surrounding the validity of psychoanalytic knowledge, others might retort that, rather than circumvent issues, they want to suggest an alternative way, perhaps a more appropriate way, of assessing the nature of psychoanalytic knowledge. A hermeneutic approach has been suggested in preference to a scientific approach.[7] In the 1960s and 1970s the hermeneutic model in psychoanalysis began, the main advocates of which included Jürgen Habermas and Paul Ricoeur in philosophy and Roy Schafter and George Klein in psychoanalysis. The hermeneutic model takes seriously Wilhelm Dilthey's distinction between sciences of nature and sciences of the spirit. The hermeneutic model mainly focuses on subjective experiences rather than behaviour, deals with meanings and has its own object of knowledge and methodology. So, for the hermeneutic model, proof of the validity of psychoanalytic theory is based on articulation of the theory, the interpretation, the therapy and clients' stories. In other words, causes and effects are not what they wish to focus on. Psychoanalysis, as far as the hermeneutic model is concerned, is not a discipline of the natural sciences.[8]

We expect that, for some time to come, the division between the scholars who insist that Freudian theory is simply untrue, unproven, mistaken or indeed a pseudo-science, and the scholars who insist that, although Freudian theory is by no means perfect, it cannot be entirely wrong, will continue to exist.[9] Amidst this division, there will be scholars who believe that there is a future for the development of psychoanalytic knowledge; as Forrester remarked: 'the more one knows about Freud . . . the more interesting and surprising and thought-provoking he becomes. The final answer to Freud's critics is that many intelligent men and women – maybe even children – have recognized and continue to recognize this' (Forrester, 1997, p. 12). In the future, psychoanalytic knowledge may evolve rather than become static or fade away, as expressed in the following: 'If psychoanalysis is not to become fossilized into received doctrine or religious practice, it will evolve. The most wonderful thing then is that in 100 or 200 years' time it will have evolved in such a way as is now quite impossible for us to imagine' (Conran, 1996, p. 122).

This book is by no means a comprehensive examination of the nature of psychoanalytic knowledge in the light of all possible topics relevant to it. Nor does it provide comprehensive literature reviews on each topic addressed. Rather, it represents a glimpse of how selected topics within psychoanalytic knowledge are being addressed in the light of contemporary philosophical views or critiques and shows something of the complexity of psychoanalytic knowledge.

Notes

1. In fact, Erwin (2002) has recently brought our attention to the fact that one can find Freudian influences in countries beyond Western Europe and the United States, including Argentina, Australia, Brazil, Chile, Poland, Hungary, the Czech Republic, Africa, Russia, Korea, Japan, India, China, the Philippines, Finland, Norway, Sweden, Peru, Venezuela, Greece and others.
2. On the other hand, Silverstein (1989) argues that Freud never abandoned dualism but remained a mind–body dualist and interactionist. According to Silverstein, Freud did make functional and psychological interpretations without making links between these interpretations and underlying brain processes. He believed that the mind was not completely controlled by the brain processes, but, on the contrary, interacted independently and actively with them. In other words, the psychical processes of the mind were intentional which, of course, echoed Freud's teacher Franz Brentano's main thesis of intentionality.
3. Freud's seemed to have focused mainly on Judeo-Christianity.
4. At that time, the Kantian tradition was a strong influence in the arenas of science and psychology. Kohut considered himself a phenomenologist and his concept of the 'Self' could be traced back to the concept of the transcendental self of Kant.
5. Glymour (1974) also believed that in principle, it is possible to test the Freudian theory.
6. Grünbaum (1984) argued that psychoanalytic theories need to be tested extra-clinically, and to this end, Smith (1996) has suggested a way to test such theories within clinical settings.
7. Instead of focusing mainly on empirical issues, Richard Wollheim (1993) looks at psychoanalysis from the angle of philosophical anthropology which, to him, provides a rich account and understanding of human nature.
8. On the contrary, Freud believed that he was offering a kind of knowledge which belonged to the arena of natural sciences.
9. Some scholars might more readily accept that there are problems with psychoanalytic knowledge, while they remain faithful to the value and importance of psychoanalysis, as Edelson stated: 'despite all of the problems and failings of psychoanalysis, what is of value in it is an intellectual treasure worth saving. I am convinced that what is of value in psychoanalysis is – when it comes to a way of understanding certain processes, certain states, and certain products of the human mind – the best we have' (Edelson, 1988, p. xvii). After all, some people might argue that there is no reason to pretend that there is perfection in psychoanalytic knowledge. Hence, there is no reason to be fearful of a day when psychoanalysis will disappear completely due to imperfection. One analyst said 'If we see Freud

as our first theorist, we may feel freer to struggle with Freud's contributions and begin to compare his contributions with those of his contemporaries, with those who came after him in the two generations since his death and with the contributions of our own generation. We might even be able to give Freud permission to be wrong without fearing that psychoanalysis will be damaged' (Schwartz, 1996, p. 60).

References

Amacher, P. (1965). *Freud's Neurological Education and its Influence on Psychoanalytic Theory*. Madison, WI: International Universities Press.

Bernfeld, S. (1944). Freud's earliest theories and the school of Helmholtz. *Psychoanalytic Quarterly*, 13, 341–62.

Bilder, R. M. and LeFever, F. F. (Eds.) (1998). *Neuroscience of the Mind on the Centennial of Freud's Project for a Scientific Psychology. Annals of the New York Academy of Sciences*, Vol. 843: New York: The New York Academy of Sciences.

Brakel, L. A. W. (1997). What is consciousness? *Journal of the American Psychoanalytic Association*, 45(3), 714–20.

Brook, A. (1998). Neuroscience versus psychology in Freud. In R. M. Bilder and F. F. LeFever (Eds.) *Neuroscience of the Mind on the Centennial of Freud's Project for a Scientific Psychology*. Annals of the New York Academy of Sciences, Vol. 843: New York: The New York Academy of Sciences.

Cavell, M. (1988). Interpretation, psychoanalysis and the philosophy of mind. *Journal of the American Psychoanalytic Association*, 36(4), 859–79.

Cioffi, F. (1998). *Freud and the Question of Pseudoscience*. Chicago: Open Court.

Conran, M. (1996). Chairman's comments: psychoanalysis – a disreputable profession? *British Journal of Psychotherapy*, 13(1), 119–22.

Edelson, M. (1988). *Psychoanalysis: A Theory in Crisis*. Chicago: University of Chicago Press.

Erdelyi, M. (1985). *Psychoanalysis: Freud's Cognitive Psychology*. New York: W. H. Freeman.

Erwin, E. (1984). The standing of psychoanalysis. *British Journal of the Philosophy of Science*, 115–28.

Erwin, E. (1985). To what degree was Freud wrong – and how much difference does it make in psychotherapy? *Journal of Contemporary Psychotherapy*, 15(2), 123–38.

Erwin, E. (1996). *A Final Accounting*. Cambridge, MA: MIT Press.

Erwin, E. (1997). Psychoanalysis: past, present and future. *Philosophy and Phenomenological Research*, LVII(3), 671–96.

Erwin, E. (Ed.) (2002). *The Freud Encyclopedia: Theory, Therapy and Culture*. London: Routledge.

Eysenck, H. J. and Wilson, G. (1973). *The Experimental Study of Freudian Theories*. London: Methuen.

Fancher, R. (1977). Brentano's psychology from an empirical standpoint and Freud's early metapsychology. *Journal of the History of the Behavioural Sciences*, 13, 207–27.

Farrell, B. A. (1981). *The Standing of Psychoanalysis*. Oxford: Oxford University Press.

Flanagan, O. (1986). *The Science of Mind*. Cambridge, MA: MIT Press.

Fonagy, P. (1996). The future of an empirical psychoanalysis. *British Journal of Psychotherapy*, 13(1), 106–18.

Forrester, J. (1997). *Dispatches from the Freud Wars*. Cambridge, MA: Harvard University Press.

Freud, S. (1891). *On Aphasia: A Critical Study*. London: Imago.
Freud, S. (1895). *Project for a Scientific Psychology*. The standard edition of the complete works of Sigmund Freud, Vol. 1. London: Hogarth Press.
Freud, S. (1912). *Totem and Taboo*. The standard edition of the complete works of Sigmund Freud, Vol. 13. London: Hogarth Press.
Freud, S. (1927). *The Future of an Illusion*. The standard edition of the complete works of Sigmund Freud, Vol. 21. London: Hogarth Press
Freud, S. (1930). *Civilization and its Discontents*. The standard edition of the complete works of Sigmund Freud, Vol. 21. London: Hogarth Press.
Freud, S. (1939). *Moses and Monotheism*. The standard edition of the complete works of Sigmund Freud, Vol. 23. London: Hogarth Press.
Freud, S. (1940). *Some Elementary Lessons in Psychoanalysis*. The standard edition of the complete works of Sigmund Freud, Vol. 23. London: Hogarth Press.
Gedo, J. E. (2001). The enduring scientific contributions of Sigmund Freud. In J. A. Winer and J. W. Anderson (Eds), *Sigmund Freud and His Impact on the Modern World*. Hillsdale, NJ: The Analytic Press.
Gedo, J. and Wolf, E. (1976). From the history of introspective psychology: The humanist strain. In J. Gedo and G. Pollock (Eds.) *Freud: The Fusion of Science and Humanism*. Madison: International Universities Press.
Glymour, C. (1974). Freud, Kepler, and the clinical evidence. In R. Wollheim (Ed.) *Freud: A Collection of Critical Essays*. New York: Anchor Books.
Grünbaum, A. (1984). *The Foundations of Psychoanalysis*. Berkeley: University of California Press.
Holt, R. R. (1965). A review of some of Freud's biological assumptions and their influence on his theories. In N. S. Greenfield and W. C. Lewis (Eds.) *Psychoanalysis and Current Biological Thought*. Madison: University of Wisconsin Press.
Jones, E. (1953). *The Life and Work of Sigmund Freud*, Vol. 1. New York: Basic Books.
Kanzer, M. (1973). Two prevalent misconceptions about Freud's project. *The Annual of Psychoanalysis*, 1. New York: International Universities Press.
Kitcher, P. (1992). *Freud's Dream: A Complete Interdisciplinary Science of Mind*. Cambridge, MA: MIT Press.
Lear, J. (1998). *Open Minded*. Cambridge, MA: Harvard University Press.
Lothane, Z. (2001). A response to Grünbaum's 'a century of psychoanalysis critical retrospect and prospect' (and other texts): requiem or reveille? *International Forum of Psychoanalysis*, 10, 113–32.
Macmillan, M. (1997). *Freud Evaluated*. Cambridge, MA: MIT Press.
Marx, O. (1967). Freud and aphasia: an historical analysis. *American Journal of Psychiatry*, 124, 814–25.
Masson, J. M. (1984). *The Assault on Truth*. New York: Farrar, Straus and Giroux.
Meissner, W. W. (1990). Foundations of psychoanalysis reconsidered. *Journal of the American Psychoanalytic Association*, 38(3), 523–57.
Moraitis, G. (2000). Knowledge and ignorance in psychoanalysis. In J. A. Winer (Ed.) *The Annual of Psychoanalysis*. Hillsdale, NJ: The Analytic Press.
Nagel, E. (1959). Methodological issues in psychoanalytic theory. In S. Hook (Ed.) *Psychoanalysis, Scientific Method, and Philosophy*. New York: New York University Press.
Nasser, A. G. (1994) Psychoanalysis after representation: The philosophical framework. *Psychoanalysis and Contemporary Thought*, 17(2), 179–214.
Neu, J. (Ed.) (1991). *The Cambridge Companion to Freud*. Cambridge: Cambridge University Press.
Popper, K. (1963). *Conjectures and Refutations*. London: Routledge & Kegan Paul.

Rachman, S. (1971). *The Effects of Psychotherapy*. New York: Pergamon Press.
Roazen, P. (1992). Freud's patients: first-person accounts. In T. Gelfand and J. Kerr (Eds.) *Freud and the History of Psychoanalysis*. Hillsdale, NJ: The Analytic Press.
Schwartz, J. (1996). What is science? What is psychoanalysis? What is to be done? *British Journal of Psychotherapy*, 13(1), 53–63.
Silverstein, B. (1989). Freud's psychology and its organic foundation: sexuality and mind-body interactionism. In L. Spurling (Ed.) *Sigmund Freud*. London: Routledge.
Silverstein, S. and Silverstein, B. (1990). Freud and hypnosis: The development of an interactionist perspective. *The Annual of Psychoanalysis*, 18. Hillsdale, NJ: The Analytic Press.
Smith, D. L. (1996). Should psychoanalysts believe what they say? *British Journal of Psychotherapy*, 13(1), 64–74.
Smith, D. L. (1999). Sigmund Freud's programme for a science of consciousness. *British Journal of Psychotherapy*, 15(4), 412–24.
Solms, M. (2000). Preliminaries for an integration of psychoanalysis and neuroscience. In J. A. Winer (Ed.) *The Annual of Psychoanalysis*, 28. Hillsdale, NJ: The Analytic Press.
Solomon, R. C. (1974). Freud's neurological theory of mind. In R. Wollheim (Ed.) *Freud: A Collection of Critical Essays*. Garden City, NY: Anchor Press/Doubleday Books.
Strachey, J. (1955). Editor's introduction to J. Breuer and S. Freud (1893–1895), *Studies on Hysteria*. standard edition, 2. London: Hogarth Press.
Vassalli, G. (2001). The birth of psychoanalysis from the spirit of technique. *International Journal of Psychoanalysis*, 82(1), 3–25.
Wallace, E. (1983). *Freud and Anthropology*. Madison: International Universities Press.
Wollheim, R. (1993). *The Mind and its Depths*. Cambridge, MA: Harvard University Press.
Young, C. and Brook, A. (1994) Schopenhauer and Freud. *International Journal of Psychoanalysis* 75, 101–18.

2
Kant and Freud

Andrew Brook

Freud gave us not just two theories of the psyche but two *kinds* of theory of the psyche. One is about the structure and function of its subsystems; the other is about the nature and management of its contents. Freud's model of psychic structure and function is closely parallel to Kant's in a number of respects. Equally, much in his theory of psychic content was anticipated by Schopenhauer. (We have explored this relationship elsewhere; Young and Brook, 1994.)

Even though not just Freud's model of the mind but also the model adopted in psychoanalysis long after Freud's death – the model adopted, for example, by ego psychology – was deeply Kantian, this feature of Freud's thought has never received much attention. The influences on Freud of German *Naturphilosophie* and Helmholtzian mechanistic materialism has received attention (Holt, 1963). *Geisteswissenshaft* (the intentional, teleological study of culture) has been discussed, and so has Darwin. The role of Machian positivism in Freud's thought has been explored. But Kant is seldom mentioned.[1] Yet Kant's models and methods dominated the German-speaking world in the nineteenth century.

Moreover, Freud referred to Kant very frequently, more frequently in fact than to any other philosopher.[2] In the form of nineteeth-century neo-Kantianism, Kant's views gained their maximum prominence just at the time when Freud was thinking through his own model of the psyche in the 1890s (Freud, 1895 and 1900: Ch. VII), the model that would guide him for the rest of his life. Herbart, Helmholtz, Meynert and even Lipps considered themselves to be Kantians.[3] For all these reasons, Freud must have been influenced by Kant. Yet Holt (1963), for example, does not even mention Kant or Kantianism. Nor does the influential Panel on The Ideological Wellsprings of Psychoanalysis (1973).[4]

Immanuel Kant was the most important philosopher in the German-speaking world from the end of the eighteenth century until at least the end of the nineteenth. His model of the mind and its knowledge was particularly influential. The parallels between Kant's and Freud's model of the structure and function of the mind run very deep. Like Kant's, Freud's model is tripartite. The three elements in Kant are Reason, Understanding and Sensibility. The first two can be readily mapped onto Freud's Superego and Ego, and there is even a connection between the third and Freud's Id. To show all this in some detail is a major goal of this chapter. Freud's theory of the relation of consciousness and language, and therefore his demarcation of the unconscious, is Kantian. Like Freud, Kant thought that a large and in many ways the most important part of the operation of the mind is 'unconscious' – not open to introspection, not conscious in Freud's sense of the term. For Kant, as for Freud, something can be or become conscious only if it is described, that is, captured in language. Freud shared Kant's interest in how the mind can tie experiences together, and even used Kant's term, 'synthesis', as his name for the process. Finally, as Freud himself was well aware, his doctrine of the unconscious (its timelessness, and so on) resonates with Kantian noumenalism (1915b, p. 171). To all of this we will return.

Freud never mentioned Kant's view of the psyche. This is intriguing but perhaps less significant than might at first appear. Freud certainly knew about Kant's model. One would expect as much on general grounds, but there is also direct evidence: Freud owned a copy of Kant's *Critique of Pure Reason* (1781/1997). It is now in the Freud Museum in London. It has some marginal markings running through the first 100 pages or so. The markings are neither extensive nor especially profound, but Freud seldom marked his books at all, so the presence of any marginal notes is significant. He bought it in 1882 (Trosman and Simmons, 1973, p. 654, p. 651), the year in which he first began to think about models of the psyche. Also, in his write-up of the Schreber case (1911a, p. 34), Freud referred to the *Critique of Pure Reason* (1781/1997) by name (the comment Freud cites is on p. A58 = B83).[5]

The reason why Freud's never mentioning Kant's model of the psyche may not be very significant is this. In Freud's time, the Kantian model of the mind was so dominant that it was the universal view of the mind in German intellectual life. On this issue, hardly any German-speaking intellectual was *not* a Kantian, and so the Kantian foundation of his model of the mind may never have struck Freud as worth pointing out. Marie Bonaparte once said to him that he was a combination of Kant and Pasteur, apparently intending to pay him an enormous compliment (Jones, 1955, II, p. 415). This makes it clear that Kant was not just well known to Freud's circle, he was a name to conjure with. The truth of Kant's model of the mind is not exactly self-evident to us now, however, so there is a need to clarify its role in Freud's thinking.

The study that follows will be hermeneutic rather than historical. That is to say, it will concentrate on relationships among texts, on drawing out parallels in doctrine and conceptual framework, rather than documented historical fact. I will not go very far into the question of why the relationships are there – whether, for example, they reflect direct influences or were just a matter of similar doctrines being developed independently. The relationships are interesting in their own right.

1. Kant's tripartite model of the psyche

Here is a sketch-map of Kant's position.[6] One can be aware only of one's own conscious states (phenomena). In order to be aware of even these, one must perform a number of intellectual operations on the raw material of them, which Kant called intuitions. First, intuitions must be 'run through and held together'. This includes locating them in time and (some of them) in space (the spatial part will appear to be external to oneself).[7] Second, earlier ones must be retained in the present so that they can be set beside current ones. Third, they must be organised under concepts, including the famous categories of the understanding. All of this yields 'representations' (*Vorstellungen*). Finally, one must tie whole groups of these representations together into a system of representations, using, for example, causal concepts to do so. Only at this stage does one have experiences, at least of the full-blown conscious variety. The general name for these intellectual operations is synthesis.

The higher levels of synthesis are performed by a faculty called apperception. Apperception must be unified in the ways required for it to operate as a single subject of experiences and for it to become aware of itself as a single subject of experience. Apperception, its being unified and the possibility of it becoming aware of itself were extremely important to Kant, but apperception plays only a minor role in Freud, so we will say no more about it. (The minor role is in Freud's description of '*double conscience*', splits of consciousness, and multiple personality (1915b, pp. 170–1), and elsewhere.)

Kant called the system which contains intuitions Sensibility. It has two subsystems, inner sense (roughly, intuitions of one's own psyche and soma) and outer sense (the intuitions which can be spatially organised).

Understanding is his name for the system which works up these intuitions into representations. It is the language-using system which does the thinking.

The Understanding in turn is governed by Reason. Kant assigned two functions to Reason. One was to generate the regulative principles which the Understanding needed to govern its operations; the other was to house the fundamental principles of morality, which could not be derived from experience. The most fundamental of these was, of course, the categorical imperative. This part of Kant's Reason is a precursor of Freud's superego. In Kant's system reason is not a system like the other two and its status is always a bit murky. The same was true of Freud's view of what underpinned morality.

2. Freud's Kantian model of psychic structure and function

Freud's model of the structure of the psyche is strikingly like Kant's. Recall the distinction between the theory of the structure and functions of the psyche – its main subsystems, driving principles, and so on – and theory of its content – phantasies, affects, dreams, introjects, character, and so on – and of how such contents are managed, the primary and secondary processes.

How different the two kinds of theory are in Freud is never clearer than in *The Ego and the Id* (1923). There is a remarkable shift between Chapters I and II and Chapter III. Chapter I gives a list of ego functions and Chapter II (simplifying) a theory of how the system that performs these functions works and how it relates to perception. This is all structure and function. However, at the end of Chapter II something new appears, the claim that the ego is first of all a bodily ego, a projection (a model) of the surface of the body. This is *not* a point about ego functions. It is a point about the *contents* of the ego, specifically, about the representations or images (*vorstellungen, bildes*) it contains. Chapter III then articulates a full theory of contents, perhaps Freud's first full theory, beginning with the idea that a key part of content, namely character, is 'a precipitate of abandoned object-cathexes'. Clearly, the two kinds of theory differ radically.

This fundamental distinction between structure and function, on the one hand, and content of representations, on the other, does not begin in 1923. Here is a clear instance of it from *Interpretation of Dreams* (1900). Freud has just warned against the dangers of picturing the psyche topographically:

> We can avoid any possible abuse of this method of representation by recollecting that ideas, thoughts and psychical structures in general must never be regarded as localized in organic elements of the nervous system but rather, as one might say, *between* them, where resistances and facilitations provide the corresponding correlates. Everything that can be an object of our internal perception is *virtual,* like the image produced in a telescope by the passage of light-rays. But we are justified in assuming the existence of the systems (which are not . . . accessible to our psychical perception) like the lenses of a telescope, which cast the image. And, if we pursue the analogy, we may compare the censorship between the two systems to the refraction which takes place when a ray of light passes into a new medium. (Freud, 1900, p. 611)

This distinction between representations and the structures and functions which produce and contain and manage them (via the primary and secondary processes) had to wait until 1923 for clear elucidation but it was already clearly present in 1900. The Kantian antecedents are to Freud's theory of psychic structure, that is, of the systems and forces and functions which generate and manage content.[8]

Although Freud's view of the structure of the psychic system underwent some shifts, it remained fundamentally the same from 1895 to 1938. He never abandoned the essentials of the model that he first laid down in 1895. Every subsequent model had a drive system like the endogenous Q of 1895 (libido, the Id) and an ego system like the ego of 1895 (the ego of 1911b and 1917, the Ego of 1923). All of them also had a self-judging element, though it took its final shape as the Superego only in 1923. And all of them remained drive-discharge theories. Though the third part of his model was fully articulated only in 1923, Freud's image of the psyche was fundamentally tripartite from start to finish. As, of course, was Kant's.

3. Freud's model face to face with Kant's

Tripartite models of the psyche have been around at least since Plato, but it was Kant who brought tripartite modelling to prominence in German thought. Few models of the psyche have ever been more influential. Freud's tripartite model, especially the final model of 1923, corresponds to it in detail. Figure 1 lays out the structure of Kant's model and shows how it relates to Freud's. The two psyches are facing each other. The arrows link each element of Freud's model to the element in Kant's to which it corresponds most closely. Not all the correspondences are perfect, of course, a matter to which we will return. From top to bottom, here is how the two models relate to one another.

Noumena-Unconsciousness

The section labelled 'Noumenal self' has been left blank because Kant taught that we cannot say anything about it. Though Freud's notion of the unconscious was certainly influenced by Kant's doctrine, he never thought it to be either as mysterious or as opaque as Kant held the noumenal to be (Freud 1915b, p. 171). We will return to this topic in section 6.

Phenomena-Pre-conscious

Though Kant did not explicitly distinguish representations that one is aware of having (consciousness) from those one is not but could become aware of having (preconsciousness) he knew of the distinction (1781/1997, p. A103, A117fn., B132), and like Freud contrasted both with something vastly larger of which we cannot become aware, namely the noumenal self. While he certainly believed that there is a great deal about psychic structure of which we are and must remain unconscious, he never spoke about whether there are *representations* which are not just pre-conscious but truly unconscious. (Pre-conscious representations that can be made conscious at will, unconscious ones cannot be.)

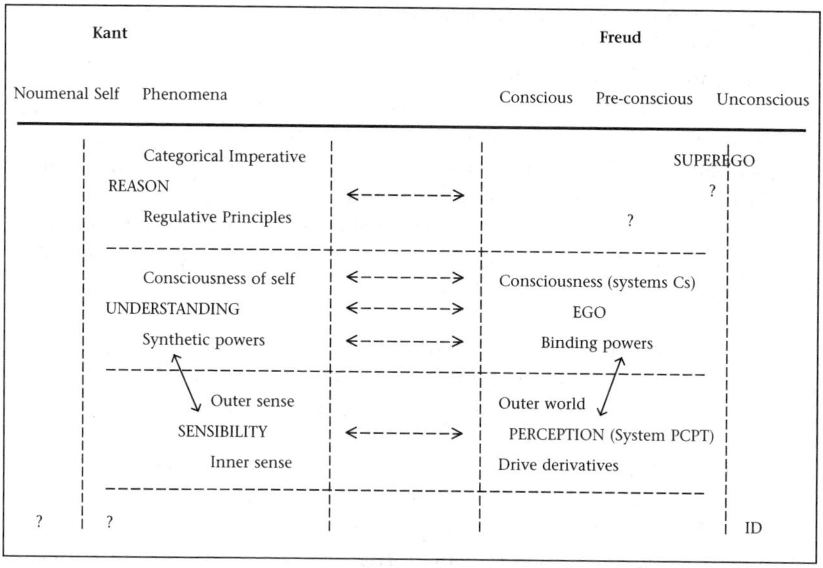

Figure 1: Kant's model face to face with Freud's
Question marks indicate that the one model contains nothing comparable to something in the other model. The lines connecting Understanding and Sensibility in Kant's model and the Ego and Perception in Freud's indicate that these subsystems are very closely related to one another.

Categorical Imperative-Superego

Freud himself saw his Superego as closely related to Kant's categorical imperative. As he once put it, 'Kant's categorical imperative is . . . the direct heir of the Oedipus complex' (1924, p. 167; see also 1923, pp. 35, 48). The Superego goes far beyond the categorical imperative, of course. Kant would never have dreamt that there even are such things as parental introjects, let alone that they could have anything to do with the categorical imperative. But it is also less than the categorical imperative. Kant used the notion to attempt to ground a certain ethical theory, namely, the deontological theory that we can deduce what we should do from extremely general first principles such as the categorical imperative. Not only did Freud not follow him in this; Freud paid little attention to the issue of *justifying* moral beliefs in any form.

For Kant, the principles with which Reason deals are necessary, or could not be otherwise, and therefore are inescapable for any rational being. Freud was also impressed by the inexorability of moral duty. Of course, his account of this inexorability was completely different from Kant's; to say the least, Freud did not think that it was a purely rational matter. None the less, the fact that he mentioned the categorical imperative a number of times shows that he saw a connection.

I have shown the Superego as extending into the Unconscious. This seems to have been Freud's dominant view. Nevertheless there is a problem here, as Freud himself came to recognise. The contents of the Superego are retained and expressed in concepts, word-presentations. But association with word-presentations is Freud's leading way of demarcating the Pre-conscious from the Unconscious (see section 4). Thus the contents of the Superego should be pre-conscious. When Freud finally got the problem clearly into focus, here is how he resolved it:

> large portions of the ego, and particularly of the superego, which cannot be denied the characteristic of preconsciousness, none the less remain unconscious in the phenomenological sense. (Freud, 1938b, p. 162)

By 'unconsciousness in the phenomenological sense', Freud must have meant what he also called the 'descriptive' unconsciousness – states that, as a matter of fact, cannot be brought to consciousness but that lack the usual trappings of the unconscious: timelessness, absence of conceptualisation ('word-representations'), and so on.

Regulative Principles-?

Kant's regulative principles of Reason have to do with a drive to completeness and generality. Freud seems never to have discussed this function of Reason, to provide rules of rational thought. That is what the question mark is meant to indicate.

Self-Consciousness-Cs

Probably the most complicated aspect of both these models is how consciousness appears in them. For in both of them it appears twice – in Kant as a heading (in the form of Phenomena; phenomenal states are conscious states) and as an aspect of the Understanding, and in Freud's as a heading and as a subsystem of the Ego. This confusing parallel is interesting.

Freud first. As is well known, he treated consciousness as both a subsystem of the Ego (Cs; the ω (omega) system of 1895), and also as a quality that some of the contents of any system can have. Though he was never very clear about the matter, he seems to have held that a representation gains the quality of being conscious by becoming available to the system Cs, the system which is sensitive to this quality.

Consciousness as a quality is in a direct line of descent from Kant's phenomena as conscious states. It contrasts with representations of which one is not aware (Freud's pre-consciousness) and, of course, with noumena or the non-conscious. Since items in any system can have or lack the quality of consciousness for Freud, it and pre-consciousness must go at the top as a heading, as with Kant's phenomena.

Cs, the system, is something quite different. Compare Kant's consciousness of self. For Kant, the apperceptive function of the Understanding gives us consciousness of self. Apperception is the application of concepts to intuitions of objects. To get consciousness of self, apperception must make one aware not just of something but also of one's being aware of it. Awareness of the thing would be Freud's perception. Awareness of being aware of it would be Freud's consciousness. What Freud called 'consciousness' is really consciousness of self. Since for Freud the system Cs is what perceives perceptions and other psychic states (1915b, p. 171), the system Cs is exactly like the aspect of apperceiving that in Kant makes us aware of ourselves.

Kant and Freud both distinguished representing the inner (one's states) and the outer (the external world), on the one hand, from awareness of having them, on the other. And they made the distinction in a similar way. Kant distinguished between experiences making us aware of objects and being aware of having the experience. For Freud, only awareness of mental states, not simply having mental states, counted as (the quality of) consciousness. All other representations were merely pre-conscious. Kant used the terms differently; what Freud called perception, he called consciousness and what Freud called consciousness, he called consciousness of self. This difference in terminology should not be allowed to mask the deep similarity in underlying picture.

Neither Freud nor Kant ever got clear about what more than simple perception is involved in consciousness of self. Both hinted that attention might be involved. In Freud, (self-) consciousness arises as follows. We have perceptions of the external world and representations of inner states – affects, drive representatives, representations of the soma and, of course, beliefs, desires and thoughts. When the system Cs, which is distinct from all of them, is 'turned on them', we become conscious of them. Otherwise, they are merely pre-conscious.

Actually, his picture is a bit more complicated than this. For Freud changed his mind about perception in the early 1900s and as a result left us two views on how it relates to Cs. In his earlier view (1895; 1900: Ch. VII), the ω system or Cs is one system and the Φ (phi) system or Pcpt. is another. But later he connected the two and called the resulting notion Pcpt.-Cs. (The first occurrence of this new term is probably 1920, p. 24, but the idea and even a possible version of the term occurs in 1917, p. 232.) This, however, was not so much a change of mind about how perception relates to consciousness as it was a change of mind about what the word 'perception' is to mean. In the earlier view, what Freud called perception (the Φ system), and also representations of the 'inner', were prior to consciousness (preconscious) and needed extra processing in the Ψ (psi) system to take on the quality of consciousness. All this corresponds closely to the outer and inner senses of Kant's Sensibility. In this earlier view, the ω system is a separate system, one related to Kant's self-consciousness. In some works, Freud also calls this the system Cs. In the later account, 'perception' becomes the name not just for preconscious inner representations and access to the outer world. It now includes *awareness of* these representations. It becomes the term for both. In short, Freud came to use the term 'perception' for both inner and outer representations and, in the form 'Pcpt.-Cs.', for self-consciousness, perception of those representations, too.

Understanding-Ego

We have shown Freud's Ego as corresponding both to Understanding and to Sensibility in Kant. The reason is that Freud included direct sensible experience, both inner and outer sense, in the Ego while Kant treated them as a separate system, Sensibility, not as part of the Understanding. We have already discussed the perceptual side of Freud's ego. The cognitive side, what he called the ego-functions, corresponds quite closely to Kant's Understanding, though Kant's theory of these functions is fuller than Freud's. These functions are what allow the ego as system to manage representations. (For Freud, prior to the growth of the ego and such secondary processing, representations are unbound, manifest the primary process.) Freud talked about ego functions a number of times (e.g. 1923, p. 17; 1926, p. 196). In computers, these functions would be the programming which allows the hardware to manage the data.

In *The Question of Lay Analysis* (1926, p. 196) and elsewhere, Freud describes the ego as 'an organization characterized by a very remarkable trend towards unification, towards synthesis'. Synthesis is the central notion in Kant's account of the Understanding. Freud not only retained Kant's concept, but even his term. Freud's interest in it was lifelong. As early as 1895, he had noted that acts of judgement bring about a 'psychological unity' by synthesising stimuli into experience of objects (p. 384) and over forty years later this still interested him (1938a, p. 276).

Outer sense-external perception

Here we will add only one comment to what we have already said – Freud did not develop a complete theory of perception, either of the inner or the outer. In 1895, he treated outer perception as a separate system, the Ø system, distinct from both consciousness and the ego. This is what we have reflected in Figure 1. Later, the only sort of perception he explicitly distinguished was the sort which involved (self-) consciousness, the system Pcpt.-Cs., though he seems to have continued to use the term to cover pre-conscious access to the external world, too, as we have seen. To the extent that he did have a theory of outer and inner perception, it was like Kant's Sensibility.

Inner sense-drive representatives

What we have called 'drive representatives' are representations of drive-derivatives, that is, desires. Freud also called them psychical representatives of the drives (1915a, p. 122). Together with affects, proprioceptive representations, beliefs, thoughts, and so on (which are not specifically identified in Figure 1), they correspond in Kant to inner sense.

?-Id

Nothing in Kant's models compares directly to Freud's notion of the Id. We will return to this issue at the end of the chapter.

4. Kant and Freud on concepts and percepts

Another significant correspondence between Kant and Freud concerns their view of the relationship between perception and description. They viewed the relationship in much the same way. Moreover, Freud used this relationship to define the unconscious. Just about the most famous remark Kant ever made was this:

> Thoughts without content are empty, intuitions without concepts are blind. (Kant, 1781/1997, p. A51 = B75)

I want to focus on the second half of this saying, that intuitions (percepts) without concepts are blind. Freud held precisely the same view. He put it this way. A 'thing-presentation' (a percept, a representation of an object or a state of affairs) cannot become conscious unless it is linked to 'word-presentations'. 'A presentation which is not put into words . . . remains . . . in the Ucs' (1915b, p. 202). Thus this view of how percepts relate to concepts also defined the unconscious for him. He gave the same account, more plausibly and with arguments, in *Project for a Scientific Psychology* (1895, 364ff.). More plausibly, because he there made clear something that he did not even mention in 1915, that it is only memories that require words to become conscious. We can be aware of perceptions of the outer, sensations of pain or unpleasure and current bodily movements, it is there quite clear, without putting them into words. (Kant would not have agreed to this exception, but here Freud has the more plausible view.)

In 1915, Freud did not argue for the link he claimed between language and consciousness. Nor is it easy to find an argument for it in Kant, plausible though it is. So the fact that Freud does argue for it in 1895 is noteworthy. His argument is complicated, but worth the effort needed to untangle it.

Freud takes cognising, coming to understand something we perceive, as the example with which to begin. To cognise, he says, we must pay attention to (hypercathect) the perception in question and then see to which mnemic images its energy (Q) flows. Put less mechanistically, to recognise what qualities we are perceiving, we must compare the perception to our memory of qualities we have encountered before and so can recognise. The process Freud is describing here of coming to recognise by comparing what is seen to memories of what was seen earlier is very much like Kant's Synthesis of Recognition in a Concept (1781/1997, pp. A103–6).

Reverting again to Freud's mechanistic jargon, to compare a perception to memory requires that the energy from the perception select (cathect) a mnemic image of a quality. But it must select the right mnemic image, one that is actually similar to the qualities of the perceived object. Just any old image won't do. Thus we have to be able to discriminate one mnemic image from another. This in turn requires that the images themselves be recognisable, that is, trigger conscious states (his qualities; qualia in more modern jargon). But this does not happen automatically; in fact, most memory-traces do not enter consciousness at all. So what is required for a memory-trace to become conscious?

The next couple of moves are important, but their importance is matched by their obscurity. For energy from the perception to be directed to the right mnemic image, namely one similar to it, the mnemic image must itself be perceptible, enter consciousness (Freud, 1895, p. 364). In addition, the information from the image thus perceived must be discharged back to the Ego, to the mechanism of attention which guides the flow of energy from the original perception to the correct memories. So far there is no reason to think that language is required.

Now comes the move that brings language in. The correlation between what is perceived in the memory image and what is discharged about it to attention (the 'indication of quality') must be tight and reliable. Input and output are systematically and tightly related in this way only in language. Only with speech is what we discharge (what we say) correlated in a systematic (Freud says exclusive) way with what we perceive (what we hear). With all other forms of perception, no such correlation exists. So, if memories are to help us recognise what we see, we must recall them in the form of descriptions of what is remembered, which 'have the closest association with motor speech-images' (Freud, 1895, p. 365).

Note what this argument actually does and does not claim. It does not claim that language is necessary for all forms of conscious recall of memories. But it does claim that language is necessary for conscious recall in any form which could be used by the secondary process. Perhaps the best way to put the point is this: a memory can be consciously *managed* only if what is remembered can be described. (Freud saw implications in this point for the nature of the processes underlying repression and splitting (Brook, 1992).) But Freud thought he had proved more. Certainly in *The Unconscious* (1915b) he felt that he had established the stronger claim that memory-traces without associations to words can never enter consciousness at all. To be sure, even this stronger claim is still weaker than Kant's. Freud applied even his stronger claim only to memory, not to perception, unpleasure and bodily/motor sensation. Kant's claim was that *all* 'intuitions without concepts' are 'blind'. Freud's weaker claim is clearly the more plausible of the two. Nonetheless, a line of descent seems very likely.[9]

In fact, the element of disagreement between them may be more apparent than real. For Freud, even if we can *have* such psychic states without having words for them, we cannot *think about* any of them without words (Freud, 1895, p. 367). That is to say, we cannot focus on them, relate them to other psychic states, identify them as instances of already familiar experiences, and so on. But it is not clear where merely being aware of an experience stops and thinking about it begins. Since it is also not clear that Kant would have denied that one can be merely aware of a psychic state without concepts, it is not clear if he and Freud really disagree.

Freud's argument would probably not stand up to scrutiny. For one thing, it seems to require that even *thinking* of a word discharges a small quotient (a very small quotient (Freud, 1895, p. 367)) of energy from one psychic system to another. But it is an argument. And that is noteworthy. Few views of Kant's are more plausible or have had more influence than the view that thinking and self-aware experiencing (consciousness in Freud's sense) necessarily involve the use of language. Yet very few arguments for the view exist, in Kant or elsewhere. The fact that Freud actually had an argument for the view is noteworthy.

The idea that consciousness requires language is connected to one further Kantian strain in Freud. Like Kant but unlike most psychologists, Freud put memory front and centre in his theory. He even used Kant's terminology, speaking for example of 'reproductive' thought (Freud, 1895, p. 319) (Kant: 'reproductive imagination', 1781/1997, pp. A100–2). Freud's theory of the nature of memory richly deserves a proper study in its own right.

5. Is the structure of the psyche innate or acquired?

One fundamental difference between Kant's and Freud's models, a difference not reflected in Figure 1, concerns innateness. Kant thought that Reason and the Understanding are innate. They must exist fully developed and ready for action prior to the first experience, since the functions they perform (organising intuitions and capturing them in concepts) are required in order to have experience at all and so must pre-exist all experience. For Kant, indeed, more is innate in Reason than its cognitive functions. Its moral side is innate, too. That the categorical imperative, the foundation of all morality, is morally binding is built into us. Freud, by contrast, held that the Ego and most of what it could do were acquired from experience, specifically from having to defend against conflicts generated by the drives.

Morality, the content of the Superego, was similarly not innate but acquired, by introjections and narcissistic projections. For Freud prior to 1920, the only innate element, beyond a general disposition to keep excitation down (the unpleasure principle), was representations caused by the drives. (There is an ironic contrast here: for Kant, representations caused by the drives were the only psychic element other than perceptions that is *not* innate!) In 1920, Freud added Eros as another innate factor. None the less, Freud's view of what is innate and what is acquired in the mind remained radically different from Kant's. Their views would have led to radically different pictures of child development had Kant ever developed such a picture. (Freud, of course, did; his theory of child psychosexual development is one of the most famous theories he developed (1905a).)

Related to this, Freud thought of his model as something discovered empirically, not derived *a priori* by reasoning about the mind and its necessary conditions. Thus, unlike Kant, he had little interest in claims as to how things have to be. He was happy enough if he could discover how they in fact are. On these issues, Kant retained vestiges of the old rationalism while Freud was already completely a child of the new *Weltanschauung* of biological empiricism that remains with us still today.

6. Freud and Kant's noumena

Earlier we said that, for Kant, all we can be directly aware of are states of our own mind, what he called phenomena. What about everything else? Indeed, is there anything else? For Kant there is. He called it the '*ding an sich*' or the noumenal. 'Noumenal' means 'unknowable'. Kant held that we cannot know things as they are, just things as they appear to us. Unknowable '*dingen an sich*' underlie two vital aspects of the mind. The source of our intuitions, intuitions both of inner sense (of our own psyche and soma) and of outer sense (of the external world), are unknowable. And the mind as it is, the thing that works intuitions up into experiences, is also unknowable. We know of the mind only as it appears to us in inner sense, not as it is. Thus, both the source of intuitions and actual nature of the apparatus that works them up into conscious experiences must remain forever beyond experience (in Freud's terms, unconscious). Though they *produce* experience, they can never themselves *be* experienced. (According to Beck (1967a, p. 305), Herbart held the same view.) This made a profound impression on Freud.

The noumenal is the source of the contents not only of outer sense but also of inner sense. Inner sense is our awareness of our own psyche and soma. Freud was certainly interested in the idea that outer sense (our experience of the external world) had a noumenal, 'unconscious' source, but he had an interesting attitude to Kant's other idea, that inner sense has a noumenal base, too. Here is what he said:

> Just as Kant warned us not to overlook the fact that our perceptions are subjectively conditioned and must not be regarded as identical with what is perceived though unknowable, so psychoanalysis warns us not to equate perceptions by means of consciousness with the unconscious mental processes which are their object. Like the physical, the psychical is not necessarily in reality what is appears to us to be. (1915b, p. 171)

In this passage Freud recognises that his ideas about the limits of the knowability of the external world are derived from Kant (see also 1920, p. 28; 1938b, pp. 150, 196; 1938c, p. 300), but says that it is *psychoanalysis* that warns us that perceptions by means of consciousness are not to be 'equated with the unconscious mental processes which are their objects'. Psychoanalysis? Kant had had this idea, too, over 100 years before Freud formulated it. Here is Kant:

> inner sense . . . represents to consciousness even our own selves only as we appear to ourselves, not as we are in ourselves. . . . I . . . know myself, like other phenomena, only as I appear to myself, not as I am . . . So far as inner intuition is concerned, we know our own subject only as appearance, not as it is in itself. (Kant, 1781/1997, pp. B152–6)

What Kant is saying here is that the sources of inner sense are as opaque to consciousness as are the sources of outer sense. That is to say, he held *exactly the same view* about the unknowability of the sources of the internal world as he held about the external world. This thought is a clear anticipation of Freud's notion of the unconscious. Indeed, Freud's ψ and Φ systems of 1895 are pretty much Kant's noumenal psyche under a different name.

Fortunately, Freud did not accept the draconian restrictions that Kant placed on knowledge of the noumenal: for Freud, 'internal objects are [merely] *less* unknowable than the external world' (my emphasis). Kant had urged that both the internal and the external world as they really are are totally unknowable. All we can be aware of is how they appear to us.

Kant's views on the nature of things as they are in themselves (the noumena) also had a direct influence on how Freud viewed the nature of the unconscious. For Kant, the noumenal cannot be spatial or temporal, space and time being merely forms imposed by the mind on sensible experience. It is notoriously difficult to make sense of these claims but notice what Freud says about them.

> As a result of certain psychoanalytic discoveries, we are today in a position to embark on a discussion of the Kantian theorem that time and space are [merely] 'necessary forms of thought'. We have learnt that unconscious mental processes are in themselves 'timeless'. This means in

> the first place that they are not ordered temporally, that time does not change them in any way and that the idea of time cannot be applied to them. . . . On the other hand, our abstract idea of time seems to be wholly derived from the method of working of the system *Pcpt.-Cs.* and to correspond to a perception on its own part of that method of working. . . . I know these remarks must sound very obscure. (Freud, 1920, p. 28)

Curiously, Freud did not take the timelessness of the unconscious literally. He did not ever deny, for example, that unconscious processes start (in time), can be modified by psychoanalysis (in time) and end with death (in time). By their timelessness he seems to have meant that these processes tend not to change over time, in particular are not modified by maturation, and they can appear out of 'normal' temporal sequence in bizarre ways. However, *Kant* would have taken the timelessness of the unconscious literally. He would have held that any idea of unconscious processes even beginning or ending would be nonsense, that the concept of time quite literally cannot be applied to them.

What Freud says here about time he later said about space. In one of the last pieces he wrote, he said: 'Space may be a projection of the extension of our psychical apparatus. No other derivation is possible' (1938c, p. 300). This is simply Kant's idea that space is imposed on reality by the mind. (Apparently Helmholtz, the founder of the school of medicine in which Freud was trained, also held this view of space (Beck, 1967b, p. 469).) In sum, Freud's notion of the unconscious psyche corresponds quite closely to Kant's doctrine that we cannot know the psyche as it really is.

7. The Id

So far we have said nothing about Freud's Id. 'Id' was a term that Freud began using in 1920. Before that, he talked about libido, the unconscious source of what he called our 'drive derivations' – our conscious desires, fears, loves, hates, and so on. There is no anticipation of this notion in Kant. To find its antecedents, we would have to turn to Schopenhauer. Unfortunately, we cannot do so here. (See Young and Brook (1994), where the doctrinal links between Freud and Schopenhauer are examined.) If we push the notion of the Id far enough back in Freud, we can eventually find a link to Kant, however. Freud developed the Id from his notion of libido, which in turn he had developed from what he called the endogenous sources of quantity of 1895. This latter notion does have a parallel in Kant. It corresponds to Kant's notion of the noumenal sources of (represented) desire, inclination and affect in inner sense. However, the first full-blown precursors of the notions of libido and the Id occur only with Schopenhauer. Starting from Kant's view of the world and self as noumenal, that is, unknowable,

Schopenhauer developed a largely new notion, his notion of the Will. To simplify, Kant provided the 'representation' part of Schopenhauer's world as will and representation, Schopenhauer the will part. There is even a loose Freudian parallel here: The *Project* of 1895 provided the ego in Freud's model and other works, especially the *Three Essays on Sexuality* (1905a), provided the libido or Id.

8. Coda on Freud's attitude to philosophy[10]

Given that Freud was well aware of major philosophers who not only knew about unconscious mental life but put it at the centre of their systems, philosophers as major as Kant and Schopenhauer, some of the things he said about philosophy are surpassingly strange. For example:

> To most people who have been educated in philosophy the idea of anything psychical which is not also conscious is so inconceivable that it seems to them absurd and refutable simply by logic . . . Their psychology of consciousness is incapable of solving the problems of dreams and hypnosis. (Freud, 1923, p. 13)

This from somebody whose youth was steeped in German romanticism! As Ellenberger notes,

> In the last decades of the nineteenth century, the philosophical concept of the unconscious, as taught by Schopenhauer and von Hartmann, was extremely popular, and most contemporary philosophers admitted the existence of an unconscious mental life. (Ellenberger, 1970, p. 311)

Freud had to have been aware of this. For example, we know that he read von Hartmann, who had popularised Schopenhauer in his widely read *The Philosophy of the Unconscious* (1869) and works of the 1870s (Brandell 1979, p. 93). Moreover, Brentano, Freud's teacher, discussed von Hartmann at length and on precisely the question of unconscious mental states in his 1874 book, finished at exactly the time Freud was attending his lectures. So what is going on?

Perhaps something like the following. One philosopher who did deny even the possibility of unconscious psychic states was Franz Brentano. While a student, Freud attended his lectures for at least two years, and at just the time Brentano was finishing his famous 1874 book in which an equation of the psychical with the conscious is central. Indeed, Brentano was the only philosopher under whom Freud studied. Though Freud referred to him only once in any of his works and even then only to a riddle (1905b) (curious in itself), Brentano may have been Freud's image of the philosopher ever after. As we said, some of what Freud attributes to philosophers in 1923 even echoes passages in the 1874 book (see pp. 101–4 for examples). Brentano was not the only nineteenth-century philosopher who equated the psychical with the conscious, but he was the only one known to have influenced Freud. If Brentano was Freud's image of philosophy, this might explain how he could overlook the views of philosophers such as Schopenhauer, von Hartmann and Nietzsche, the impact they had had on him in his youth notwithstanding.

To conclude. The burden of our argument has been that the model of the structure and function of the psyche that governed Freud's thought throughout his whole career was essentially Kantian. On the question of what actual historical influence Kant's thought had on Freud, we have offered some tentative suggestions but many questions still remain open.

Notes

1. Another major influence on German-speaking intellectual life in the latter part of the nineteenth century was the Romantic idealism of Hegel and his followers. Interesting, this school of thought seems to have had almost no influence on Freud. Hegel and Hegelian philosophy are only mentioned twice in the entire Standard Edition (S.E. 4, p. 55 and S.E. 22, p. 177), and the only obviously Hegelian idea in Freud's work is the idea of projection. German intellectuals seem to have roughly divided into a Kantian camp and a Hegelian camp: science-lovers and speculators. In such a split, Freud would clearly have been a Kantian, despite a strong speculative streak in both his youth and his old age.

   Freud's library, the part of it he took with him to London, is interesting with regard to the influences on him. (What information we have about the part he left behind is not reliable (Trosman and Simmons, 1973; Bakan, 1975).) He took Darwin's *Gesammelte Werke* (a translation), and most of Mach's works but, curiously, only one late work by Helmholtz and only two by Meynert. No Hegel, no Fichte, no Schelling, only one early work of Schopenhauer's. However, he took Nietzsche's *Gesammelte Werke* in 23 volumes and two books of Kant's, *The Critique of Pure Reason,* and *Short Writings on the Philosophy of Nature* (both in German, of course). The significance of the first of these will emerge shortly.
2. Here are the figures: Plato (17), Aristotle (19), Schopenhauer (25), Lipps (26), Nietzsche (17), and Kant (28+, 16 by name plus at least a dozen more to his doctrines). Lipps is included, though he was a psychologist, because he was a prominent Kantian. Many of Freud's references to Kant or his doctrines are not mentioned in Strachey's indexes, which are not entirely reliable.
3. See Beck (1967b). Jones (1953, I, p. 375) indicates that Meynert in particular was well known as a Kantian. He was one of Freud's principal teachers (Amacher, 1965). Beck (1967a and especially 1967b) gives a good description of neo-Kantianism in the German-speaking regions in the late nineteenth century.
4. The situation with respect to Schopenhauer is different. Parallels between Schopenhauer's views and Freud's have been known for a long time. Freud himself was aware of them. One of the things that make the study of *these* correspondences interesting is that Freud denied that he read Schopenhauer until late in life (for both points, see Freud, 1925).
5. 'A' before a number gives pagination of the first edition of 1781 and 'B' the pagination in the second edition of 1787.

6. This sketch is drawn from sections called 'Transcendental Aesthetic', 'The Pure Concepts of the Understanding, or Categories', and 'The Transcendental Deduction of the Pure Concepts of the Understanding', especially the latter, in (1781/1997). Kant's views on Reason are not well represented in these sections, but they are not completely presented in any other single place either. The Introduction and Book I The Concepts of Pure Reason of the part of the work called the Transcendental Dialectic discuss it in more detail. For a thorough exploration of Kant's model of the mind, see Brook (1994).
7. There is an interesting problem about what the word 'external' in 'external world' can mean in Kant. It cannot mean 'located outside me' because for Kant the whole of space is a state *of the mind*; intuitions are not spatial when they arrive in Sensibility but have spatial location imposed on them. (Kant says the same thing, even more bewilderingly, of time.) So 'external' can only mean 'not states of myself'. The notion cannot have any spatial connotation.
8. The distinction between structure and content should not be pushed too far. Character is a case in point. Though it was for Freud an *entreé* into content theory, it actually has a foot in both camps. It is a matter of contents, representations – what else would abandoned object-cathexes be? Yet it is more than just content, because character shapes and controls how content (experiences, thoughts, desires) is managed. Perhaps a computer analogy might be helpful. Computers have not two main elements but three. They have data (the analogue of content) and hardware (the analogue of structure). But they also have programming. This programming gives the hardware its functions, it capabilities. But it is also content. Character seems in a similar way to be both function and content.
9. Note that the other half of Kant's saying, that thoughts without content are empty, also anticipated a doctrine of Freud's, this time about schizophrenia. In schizophrenia, Freud held, word-presentations have become detached from thing-presentations, that is, from their referents, their content. Moreover, Freud made this claim in the same passage in which he laid out the doctrine of the unconscious which parallels the other half of Kant's famous remark (1915b, pp. 196–204).
10. My thanks to Chris Young for his central contribution to this coda.

References

Amacher, P. (1965). *Freud's Neurological Education and its Influence on Psychoanalytic Theory*. New York: International Universities Press.

Bakan, D. (1975). The authenticity of the Freud memorial collection. *Journal of the History of the Behavioral Sciences* 11, 365–7.

Beck, L. W. (1967a). German philosophy. In P. Edwards (Ed.) *The Encyclopaedia of Philosophy*. New York: Macmillan and the Free Press, 3, 291–309.

Beck, L. W. (1967b). Neo-Kantianism. In P. Edwards (Ed.) *The Encyclopaedia of Philosophy*. New York: Macmillan and the Free Press, 5, 468–73.

Brandell, G. (1979). Freud: *A Man of his Century*. Englewood Cliffs, NJ: Humanities Press.

Brentano, F. (1874/1973). *Psychology from an Empirical Standpoint*. London: Routledge and Kegan Paul.

Brook, A. (1992). Freud and splitting. *International Review of Psychoanalysis* 19, 335–50.

Brook, A. (1994). *Kant and the Mind*. Cambridge and New York: Cambridge University Press.

Ellenberger, H. (1970). *The Discovery of the Unconscious: The History and Evolution of Dynamic Psychiatry*. New York: Basic Books.
Freud, S. (1895). *Project for a Scientific Psychology*. The standard edition of the complete works of Sigmund Freud, Vol. 1. London: Hogarth Press.
Freud, S. (1900). *Interpretation of Dreams*. The standard edition of the complete works of Sigmund Freud, Vols 4 and 5. London: Hogarth Press.
Freud, S. (1905a). *Three Essays on the Theory of Sexuality*. The standard edition of the complete works of Sigmund Freud, Vol. 7. London: Hogarth Press.
Freud, S. (1905b). *Jokes and their Relation to the Unconscious*. The standard edition of the complete works of Sigmund Freud, Vol. 8. London: Hogarth Press.
Freud, S. (1911a). *Psychoanalytic Notes on an Autobiographical Account of a Case of Paranoia (Dementia paranoides)*. The standard edition of the complete works of Sigmund Freud, Vol. 12. London: Hogarth Press.
Freud, S. (1911b). *Formulations on the Two Principles of Mental Functioning*. The standard edition of the complete works of Sigmund Freud, Vol. 12. London: Hogarth Press.
Freud, S. (1915a). *Instincts and their Vicissitudes*. The standard edition of the complete works of Sigmund Freud, Vol. 14. London: Hogarth Press.
Freud, S. (1915b). *The Unconscious*. The standard edition of the complete works of Sigmund Freud, Vol. 14. London: Hogarth Press.
Freud, S. (1917). *A Difficulty in the Path of Psycho-analysis*. The standard edition of the complete works of Sigmund Freud, Vol. 17. London: Hogarth Press.
Freud, S. (1920). *Beyond the Pleasure Principle*. The standard edition of the complete works of Sigmund Freud, Vol. 18. London: Hogarth Press.
Freud, S. (1923). *The Ego and the Id*. The standard edition of the complete works of Sigmund Freud, Vol. 19. London: Hogarth Press.
Freud, S. (1924). *The Economic Problem of Masochism*. The standard edition of the complete works of Sigmund Freud, Vol. 19. London: Hogarth Press.
Freud, S. (1925). *An Autobiographical Study*. The standard edition of the complete works of Sigmund Freud, Vol. 20. London: Hogarth Press.
Freud, S. (1926). *The Question of Lay Analysis*. The standard edition of the complete works of Sigmund Freud, Vol. 20. London: Hogarth Press.
Freud, S. (1932). *New Introductory Lectures*. The standard edition of the complete works of Sigmund Freud, Vol. 22. London: Hogarth Press.
Freud, S. (1938a/1940). *An Outline of Psycho-analysis*. The standard edition of the complete works of Sigmund Freud, Vol. 23. London: Hogarth Press.
Freud, S. (1938b/1940). *Some Elementary Lessons in Psycho-analysis*. The standard edition of the complete works of Sigmund Freud, Vol. 23. London: Hogarth Press.
Freud, S. (1938c/1941). *Findings, Ideas, Problems*. The standard edition of the complete works of Sigmund Freud, Vol. 23. London: Hogarth Press.
Hartmann, E. von (1869/1931). *Philosophy of the Unconscious: Speculative Results According to the Inductive Method of Physical Science*. New York: Harcourt, Brace & Company.
Holt, R. R. (1963). Two influences on Freud's scientific thought: a fragment of intellectual biography. In *Essays on Personality in Honour of Henry A. Murray*. New York: Atherton Press.
Jones, E. (1953/1955). *The Life and Work of Sigmund Freud*, Vols I & II. New York: Basic Books.
Kant, I. (1787/1997). *Critique of Pure Reason*. P. Guyer and A. Wood (Eds.) Cambridge: Cambridge University Press.

Panel on the Ideological Wellsprings of Psychoanalysis. (1973). *Psychoanalytic Quarterly*, 43, 167–242.

Trosman, H. and Simmons, R. D. (1973). *The Freud Library. Journal of the American Psychoanalytic Association* 21, 646–87.

Young, C. and Brook, A. (1994). Schopenhauer and Freud. *International Journal of Psychoanalysis* 75, 101–18.

3
Psychoanalysis as Philosophy, Psychoanalysis as Worldview

C. Fred Alford

What makes the world go round, the human world that is? What are the leading forces that act in, on and possibly through humans? How do we know them? These are fundamental questions, almost but not quite as fundamental as it gets. They are the questions asked, and sometimes even answered, by the major psychoanalytic theories. There is a more fundamental question still: what is the relationship between the forces that act in, on and through humans and the forces that reign in the cosmos? How humans can and should align their lives with cosmic principles is a religious question that psychoanalysis for the most part does not address, though Freud gave it a start. All the other questions are the province of psychoanalysis.

In what follows I treat psychoanalytic theory as though it were a philosophy. Like all philosophy, psychoanalytic theory tells a story. The story that I trace is the story that moves from Athens to Jerusalem to postmodernism: that is, the story that runs from Sigmund Freud to Melanie Klein to Jacques Lacan. The story begins with faith in reason (Freud), moves to an account of salvation through reparation (Klein) and finally to an account that expresses the gravest doubt about humanism in all its guises (Lacan).

In an era in which mental distress is increasingly attributed to 'biochemical imbalance' and the like, in which not just mind but self has become tantamount to chemicals in the brain, an interpretation of psychoanalysis as worldview and philosophy may seem an old and unlikely enterprise. It is both, one that sees psychoanalytic knowledge not as mental technology, but as world philosophy. If psychoanalysis does not always relieve us of our misery, we might consider that is not its true purpose. Its purpose is to help us understand what it is to be human. Even Lacan's anti-humanism is about this.

1. Freud and Marcuse: from superego to utopia

For Freud, it's all about sex. Or at least that is how he is frequently interpreted, and with good reason. Until, that is, one arrives at *Beyond the*

Pleasure Principle (1920). There everything changes with the introduction of the death drive (*Todestrieb*). It's easy to interpret the death drive as aggression. This is what Melanie Klein does, and Freud's introduction of the concept after the First World War, about which he was admittedly, and later ashamedly, enthusiastic during its early months, certainly shows this to be a partial explanation. But the *Todestrieb* isn't just, or even primarily, about aggression, the pleasure in destruction. The *Todestrieb* is about the pleasure of non-being.

One sees this most clearly in Freud's account of where he got the idea of the *Todestrieb*. Not from watching soldiers kill each other, but from watching his eighteen-month-old nephew play a game when his mother left him. Freud calls it the *fort-da* game, which might best be translated as the gone-there-it-is-again game. Evidently anxious in his mother's absence, Freud's nephew would take a reel of string, throw it out of his cot, and retrieve it by pulling on the string. When he threw the reel he would say 'gone', when he retrieved it he would coo 'there it is'. Over and over the child played as this game of disappearance and return (Freud, 1920).

Freud calls this game a great cultural achievement, as the child substitutes symbolic control of his mother's goings and comings (as though his mother were the reel of string) for actual control, a representation for the real thing. On this principle of substitution, society is built, as we renounce immediate satisfaction for substitutes. But where does the *Todestrieb* fit in?

Here we have to understand the importance of the pleasure principle to Freud's thinking. If we aim at pleasure, asks Freud, then why did his nephew, why do we all, repeat unpleasant experiences, such as mother's absence? 'How then does his repetition of this distressing experience as a game fit in with the pleasure principle?' (Freud, 1920). One answer might be that the repetition evokes a feeling of control over the mother's absence, but Freud doubts that this is the entire answer. There must be a part of the mind that longs to restore an earlier state of things, to remember even the most unpleasant experiences because they came first. Taken to its logical (psychological) conclusion, this line of thinking suggests that what people want is not just pleasure, but a restoration of the earliest state of things. We remember unpleasant experiences because we desire to recall not the experience itself, but what it represents, the earliest state of being, and that state is non-being, a state prior to existence (Freud, 1920).

It's a long and audacious passage from a little boy's game to the hypothesis that humans seek not just pleasure but nirvana, a state of non-being which Freud generally equates with death. One might argue that it is unlikely, as it certainly is, though Freud adds that each creature seeks not simply death, but its own path to death, one that generally takes a long detour through life. Most analysts have rejected the *Todestrieb* as speculation, as it surely is, though this has not stopped many analysts from accepting other less somber speculations. My point, in any case, is not that Freud is correct, but that from 1920 on he divided the world into two forces, Eros and the *Todestrieb*, what Jung called Thanatos. It is the conflict between these two forces that makes the world go around.

> The aggressive instinct is the derivative and the main representative of the death instinct which we have found alongside of Eros and which shares world-dominion with it. And now, I think, the meaning of the evolution of civilization is no longer obscure to us. It must present the struggle between Eros and Death, between the instinct of life and the instinct of destruction, as it works itself out in the human species. This struggle is what all life essentially consists of, and the evolution of civilization may therefore be simply described as the struggle for the life of the human species. And it is this battle of the giants that our nurse-maids try to appease with their lullaby about Heaven. (Freud, 1929, p. 82)

Not sex but aggression is the main problem that civilisation has to deal with. 'I am convinced that many processes will admit of a simpler and clearer exposition if the findings of psycho-analysis with regard to the derivation of the sense of guilt are restricted to the aggressive instincts' (Freud, 1929, p. 103). We feel guilty because we long to harm others, and so we turn this aggression back against ourselves, accounting for the malaise of civilisation, what Freud means by guilt. The discontent of civilisation is this guilt, and that is as it must be, as the alternative is no civilisation at all.

Though I write frequently about psychoanalysis, I am a political theorist, for whom Freud is as fundamental as Hobbes, Locke or Rousseau, the more familiar state of nature theorists. The state of nature is, of course, a trope, a way of talking about human nature. From a Freudian perspective, the choice is simple: superego or superstate. Either humans impose a harsh aggressiveness on themselves, or the state will have to do it for them, lest civilisation itself perish. Freud believed that most people were incapable of this self-discipline. Consequently, he was pessimistic about democracy (Freud, 1929, pp. 74, 110–12). We may be more optimistic, but it is well to remember the costs in human happiness.

Philosophers don't just criticise each other. They love to turn each other upside down, or rather right side up, as Marx famously puts it about Hegel. Herbert Marcuse (1966) does something similar with Freud in *Eros and Civilization*, his rewriting of *Civilization and its Discontents*. We won't, says Marcuse, create a utopia out of Freud's account (who else would even try?) by ignoring the darker passages. Instead, we must embrace Freud's account of the *Todestrieb*, while trying to explain why humans might seek the nirvana of non-being. Isn't it because life is so painful, requiring so much instinctual renunciation that the pain hardly seems worth it? If true socialism were ever to come, if all labour were to become satisfying (or rather, if all labour were to be taken over by machines, so that men and women could engage in meaningful work), then the *Todestrieb* might become merely the nirvana principle, another aspect of Eros, the pleasures of Orpheus and Narcissus. Never, concludes Marcuse, have love and death come so tantalisingly and dangerously close as in Freud's late metapsychology. But it is only by positing this hazardous intersection that utopia becomes possible.

> As suffering and want recede, the Nirvana principle may become reconciled with the reality principle. The unconscious attraction that draws the instincts back to an 'earlier state' would be effectively counteracted by the desirability of the attained state of life . . . Death would cease to be an instinctual goal. It remains a fact, perhaps [?] even an ultimate necessity, but a necessity against which the unrepressed energy of mankind will protest, against which it will wage its greatest struggle.
>
> (Marcuse, 1966, p. 235)

In Marcuse's utopia, even the necessity of death remains up for grabs, the subject of a 'perhaps'. Marcuse is perhaps mistaken to ask for so much, and to go so far. Nevertheless, it reveals that Freud's legacy includes not just a clinical method, but a vision of the cosmos so complete that turned upside down its human inhabitants might at least hope to join the immortals. Like most utopias, Marcuse's has the quality of a this-worldly heaven. This doesn't make it wrong; it just means that we should not take it literally. *Eros and Civilization* is a cultural achievement akin to that of Freud's nephew with his reel of string, as though to say 'I want to live forever in pleasure and satisfaction' were almost an acceptable substitute for doing it, almost consolation for the knowledge that we can't.

3. Klein and the theological model of mind

Of all the psychoanalytic theorists, it is Melanie Klein who poses the greatest challenge to Freud. Not because she disagrees with him more than those who followed, for she doesn't, but because of the subtle way she transformed his account of the conflict of love and hate into an account of human salvation through reparation. In reading Klein along these lines, I follow the lead of Greenberg and Mitchell (1983, pp. 119–36) in *Object Relations in Psychoanalytic Theory*, who argue that Klein's object-relations theory, as it is called out of deference to Freud, who wrote of the object of a drive, is really a relationship theory, an account of the way we love and hate those most intimately involved in our lives. When we consider that Freud developed his theory after observing a little boy cope with his longing for his mother, it makes sense. Not just love and hate, but the love and hate for particular others, love and hate for the same person at almost the same time, are what make the world go round. How, in other words, do we come to terms with, and make amends for, the hate we feel, and often express, toward those we love? Can we ever make amends for the fact that we have wanted to destroy the world and everyone we have ever cared out? This is the question Klein answers. It is at heart, I think, a religious question, even if hers is not a strictly religious answer. If Freud is a materialist and atheist, and Marcuse a utopian, then Klein is an idealist in the spiritual vein.

Generally seen as a theorist of aggression and paranoia, the central role of love and reparation in her thinking should not be overlooked. Joan Riviere (1952, p. 60), one of Klein's associates, argues that her studies on reparation are 'perhaps the most essential aspect of Melanie Klein's work'. The psychoanalyst Elliott Jaques, student and friend of Mrs Klein, agrees (personal communication). Just as much as aggression, care and concern for others are inherent features of the child's earliest relationships. 'Feelings of love and gratitude arise directly and spontaneously in the baby in response to the love and care of his mother,' says Klein (1964, p. 65). Love is neither an aim-inhibited expression of libido nor merely an attempt to identify with a powerful other. Love expresses concern, what Christians came to call caritas, regarding the welfare of the other as other. Furthermore, caring is not simply a reflection of the child's great dependence on others; the child does not care for others solely to have his desires satisfied. Care and concern express 'a profound urge to make sacrifices', to make others happy out of genuine sympathy for them (1964, p. 65).

Donald Meltzer (1981, p. 179) calls Klein's a 'theological model of the mind'. By this he means that a person's internal objects, his ideas of others and their relationship to him, are his gods, giving meaning and purpose to his life. We might, however, extend this observation to include the recognition that Klein's basic categories are fundamentally ethical or moral in character. As Michael Rustin (1982, pp. 82–3) observes, 'Kleinian theory is impregnated with moral categories, and its developmental concepts . . . incorporate moral capabilities (notably concern for the well-being of other persons) into their theoretical definition.'

One might argue that Klein, or Rustin, commits the naturalistic fallacy, deriving ought from is. That would not be correct. Rather than deriving morality from human nature, Klein discovers morality in the earliest human relationships. Whether it is the right morality cannot, of course, be answered by Kleinian analysis alone. What is clear is a morality of caritas – unselfish concern for others, coupled with a willingness to sacrifice for them – uncovered by Klein in the child's earliest relationships connects her work with the Judeo-Christian tradition.

Jürgen Habermas (1980, pp. 11–12) has stated that in his last philosophical conversation with Herbert Marcuse, shortly before Marcuse's death, Marcuse said, 'I know wherein our most basic value judgements are rooted, in compassion, in our sense for the suffering of others.' It is precisely this sense of morality whose roots Klein uncovers. It is a morality based not merely on the desire to make sacrifices, in order to make reparation for phantasied acts of aggression. It is also based on an ability to identify deeply with others, to feel connected with their fates. Their pain becomes our pain.

Marcuse's observation that morality stems from compassion is an insight also expressed by Jean-Jacques Rousseau when he posit pity (*pitié*) as the pre-rational basis of all morality.

> Thus is born pity, the first relative sentiment which touches the human heart according to the order of nature. To become sensitive and pitying, the child must know that there are beings like him who suffer what he has suffered, who feel the pains he has felt, and that there are others whom he ought to conceive of as able to feel them too.
>
> (Rousseau, 1979, p. 222)

This is the morality of the depressive position, as Klein calls it, reparative morality. It depends on the interaction of pity and identification.

Reparative morality is not the only Kleinian morality. There is also a morality associated with the paranoid-schizoid position. That is talion morality, the morality of revenge rather than of reparation, based upon the most primitive aspects of the superego. Like Freud in *Civilization and its Discontents*, Klein bases morality on guilt. Unlike Freud, Klein systematically distinguishes between two kinds of guilt: paranoid-schizoid and depressive. The guilt associated with the paranoid-schizoid position is based on the child's fear that what he would do to others will be done to him. It is not a pretty picture:

> The child lives in dread of his objects destroying, burning, mutilating, and poisoning him, because these activities dominate his own phantasies toward them . . . Thus, in the child's psychic economy, as on the Lord High Executioner's list, the punishment always fits the crime.
>
> (Greenberg and Mitchell, 1983, pp. 132–3)

Though Freud does not put it in such dramatic and evocative terms, this is the source of what Freud calls the discontent of civilisation, the guilty malaise that stems from having to turn one's aggression back against oneself in order to live in civilised society.

Psychoanalysis can reduce paranoid-schizoid anxiety by uncovering its origins in unconscious and unrealistic fears of persecution. Analysis cannot, however, do much to reduce depressive guilt, because the analysand, in reality, did want to ravage and destroy those he loves. Saint Augustine says in his *Confessions* that he still felt guilty for stealing pears as a youth. Not because stealing pears was such a terrible thing, but because he knew that what he really wanted to do was transgress, not just this boundary but any boundary. From this perspective, suggests Klein (who does not invoke

Augustine, but might have; he fits her tone), one *should* feel guilty for one's phantasies, whether one has acted on them or not. Or rather, one will feel guilty about them no matter how many times the therapist says one need not. The real goal of analysis is not the reduction of depressive guilt, but the mobilisation of compensatory reparative activities. In this respect, Freud's classic characterisation of emotional maturity as the ability to do creative work and to love takes on new meaning. Creative work and love are signposts of maturity because they are the primary ways in which adults may make reparation, symbolic and real, in our culture. If the reel of string that Freud's nephew threw from his cot represents the primordial achievement of culture, the representation of fear and need in a new symbolic register, then reparation represents the pinnacle of civilisation, the way we use the creative achievements of culture to make amends for all the harm we have done to others.

Yet, about reparation we must be careful. One way we may make reparation for the extermination of native peoples, suggests Klein (1964, p. 105), is to repopulate the land with one's own people! Reparation is a moral impulse, which does not make it automatically moral. For that it must be educated and refined, which means made more aware of the suffering of others. Klein's idealism is not always helpful in this regard. I use the term 'idealism' in the philosophical sense, the sense in which Meltzer (1981, p. 179) calls Klein's model of the mind 'Platonic', because for Klein it is one's internal objects or ideas of people that are most real. The result is that she tends to equate the idea with the act, a doctrine more suitable for children than adults. For adults, reparation must be directed at those I have harmed, lest it become mere sentimentality.

Flawed and limited as it is, it is clear that Klein's is a moral model of the mind, an account of the roots of what we call Judeo-Christian morality (but which we might just as well call Buddhist or Islamic morality) in a primordial ethical experience she calls reparation. Like Freud, Klein divides the world into love and hate. Unlike Freud, she sets love loose to care for others. Everything else is detail.

4. Lacan: the self as all or nothing at all

Freud is modern man *par excellence,* willing to see the world in terms of a reason that knows man to be one more struggling piece of nature, lifted out of nature only by his willingness to use his reason to know this. Klein, by contrast, teaches a fugitive salvation, the world rendered subject to redemption by the power of love. Into this modern world, whose bifurcation between Freud and Klein signifies the bifurcation of the West into the spheres of Athens and Jerusalem, reason and religion, steps Jacques Lacan, epitome of postmodern man. For Lacan, man does not exist, nor does woman. Men and women don't exist because the self does not exist; it is but an artifact of language, like the 'I', that slippery signifier that belongs to whoever happens to be speaking at the moment.

One of Lacan's most influential and intriguing works remains his early (1936–40) work on the mirror stage of development (*le stade du miroir*). The mirror stage runs from about six months to two years of age. At some time during this stage the young child recognises the image of himself (*moi*) in a mirror (even if this recognition is superficial, even illusory). ('Lipstick experiments', in which the child's nose is smeared with lipstick as he is placed before a mirror, generally support Lacan's timing of this stage; children younger than six months do not respond with embarrassment (Stern, 1985, pp. 82–9).) The child is impressed by the wholeness of his image, the appearance of definite boundaries, form and control seen in the mirror. Yet this wholeness is really an illusion. He is none of these things. Sometimes he even confuses his own image with the image of the mother who, in one of Lacan's (1977, pp. 1–7) versions, is holding him before the mirror. Nor does the image in the mirror anticipate a future wholeness. As Benvenuto and Kennedy (1986, p. 55) put it, 'the infant's mastery is in the mirror image, outside himself, while he is not really master of his movements. Alienation is this lack of being by which his realization lies in another actual or imaginary space.'

Although it would go too far to regard the mirror stage as mere metaphor, it is apparent from the context of Lacan's discussion that it need not always be an actual mirror. It could just as well be what Heinz Kohut (1984) calls the mirroring response of the parents, a response that seems to confirm the child's own grandiose, narcissistic ideas of himself as whole and perfect. It is, continues Kohut, the parents' treatment of the young child as though he were a coherent self that teaches him that he is one, as the parental mirroring is internalised in the child as a part of himself.

It is this concept of internalisation that Lacan challenges. The coherence and control of the self that one feels when looking in the mirror, or when in the presence of mirroring and admiring others, is never internalised, but always remains alienated in the other. In this sense the experience of wholeness and completeness is an illusion (*méconnaissance*), for it can never become one's own.

Here is the source of a fundamental lack (*manque*) in human existence, a lack that is never overcome, for it represents the distance between what we desire to be, whole and complete, and what we are, incomplete and fragmented. Into this gulf rushes rage and desire, which Lacan sees not as biological givens, but responses to the lack in human existence. With the experience of the mirror image, rage is born in the envy we have of an image of ourselves that will always remain alienated. The discord and distance between the child's ideal image of his body and his actual experience of being fragmented by desire is experienced by the child as a sadistic attack on his own body from the inside. For a moment Lacan (1977, pp. 6, 12) sounds like Klein, but only for a moment, as he goes on to explain aggression as a 'correlative tension of the narcissistic structure in the coming-into-being of the subject'. We rage and hate because we are not, never will be, and know we will never be, whole and complete. Unlike Klein, or even Freud, relationships with others are not central in Lacan's story. It is ourselves, whole and perfect, that we most desire.

Lacan claims to have returned psychoanalysis to Freud, particularly Freud's early work, a claim about which there is much disagreement. In one respect, however, Lacan may be correct. As Muller (1982) points out, Freud's early work stressed the defensive functions of the ego. For example, the ego organises the defences against remembering certain experiences. This leads to more organised repression by the ego, such as the repression of threatening possibilities and fantasies. Surely this is an adaptive function, even a coordinating functioning, but it seems misleading to suggest that it implies such ego functions as autonomy, self-control and self-direction. In fact, these latter functions play a less significant role in Freud's work than in that of the ego psychologists, such as Heinz Hartmann and Erik Erikson. 'In pointing this out, the Lacanians argue that the Americans have missed the ego's fictional, alienating and distorting role' (Muller, 1982, p. 237).

For Lacan, the ego is itself the symptom, the disease. 'The ego is structured exactly like a symptom. Interior to the subject, it is only a privileged symptom. It is the human symptom par excellence, it is the mental malady of man' (Lacan, in Muller, 1982, p. 240). Hume (1993) states that whenever he looks inside himself, there is no self to be found. Lacan might put it this way. 'If I am honest with myself, every time I think I find myself, I realise that I have found only one more defence, one more symptom, one more layer of rationalisation protecting me from the truth: that what I desire and long for above all else, my self, does not exist.'

In one respect, Lacan is just taking the Freudian revolution further, assaulting humanity's pride and self-esteem for a third time. The first time, says Freud (1925), was when Copernicus showed that the earth, and with it man, was not the centre of the universe. The second time was when Freud showed that man is not the master of himself, but subject to powerful unconscious forces. To be sure, Freud seems to have believed that a few exceptional individuals might come to master themselves, a possibility expressed in his famous characterisation of the successful outcome of analysis as '*Wo es war, soll ich werden*', usually translated as 'Where id was, there ego shall be.'

Arguing that Freud has generally been misinterpreted on this point, Lacan states that one could better read Freud's intent this way. 'There where it [id] was just now, there where it was for a while, between an extinction that is still glowing and a birth that is retarded, "I" can come into being and disappear from what I say' (1977, p. 300). We become authentic, Lacan seems to be saying, to the degree that we abandon the illusionary attempt at control, the attempt, bound to fail, to be more than the desiring, lacking subject. Or as Sass (1988) puts it, the point is not that the ego should replace the id, but that the ego should come to exist in the realm of the id. 'That is, it should shed the illusion of integral, controlled selfhood and dissolve into those associative chains normally repressed into the unconscious' (Sass, 1988, p. 602).

This is, of course, the third great narcissistic injury. Not only is man not master of himself, but 'himself' does not exist. How depressing! Modernity has run its course, even (or especially) in psychoanalysis, to be replaced by a postmodern vision of man as not even the sum of his parts. Yet, let us think for a minute about what 'postmodern' means. It means a reaction to modernity, a reaction defined by modernity itself. Postmodernity couldn't exist, doesn't exist, except in contrast to modernity. Postmodernity means the dashing of modernity's hopes for rational understanding, if not mastery, of the irrational forces that dominate us all, forces that operate everywhere in nature including human nature.

Seen from this perspective, as a disappointed reaction to the failure of the modern project, it is interesting to ask what the self would be like for Lacan if it were to exist. In *Not Saussure: A Critique of Post-Saussurean Literary Theory*, Raymond Tallis (1988) argues that it would be a self in which there was a complete coincidence of desire and the self that desires. It would be immediately present to itself, completely transparent, like 'Rilke's angel "a perfect consciousness . . . a being in whom thought and action, insight and achievement, will and capability, the actual and ideal, is one"' (Tallis, 1988, p. 231). Obviously, such a self is impossible, and that is Tallis's point. Because the self is split, torn with desire, rarely transparent to itself, means neither that the self does not exist nor that it is never present to itself. To conclude this, says Tallis, is a giant synecdoche, in which absolute unmediated presence is confused with presence. Since the former is impossible, so is the latter. Or so many postmodernists, including Lacan, seem to have concluded. In effect, postmodernism means that if the claims of modernity for transparency and self-understanding were inflated and naive, then they shall have meant nothing at all. Or at least this is what Lacan seems to have concluded. And he's not all wrong. But he's not all right either. In fact, it is this schizoid tendency within postmodernism thought that is itself the problem, the tendency to see the modern project as an illusion and failure because it was not a success. Could it not be both?

5. Conclusion: what kind of knowledge is this?

One could read the preceding as a summary of leading psychoanalytic theories, and it certainly is that. It is, I hope, something more, an account of the transition from modern to postmodern thought. It is not a particularly satisfying story. If, that is, we equate satisfaction with resolution.

If, however, we seek not resolution, but a deeper understanding of the psychoanalytic project, then it is an interesting story, reminding us why psychoanalysis remains alive and vital in an era of Prozac and managed care, when hardly anyone undergoes a traditional five days a week psychoanalysis. Hardly anyone, that is, but those who are training to be analysts themselves. (Could psychoanalysts create their own psychic economy, so to speak, paying to analyse each other?) Psychoanalysis is an account of the meaning of life. This is as true for Lacan as for Freud; it's just a different meaning, and Lacan's is not necessarily the darker one.

I have sought to distinguish psychoanalytic theory as an account of the meaning of life from its clinical practice, but this is perhaps misleading. Sometimes theory and clinical practice converge, and nowhere more so than in Lacan. Let's imagine what a Lacanian analyst might say to a patient. 'Grow up. You cannot overcome your lack (*manque*), and if you spend your entire life trying to do so, you will live an inauthentic, miserable, symptom-plagued existence. If, however, you can learn to accept this lack you can experience a certain fugitive authenticity (the authenticity of knowing one's lack), and occasionally a certain joy. Your desires need not tear you apart, and you can learn to "organise your menu". To do this, however, you must recognise that you do not really exist as a subject, but are "in the position of the dead".' One is reminded here of Freud's statement that a successful cure will consist of transforming the analysand's hysterical misery into ordinary human unhappiness.

This is, I think, what joins Lacan to Freud: the terrible honesty, the absolute rejection of bourgeois sentimentality. In this regard, Klein is a little different, her own category. About the young child's hate and anger, his or her eagerness to destroy the world, Klein is unsentimental. Aspects of reparation, however, especially those that fail to distinguish between the impulse and the act (such as making reparation to native peoples by repopulating the land with one's own), have the quality of bourgeois sentimentality, for which having good and noble feelings is everything. We should not, however, mock sentimentality. The term comes from the French *sentiment*, and it means to feel, above all the ability to feel pity. There is a type of honesty, shared by Freud and Lacan, that finds it easier to see the bad than the good, the tough but not the tender. In this, at least, they are both male and modern. Reason has always been this way, so afraid of being tender-hearted that it leaves no room for heart at all. In this regard Klein is the odd woman out, and we are the better for it.

A question raised throughout this collection is, what kind of knowledge is psychoanalytic knowledge? I've looked at the most abstract and philosophical aspect of psychoanalysis, its metapsychology as it is often called, and my conclusion is that psychoanalytic knowledge is nothing special. Not that it is not profound, but that it is profound in the same way that the knowledge of poets and novelists and playwrights is profound, generalisations about the world originating in the knowledge we come by in families. (Freud's nephew was the inspiration for his account of the *Todestrieb*, and Klein's first case study was an account of her therapy with her own child, a fact she withheld for years.) Habermas (1971) writes of the emancipatory cognitive interest, a special type of knowledge based on the power of reflection to liberate itself. Reflection is not magic, and about language Lacan (1953, pp. 11–12) comes closer to the mark when he says, 'our researches justify the epigram of the philosopher who said that speech was given to man to hide his thoughts; our view is that the essential function of the ego is very nearly [a] systematic refusal to recognize reality.'

The power of psychoanalytic thought stems not from its special closeness to the human interest in emancipation (if that's what humans are truly interested in), but from its willingness to see the family drama everywhere, much as the Greek tragic poets did. What else is Greek tragic drama but the love and hate of families projected into the cosmos, where it is discovered in the life of the gods, and brought back to earth in the gods' intervention in the lives of royal families (Simon, 1988; Alford, 1992)? One might argue that is itself a narcissistic assumption, and perhaps it is. Why should the cosmos mirror the life of human families? As I argued in the beginning, psychoanalytic theory is not coincident with philosophy and religion *per se*, but with philosophy that puts the lives of men, women, and children at the centre of this account. This, of course, is not the same as a humanistic account, as Lacan's work testifies.

Psychoanalytic knowledge is the knowledge of poets, novelists and playwrights, rendered more systematic, and for this reason somewhat less subtle. One cannot have all of every good thing. Psychoanalytic knowledge is an account of the meaning of human existence (this is as true of Lacan as Freud), made more systematic (and hence possibly more useful) but less beautiful than in the work of artists.

One advantage of seeing psychoanalysis in these terms is that it is not readily transformed into what Michel Foucault (1979) calls discipline, a technology of human control by means of categorisation and diagnosis. As in, 'you protest against your working conditions because you have a histrionic personality disorder'.[1] Not just the abstraction, but the fact that it is not addressed to individual sufferers, but to humanity at large, means that the psychoanalytic theories discussed here have more to do with the meaning of life than with disciplining its subjects.

To be sure, the distinction is not quite so simple. In *Eros and Civilization*, Marcuse discovers ideology in Freud's assumption that repression will always be necessary. That assumes, says Marcuse, that labour and social hierarchy will always be necessary. But who could argue that the metapsychologies of Freud, Klein and Lacan are free of ideology? On the contrary, they are grand ideologies, systems of ideas that reflect (indeed, are) the worldviews of the age, the worldviews associated with Athens, Jerusalem and postmodernism.

(Postmodernism may be defined as incredulity towards metanarratives, but of course it too is one more metanarrative to be incredulous about.) Indeed, it is precisely because they are such comprehensive visions that these metapsychologies do not readily lend themselves to discipline. We best criticise these metapsychologies as ideologies are best criticized: as mistaking a historical era for eternity, empirical regularity for ontology.

From this perspective it may not be so important to ask whether Freud is correct that the ego is a centre of self-control and mastery (even if it is not a very big centre, but more akin to a little man riding a gigantic horse, as Freud compared the ego to the id), or whether Lacan is correct that the ego is but a symptom. Not who is correct, but what is happening in the world we live in that something once taken as unproblematic, the ego or self, suddenly becomes precarious? Seen from this perspective, psychoanalytic theory becomes the mirror of the hopes and fears of the age. So is the *Diagnostic and Statistical Manual of the American Psychiatric Association*, in which, for example, homosexuality was once a disorder, but no longer is. The difference is that the metapsychologies we have considered reflect a more profound and subtle set of hopes and fears, the social anxieties themselves so to speak, rather than their symptoms. What could be more interesting than that?

Note

1. I (Alford, 2001) recently completely a research project that involved interviewing a large number of whistleblowers, men and women who speak out against unethical or illegal conduct where they work. Most referred to the strategy of 'nuts and sluts' deployed against them, as one called it. Instead of taking up their ethical arguments, the organisation sought to diagnose them as mentally or morally ill, and so dismiss them and their charges. This is what Foucault means by discipline, and it is hard to imagine that discipline gains much support from the metapsychologies considered here. The *Todestrieb* is not a disciplinary category as, for example, narcissistic personality disorder might be.

References

Alford, C. F. (1992). *The Psychoanalytic Theory of Greek Tragedy*. New Haven, CT: Yale University Press.

Alford, C. F. (2001). *Whistleblowers: Broken Lives and Organizational Power*. Ithaca, NY: Cornell University Press.

Benvenuto, B. and Kennedy, R. (1986). *The Works of Jacques Lacan*. New York: St. Martin's Press.

Foucault, M. (1979). *Discipline and Punish: The Birth of the Prison*. New York: Vintage Books.

Freud, S. (1920/1961). *Beyond the Pleasure Principle*. New York: W. W. Norton.

Freud, S. (1925/1953). *The Resistances to Psycho-analysis*. The standard edition of the complete works of Sigmund Freud, Vol. 19. London: Hogarth Press.

Freud, S. (1929/1961). *Civilization and its Discontents*. New York: W. W. Norton.

Greenberg, J. and Mitchell, S. (1983). *Object Relations in Psychoanalytic Theory*. Cambridge, MA: Harvard University Press.

Habermas, J. (1971). *Knowledge and Human Interests*. Boston: Beacon Press.

Habermas, J. (1980). Psychic thermidor and the rebirth of rebellious subjectivity. *Berkeley Journal of Sociology*, 24–25, 11–12.

Hume, D. (1993). *An Enquiry Concerning Human Understanding*. Indianapolis: Hackett.

Klein, M. (1964). Love, guilt and reparation. In M. Klein and J. Riviere (Eds.) *Love, Hate and Reparation*. New York: W. W. Norton.

Kohut, H. (1984). *How Does Analysis Cure?* Chicago: University of Chicago Press.

Lacan, J. (1953). Some reflections on the ego. *International Journal of Psycho-Analysis*, 34, 11–17.

Lacan, J. (1977). *Ecrits*. New York: W. W. Norton.

Marcuse, H. (1966). *Eros and Civilization: A Philosophical Inquiry into Freud*. Boston: Beacon Press.

Meltzer, D. (1981). The Kleinian expansion of Freud's metapsychology. *International Journal of Psycho-Analysis*, 62, 177–84.

Muller, J. P. (1982). Ego and subject in Lacan. *Psychoanalytic Review*, 69(2), 234–40.

Riviere, J. (1952). On the genesis of psychical conflict in early infancy. In M. Klein, P. Heimann, S. Isaacs and J. Riviere (Eds.) *Developments in Psycho-analysis*. London: Hogarth Press.

Rousseau, J. (1979). *Emile*. New York: Basic Books.

Rustin, M. (1982). A socialist consideration of Kleinian psychoanalysis. *New Left Review* 131, 71–96.

Sass, L. A. (1988). The self and its vicissitudes: an 'archaeological' study of the psychoanalytic avant-garde. *Social Research*, 55 (Winter), 551–608.

Simon, B. (1988). *Tragic Drama and the Family: Psychoanalytic Studies from Aeschylus to Beckett*. New Haven, CT: Yale University Press.

Stern, D. (1985). *The Interpersonal World of the Infant: A View from Psychoanalysis and Developmental Psychology*. New York: Basic Books.

Tallis, R. (1988). *Not Saussure: A Critique of Post-Saussurean Literary Theory*. Basingstoke: Macmillan.

4

'Some Unimaginable Substratum': A Contemporary Introduction to Freud's Philosophy of Mind

David Livingstone Smith

Sigmund Freud is a philosopher, but became one posthumously. This odd state of affairs came about because philosophy underwent a transformation during the late twentieth century, with the result that a good deal of what is considered the legitimate business of twenty-first-century philosophers was not considered their business a century before. Ever since the rise of Logical Empiricism in the early decades of the twentieth century, philosophy has moved into an ever more intimate embrace with science, and it has become increasingly difficult to draw a hard-and-fast line between them. This intellectual trajectory was hastened by the birth of cognitive science in the 1950s. The new cognitivists worked in the borderlands between philosophy and science and could be describe equally well as philosophical scientists or scientific philosophers. They investigated, and continue to investigate, issues such as the neural instantiation of mental functions, the relationship between language and consciousness, the nature of non-conscious information processing, the structure of cognitive architectures, and so on. These issues, and others like them, were also given careful consideration by a vibrant intellectual community of philosophically sophisticated scientists and scientifically sophisticated philosophers that flourished in Europe during late nineteenth and early twentieth centuries, a community that included, among many others, Sigmund Freud. It is only relatively recently that historians of psychology have begun to realise that Freud was a philosophically savvy cognitive scientist who attended to many of the same fundamental questions that preoccupy philosophers and cognitive scientists today (Glymour, 1991; Kitcher, 1992; Smith, 1999a). Freud deserves attention from philosophers and cognitive scientists not only because of the issues that he wrestled with, and in some instances the contemporary theories that he anticipated, but also because this neglected dimension of his legacy may yet have things to contribute to attempts to solve the problems that continue to vex philosophers today. As Clark Glymour sums up:

> Freud's writings contain a philosophy of mind, and indeed a philosophy of mind that addresses many of the issues about the mental that nowadays concern philosophers and ought to concern psychologists. Freud's thinking about the issues in the philosophy of mind is better than much of what goes on in contemporary philosophy, and it is sometimes as good as the best. . . . Even when Freud had the wrong answer to a question, or refused to give an answer, he knew what the question was and what was at stake in it. And when he was deeply wrong it was often for reasons that still make parts of cognitive psychology wrong.
>
> (Glymour, 1991, p. 46)

In this chapter I will explore and delineate aspects of Freud's philosophical reflections on the mind–body problem, the nature of unconscious mental events, the constitution of consciousness and the scientific status of folk psychology. These four closely interwoven philosophical themes lie at the very heart of Freud's theory of mind. In my opinion it is simply not possible to understand fully what it was that Freud was trying to do without a clear understanding of the four themes and their logical, epistemological and ontological ramifications.

Although this chapter aims at being thorough it cannot, alas, given the inevitable expository constraints of an introductory paper, lay claim to being comprehensive. For this, the interested reader must consult the wider literature (Natsoulas, 1984, 1985, 1989a, 1989b, 1991, 1992; Glymour, 1991; Greenberg, 1997; Smith 1999a, 1999b, 1999c, 1999d, 2000, 2001, 2002).

1. Freud and philosophy

Contrary to the claims of several writers, Freud was not opposed to philosophy *per se*. In common with his contemporaries of the Vienna Circle, he was sharply critical of many aspects of the philosophical methods and doctrines promulgated in his day, particularly speculative metaphysics. The following passage, from a letter that Freud wrote to Werner Achelis in 1927, could easily have come from the pen of a member of the *Wiener Kreis*.

> What I have to say about your argument will not surprise you, as you seem to be familiar with my attitude towards philosophy (metaphysics). Other defects of my nature have certainly distressed me and made me feel humble; with metaphysics it is different – I not only have no talent for it but no respect for it either. In secret – one cannot say such things aloud – I believe that one day metaphysics will be condemned as a nuisance, as an abuse of thinking, as a survival from the period of the religious *weltanschauung*. I know well to what extent this way of thinking estranges me from German social life. (Freud, E. L., 1970, p. 375)

Freud's other main targets were rationalism (the view that the mysteries of the world can be solved by the power of thought alone), anti-naturalism (the view that human beings are somehow special and stand outside the natural world) and dualism (the idea that mind and body are separate).

As it happens, the Vienna Circle philosophers were generally hospitable to psychoanalysis. Rudolf Carnap and Otto Neurath in particular spoke well of it (Frank, 1959; Schlipp, 1963). Several of them entered into psychoanalytic treatment, including Carnap (Neider, 1977). Slightly further afield, the great logical empiricist philosopher Hans Reichenbach considered psychoanalysis worthy of philosophical inquiry and after emigrating to the United States co-founded the Los Angeles Psychoanalytic Association (Grünbaum, 2002). Although Freud was a member of the Society for Positivist Philosophy, he was not a logical positivist and it is unclear to what extent he was aware of the activities of the Vienna Circle.

Freud's exposure to philosophy began under the tutelage of Franz Brentano, who expressed very strong opinions about what was and was not worthwhile for his student to study. Brentano favoured positivism and empiricism, informing the young Freud that David Hume was the 'most precise thinker and the most perfect writer of all the philosophers' (Freud, 1989, p. 103). He also thought highly of John Locke and the French positivist August Comte. Brentano reserved his fiercest criticism for the rationalists and idealists. Kant was damned with faint praise: all that was of value in his works had been lifted from Hume. Spinoza was 'not worth reading', but not as bad as Fichte, Shelling and Hegel, who are described as downright 'swindlers' (Brentano, 1874, p. 103).

Freud's philosophical thinking was probably influenced by Brentano (Smith, 1999a; Cohen, 2002). The other philosopher who definitely had a strong impact on his thinking was Theodor Lipps (Flügel and West, 1964; Ellenberger, 1970; Spiegelberg, 1982). Freud described Lipps as having 'the clearest mind among present-day philosophical writers' (Masson, 1985, p. 324). When Freud was hammering out his fundamental philosophical and psychological position in 1896, he found that Lipps had reached the same ideas as himself. Specifically, both Lipps and Freud argued for the thesis that consciousness is an inner sense-organ, that all cognitive processes are unconscious and that all mental items are representations (Masson, 1985, p. 325).

Freud cited Kant more frequently than any other philosopher and certainly read him. He also often used the Kantian trademark locution '*an sich*' ('as such') when discussing the unconscious. Kant's influence on the structure and content of Freud's has certainly been underestimated. Brook (this volume) identifies a number of points of contact between Freudian and Kantian views on the mind. However, Freud was no Kantian and did not endorse what is central to Kant: his metaphysics. Kant's transcendental idealism sits very uneasily with Freud's materialism, and Kant's view that a science of psychology is, strictly speaking, impossible is quite incompatible with Freud's claim that psychoanalysis partakes of the scientific *weltanschaaung* (Freud, 1933). Freud appears to have employed the Kantian idiom in much the same way as the French mathematician/physicist André-Marie Ampère, whom he cited in the 'New introductory lectures on psychoanalysis' (Freud, 1933). Ampère equated Kant's unknowable noumena with theoretical entities deduced from scientific experimentation (Williams, 1989).

Other alleged influences are debatable. Many authors have been struck by the similarity between aspects of Freudian theory and the philosophy of Friedrich Nietzsche. Ellenberger (1970), Esterson (1993) and Sulloway (1979) claim that Freud borrowed psychological ideas from Nietzsche without giving him credit. Freud was exposed to Nietzschian thought during his student years, and three of his university friends, Josef Paneth, Heinrich Braun and Siegfried Lipiner, were deeply immersed in Nieztsche's philosophy (McGrath, 1967; Lehrer, 1995). In 1900 Freud purchased a set of Nietzsche's *Collected Works* and he was given a second set by Otto Rank on the occasion of his 70th birthday (Jones, 1953). However, the weight of evidence suggests that Freud did not begin to read Nietzsche seriously prior to about 1925 (Smith, 1999a). Freud's theories also have a striking similarity to those of Arthur Schopenhauer (Brook and Young, 1994; Brook, this volume). Freud mentions Schopenhauer at several points in his writings, but states that he read Schopenhauer only late in life (Freud, 1925a). Although several writers have claimed that Freud must have been directly influenced by Schopenhauer (for example, Ellenberger, 1970; Gupta, 1980; Magee, 1989), there is no firm evidence for this.

2. Freud and the mind–body problem

The secondary literature on Freud's approach to the mind–body problem has been, to say the least, inconsistent. Freud has been described as a materialist (Amacher, 1965; Solomon, 1974; Natsoulas, 1984; Flanagan, 1986; Wallace 1992) and a dualist. Amongst the advocates of the dualist interpretation, some describe him as an epiphenomenalist (Anderson, 1962), others claim that he was a psycho-physical interactionist (Silverstein, 1985, 1989), while yet others inform us that he was a psycho-physical parallelist (Sulloway, 1979). A few scholars argue that Freud's position shifted over time (Mackay, 1989). In fact, Freud's position on the mind–body problem is rather easy to discern, if one is prepared to pursue it carefully and chronologically though his corpus: he was a dualist prior to April 1895, and a consistent materialist after that.

The mind–body problem was a matter of grave concern for many serious thinkers during the nineteenth century, not just for professional philosophers but also for workers in the new disciplines of neuroscience and psychology. Cartesian and neo-Cartesian doctrines of body–mind dualism had dominated the philosophical *weltanschauung* for more than three centuries, and although Locke had argued as early as the early seventeenth century in his *Essay Concerning Human Understanding* that it might be possible, if God wills it, for a purely material thing to think, and others later made similar points, materialism was not widely regarded as a viable option. The idea that a purely material system could think, much less have a subjective inner life, was simply inconceivable for most thinkers in an era pre-dating the invention of the electronic computer. (Charles Babbage could not obtain funding to build his 'analytical engine', the Victorian prototype of the modern computer.) In effect, then, dualism was the only game in town. As a fledgling neuroscientist Freud hopped aboard the dualist bandwagon, as is evidenced by remarks found in a number of his works written prior to the spring of 1895 (for example, Freud, 1888, 1890, 1891, 1894). Freud wrote in 'Gehirn' (1888) that:

> If a specific change in the material state of a specific brain element connects with a change in the state of our consciousness, then the latter is entirely specific as well; however *it is not dependent on the change in the material state alone whether or not this connection occurs*. If the same brain element undergoes the same change at different times, then the corresponding mental process can be linked with it on one occasion (it can cross the threshold of consciousness), [at] another time not. . . . For the present we are unable to formulate the ruling over the laws governing this [any] closer. We do not know whether or not the ruling only depends, apart from [depending on] the change in the state of the considered elements, upon the simultaneous states and changes in the state of the other brain elements, *or, moreover depends upon still something else*.
> (pp. 62–3, emphasis added)

Two years later, in 'Psychical (or mental) treatment' (1890), we find him advocating psychophysical interactionism:

> The relation between body and mind (in animals no less than human beings) is a reciprocal one; but in earlier times the other side of this relation, the effect of the mind upon the body, found little favor in the eyes of the physicians. They seemed to be afraid of granting mental life any independence, for fear of that implying an abandonment of the scientific ground on which they stood. (p. 294)

Whereas Freud embraces the psychophysical parallelism of John Hughlings Jackson in his 1891 monograph *On Aphasia* in stating that 'the psychical is a process parallel to the physiological' (Freud, 1891, p. 55).

However, all this soon changed. In a passage of the 'Studies on Hysteria' written in March 1895, Freud announced his intention to clarify his basic psychological views, particularly with regard to the nature of consciousness (Freud and Breuer, 1895, p. 300) and early in April began work on the posthumously published manuscript that is now known as the 'Project for a Scientific Psychology' (Freud, 1950). Freud's new anti-Cartesian battle cry is sounded in the opening passage:

> The intention is to furnish a psychology that shall be a natural science: that is, to represent psychical processes as quantitatively determinate states of specifiable material particles, thus making those processes perspicuous and free from contradiction. (Freud, 1950, p. 295)

The 'Project' represented a philosophical revolution in Freud's thinking. First, he exchanged dualism for materialism, the view that mental events are the activities of a physical brain. Second, he argued that consciousness and cognition are functionally distinct, and that all thinking is intrinsically unconscious. Third, as we shall see, he used his materialism and his conception of unconscious cognition to undermine the centrality of introspection for psychological research and self-understanding.

3. The unconscious

The revival of Mesmerism in the new and more scientific form of hypnosis during the late nineteenth century coupled with developments in psychology, psychiatry and neuroscience produced an intellectual climate in which concepts of the unconscious were widely debated and discussed (Ellenberger, 1970; Decker, 1977; Whyte, 1979). However the term 'unconscious' and related terms (subconscious, subliminal self, non-conscious, and so on) were used in a variety of senses. For example, metaphysicians like von Hartmann and Schopenhauer spoke of 'the unconscious' in abstract and often mystical terms. Eissler, cited in the first volume of James Mark Baldwin's monumental *Dictionary of Philosophy and Psychology* (1902), describes the unconscious as:

> The absolute principle, active in all things, the force which is operative in the inorganic, organic and mental alike, yet not revealed in consciousness. . . . The unconscious exists independently of space, time and individual existence, timeless before the being of the world. . . For us it is unconscious, in itself it is superconscious. (p. 725)

This quasi-religious story could not be further removed from Gustav Fechner's account of unconscious states as neurophysiological dispositions:

> Sensations, ideas, have, of course, ceased actually to exist in the state of unconsciousness, insofar as we consider them apart from their substructure. Nevertheless something persists within us, that is, the psychophysical activity of which they are a function, and which makes possible the reappearance of sensation, etc.
>
> (Fechner, cited in Brentano, 1874, p. 104)

On the whole, nineteenth-century concepts of the unconscious were embedded in broadly Cartesian conceptions of the mind. We have already discussed one component of the Cartesian package, the dualistic view that mind and body are two distinct and separate things. The second component is the notion that the mind is transparent to itself and possesses an incorrigible knowledge of its own workings. In other words, the mind was regarded as being *all consciousness*. This view of the mind went hand-in-hand with a valorisation of the role of introspection in psychological research. After all, if each of us is inevitably and infallibly aware of the contents of our mind, the psychological researcher need only peer inside his or her own head or, as Wundt did, train experimental subjects to peer inside their heads. According to Cartesian or neo-Cartesian metaphysics, then, *a mental state simply cannot be unconscious*. What appear to be unconscious mental states must therefore either not be genuinely mental or not be genuinely unconscious.

Although working scientists paid little attention to the florid rhetoric of the metaphysicians, there were two other theories, the dispositionalist and dissociationist theories, that were taken far more seriously.

The group of thinkers whom I have called the *dispositionalists* (Smith, 1999a, 2001) preserved the Cartesian framework by denying that apparently unconscious mental states were genuinely mental, and claimed that they are actually neurophysiological dispositions for (by definition, conscious) mental states. It was embraced by a number of psychologists, philosophers and neuroscientists during the closing decades of the nineteenth century. The passage from Fechner quoted above exemplifies the dispositionalist position. Brentano was also a dispositionalist. He wrote in his famous *Psychology from an Empirical Standpoint* that:

> There are undoubtedly habitual dispositions resulting from previous actions. . . . If we want to admit generally that it is certain that these acquired aptitudes and dispositions are tied up with real things . . . we must also grant that they are not mental phenomena, because otherwise, as we shall show, they would be conscious. Psychological reflection informs us only that they are causes, unknown in themselves, which influence the rise of subsequent mental phenomena, as well as that they are in themselves unknown effects of previous mental phenomena.
>
> (Brentano, 1874, p. 60)

Contrary to Fechner, Brentano, Mill, Carpenter, Maudsley and the other dispositionalists, Freud argued that unconscious mental states are not just neural dispositions for conscious mental events but are genuinely occurrent.

The other neo-Cartesian option was to deny that the states in question were truly, that is, intrinsically, unconscious. This tack was taken by the group whom I call the *dissociationists* (Smith, 1999a), who believed that a single consciousness can under certain circumstances divide itself into two or more subsidiary or competing consciousnesses. They regarded consciousness as amoeba-like in its capacity to effect what these writers described as 'doubling' or 'splitting' ('*double conscience*', '*doublement de la vie*', '*dédoublement de la vie*' or '*dédoublement de la personnalité*'). Pierre Janet was perhaps the most famous proponent of this thesis, although he later repudiated it. Other dissociationists were William James, Prince, Taine, Azam, Binet and Ribot. According to this view, each of a person's multiple consciousnesses is fully aware of its own mental contents. However, even though they all belong to the same person, each consciousness is unaware or 'unconscious' of the contents of the others for precisely the same reason that one is 'unconscious' of the mental states that another person is experiencing: each sub-consciousness has direct, unmediated access only to *its own* mental states. Dissociationism was closely associated with psychopathology, and was rather popular amongst psychiatrists and neuropathologists. 'An hysterical woman,' wrote William James, 'abandons part of her consciousness because she is too weak nervously to hold it together. The abandoned part meanwhile may solidify into a secondary or subconscious self' (James, 1890, Vol. I, p. 210). Dissociationism is presently undergoing something of a renaissance in the wake of popular and psychiatric interest in so-called dissociative disorders (Hacking, 1995). In contemporary philosophy Donald Davidson has give a dissociationist interpretation of the Freudian theory of mind (Davidson, 1982; Smith, 1999a).

Freud occasionally drew on the dispositionalist theory (for example, Freud, 1891, 1894) but found more use for the dissociationist account, which is the organising model for the 'Preliminary Communication' and 'Studies on Hysteria' (Freud and Breuer, 1893, 1895). The idea of intrinsically unconscious mental states does not appear until the 'Project' in which he, having abandoned Cartesian dualism, was emboldened to discard the dogma that the mind is coextensive with consciousness. The obvious methodological spin-off of this move is the demotion of introspection as a method for psychological investigation:

> We at once become clear about a postulate which has been guiding us up to now [in the present work]. We have been treating psychical processes as something that could dispense with this awareness through consciousness, as something that exists independently of such awareness. We are prepared to find that some of our assumptions are not confirmed

> through consciousness. If we do not let ourselves be confused on that account, it follows, from the postulate of consciousness providing neither complete nor trustworthy knowledge of the neuronal processes, that these are in the first instance to be regarded to their whole extent as unconscious and are to be inferred like other natural things.
>
> (Freud, 1950, p. 308)

This was a radical and daring epistemological move. The phenomena of consciousness are seen as the *output* of the mind. In themselves, they tell us little or nothing about the mental processes that have brought them about. Consciousness is the relatively passive recipient of whatever information that the psychical apparatus throws it way. As Dennett (1979) has emphasised, there is a vast difference between the *feeling* of authority that normally accompanies our introspective reports, and the capacity of introspection to deliver an accurate account of what is really going on in the depths of the mind. The 'Project' was Freud's point of departure from introspectionism. The *Oxford English Dictionary* defines introspection as the 'examination or observation of one's own mental processes'. In light of this, Freud can be considered an anti-introspectionist, as he considered that we have no direct access to mental processes themselves.

4. Freud's critique of dissociationism

Freud objected to the dissociationist thesis of an 'unconscious consciousness' as an alternative to the theory of radically unconscious mental events on three grounds. First, he argued that there is something incoherent about the notion of 'a consciousness of which its own possessor knows nothing' (1915, p. 170). On the face of it, this claim does not appear to hold water, for Freud simply asserts that the idea is incoherent without logically justifying it. Second, he objects that the idea of unconscious consciousness requires us to multiply entities needlessly, particularly in light of the fact that it allows us to 'assume the existence not only of a second consciousness, but of a third, fourth, perhaps of an unlimited number of states of consciousness, all unknown to us and to one another' (1915, p. 170). The need to multiply these theoretical entities is just a byproduct of the dogmatic *axiomatic* equation of mind with consciousness, the 'preconceived belief that regards the identity of the psychical and the conscious as settled once and for all' (1923, p. 16n), so Freud has parsimony on his side. This criticism has further implications which are far more profound and damaging than the violation of Occam's razor. The startling observation that as soon as we open the metaphysical door to the possibility of multiple consciousnesses inhabiting a single person, the number of consciousnesses inhabiting them becomes *indeterminate,* was brilliantly elaborated by Peter Strawson's (1962) attack on Cartesianism. If, writes Strawson, we are unable to distinguish between one of an item and more than one of an item, it is not possible to talk intelligibly about that item. Because the idea of a consciousness is logically dependent on the idea of a person, we can count consciousnesses by invoking the rule that there is a one-to-one correspondence between consciousnesses and persons. Strawson notes that the Cartesian theory, in which the idea of a consciousness is logically independent of the idea of a person, gives us no way of even in principle distinguishing how *many* consciousnesses a person has, and therefore makes it impossible to speak intelligibly about consciousnesses. Freud, then, is quite right in insisting that violating the one-to-one constraint by flinging the door open to multiple consciousness leads to an unconstrained multiplication of consciousnesses, because there is no longer an epistemological technique for numbering them, although he did not recognise that this was a logical consequence of dualism *per se*. Freud's third argument against dissociationism was based on the striking differences between conscious mental life and psychoanalytic inferences about at least some forms of unconscious mental activity. Many unconscious mental events possess properties which conscious mental events do not share. Specifically, Freudian theory claims that some forms of unconscious mental activity are exempt from mutual contradiction and negation make ample use of displacement and condensation, are 'timeless' (not temporally ordered) and disregard reality (Freud, 1915). Given these dramatic differences, it is not legitimate to assume that the property of consciousness can reasonably be extrapolated from one set of mental events to the other.

5. Freud's critique of dispositionalism: the continuity argument

Freud (1915, 1926a, 1926b, 1940) used a powerful philosophical argument against the dispositionalist theory, which I refer to as the 'Continuity Argument' (Smith, 1999a, 1999c, 2001, 2002). Freud may have derived the argument from Sir William Hamilton (1853). He purchased a copy of John Stuart Mill's *Examination of the Philosophy of Sir William Hamilton* (1865) in 1889, apparently while researching his book *On Aphasia* (1891), which cites it. Other possible sources were Ewald Hering's 'On Memory as a General Function of Organized Matter' (Hering, 1870) and Lipps' *Grundtatsachen des Seelenlebens* (1883), both of which Freud had read.

The Continuity Argument addresses the fact that conscious cognition is phenomenologically discontinuous. One such discontinuity, which occurs on a daily basis, is sleep. Another common example, singled out by Freud, is the experience of giving up work on a problem and putting the problem out of mind only to have the answer involuntarily flash across one's consciousness, unbidden and seemingly out of nowhere. Freud argues that in such cases we are logically compelled to conclude that occurrent unconscious mental activity is responsible for the result. Freud's reasoning proceeds as follows:

1. There are discontinuities in the flow of conscious mental events.
2. Only mental processes can provide mental continuity.
3. All mental events are caused.
4. In cases where an attempt to consciously solve an intellectual problem at time T^1 is followed by (a) a period of conscious mental activity semantically discontinuous with it, or a period during which conscious mental activity has ceased entirely, and (b) which is in turn followed by the involuntary occurrence of a conscious mental event at time T^2 the content of which provides a solution to the problem addressed at T^1 and which (c) cannot reasonably be attributed to any cause other than the subject's own mental activity, then (d) it is legitimate to conclude that the subject's unconscious mental activity is a necessary cause for the event at T^2. Therefore, unconscious mental states can be occurrent and the dispositionalist thesis is refuted.

6. Freud's theory of consciousness

In 1915 Freud wrote an essay devoted entirely to the subject of consciousness. The paper was one of six that were never published, and it is presumed to have been destroyed. Freud's most complete surviving discussion of consciousness is found in the 'Project for a Scientific Psychology', and the more cursory discussions found in his later works suggest that he retained this theory, perhaps with minor modifications, until his death in 1939 (Smith, 1999a). Freud's concept of the nature of consciousness and its functional relationship with other neuropsychological modules is fundamental to his entire theoretical edifice, and is intimately entwined with his better known notions of the unconscious and repression. Furthermore, because of its strikingly prescient character, the theory also provides a bridge between psychoanalysis and contemporary work in cognitive science and consciousness studies (Natsoulas, 1984, 1985, 1989a, 1989b, 1991, 1992; Smith, 1999a, 1999b, 2000; Crick and Koch, 2000).

The architecture of the mind described in the 'Project' has its foundation in the time-honoured distinction between perception and memory invoked by Aristotle, Locke, Kant and others. Perception requires a clean slate for the accurate registration of sense impressions: the nervous system must be prepared to receive fresh information and thus be relatively free of the effects of previous sensory experiences. Consistent with his newfound commitment to philosophical materialism, Freud reasoned that perceptual neurons must be able to return to their initial state after being stimulated in order to be ready to receive fresh information, whereas the neurons responsible for memory must undergo permanent modification. Memory itself, he reasoned, must be identical to some sort of material alteration of the brain which effects the ease with which excitation is able to flow along particular neural vectors. Freud therefore distinguished between an input system, which he called the Φ system, which is responsible for perception and carries information from the sense organs to the brain, and a memory system, which he called Ψ, which stores information. The Ψ neurons must have the physical property of being permanently modified each time a new excitation passes through them (they must be able to 'remember' being stimulated), whereas the Φ neurons must be 'permeable' to stimulation, and quickly return to their initial state so as to be fresh for the reception of new information. On this account, mental processing is nothing more than the passage of information through a brain that has been modified by previous perceptual experiences. Information is assimilated to the structure already established by the selective weighting of neural firing thresholds while also having the potential to modify that structure through the impact of its passage through the system. Freud portrayed the mind as what is now called a 'connectionist' architecture, in which mental representations are not localised but distributed through the entire system. It is for this reason that Freud was critical of the 'localisationist' approach in neuroscience, which held that specific mental contents were located in particular parts of the brain, or even in particular neurons (Solms and Saling, 1986). Like Freud, contemporary connectionism conceives of mental events as activation pathways through a massively ramifying neural network. His conception of perception, memory, processing and learning are much the same as those advanced by present-day connectionists (Spitzer, 2000).

> Thoughts and psychical structures in general must never be regarded as localised in organic elements of the nervous system but rather, as one might say, between them, where resistances and facilitations [*Bahnungen*] provide the corresponding correlates. Everything that can be an object of our internal perception is virtual. (Freud, 1900, p. 611)

In common with his contemporaries William James (1892) and Sigmund Exner (1894), Freud believed that learning and memory are brought about by physical modifications of neural firing thresholds and described what are now called Hebbian and non-Hebbian learning mechanisms. As Clark Glymour (1991) has noted, contemporary connectionists take Lashley (1956) and Hebb (1949) as their historical points of departure, but 'Freud himself anticipated both the views of Lashley and Hebb, and presented them in detail that is more congruent to current thinking' (Glymour, 1991, p. 59).

So far, I have described how Freud's neuropsychological model dealt with perception and memory. But what about consciousness? Freud identified consciousness with mental 'qualities', nowadays referred to as qualia, and clearly meant what Block (1995) calls 'phenomenal consciousness', which is simply felt experience, '*Erlebnis*' or 'experiential sensitivity' (Flanagan,

1992). Consistent with his functionalist and modular take on the mind, Freud ascribed this to a third neural system, the ω system.

He further suggested that all qualia are sensory, and that only sensations have access to consciousness. Freud believed that qualitative information is represented in the central nervous system by a *temporal* code, while cognitive content is represented by the spatial code of neural activation pathways. Freud believed that the *frequency* of neural firings transmits qualitative information, whereas the activation vector – the pathway through the brain – transmits cognitive information. It follows that the ω system is equipped with a neural mechanism that transduces the temporal code into qualitative information. The notion that sensory information is represented in the brain by a temporal code based on neural firing frequencies is supported by some contemporary neuroscientists (Mountcastle, 1967; Perkell and Bullock, 1968; Hardcastle, 1994; Cariani, 1995, 1997; Cariani and Delgutte, 1996; Rieke et al., 1997). Stuart Hameroff (1995), who considers that qualia may be represented by specific frequencies of boson-condensed field excitation, has advanced a different version of frequency-dependent coding. Freud (1950) believed that qualitative information propagates across synaptic barriers by electromagnetic induction or an induction-like process, a suggestion that has turned out to enjoy support from the work of Pribram (1971) and Libet (1995) as well as Hameroff's (1995) hypothesis of non-local, quantum-level interactions within the brain.

We experience perceptions of the world external to the mind when information proliferating along Φ arouses ω. But how do we become conscious of *cognitive* states that are not in themselves endowed with sensory qualia? Freud suggests that cognition is the brain's manipulation of a neural code that is structured like a language, rather like Jerry Fodor's (1975) concept of the language of thought (or 'mentalese'). In order for bare unconscious mental representations in Ψ to 'become' conscious by impinging upon ω they must somehow become clothed in qualia. A cognition needs, in effect, to 'transform itself into a perception' (Freud, 1923, p. 20) and thus 'be reinforced by new qualities' (Freud, 1915, p. 202). The factor that renders this especially problematic lies in the structure of language itself. If it were the case that the language of thought consisted entirely of object-representations (the mentalese equivalent of names), then conscious thinking might proceed by taking the straightforward route of qualia-laden mental images. But as soon as predicates enter the picture, things get much more complicated. If the thought that 'the cat is on the mat' were represented in consciousness by a picture of a cat on a mat, this picture would also have to stand for thoughts like 'the cat *was* on the mat', or 'the cat *will be* on the mat'. Furthermore, language is arranged in propositionally ordered sentences, the syntax of which contains logical operators such as 'and', 'or', 'if . . . then', and so on, as well as representations of properties and relations (for example, 'is bigger than . . .'). These entities simply cannot be represented in a pictorial fashion (consider the impossibility of representing 'it is not the case that the cat is on the mat', or 'if it is on the mat, then it is a cat' or 'if it is not on the mat, then it is not a cat' by pictures alone) so the simple evocation of mental images does not suffice for making thoughts conscious.

Freud's proposed solution to this problem was the thesis that thought becomes conscious by becoming indexed to appropriate linguistic representations.[1] Language is suited to the task because it possesses the same propositional structure as thought, but it is also richly sensory. Language is double-sided, possessing both intentional content and qualia. For an unconscious thought to 'become' conscious, then, it must activate a corresponding linguistic representation which, having qualitative content, is able to impact upon consciousness. Conscious thinking is thus a form of talking to oneself.[2] Strictly speaking, Freud, like Lipps before him and Lashley after him, believed that thoughts are *never* conscious; they merely produce conscious effects which co-vary with unconscious information structures, a view that is shared by the contemporary psycholinguist Ray Jackendoff (1987, 1996a, 1996b), whose theory of mind is in several respects uncannily similar to Freud's.

7. Folk psychology versus metapsychology

The term 'folk psychology' is used to denote the psychological assumptions that we spontaneously deploy to make sense of human behaviour, including our own. These assumptions are not formal theories of the kind that one reads about in textbooks of psychology, but are arguably theories none the less, theories that we learn at our mother's knee, imbibe with the acquisition of language, and are perhaps to some extent hard-wired into our nervous systems.

We tend to take folk psychology so completely for granted that it can come as a shock to realise that it is just a theory, or rather a collection of theories, and therefore in principle open to revision and refutation. Furthermore, if we did not have access to folk psychological theory (or some other formal theory to replace it), we would be quite unable to make sense of human behaviour. It is our intuitive mastery of folk psychological theory that allows us to perform those everyday acts of mind reading that form the core of social life. Dennett (1987, p. 8) invites us to 'Imagine seeing two children tugging at the same teddy bear and not having it occur to you that they both *want* it.' The idea that people 'have' desires is a folk psychological theory. No one has ever seen or measured a desire. Desires are every bit as hypothetical as quarks or gravitational fields.

The application of folk psychology is not restricted to human beings. We also use it to make sense of the behaviour of animals. On some occasions when overwhelmed with exasperation I have even used folk psychology to draw paranoid conclusions about the malevolent intentions of my personal computer.

The question of whether or not folk psychology is best regarded as a *theory* remains a matter of debate amongst philosophers of mind which I will neither survey nor join here. Suffice it to say that amongst those who affirm the theoretical status of folk psychology there is a whole spectrum of views running from the sanguine assessment that it is an exceptionally good theory to the damning verdict that it is a particularly bad one. Paul Churchland, who is one of the more outspoken representatives of the latter view, has written in a passage that has become famous amongst connoisseurs of the debate that:

> The story [of folk psychology] is one of retreat, infertility and decadence. The presumed domain of FP used to be much larger than it is now. In primitive cultures, the behavior of most of the elements of nature were understood in intentional terms. The wind could know anger, the moon jealousy, the river generosity, the sea fury, and so forth. These were not metaphors. Sacrifices were made and augeries undertaken to placate or divine the changing passions of the gods. Despite its sterility, this animistic approach to nature has dominated our history, and it is only in the last two or three thousand years that we have restricted FP's application to the domain of the higher animals. (1981, p. 211)

Churchland implicitly defines animism as something more thoroughgoing than simple anthropomorphism. Animism is just the misapplication of folk psychology and, as Churchland regards *all* applications of folk psychology as misapplications, he implicitly regards folk psychology itself as irredeemably animistic, falsely attributing non-existent processes, entities and states to human subjects. And so with Freud:

> The psycho-analytic assumption of unconscious mental activity appears to us on the one hand, as a further expansion of the primitive animism which caused us to see copies of our own consciousness all around us, and on the other hand, as an extension of the corrections undertaken by Kant of our views on external perception. Just as Kant warned us not to overlook the fact that our perceptions are subjectively conditioned and must not be regarded as identical with what is perceived though unknowable, so psycho-analysis warns us not to equate perceptions by means of consciousness with the unconscious mental processes which are their object. Like the physical, the psychical is not necessarily in reality what it appears to us to be. (1915, p. 171)

As we have seen, Freud proposed that introspective awareness of one's own thoughts is brought about by information from Ψ activating language representations and riding piggyback on them into ω and that introspective awareness is therefore identical to the effects of unconscious mental processes upon a particular neuropsychological system (the ω system). Consciousness thus does nothing more than selectively *display* cognitive output from Ψ, and no more provides us with information on the workings of the mind than the image on a computer monitor informs us of the material processes in the processing unit. We do not have direct, non-inferential knowledge of the unconscious cognitive processes themselves, and anything that we say about them must inevitably be at best theoretical in nature. Psychoanalysis is 'an expansion of primitive animism' because it uses the folk psychological categories enshrined in natural languages to describe unconscious mental states. It is an expansion of Kantian insight because it simultaneously recognises that these categories are inevitably imposed upon the true psychical reality as a condition for their becoming conscious. Psychoanalysis is a prisoner of language.

The deep structure of consciousness is unconscious, and whereas 'the psychology of consciousness never went beyond the broken sequences which were obviously dependent upon something else', the understanding that cognition is intrinsically unconscious (unconscious '*an sich*', 'in itself') allows psychology to become 'a natural science like any other' (1940, p. 158). These intrinsically unconscious processes are the 'true psychical reality' and are 'as incompletely presented by the data of consciousness as is the external world by the communications of our sense organs' (1900, p. 613).

The information gained through consciousness is thus not only unreliable, discontinuous, constrained by various filtering mechanisms (censorship) and in any case at least one step removed from the cognitive processes themselves, it is also misleadingly *translated* into the language that makes conscious cognition possible. Ultimately, Freud the materialist understood 'true psychical reality' as the neuroscientific level of description. However, he was well aware that in his day it was not possible to give even a very rudimentary neuroscientific account of mental processes, an issue that he predicted in 1909 'may be on the agenda a century after us' (Nunberg and Federn, 1962, p. 280). Given this constraint, Freud was limited to mentalistic accounts of the deep structure of cognition, and described himself as attempting to 'translate into *the language of our thinking* what must in fact be a process that is neither conscious nor preconscious, taking place between quotas of energy in some unimaginable substratum' (Freud, 1933, p. 90; emphasis added). Freud was, therefore, in the final analysis, an eliminativist; he believed that the only natural kinds are physical kinds, and that folk psychological entities do not denote physical kinds (they are not reducible to neuroscientific terms) and therefore should ideally be eliminated from scientific discourse, although he realised that this was hopelessly overambitious in practice. 'The deficiencies in our description [of the mind] would probably vanish if we were already in a position to replace the psychological terms by physiological or chemical ones' (Freud, 1920, p. 60). As it stands, when we refer folk psychologically to the causal impact of an unconscious memory, we are actually referring to 'something of which we are totally unable to form a conception' (Freud, 1940, p. 197).

In light of the foregoing analysis I cannot agree with those philosophers who describe psychoanalysis as simply an extension of folk psychological reasoning. Although Freud could never effectively manage to get beyond a version of folk psychological discourse, he felt this to be a shortcoming of his enterprise, rather than its essence. Thus Fodor's attempt to recruit Freud for his cause by claiming that 'Freud . . . anticipated, and roundly refuted, the charge that Granny-psychology [that is, folk psychology] is stagnant science' (1991, p. 277) rests on a deep misunderstanding of his project. Although he may have succeeded in creating an enlarged version of folk psychology, this was, by Freud's lights, probably a Pyrrhic victory. By the same token, although Freud described his metapsychology as a 'speculative superstructure' erected over the methodological core of psychoanalysis, 'any portion of which can be abandoned or changed without loss or regret' (1925, pp. 32–3), these remarks were intended to apply to specific metapsychological models rather than the idea of metapsychology *per se*, on which Freud futilely pinned his eliminativist hopes. Those hermeneutic psychoanalysts who have opined that metapsychology should be discarded and that psychoanalysis be restricted to so-called 'clinical theory', therefore, do violence to Freud's fundamental philosophical vision for his discipline. Freud has far more in common with contemporary neuropsychologists than with such erstwhile guardians of his legacy.

Folk physics – the shared set of rough-and-ready beliefs 'about how middle-sized physical objects in our world react to middle-sized events' (Dennett, 1987, pp. 7–8) – gave birth to scientific physics with the assistance of two midwives: scientific methodology and formal, mathematical languages that allowed investigators to get beyond the crude and misleading assumptions built in to ordinary language. The starkly counterintuitive claims of quantum theory would be unthinkable if physicists were confined to the languages of the folk, from which standpoint they often appear paradoxical or incoherent. The creation of metapsychology expressed Freud's forlorn hope of creating a formal language for psychoanalysis which 'approximates more closely to what may be supposed to be the real state of affairs' (Freud, 1940, p. 196). However, metapsychology was never the success that Freud hoped it would be. Metapsychology remained nothing more than a physicalistic redescription of folk psychological accounts of unconscious mental life, an alternative notational system that nevertheless remained parasitic on ordinary forms of psychological description. If it worked, metapsychology would at best provide a method of *reducing* folk psychological to neurophysiological descriptions of mental phenomena, but it was doomed to failure for far deeper reasons than the shortcomings of the specific scientific assumptions from which its concepts were derived. Freud's ambitious goal of *eliminating* folk psychological discourse could not possibly be realised without the benefit of specifically neuroscientific investigations, which would provide the necessary alternative framework. As Freud summed up at the end of a long life of psychological and philosophical reflection, we are unable to describe the unconscious as it is because 'everything new that we have inferred must nevertheless be translated back into the language of our perceptions, from which it is simply impossible for us to free ourselves. But herein lies the very nature and limitation of our science' (Freud, 1940, p. 196).

Notes

1. A similar, although far less fully articulated theory was suggested by Nietzsche (1882) in section 354 of *The Gay Science*.
2. In the 'Project' Freud describes these specifically as *motor* representations, the idea was presumably that afferent feedback from motor speech-impulses generate the required qualia. In later works he speaks more generally of 'verbal residues'.

References

Amacher, P. (1965). Freud's neurological education and its influence on psychoanalytic theory. *Psychological Issues* 4(4) (Monograph 16). New York: International Universities Press.

Anderson, O. (1962). *Studies in the Prehistory of Psychoanalysis: The Etiology of Psychoneuroses and Some Related Themes in Sigmund Freud's Scientific Writings, 1886–1896*. Stockholm: Svenska Bokforlaget.

Baldwin, J. M. (Ed.) (1902). *Dictionary of Philosophy and Psychology*, Vol. II. London: Macmillan.

Block, N. (1995). On a confusion about a function of consciousness. *Behavioral and Brain Sciences*, 18, 228–87.

Brentano, F. (1874/1973). *Psychology from an Empirical Standpoint*. London: Routledge & Kegan Paul.

Brook, A. (2002). Kant and Freud. This volume.

Brook, A. and Young, C. (1994). Schopenhauer and Freud. *International Journal of Psychoanalysis*, 75, 101–18.

Cariani, P. (1995). As if time really mattered: temporal strategies for neural coding of sensory information. Communication and Cognition – Artificial Intelligence (CC-AI) 12 (1-2), 161–229. Pre-printed in K. Pribram (Ed.) *Origins: Brain and Self-organization*. Hillsdale, NJ: Lawrence Erlbaum.

Cariani, P. (1997). Temporal coding of sensory information. In J. M. Bower (Ed.), *Computational Neuroscience: Trends in Research*. New York: Plenum.

Cariani, P. and Delgutte, B. (1996). Neural correlates of the pitch of complex tones. I. Pitch and pitch salience. *Journal of Neurophysiology*, 76(3), 1698–1716.

Churchland, P. (1981). *Scientific Realism and the Plasticity of Mind*. Cambridge: Cambridge University Press.

Cohen, A. (2002). Franz Brentano, Freud's philosophical mentor. In G. Van de Vijver and F. Geerardyn (Eds.) *The pre-Psychoanalytic Writings of Sigmund Freud*. London: Karnac.

Crick, F. and Koch, C. (2000). The unconscious homunculus. *Neuro-psychoanalysis*, 2(1), 2–10.

Davidson, D. (1982). Paradoxes of irrationality. In R. Wollheim and J. Hopkins (Eds.) *Philosophical Essays on Freud*. Cambridge: Cambridge University Press.

Decker, H. (1977). *Freud in Germany: Revolution and Reaction in Science, 1893–1907*. New York: International Universities Press.

Dennett, D. (1979). *Brainstorms: Philosophical Essays on Mind and Psychology*. Brighton: Harvester.

Dennett, D. (1987). Starting off on the right foot. In *The Intentional Stance*. Cambridge, MA: MIT Press.

Ellenberger, H. F. (1970). *The Discovery of the Unconscious: The History and Evolution of Dynamic Psychiatry*. New York: Basic Books.

Esterson, A. (1993). *Seductive Mirage*. Chicago: Open Court.

Exner, S. (1894). *Entwerf zu einer physiologischen Erklärung der psychischen Erscheinungen*. Vienna: Franz Deuticke.

Flanagan, O. (1986). *The Science of the Mind*. Cambridge, MA: Harvard University Press.

Flanagan, O. (1992). *Consciousness Reconsidered*. Cambridge, MA: Bradford/MIT.

Flügel, J. C. and West, D. (1964). *A hundred Years of Psychology: 1833–1933*, with an additional Part: 1933–1963. New York: Basic Books.

Fodor, J. A. (1975). *The Language of Thought*. New York: Thomas Y. Crowell.

Fodor, J. A. (1991). Replies. In B. Loewer and G. Rey (Eds.) *Meaning in Mind: Fodor and his Critics*. Oxford: Basil Blackwell.

Frank, P. (1959). Psychoanalysis and logical empiricism. In S. Hook (Ed.) *Psychoanalysis, Scientific Method and Philosophy*. New York: New York University Press.

Freud, E. L. (Ed.) (1970). *The Letters of Sigmund Freud*. London: Hogarth Press and the Institute of Psycho-Analysis.

Freud, S. (1888/1990). Gehirn. In M. Solms and M. Saling (Eds.) *A Moment of Transition: Two Neuroscientific Articles by Sigmund Freud*. London: Karnac.

Freud, S. (1890). *Psychical* (or *Mental*) *Treatment*. The standard edition of the complete works of Sigmund Freud, Vol. 7. London: Hogarth Press.

Freud, S. (1891). *On Aphasia: A Critical Study*. New York: International Universities Press, 1953.

Freud, S. (1894). *The Neuropsychoses of Defence*. The standard edition of the complete works of Sigmund Freud, Vol. 3. London: Hogarth Press.

Freud, S. (1895). *Studies on Hysteria*. The standard edition of the complete works of Sigmund Freud, Vol. 2. London: Hogarth Press.

Freud, S. (1900). *The Interpretation of Dreams*. The standard edition of the complete works of Sigmund Freud, Vols 5 and 6. London: Hogarth Press.

Freud, S. (1912). *A Note on the Unconscious in Psychoanalysis*. The standard edition of the complete works of Sigmund Freud, Vol. 12. London: Hogarth Press.

Freud, S. (1913). The Claim of Psychoanalysis to Scientific Interest. The standard edition of the complete works of Sigmund Freud, Vol. 13. London: Hogarth Press.

Freud, S. (1915). *The Unconscious*. The standard edition of the complete works of Sigmund Freud, Vol. 14. London: Hogarth Press.

Freud, S. (1920). *Beyond the Pleasure Principle*. The standard edition of the complete works of Sigmund Freud, Vol. 18. London: Hogarth Press.

Freud, S. (1923). *The Ego and the Id*. The standard edition of the complete works of Sigmund Freud, Vol. 19. London: Hogarth Press.

Freud, S. (1925). *Autobiographical Study*. Standard edition of the complete works of Sigmund Freud, Vol. 20. London: Hogarth Press.
Freud, S. (1926a). *Inhibitions, Symptoms and Anxiety*. The standard edition of the complete works of Sigmund Freud, Vol. 20. London: Hogarth Press.
Freud, S. (1926b). *The Question of Lay Analysis*. The standard edition of the complete works of Sigmund Freud, Vol. 20. London: Hogarth Press.
Freud, S. (1933). *New Introductory Lectures on Psycho-analysis*. The standard edition of the complete works of Sigmund Freud, Vol. 22. London: Hogarth Press.
Freud, S. (1940). *An Outline of Psycho-analysis*. The standard edition of the complete works of Sigmund Freud, Vol. 23. London: Hogarth Press.
Freud, S. (1950). *Project for a Scientific Psychology*. The standard edition of the complete works of Sigmund Freud, Vol. 1. London: Hogarth Press.
Freud, S. (1989). *The Letters of Sigmund Freud to Edouard Silberstein, 1871–1887*. Cambridge, MA: Belknap Press.
Freud, S. and Breuer, J. (1893, 1895). *Preliminary Communication*. The standard edition of the complete works of Sigmund Freud, Vols 1 and 2. London: Hogarth Press.
Glymour, C. (1991). Freud's androids. In J. Neu (Ed.) *The Cambridge Companion to Freud*. Cambridge: Cambridge University Press.
Greenberg, V. D. (1997). *Freud and his Aphasia Book*. Ithaca, NY: Cornell University Press.
Grünbaum, A. (2002). A brief autobiographical narrative. Keynote address delivered at 'The Adolf Grünbaum Symposium' held at the Center for Philosophical Education, Santa Barbara, California, on 18 and 19 October 2002.
Gupta, R. (1980). Freud and Schopenhauer. In M. Fox (Ed.) *Schopenhauer: His Philosophical Achievement*. Totowa, NJ: Barnes & Noble.
Hacking, I. (1995). *Rewriting the Soul: Multiple Personality and the Science of Memory*. Princeton, NJ: Princeton University Press.
Hameroff, S. (1995). Quantum coherence in microtubules: a neural basis for emergent consciousness? *Journal of Consciousness Studies*, 1(1), 91–118.
Hamilton, W. (1853). *Discussions on Philosophy and Literature, Education and University Reform, Chiefly from the* Edinburgh Review; *Corrected, Vindicated, Enlarged in Notes and Appendices*. Second edn. London: Longman, Brown, Green & Longmans.
Hardcastle, V. G. (1994). Psychology's binding problem and possible neurobiological solutions. *Journal of Consciousness Studies*, 1(1), 66–90.
Hebb, D. O. (1949). *The Organisation of Behavior*. New York: Wiley.
Hering, E. (1870). *Über dass Gedächtniss als allegemeine Funktion der organiserten Materie*. Vienna: K. K. Hof- und Staatsdrukerei.
Jackendoff, R. (1987). *Consciousness and the Computational Mind*. Cambridge: Cambridge University Press.
Jackendoff, R. (1996a). How language helps us think. *Pragmatics and Cognition*, 4, 1–34.
Jackendoff, R. (1996b). *Languages of the Mind: Essays on Mental Representation*. Cambridge, MA: Bradford/MIT.
James, W. (1892/1984). *Psychology: Briefer Course*. Cambridge, MA: Harvard University Press.
Jones (1953). *The Life and Work of Sigmund Freud*. New York: Basic Books.
Kitcher, P. (1992). *Freud's Dream: A Complete Interdisciplinary Science of Mind*. Cambridge, MA: Bradford/MIT.
Lashley, K. S. (1956). Cerebral organization and behavior. In H. Solomon, S. Cobb and W. Penfield (Eds.) *The Brain and Human Behavior*. Baltimore, MD: Williams and Wilkins.

Lehrer, R. (1995). *Nietzsche's Presence in Freud's Life and Thought.* Albany, NY: SUNY Press.

Libet, B. (1995). A testable field theory of mind-brain interaction. *Journal of Consciousness Studies*, 1(1), 119–26.

Lipps, T. (1883). *Grundtatsachen des Seelenlebens.* Bonn: Max Cohen & Sohn.

Mackay, N. (1989). Freud, explanation and the mind-brain problem. *Psychoanalysis and Contemporary Thought*, 9, 373–404.

Magee, B. (1989). *The Philosophy of Schopenhauer.* New York: Oxford University Press.

Masson, J. M. (Ed.) (1985). *The Complete Letters of Sigmund Freud to Wilhelm Fliess, 1887–1904.* Cambridge, MA: Harvard University Press.

McGrath (1987). *Freud's Discovery of Psychoanalysis: The Politics of Hysteria.* Ithaca, NY: Cornell University Press.

Mill, J. S. (1865/1979). *An Examination of Sir William Hamilton's Philosophy and of the Principal Philosophical Questions Discussed in his Writings.* Toronto: University of Coronto Press.

Mountcastle, V. (1967). The problem of sensing and the neural coding of sensory events. In G. C. Quarton, T. Melnechuk and F. O. Schmitt (Eds.) *The Neurosciences: A Study Program.* New York: Rockefeller University Press.

Natsoulas, T. (1984). Freud and consciousness I: Intrinsic consciousness. *Psychoanalysis and Contemporary Thought*, 7, 195–232.

Natsoulas, T. (1985). Freud and consciousness II: Derived consciousness. *Psychoanalysis and Contemporary Thought*, 8, 183–220.

Natsoulas, T. (1989a). Freud and consciousness III: The importance of tertiary consciousness. *Psychoanalysis and Contemporary Thought*, 12, 97–123.

Natsoulas, T. (1989b). Freud and consciousness IV: A propedeutic for functions of consciousness in hypercathected speech-imagery. *Psychoanalysis and Contemporary Thought*, 12, 619–62.

Natsoulas, T. (1991). Freud and consciousness V: Emotions and feelings. *Psychoanalysis and Contemporary Thought*, 14, 69–108.

Natsoulas, T. (1992). Freud and consciousness VI: A present-day perspective. *Psychoanalysis and Contemporary Thought*, 15, 305–48.

Neider, H. (1977). *Gesprach mit Heinrich Neider: Persönliche Erinnerungen an den Wiener Kreis.* Conceptus, 1.

Nietzsche, F. (1882). *The Gay Science.* New York: Vintage, 1974.

Nunberg, H. and Federn, E. (Eds.) (1962–75). *Minutes of the Vienna Psychoanalytic Society*, 4 vols. New York: International Universities Press.

Perkell, D. H. and Bullock, T. H. (1968). Neural coding. *Neurosciences Research Program Bulletin* 6(3), 221–348.

Pribram, K. (1971). *Languages of the Brain: Experimental Paradoxes and Principles in Neurophysiology.* New York: Brandon House.

Rieke, F., Warland, D., de Ruyter van Steveninck, R. and Bialek, W. (1997). *Spikes: Exploring the Neural Code.* Cambridge, MA: MIT Press.

Schlipp, P. A. (1963). *The Philosophy of Rudolf Carnap.* London: Cambridge University Press.

Silverstein, B. (1985). Freud's psychology and its organic foundation: sexuality and mind-body interactionism. *Psychoanalytic Review*, 72, 203–28.

Silverstein, B. (1989). Freud's dualistic mind-body interactionism: implication for the development of his psychology. *Psychological Reports*, 64, 1091–7.

Smith, D. L. (1999a). *Freud's Philosophy of the Unconscious.* Dordrecht, NL: Kluwer Academic Publishers.

Smith, D. L. (1999b). Sigmund Freud and the Crick–Koch hypothesis: a footnote to the history of consciousness studies. *International Journal of Psycho-Analysis*, 80(3), 543–8.
Smith, D. L. (1999c). John Searle's unconscious: a Freudian philosophical critique. *PS: Journal of the Universities Association for Psychoanalytic Studies*, 1(2), 64–79.
Smith, D. L. (1999d). Sigmund Freud's programme for a science of consciousness. *British Journal of Psychotherapy*, 15(4), 1999, 412–24.
Smith, D. L. (2000). Freud's science of consciousness then and now. *Neuro-psychoanalysis*. 1(2), 45–8.
Smith, D. L. (2001). The unconscious. In E. Erwin (Ed.) *The Freud Encyclopaedia*. New York: Garland Press.
Smith, D. L. (2002). The ontology of the unconscious: Freud vs. Searle. In J. Mills (Ed.) *Psychoanalysis, Science, and Epistemology*. Albany, NY: SUNY Press.
Solms, M. and Saling, M. (1986). On psycho-analysis and neuroscience: Freud's attitude towards the localizationist tradition. *International Journal of Psycho-Analysis*, 67, 397–416.
Solomon, R. C. (1974). Freud's neurological theory of mind. In R. Wollheim (Ed.) *Freud: A Collection of Critical Essays*. Garden City, NY: Anchor Press/Doubleday Books.
Spiegelberg, H. (1982). *The Phenomenological Movement: An Historical Introduction*. The Hague: Martinus Nijhoff.
Spitzer, M. (2000). *The Mind Within the Net*. Cambridge, MA: MIT Press.
Strawson, P. F. (1962). *Self, Mind and Body. Freedom and Resentment and Other Essays*. London: Methuen & Company, 1974.
Sulloway, F. (1979). *Freud: Biologist of the Mind: Beyond the Psychoanalytic Legend*. New York: Basic Books.
Wallace, E. (1992). Freud and the mind–body problem. In T. Gelfand and J. Kerr (Eds.) *Freud and the History of Psychoanalysis*. Hillsdale, NJ: The Analytic Press.
Whyte, L. (1979). *The Unconscious Before Freud*. London: Julien Friedman.
Williams, L. P. (1989). André-Marie Ampère. *Scientific American*, 260, 72–9.

5

Freud and the Neurological Unconscious

Grant Gillett

There is at present, in both philosophy and psychology, a resurgence of interest in the unconscious mind and a parallel interest in the work of Freud. Contemporary work on the unconscious tends, however, to focus on the cognitive unconscious rather than the dynamic unconscious and discussion concerns tacit knowledge, preconceptual content, automatised cognitive representations, and so on. In fact, those who devote thought to the problem of non-conscious representations are divided between thinkers who would view this as a cognitive phenomenon and those who would see only neurophysiology operating at the levels beneath consciousness. Freud was a neurologist before he was a psychiatrist and, as with any other neurologist of his time, he thought deeply about human being and the human brain as focal points of studies in biology, psychology and philosophy. He himself was deeply influenced by the rise of evolutionary thought, the burgeoning psychology of his time and increasingly sophisticated philosophical reflection on cognitive processes. The last was much more developed in continental Europe (following Kant) than in Britain (following the empiricists). These diverse influences played key roles in Freud's development and refinement of psychoanalysis as a theoretical account of the function of the mind and its relation to the brain. He was careful, for instance, to take note of the phenomenology of, his teacher, Franz Brentano, who was actively working on the science of consciousness in relation to logic and philosophy. Brentano's insistence that the psyche was something distinct in essence from, and irreducible to, physical events and objects and that it must be understood in its own terms had to be married with Freud's commitments as a neurobiologist in laying out a framework for his own distinctive understanding of the mind and brain.

> We know two kinds of things about our psyche (or mental life): firstly, its bodily organ and scene of action, the brain (or nervous system) and, on the other hand, our acts of consciousness, which are immediate data and cannot be further explained by any sort of description.
>
> (Freud, 1986, pp. 375–6)

The crucial distinctions and connections between the level at which philosophical understanding could illuminate experience and the level at which psychoanalytic synthesis could explain it would remain largely unexplored by Freud, but the latter would come to occupy a pre-eminent position in psychology. For Freud, the bill of fare in the latter type of inquiry would be filled out in terms of the subconscious forces and events which influenced the direction and dynamics of conscious thought. This was to remain a dominant theme, with the implicit presupposition that the causal underpinnings of events in the psyche might be as open to scientific investigation as any other biological field in which causal forces operated. Freud thought that the world of conscious phenomena was, as the phenomenologists claimed, a world in which we conceptualised and dealt with objects according to laws of normative psychology which could be investigated by traditional philosophical analysis (a point laid out quite carefully by Jaspers in his critiques of Freud). It was otherwise for the machinery at work beneath consciousness, which had to be treated more like a realm of biological phenomena understandable in the terms we might derive from neuroscience. I will examine this view and suggest that it has a remarkably contemporary ring to it. What is more, just as Freud and Jaspers both suggested, it does not pose the crass reductive threats that some have been too quick to trumpet as an implication of scientific psychology.[1]

1. The roots of the psychoanalytic tree[2]

We might begin our exploration of psychoanalytic knowledge by noting some of the more important influences on Freud and their effect on psychoanalytic theory.

Darwinism swept through the scientific world of the latter half of the nineteenth century and firmly established within the naturalistic ethos the continuity between human beings and other animals. This underpinning of the human sciences extended to our knowledge of the cognitive structures controlling human behaviour. Reserved for the future were detailed theoretical arguments about the selection and transmission of traits, the idea of cultural evolution and the innateness or otherwise of natural language. These later debates would focus on such issues as the relative merit of fairly simplistic theories concentrating on gene-based variation in individuals as the basis of fitness as over against those that posited the existence of multiple gene-based but variously realisable phenotypes which would respond to environmental selective forces in order to express their potential. In Freud's time some basic axioms of Darwinian theory were clear, unopposed by serious scientific opinion and of direct relevance to the study of the mind:

(a) There was a deep continuity between the human and the animal brain.
(b) The brain was the informational mechanism that conferred survival advantages on a species.
(c) The brain had a basis of instinctual or inherited behaviour patterns upon which learned responses supervene.
(d) The human brain was designed to be profoundly influenced by early learning experience.
(e) The most recent and ratiocinative adaptations would be encoded in the most phylogenetically recent areas of the brain.

We can spell these out in a little more detail to arrive at the picture that was to shape psychoanalysis. Animal species clearly had instincts which met the basic demands for nutrition, survival and procreation. In service of these basics of survival, the animal brain has developed a repertoire of cognitive skills which are exhibited as and when the environmental conditions warrant it. The idea of an objective, reality-based representation of the environment which will stand up to increasingly elaborate scrutiny is not nearly as important as having a ready response for any challenge and therefore we, and Freud, tend to think of animal behaviour as mainly instinctual. The human situation is quite different. Our main adaptation is flexibility in the face of diverse environmental challenges and we base this flexibility on the good tricks that members of our species have learned around here. We therefore emphasise bonding between offspring and their care-giving adults and the assimilation by human infants of what those adults have to impart. Along with assimilation by imitation and direct shaping of behaviour, we have an all-important mechanism for inter-generational improvement which is the ability to reflect on what we do and how it might be improved. This mechanism allows us to use multiple sources of information and association (some cultural and linguistic) to construct a response to any given situation. The net result of this is conscious active transformation of information in ways that facilitate novel solutions and perspectives or cognitive tricks not learnt at our parents' knees.

The Darwinian thought underlying early twentieth-century neuroanatomy was that the higher brain overwrote and subsumed more primitive functions using the information and connections that they embodied, but submitting them to modification by levels of function which represented higher adaptations to the environment. Thus the relatively primitive information in lower centres became engaged with the more detailed and adaptive information-gathering and strategy-forming centres of the neocortex. Translated into the concepts of psychoanalysis this structure parallels the relation between the (relatively simple and primitive) pleasure principle and the (relatively sophisticated and complex) reality principle which both operate in the psyche.

Throughout his writing Freud held himself accountable to neurobiology in discussing the psyche. 'Like Wundt, he believed that all his hypothesizing was constrained by known properties of the nervous system' (Kitcher, 1992, p. 59). With that in mind we must visit in brief the tenets of the neurophysiology of his time in order to appreciate this influence on psychoanalytic thought.

The *neuronal theory* was firmly established by neuroanatomists just as Freud began his major work. This theory maintained that the brain comprised discrete neurons which were connected to each other in organised ways to enable information processing in the central nervous system (CNS). Freud accepted that important information was captured in the connections between neurons which were affected by experience according to certain basic principles.

The most important of these principles was the *principle of association* and Freud was convinced of its truth and its usefulness in explaining both normal and abnormal mental phenomena (Spitzer, 1999, p. 5). Subsequently, this doctrine became established in psychology through the work of Hebb and others. The principle is simple and, as a basic theoretical model of the mechanism principally responsible for central nervous system organisation, has survived the coming and going of other theories of neural function:

The *principle of association*: Any two neurones which tend to fire together will strengthen their association or the likelihood that they will fire together in the future. This principle allows the brain to capitalise on coincidence provided only that the coincidence reflects a genuine probability of co-occurrence rather than a random event. Obviously, this basic principle is only the beginning but most other significant doctrines of neural organisation are built on it rather than overturning it. The advent of the computer age obscured this basic principle and substituted classic computational theories of cognition which relied on syntactic relations between structured representations of the environment. The transitions that occurred in classic computational series were formal and based entirely on the representational shape according to which the relevant environmental conditions were encoded (Fodor, 1981). This theory cuts cognition off from its primal roots replacing the well-established principles of probabilistic association with formal syntactic representation. But this is not the kind of mistake that Freud was prone to make. Freud needed association to account for the working of the Unconscious (Ucs) just as both he and contemporary psychoanalysis need linguistic encoding and symbolic content to fill out the picture. Both were available once the philosophy of Brentano and Husserl was mixed with the scientific dominance of Darwinian thinking.

It is interesting, in the light of the debates and influences prevalent at Freud's time, that the tide has turned again and connectionist and neo-associationist models are now again resurgent and proving robust in the face of neuro-cognitive and psychological data (Churchland and Churchland, 1998; Clark, 1997). The central tenets of associationism are well suited to Freud's doctrine of the primary process which is the dominant mode of information transfer in the Ucs. The central tenets of the new cybernetic associationism (of embodied cognition) are equally suited to our current understanding of the cortex and the conscious work of the psyche.

Recapitulation was the doctrine that the human being recapitulated in its ontogeny the evolutionary history of the species with older and more primitive modes of response to the environment persistent in the developing repertoire of behaviours exhibited by any individual. The primary process in particular worked by mechanisms that bore little relation to the articulate and environmentally specific sensitivities of the more developed centres and is directly reminiscent of the more impressionistic and affect-laden responses of instinct based agents.

Functional differentiation flowed from the connections established by neuronal assemblies and therefore was moderated by the way cell assemblies formed during a learning history rather than reflecting direct effects of environmental stimulation. The idea is that any neurone or neuronal assembly comes to realise a firing pattern that is based on presented environmental conditions but also the coincident patterns of stimulation (such as auditory stimuli) that typically accompany those conditions. In this way the firing patterns of neurones can be subtly differentiated from each other in myriad ways, depending on their connections to other functionally discrete neurones. Among the moderating effects were the influences of the pleasure/pain mechanisms and the affective tone they imparted to any representation linked to a set of environmental conditions. Also the effects of (potentially emotionally-laden) sound patterns from care-givers would have a complex interlacing set of associations with sets of environmental conditions. Only some of these associations would be accessible to conscious reflection on the basis of the habits of reality testing that are characteristic of consciousness. To appreciate this we need briefly to digress into the phenomenological studies that surrounded the young Freud and were to transform psychology and philosophy at the turn of the century.

2. Phenomenology, consciousness and reflection

We cannot begin to appreciate the philosophical psychology of Franz Brentano, or indeed any of the turn-of-the-century continental philosophers such as Husserl (Brentano's pupil) or Frege, without recalling the main tenets of Kantianism. Kant had argued that the contents of conscious thought were shaped on the basis of rule-governed judgements about the environmental conditions confronted by the subject. These judgements were principled and subject to critical scrutiny and only when they met the tests imposed on right judgement did they form the basis of a picture of the objective world.

The problem he bequeathed to his followers was to understand the norms that shaped judgement, which he himself linked to the judgements of other rational subjects and universal tenets of reason. Brentano was more interested in the cognitive structure of experience and the truths about psychology that could be discovered by examining it.

Brentano realised that consciousness was essentially intentional in the sense that its contents were objects about which judgements could be made which delineated the character of those objects. In order to make such judgements, the subject had to exercise certain developed cognitive skills in relation to the conditions it encountered in the environment. The subject first had to attend to the aspects of the presentation grounding the experience of the object and then differentiate the object from the background of conditions against which it appeared. That then allowed an implicitly comparative judgement about the nature of the object as compared with the categories of objects of which the subject had cognisance. This complex performance then allowed the object to be cognised as being an object of a certain type with certain general features (that it shared with other objects of the relevant type or classification) defining its nature.

The conscious ego and its operations which delineate and then classify objects as having this or that characteristic and being of this or that nature in part determine the reality with which the mind is in contact. This is a reality which has recognisable characteristics and essentially discursive or thinkable features comprising particular objects and general properties of objects. Kant realised that both types of judgement involved cognition in that (1) a particular object becomes thinkable (as an object) only when the subject unifies different experiences in which that object is encountered, and (2) general properties emerge when some principle of grouping is applied to different objects from which the mind distils a common feature.

Husserl developed this view and analysed the contents of consciousness as being conformed or informed by norms (*noemata*) which stand in a normative relationship to *noesis* or the cognitive faculty which gave rise to contents rather than a flux of unformed and uninformative impressions (*hyle*). Husserl noted that hyle and noetic productions were real contents of the individual psyche but noemata had an ideal existence essentially independent of individual subjects and definitive of the logically analysable intentional contents of the mind. One can make a compelling case that noemata are public phenomena (Gillett, 1997)[3] which are socio-culturally produced and discursive in nature. That view implies that the norms governing cognition are subject to rational correction and prescriptive transmission enshrining categories which are used to classify objects in relatively objective (or widely shared) ways. The material informed by these categories is subjective, but the contents which result in consciousness are much less so with essential links to language and validated ways of conceptualising experience. It is this validation that forges a link between reflection and the nature of consciousness. Reflection is normally taken (at least in phenomenological circles) to require that the individual can take his or her own mental states as the proper objects of attitudes and thoughts and therefore make judgements about those states. Thus we might conclude that the contents of those mental states which become conscious are subject to a reflective appraisal that judges their adequacy to a situation in terms of publicly endorsed criteria of truth or propriety. It is, of course, otherwise with the somewhat murky contents which affect us unconsciously.

We cannot undertake an analysis of the ideas informing the philosophical psychology of Freud and relating those to current thought in cognitive neuroscience without one further piece in the jigsaw of turn-of the century philosophy. Frege was a dominant figure in late nineteenth- and early twentieth-century philosophy and emphasised (as did Husserl) the difference between the contents of thought which were truth-assessable and subject to objective judgements and the less objectively grounded mental contents appearing in the minds of a particular individual at any given point in time. The thinking going on in the mind of any individual would, in becoming conscious thought, be judged against the standards of objectivity and rectitude, but mental activity might be going on in an individual with far less respectable credentials. The former contents were tied to language and the objective meanings established for words and therefore to well-formed sentences which may be assessed for their truth. Unequivocally conscious thoughts would be clear and distinct in that they could be mapped on to the clear lines of publicly validated meaning and rational connection. Mental acts and contents which fell short of this standard were much more the domain of psychological association, imagination (not in Kant's technical sense) and the poetic or rhetorical use of language. Philosophy (and therefore science) was mainly concerned with what could be established objectively and argued about against the framework of logical deduction and truth. Frege, unlike Husserl, did not speculate in his writing on the social and cultural and therefore inter-subjective means by which we establish truth and preferred to leave the anthropological or naturalistic turn in the understanding of truth and meaning to others. He was allergic to the idea that human subjectivity (whether individual or collective) could play a significant role in thought (as discussed by logicians and other philosophers) and therefore psychosemantics (of vast interest to Freud, Wundt, Head and the aphasiologists) was not something he concerned himself with. Some would therefore say that Frege, and the analytic philosophers that follow him, have little to say which is of interest to real human psychology.

We can now, in the light of this brief survey, define a clear philosophical framework against which Freud's understanding of the psyche can be outlined.

(a) The contents of consciousness are intentional and essentially concern objects in and features of the world of the subject.
(b) The ways in which these environmental features are classified and enter conscious thought are discursive and subject to norms or ideals.
(c) The norms are socio-culturally determined and conveyed by prescriptive practices which crucially involve language – thus they are supra-individual norms.
(d) The contents of the individual psyche are transformed into suitable material for conscious thought and reflection by the structuring influence of these discursive norms.
(e) The mind is the locus of and is, to some extent, free to shape subjective psychic content somewhat unconstrained by these norms but such material is not conscious intentional content.
(f) The mind is in causal interaction with the world in that its functions are realised by the workings of the CNS.

Once these foundations are in place we are well placed to understand the Freudian psyche, its structure, its function, and its principles of operation. It is this understanding that is the formative ground for the assessment of psychoanalytic knowledge.

3. The unconscious mind

Freud's summary of the system Ucs is as follows:

> To sum up: exemption from mutual contradiction, primary process (mobility of cathexes), timelessness, and replacement of external by psychical reality – these are the characteristics which we may expect to find in processes belonging to the system Ucs. (1986, p. 160)

Freud is quite clear that language plays a crucial role at the border between Ucs and Cs.

> The conscious presentation comprises the presentation of the thing plus the presentation of the word belonging to it, while the unconscious presentation is of the thing alone. The system Ucs contains the thing-cathexes of the objects, the first and true object-cathexes, the system Pcs comes about by this think-presentation being hyper-cathected through being linked with the word-presentation belonging to it. (1986, p. 172)

When we recall the philosophy of Husserl (and Frege) it becomes apparent that in the passage from Ucs to Cs there is discursive transformation and abstraction so that the causal immediacy of the thing presentation is to some extent replaced by the legitimated or conventional relations and associations of words and their connectedness in streams of thought.

> Probably . . . thought proceeds in systems so far removed from the original perceptual residues that they no longer have retained anything of the qualities of those residues and in order to become conscious, need to be reinforced by new qualities. Moreover, by being linked with words, cathexes can be provided with quality even when they represent only relations between presentations of objects and are thus unable to derive any quality from perceptions. (1986, p. 173)

The Kantian and Husserlian thought that words represent unifications of judgements constrained by ideal norms is evident in this passage. Freud notes that the original encounter with the object or thing that is the focus of an experience is displaced by a verbal or discursive representation. This representation functions in part by an abstraction from the thing in favour of the linking relation that allows different things (say a black cat, a Siamese, a tabby and an ocelot) to be represented by a term ('cat') which neglects the differences between them. The word also directs the mind away from the immediate perceptual individuality of the thing encountered to a colourless substitute with its own connections to other fragments of discourse rather than fragments of the perceptual world.

The replacement of the causal and perceptual or organic reality by the discursive representation is necessary for the process of reasoning and allows us to produce trains of conscious thought. In doing so it locks us in our thinking into the reflective and causally mediate discursive world rather than the world in which the direct effects of the real world encounter resonate within us as embodied organic beings.

But we ought not to overstate this as there is a core or nucleus of meaning that resides in the original associations which arise as a word is used in a set of conditions which ground that use and therefore its meaning. Freud's atomism reflects this focus on the original reference of the word.

> A word . . . acquires its meaning by being linked to an 'object-presentation', at all events if we restrict ourselves to a consideration of substantives. The object-presentation itself is once again a complex of associations made up of the greatest variety of visual acoustic, tactile, kinaesthetic and other presentations. (1986, p. 182)

Whereas thought at the conscious level is very much constrained by the discursive relations between content (replete with the logical relations beloved of Frege and the noematic or ideal prescriptions of Husserl), the nature of the processes in the unconscious was quite different. In the unconscious the primary process and modes of thought which were both associationist and directly responsive to the idiosyncrasies and emotional colours of individual experiential history were *à la mode*. This led to a breakdown on the public, rational and relatively objective constraints on conscious thought:

> . . . we are dealing here with modes of expression that are closer to hallucination than they are to thinking in words; opposites become one and the same thing; temporal relationships and sequences are disregarded; logical thinking and consequential cause-effect connections are missing; emotions are easily displaced from their real object to another; mixed figures are formed as the result of condensation of several single figures. Altogether this mode of thinking characteristic of the unconscious strikes one as extraordinarily primitive; it is not different from what we presume to prevail in the infant before the acquisition of language. In psychoanalytic terminology, we call it the primary process. (1986, p. 132)

Freud has here related the primitive nature of the primary process to ontogeny as is consistent with the overall aim of tracing the genesis of the forces in the Ucs affecting the behaviour of a person under analysis. We can see that, from a theoretical point of view, a phylogenetic sense of 'primitive' might also be invoked. In any event we can identify certain key features of the psychic processes in Ucs; these include:

- mobile cathexes and the prevalence of association over implication;
- pre-reflective influences on behaviour via the content of experience;
- non-moderation by the other conscious contents of the ego.

Ucs is therefore a domain of influences on the psyche which operate according to relatively primitive associative links derived from internal and external stimuli or conditions. The psychological or mental laws which govern rational and valid transactions in thought do not preside over the Ucs and therefore there are differences which 'cannot be overestimated' in the operation between this area and the field of the ego with its discursive structure. The contents of the Ucs are intentional in the sense that they relate to objects and have significance or meaning for a subject but the meanings are not subject to the Kantian norms of rationality that are definitive of intentional content as it appears in consciousness.

What is more, there is a process of censorship operating between Ucs and Cs and normative judgements – which are not only epistemic but also evaluative – are constantly being made about the suitability of the psychic material and its connections for representation in the domain of the ego. Moral and cultural norms interpose at the boundary between Ucs and the ego processes of Pcs and Cs and, even though the material pressing to be represented is to some extent ill-formed (in Frege's or Husserl's sense) its psychic moments are sufficient to activate ego-protective mechanisms when it threatens to be highly disruptive.

4. Critics and exponents of the Ucs

Both within and outside of psychotherapeutic circles the Freudian picture of the unconscious has attracted fierce criticism. It is not relevant at present to be at all comprehensive in my coverage of these criticisms as I have a much more limited aim.[4] In the present work I am attempting to sketch a reasonable interpretation of Freud's major claims that can be shown to be compatible with current philosophical thinking about the mind and its relation to the brain. It is however germane to my task to register some of the major critiques which lay some foundations for the view I hope to commend (itself not wholly critical).

In the 1940s and 1950s both Wittgenstein and Jaspers noticed that the Freudian claims for the Ucs as the locus of the real causes of current conscious states and behaviour were not well grounded. Wittgenstein (1970) discusses Freud's view in relation to the finding of meanings and explanations for what is puzzling in a psychological life. He objects to Freud's causal claims on the basis that Freud does not do the kind of experimental and statistical work that allows causality to be asserted. Jaspers (1997) makes a similar point. He notes that Freud manages to make meaningful connections between current disorders or behaviour and past events (or relationships) in the subject's life. These connections are, in the main, unnoticed by the naïve subject. Freud then claims that the resulting gaps in conscious life and explanation of behaviour are all meaningful in the posited way and that, in fact, the life events and experiences he identifies in analysis (some of which may not have been actual) have a causal influence on the psychic life of the individual concerned. He then derives a typology of such connections (Oedipal complex, castration anxiety, and so on) and transforms the explanatory connections into a theory of the psychological life of human beings. By this means the hypothetical understanding which allows us to integrate and explain what is going on in a puzzling psychological profile becomes hypostasised as a causal theory of the individual psyche and its moments.

Contemporary sceptical thoughts on the Ucs are largely identified with the work of Searle (1992). As a follower of Frege and Wittgenstein, we can expect him to be well aware of the problems besetting mental ascriptions in general and the idea of unconscious content in particular. He makes these problems vivid by pursuing a particular aspect of intentionality which leads him to conclude that the system Ucs does not contain the kind of formed psychic contents that Freud and his followers posit. His major argument turns on a feature of intentional content which was well known to the phenomenologists (such as Husserl) and therefore well understood by Freud: the object of thought is always thought about in some particular way. Thus (to use Frege's example), if I am thinking of the object in the sky which happens to be the planet Venus, I may be thinking about the evening star, the morning star or the planet Venus. There is only one object involved but there are three distinct conscious acts. Normally, one can easily decide which content aptly describes my mental state because I will be able to tell you or you will discern from my speech or actions just what I think of the object of my current attention. The same does not hold of the alleged contents of Ucs.

Consider the following example:

> *The primal wound:* A 39-year-old man, call him Gregor, goes to see a psychotherapist. He outlines a life in which he has constantly regarded himself as a misfit who feels that he has to make himself agreeable to whomever he is currently in any relationship with. Sometimes this has meant doing things about which he felt uncomfortable but he describes a constant fear of rejection and need to prove himself. He also describes problems in emotional relationships such that he feels detached or lacking in emotional engagement and has chronic feelings of insecurity and suspicion of his partners. He recounts dream experiences of betrayal and cruel abandonment in situations where he ought to feel loved and nurtured.
>
> The therapist finds out that Gregor was adopted soon after birth and relates much of what he is feeling to a 'primal wound'. This, according to the therapist, is the unconscious awareness carried from the time of adoption that his real mother has departed and abandoned him so that from that time onwards he has felt the loss of that broken relationship.

It is possible that the therapist is correct here, but one is entitled to ask what evidence she has that this is the correct reading of some thought (or more properly mental content) lodged in the Ucs. To be sure, such content may explain a number of Gregor's current conscious feelings, attitudes and behaviours, but there may be other explanations and there is no way of deciding between them independent of the theoretical context posited. Gregor himself cannot, *ex hypothesi*, tell us why he acts in the way he does and will not have any clear knowledge of the thought that is being attributed to him, as he would if he was thinking of the evening star as the evening star rather than the planet Venus. Thus the most that one can conclude is that there is something in his psyche which is affecting him *as if* he were aware at some deep level of a sense of abandonment as an infant. We cannot reify the 'primal wound' and the content involved any further than that. But this raises a problem which is central in the understanding of mind and world and the formation of conscious content on the basis of experience in the physical environment to which we are adapted and of which we are cognisant. The problem is the problem of psychic content in Ucs, proto-content or content which is essentially not conscious.

The problem of proto-content is a dilemma for theorists of mind and mental content. Is there material which is properly called mental content but which occurs in the mind prior to the application of concepts and the classification of that material according to those concepts? It seems that there must be because we can talk of ourselves, for instance, as being justified by the evidence before us that we are seeing a musk ox. Now if we are justified, then we are not merely caused to think we have witnessed a musk ox and must take ourselves to have some reason for thinking that. But reasons are framed in terms of conceptualised experience (it was a musk ox because I saw the fur and the horns) and yet the very same experience might turn out to be mistaken – 'Oh, I see now it was only a clump of grass with a branch sticking out of it'. In such a case it is more than plausible that there is some presentation or set of environmental conditions registered by the mind but indeterminate between an experience of a musk ox and the grass and branch ensemble. Now what do we say about this? Although I spelt out a possible explicit inference to the presence of a musk ox, perception far more often just presents us with an appearance which does not have any discursive preliminaries and explicit inferences. However, the possibility of doubt and our methods of dealing with it reveal the discursive nature of perception even though it is normally so assured and practised that its cognitive nature can pass unnoticed (as it seems to have done by Descartes, Locke and Hume). Kant was clearly aware of the cognitive skills inherent in perception and, as I have noted, it is his legacy that informed Freud. (See also Brook's discussion of Kant and Freud in this volume, Chapter 2.) In any event we must now acknowledge the paradox that to see the presentation before one as a musk ox is far more well grounded (in some sense) than to see it as a flamingo. In some sense the subject is epistemically better off if he makes the one mistake rather than the other, but it does not seem plausible that this is a matter of quality of inference, rather it has to do with the transformation of sensory contact with the environment into mental or experiential content, *in the right kind of way*. I consider this to be a skill at which one might be more or less adept and which is most likely to be well developed in familiar contexts and with familiar perceptual objects. When we see it in this way, the idea of an unconscious life which is, as Searle claims, neuro-physiological can become both plausible and attractive. That is part of the theory of mind which I will recommend.

Dennett (1991) has also explored the problem of reconciling a neurophysiological or neuropsychological account of what is happening with traditional phenomenological accounts of conscious experience. He has an underlying view which favours the explanatory basicness of the biological or physiological level. However, the material he presents does not offer clear support for this view. Dennett notices that the physical events registered by the brain, taken just on their own merit, under-determine the conscious phenomenology experienced. Thus, for instance, a record of the stimuli exhibited do not tell us how the percept or experience will be registered by the subject. To Dennett this suggests that the level of brain function is to be interpreted realistically and the psychological level is to be interpreted instrumentally. However we could argue (*contra* Dennett) that conscious phenomena are both genuinely explanatory and represent a meeting of two strands of events each of which can be understood to some extent in its own terms. The picture I suggest is as follows:

Brain events →		→ brain events
	{conscious moments}	
Discursive skills →		→ meaningful experience

According to this picture there is a meeting in the human subject of two distinct series of events:

1. a causally produced stream of neural activity which arises from the interaction between the brain and the environment (some brain events give rise to others);
2. a stream of discursive activity which renders that neural stream in terms apt for the meaningful experience that becomes my autobiography.

Stream 1 – the neural stream – is only misleadingly cast as a stream of discrete events; it is really a shifting seamless web of neural activity obeying laws of association and possible neuro-cognitive vector transformation (the details do not matter once the parsing is gone). Importantly, this stream gives us real-time access to the world around us and grounds one's consciousness in one's actual situation.

Stream 2 – the discursive stream – is rooted in our interactions as persons, one with another, and results in each of us commanding a set of skills on the basis of which we figure out what is happening around us. These skills are discursive and therefore, as Kant observed, intrinsically connected with our epistemic justifications, but they are skills and operate like any other skills. They are means by which we use tools and techniques to transform a stream of physical activity into a form more suited to our cognitive needs. In this case, the tools are notional or abstract involving mapping rules which take in raw causal data from the brain–world stream and work with it until it fairly reliably reveals what is happening to us and around us in terms of the things we have learned to think about.

The focus on skills links us with the non-discursive animals in that all intentional creatures deploy cognitive techniques which take what is currently happening to them and assimilate it to previously encountered situations. This allows new situations to be met by congenital or ontogenetically developed strategies which are likely to deal successfully with the environmental challenges that are posed. That process is the pragmatic or adaptive essence of representation and makes ontogeny an important time of learning. As human beings, we have (to an extent unprecedented in nature) a pooled cultural resource for dealing with the complex things that tend to happen around here, but there is no mystery about that. It is part of our natural history to be social and discursive creatures and that expands our range of experience (we can have vicarious experience as a result of story-telling, and so on) and equips us with good tricks that others in our cultural group have tried and proved in their dealings with the world. And here we ought to recall that if a species designer were to build one pre-eminent survival trick into human beings it would be to learn to do what other human beings are doing. We shall return to this outline picture in the light of Freud's structure of the psyche once we have put in place some further conceptual apparatus.

Jacques Lacan (1981) has transformed psychoanalytic theory by introducing ideas from structuralism and existentialism to generate a novel and modified derivative of classical Freudianism. Jointly these have had the effect of weakening the strong emphasis on the biological determinism and the bottom-up explanation of psychic life in terms of instinctual and unconscious forces (Gillett, 1999). Lacan has a great deal of respect, even reverence, for the Freudian corpus but he has a keen appreciation for the importance of recent work in the philosophy of language. This has opened psychoanalytic theory to the possibility that the contents of the unconscious are negotiable in the light of (1) the constantly evolving network of meanings that is inherent in any living language; and (2) the role of the subject in linking words to the moments of his or her psychological life. A few key concepts will suffice to outline the essential favour of the Lacanian revolution in psychoanalytic theory.

Lacan's structuralist leanings have added a great deal of detail and resonance to Freud's remarks on the role of language in the ego. Structuralism emphasises the fact that language is a complex network of signifiers each of which draws meaning in part from the distinctions and similarities between its signification and that of others (Saussure, 1983). This holism about meaning implies that the individual's immersion into language is like an immersion into a 'braided' or many currented, river in which life takes on its experiential shape. Each individual increasingly (in ontogeny) grasps more and more of the linked significations prevalent in a linguistic group. These provide the terms in which that individual articulates conscious experience. However, even though each individual increasingly masters the tools used to articulate experience, the whole is not the possession of any individual and is in fact something enveloping, contextual and almost infinite in its potential complexity which pre-dates the individual's arrival, provides the setting for the individual's existence and significantly conforms the psyche.

The medium through which language forms and continually transforms the psyche is social – those relationships in which we imbibe language. These are primarily the relationships of close kinship and therefore the forces which Freud emphasised, focusing as they do on primary group relationships, have great importance in the development of mind and personality. For Lacan (1981), and his anthropological mentor Lévi-Strauss (1978), the structure and rituals of kinship play a hugely important part in this development, but we need not pursue that at this point. For the minute we need only note that the psyche, and particularly those parts of it significantly formed before the development of self-critical and reflective awareness, is a palimpsest of significations whose contributory texts are linguistic and heavily coloured by emotional overtones.

The network of signifiers that form and become realised in the individual psyche is not separable from the immersion of the individual in two worlds – an actual causal world and a world of meaning. These worlds are not wholly separable and interpenetrate at every point. The brain – as the repository of experience – can therefore be thought of as keeping a cumulative record of significance-laden encounters with the world. In this way Lacan can pay due attention, on the one hand, to the human world of meaning and socio-cultural interchange and, on the other, to the physico-causal impact of the environment on the organism as organism. Lacan's existentialist leanings allow him to pick up, in Freud's writings about memory, the hints of anti-realism about the contents of the psychic Ucs that makes one wary of attributing real historical significance to the memories and traumata unearthed in analysis. If we accept that the psyche is configured by a conjoint product of the actual impact of the environment on the organism and the significances attached to those moments of brain–world interaction, then we can endorse this suggestion. Just as one's individual grasp of language and the complexities of social life are constantly being updated and refined, we can infer that the psychic life and its contents, even at the level of Ucs, is constantly being reconfigured. This theoretical position is tenable as a development of the (Freudian and psychoanalytic) view that any individual can become stuck and have points in their psyche at which pathological or maladaptive complexes of psychic material have congealed and represent barriers to personal growth and well-being.

In the light of the general position I want to recommend, this allows us to formulate a plausible view of the problem of proto-content that we encounter in the philosophy of mind. One might argue that the impact of world and culture or Language (Grand L) on the individual provides a framework for thought and experience which is complementary to that of the actual environment. Together, environment and culture potentiate the articulation of certain psychic or mental content which requires the endorsement of conscious cognitive recognition to fix it as part of the conscious life of the individual. In some cases this endorsement is automatic (such as well-practised perceptual recognition), but in others there is conscious cognitive work to be done. In some cases it is plausible that the mind is in a mode such that the material which most people would naturally cognise as having content A (anger, say) remains to some extent unformed, but with some of the causal force that would normally attach to A. We might conjecture that this would be more likely to occur when the experiences concerned were potentially conflict-ridden at some level or another. To clarify: at certain points the conjoint effect of the encounter with certain environmental conditions and the normal mechanisms of signification would tend to produce a given intentional content, but for reasons inherent in the psyche/neural network of the person concerned that content does not result in any form which is consciously recognisable. This material is the material which lurks in what Freud calls Ucs. The work of psychotherapy is to clarify this material and to rework the significant dimensions of the experiences which have led to it being formed. By so doing one may reconfigure the psyche such that the consciously lived narrative becomes more adequate to deal with the ongoing encounter between the subject and the world.

Both Lacan and Jaspers pick up the hints of agnosticism in Freud's writing about the determinacy of the content of such material. We can now recap and move directly to the development of a neo-Freudian view that does justice to the intellectual currents within which he formed his own theory.

5. The neuro-cognitive Ucs

The argument to date is as follows:

1. Freud was a child of late nineteenth-century biology, neurology, psychology and philosophy.
2. The theoretical context of Freud's work requires us to take Darwinism seriously, to attend to the structure of the brain in developing a theory of mental function, to work from the basis of the principle of association and to notice the logical constraints on the content of conscious phenomenal content.
3. Freud argued that conscious life was just part of the whole life of the psyche and that the gaps in conscious thought and the explanation of behaviour could be filled in by close attention to childhood events and biological instincts.
4. Freud posited complexes in the unconscious whose content could elucidate the meaning of conscious behaviour and attitudes and which caused those phenomena.

5. Critics have noted the lack of evidence for causal explanations in Freudian theory and the immodest presumption of meaningfulness that pervades his view of conscious life.
6. There is a growing body of opinion that posits neural networks and connections working on associationist principles underlying mental life.
7. It is plausible that the meanings one finds in life and the cultural setting in which one lives significantly alter the way that events are connected in the mind/brain.
8. The possibility of self-creation and reflective revision of one's thought life affects both the contents of conscious life and the deeper levels of neuro-cognitive association which shape that life.
9. The mind is a joint product of the narrative skills of the subject (drawn from those available in a culture and the seamless neurophysiological stream arising from the brain–world interaction).
10. Some aspects of mind are not fully articulated by conscious narrative skills and yet play an important role in mental life.
11. It is these last aspects which are the topic of specifically psychoanalytic knowledge.

This position is consistent with Freud's writings on the relation between the psychic and the physiological levels of human function:

> It is probable that the chain of physiological events in the nervous system does not stand in causal connection with the psychical events. . . . What happens is simply that, after a certain point of time, each (or some) of its links has a psychical phenomenon corresponding to it. Accordingly, the psychical is a process parallel to the physiological – 'a dependent-concomitant'. (1986, pp. 176–7)

I have argued that there is a very contemporary ring to this thought although the idea of psychophysical parallelism is no longer fashionable. According to my synthesis, parallelism is not the most helpful way to look at what is going on. I have argued that consciousness is a lived narrative in which one has used discursive techniques to inform (or give form to) a stream of activity which functions to keep me in contact with my environment. Faced with the concept of parallelism, Freud naturally concluded that the physical was more basic, but when we regard consciousness as rooted equally in the physical world and in the realm of discourse and self-narrative then the relation between these two influences looks less obvious. Given Freud's recognition of the negotiability of the contents of the unconscious and the Lacanian emphasis on the creation of the structures of Ucs by the ongoing meaning giving activity of the subject as engaged subject, we end up with a picture of the co-production of mental life rather than a basic level and a level which supervenes or depends on it. If, in fact, we argue that the neurocognitive stream is insufficient to unilaterally determine the contents of consciousness and if Searle is right to argue that mental content is related to the conscious intentional states that the subject would experience (or I would say 'produce') in relevantly similar situations, then the participation of the discursively located subject is an important factor in determining the contents of the mind. On this reading the contents of Ucs would move us according to their connections to relevantly similar meaningful or conscious contents. The difference is that they would move us in ways that are not subject to our normal habits of self-censure and reflective self-scrutiny. Because the contents of Ucs are, on this view, somewhat opaque to the conscious self, they might be expected to move us in ways we do not fully understand and imbue things with non-transparent significance. The evasion of critical self-scrutiny is also likely to mean that they show characteristics of rigidity, disharmony, immaturity and inauthenticity with respect to one's lived narrative and sense of self.

Psychoanalytic knowledge concerns the dynamic interplay between the various influences on the human psyche. Those influences importantly include events in the individual's past and the meanings which have structured the associations and connections informing mind and behaviour. The structure that is produced from this interplay of forces is realised in the neurocognitive microprocessing function of the brain which effectively becomes the physical substrate of mind. This substrate, I have argued, is inscribed by the ongoing encounter between the individual and the environment but also by correlations between patterns of activity which reflect the rules governing meanings and their interrelationships in the microcultural context of that individual. The conscious narrative that results from the use of this rich resource is a central feature of any lived human life and it expresses or exhibits both the discursive skills of the subject and effects arising in the domain of extraconscious forces that Freud sought to understand. Each human being is in the business of fulfilling the dictum 'know thyself', but at various times and for many different reasons one might enlist the help of a skilled interpreter in essaying that task. Psychoanalysis has always provided a cadre of such interpreters who have painstakingly built, on diverse foundations, a complex understanding of the human condition intimately tied to the stories we live by. For these practitioners there is a special place to be given to the theoretical understanding of the complex relationship between consciousness and the substrate on which it is built. On the present account this substrate is the brain, but it is the brain as inscribed by causal and cultural influences and not just the brain of the neurobiologist. Freud, having begun as a neurobiologist, moved during his career to the more inclusive understanding I have sketched and so made an invaluable contribution to the future of psychoanalytic knowledge.

Notes

1. The reductive thesis is evident in the work, for instance, of Colin Blakemore, J. Z.Young and Richard Dawkins.
2. Patricia Kitcher (1992) has done a marvellous job of discussing the milieu of theory and scholarship that shaped Freud's ideas on the brain/mind and I can only highlight the one or two strands that are germane to the present argument.
3. A view to which Husserl himself gravitated.
4. I have been more comprehensive in *The Mind and its Discontents* (1999).

References

Blakemore, C. (1982). *The Mechanics of Mind*. London: Penguin Books.
Clark, A. (1997). *Being There*. Cambridge, MA: MIT Press.
Churchland, P. and Churchland, P. (1998). *On the Contrary*. Cambridge, MA: MIT Press.
Dawkins, R. (1976). *The Selfish Gene*. Oxford: Oxford University Press.
Dennett, D. C. (1991). *Consciousness Explained*. London: Penguin Books.
Fodor, J. A. (1981). *Representations*. Cambridge, MA: MIT Press.
Freud, S. (1986). *The Essentials of Psychoanalysis*. London: Penguin Books.
Gillett, G. (1997). Husserl, Wittgenstein and the snark. *Philosophy and Phenomenological Research*, LVII, 331–50.
Gillett, G. (1999). *The Mind and its Discontents*. Oxford: Oxford University Press.
Jaspers, K. (1997). *General Psychopathology*. Baltimore: Johns Hopkins University Press.
Kitcher, P. (1992). *Freud's Dream*. Cambridge, MA: MIT Press.
Lacan, J. (1981). *The Four Fundamental Concepts of Psychoanalysis*. London: Norton & Co.
Lévi-Strauss, C. (1978). *Myth and Meaning*. New York: Schocken.
Saussure, F. de (1983). *Course in General Linguistics*. Chicago: Open Court.
Searle, J. (1992). *The Rediscovery of Mind*. Cambridge, MA: MIT Press.
Spitzer, M. (1999). *The Mind within the Net*. Cambridge, MA: MIT Press.
Wittgenstein, L. (1970). *On Certainty*. Oxford: Blackwell.
Young, J. Z. (1987). *Philosophy and the Brain*. Oxford: Clarendon Press.

6

The Etiology of Emotion and Ossification of Self: You Can't Change People because People Don't Change

Michael P. Levine

1. Introduction: do people change?

It is not surprising that this chapter's title riles people. Among an individual's cherished beliefs are the beliefs that in fundamental ways relating to character and emotion (1) they are capable of change and, more narcissistically, (2) they are capable of changing others. The strength of these convictions should make one wary. After all, one doesn't really need Freud to tell us that our strongest affirmations are *often* (not always) our strongest denials (cf. Sachs, 1982, p. 92). On this matter, psychoanalytic theory seems not so much an extension of common-sense psychology as part of it. For psychoanalysis, the strength with which these beliefs are held is indicative of repression – a defensive self-deceptive strategy that serves the ego.

The title of the chapter notwithstanding, I have no intention of arguing that people cannot and do not change in various ways, or that they may not be instrumental in changing themselves or others. That they can and do is obvious. The more interesting issue, especially in relation to character – of which emotion is an important part – is to show why fundamental aspects of an individual do not change, or change very little. It is useful to distinguish between (a) changes that occur in people as a matter of course over time with little in the way of focused effort on their part and (b) the significant changes that people seek consciously to bring about. When it is said that people do not change it is usually the latter that is being referred to. But of course, there is nothing incongruous in maintaining that in some respects people change, sometimes as a matter of course over time, while also maintaining that basically people do not change.

Someone once said to me, 'People do not change; they just become more so.' It is what is right about this that is worth examining. It is part of the perennial question of whether character is destiny. In relation to emotion, it turns out that the possibility of change and the manipulation of one's emotional repertoire is far more significant than whether or not emotions are rational. The answer to the latter question is simply that in some ways they may be rational and in other ways they are not.[1] It depends – no surprise – on what is meant by 'rational'. But seeing why emotional change is problematic tells us a great deal about our lives. Indeed, much of what one expects or hopes to find out in regard to the question of the rationality of emotions can be better gleaned by looking at the possibility of emotional change. Questions about the rationality of emotion are linked closely to hypotheses about the etiology of emotion. There are closer links, however, between considerations of etiology and views about the ability to change emotionally.

Tamas Pataki says 'that although the rigidity of emotional disposition obviously is a component of the rigidity of character, getting at the latter through the former is probably the hard way. Coming at character through the rigidity of internalised object relations, of instinctual fixations, habitual character defences, and so on, would be easier, and in some sense these are more fundamental than emotion.'[2] This may be true, although I do not see why they would be more fundamental. But isn't it plausible to suppose that the rigidity of internalised object relations, instinctual fixations and the like are themselves to be explained at least partly in terms of the rigidity of emotions? At any rate, I am not necessarily claiming that emotion is the only or even primary thing that fixes or affects character – only that it is one important factor.

I am focusing on the extent to which we can change emotional responses and why it is exceedingly difficult to do so. By this I mean not if and how we can control our *display* of emotions, but rather to what extent we can control what emotions are evoked in certain situations. This is narrower than questions about the extent to which we can control or change character traits that have generally occupied philosophers.[3] Changing emotions is crucial to altering character. However, changing aspects of one's character involves more than this.

There are three distinctions to be made: (1) undergoing changes in emotional dispositions and therefore to a degree in character; (2) changing one's own character, 'directly' as it were; and (3) changing somebody else's emotional disposition or character or being changed by somebody else. It is primarily (2) that I focus on, but the arguments I present tend to support (1) and (3) as well. Because (1)–(3) are interrelated and subject to many of the same factors, the distinctions made here are somewhat arbitrary. The same or similar reasons that are offered in support of (2) will be operative in (1) and (3) as well – and similarly with any other permutation of (1)–(3). If it is going to be difficult to change one's own dispositions, then it will be difficult to change those of others or have others change one's own. The thrust of my argument, in general terms, is that it is extraordinarily difficult to change.

At the outset one faces the formidable objection that as it stands (1) is obviously false. We do change radically in emotional disposition and character. I am hardly anything like the way I was as an adolescent, as a seven-year-old, as a baby. Analysts sometimes say a person's character doesn't gel until middle age. The objection is formidable and the way to deal with it is to meet it head on. It is not at all clear that (1) is altogether false. Although in some ways you are not like the adolescent you were, this chapter suggests you are more like the seven-year-old and adolescent you were than you realise or can realise. Subject to maturation, various kinds of acculturating influences and reason, you may well have largely (not wholly) the same kinds of emotional dispositions and character you had early on. This chapter tries to establish that when we look at the etiology of emotion there are strong theoretical reasons to suppose that the changes we would like to believe occur, and that we would like to believe we can influence, do not really occur (all that much). Appearance notwithstanding – although appearances are of little help in deciding how much we change – there are important ways in which people do not change much. As would many others, I reject the formidable objection above. It is an objection that merely supposes the thesis of this paper is flat out wrong at the outset.

Having said that I do not want to deny that that there are periods of greater and lesser liability, even as regards emotional change. Nor do I contend that it is utterly impossible to choose to alter intentional sets and even succeed on occasion in doing so – though how this comes about is, I take it, not easily explained. Finally, the fact that we do undergo certain kinds of changes, like those in sexual feelings – and even that these in turn influence character development in some ways is perfectly compatible with the view that, in the relevant sense, and for the reasons given in this chapter, change is extraordinarily difficult. Remember: what we are looking for is the truth in the assertion that people do not change, not the falsity in it.

I shall discuss three accounts of the etiology of emotion. Despite significant variations these accounts are broadly compatible and in some ways similar. Although they are all psychoanalytically oriented, Gardner's explicitly so, there is much in each that seems plausible even in terms of common-sense psychology. Indeed, the accounts they give are, in my view, insightful and more or less correct. What is less clear in varying degrees in each account, and what I intend to supply, is further discussion of the accounts' implications for the possibility of emotional change.

2. Amélie Rorty: why it is difficult to change

Rorty (1980, p. 103) claims that the intentionality of emotions, what an emotion is mentally directed towards and is partly about, has a complex structure.[4] This is revealed in focusing on cases of what she terms 'unexpected conservation of emotions'. Such emotions appear to be inconsistent or conflict with judgements and beliefs a person has. They also distort a person's perceptions and beliefs in ways that make those emotions difficult to alter or correct in view of one's considered beliefs. To use Rorty's cases: An example of the former would be when a person continues to have an emotion even after changing the belief apparently necessary to generate the emotion at the time. A spouse continuing to grieve even after they find out their spouse was not killed, where the belief that they were killed appears to have been the immediate cause of the grief, is a case of unexpected conservation of the emotions. An example of the latter is a case in which an employee feels resentment at a female boss whom he sees as domineering when objectively speaking there are no grounds to perceive her this way. Jealousy that appears ungrounded, even from the jealous person's own perspective, is another example of the latter.

Although the complex structure of the intentionality of emotions is best revealed in these puzzling cases, Rorty's account suggests that the structure is essentially the same in quite ordinary cases of emotion. Components of the structure may have different degrees of significance in accounting for the emotion in puzzling versus ordinary cases, but the structure is the same. Additionally, Rorty's account of anomalous and ordinary emotional response is equally applicable, and applicable in the same way, to explaining (in part) why people in a similar situation may react with different emotions. It explains why, though similarly situated, you react with jealousy or anger and your friend does not. There is a sense in which, given Rorty's explanation, you and your friend are not in the same situation. Emotional responses are not merely or primarily a product of present circumstances, but of past circumstance as well. It is because different histories and constitutional (genetic) dispositions result in different intentional sets and magnetising dispositions (see below), that people have different emotions in similar situations.

The problem cases are those in which we are puzzled about how (1) the immediate target of the emotion (that is, what the emotion appears to be, and is in fact in some sense, directed at), and (2) the precipitating or immediate cause of the emotion, can actually explain or justify the emotion in some rational way. So how are these cases of emotion to be explained? Rorty (1980, pp. 106–7) terms the entire causal history of an emotion its 'significant cause'. This is what explains the 'efficacy' of the emotion's precipitating or immediate cause. The significant cause, however, can *often* not be located in the events immediately leading up to an emotion's occurrence – that is in the 'immediate past'. (Rorty says the significant cause 'often' cannot be located in the immediate past, but why it is not always the case that it cannot be located there, given her account of what a 'significant cause' is, is not clear.) Instead, it will often be a series of events in the distant past; an event or series of events forgotten 'that formed a set of dispositions that are triggered by the immediate cause'.[5]

Rorty (1980, pp. 106–7) employs the notion of a 'magnetizing disposition' to further explain an emotion's significant cause. These dispositions 'gravitate toward and create conditions that spring other dispositions'. If one has such a disposition towards irascibility, then not only does one tend to be irascible – have a 'low threshold' towards irascibility – but one also tends to gravitate towards or look for conditions that trigger irascibility. Such dispositions do not necessarily explain by themselves why one reacts, through actions or attitudes, in the particular ways one does. But they can help explain such reactions 'indirectly' by accounting for the range of desires, beliefs and perceptions one is inclined to have. Magnetising dispositions are, in varying degrees, a result of a person's psychological history. However, they can also be acquired 'along with other characteristically culture-specific intentional sets and motives, as part of a person's socialization'. Significant causes produce such dispositions – which is why they can explain how an immediate cause is able to produce an emotion in a particular person but not in another. Magnetising dispositions go some way towards explaining a particular emotional response along with 'the tendencies to structure experience in ways that will elicit that characteristic response' in a particular person.

Thus, according to Rorty (1980, p. 108), to explain peculiar emotional responses – anomalous or intractable emotions – one must have recourse to the emotion's significant cause. The emotion is grounded in the significant causes of magnetised dispositions that explain 'habits of selective attention and interpretation' and how they are activated in certain situations. Summarising, she says (1980, p. 108): 'When in doubt about how the immediate target and precipitating cause explain the emotion, look for the significant cause of the dispositional set that forms the intentional component of the emotion.'[6]

As Rorty describes it, both the gravitational and creation aspects of magnetising dispositions are to be explained by the combination of genetic and other constitutional factors, socialisation and individual history. Which factors causally predominate in particular individuals will itself be a function of these factors.[7]

Rorty (1988, pp. 114–15) argues convincingly that even if one chose to explain 'intractable, inappropriate emotions more simply and elegantly by specifying the relevant belief that fixes the description of the target', this would not really simplify matters. Indeed, it would obfuscate them in the long run since the same issues addressed in her analysis would at some point have to be addressed anyway. To explain the resistance of certain emotions to considerations that would or should ordinarily change the emotion, or to explain the 'anomalous conservation of belief', one must have recourse to 'exactly the same sort of schema of causal explanation that we use in understanding the conservation of emotions'.

Once Rorty's definitions and account of 'significant cause' are grasped, it is surprising how commonsensical her explanation is. When an emotion appears utterly unwarranted or disproportionate, the first thing that comes to mind in attempting to understand it is to posit something like what Rorty means by a significant cause. We say that the person has a problem, and to understand it we have to understand its source. Except in cases where we suspect brain damage or psychosis, there is rarely doubt that the reaction does have an explanation along the lines of Rorty's 'significant cause'.

Rorty's explanation of emotions has implications for assessing the degree of difficulty in changing both emotional response and the part of one's character determined by emotional makeup. She says (1980, p. 121) that an explanation of the ways people go about changing emotions they take to be irrational or inappropriate is similar to the explanation of how people go about changing habits. Changing such emotions, like changing habits, is difficult and complex. Understanding the significant cause of an emotion and its magnetising dispositions helps explain the difficulty. Furthermore, the difficulty in bringing about such change in the face of 'the deep conservation of emotional habits' indicates why the claim that we choose our emotions, or that emotions are 'voluntary judgements' is likely to be false. Rorty says (1980, p. 121), 'Sometimes – rarely – it is possible for some people – a happy few – to take steps to restructure their intentional sets, to revise their emotional repertoire.'

In simple cases emotions are causally linked to beliefs in such a way that when the belief immediately causing the emotion changes, then so does the emotion. But even in such cases one may want to change the kind of emotional response that one has to such beliefs, and this requires something different than merely changing one's beliefs – even if, as seems neither likely nor desirable in most cases, one can change the relevant beliefs one has. The best way to effect change, when change is possible, may not be by attempting to influence one's emotions with beliefs, or solely with beliefs, but with other emotions. Emotions not only influence what beliefs one holds, they may also influence the strength or intensity of beliefs, and their intractability. Emotion influences how one perceives and processes information involved in forming and supporting beliefs (cf. Frijda et al., 2000). Often – much more often than people like to believe – it is emotion that influences what we believe rather than vice versa. A worldview (of which beliefs are a part) intellectually supports an ethos (of which emotions are a part), but at the same time an ethos supports a worldview.

George Sher (1998, p. 9) says, 'even when people do change, the cause is far more often pressure from the world than their own hopeful efforts'. But resistance to change does not suggest that when it occurs it must come primarily from extrinsic pressures. As psychoanalysis would have it, it is 'hopeful efforts' that combine with the intractability of the external world to conform to one's desires that may lead to change or a reshaping of one's desires. People seek change due to both internal and external pressure, but the question is, how successful are they likely to be? Given Rorty's account of the causal history of emotion, is there reason to believe that change is likely to occur as a result of hopeful efforts? Is such change likely to be under a person's control? Rorty doesn't think so, and her account explains why. Compared to these questions, whether one changes primarily because of external rather than internal causes or reasons is less significant.

It is important to distinguish between the possibility of changing the actual emotions one undergoes on the one hand, from the way one expresses the emotion in outward behaviour on the other. Rorty (1980, pp. 121–2) notes that for various reasons a person may want, and be able, to alter the usual expression and consequences of first or second order emotions without wanting to change the habits or intentional sets that give rise to the emotions. A person may distinguish between appropriate and inappropriate emotional responses by observing that different cases (appropriate and inappropriate) of the same type may group together because of a shared casual history. Rorty (1980, pp. 121–2) says, 'If he tackles his problem of identifying and overcoming inappropriate resentments separately each time . . . [he] is unlikely to make much headway . . . Because he thinks some cases of resentment are perfectly justified by their causes and objects, he is unlikely to solve his problem by setting himself the task of avoiding resentment altogether.' By understanding the causal history of the problematic (inappropriate) kinds of resentments one can become aware of the kinds of situations 'that trigger magnetized dispositions he regards as inappropriate'.

By alerting oneself to such situations one may, of course, attempt to alter one's outward behaviour. But even if one is alert and sensitised, is there good reason to suppose that one can also alter one's actual emotional response internally as well – I mean not have the emotion or have a different emotion? In fact, isn't the change we often seek – the change we are really after – a change in 'the habits or intentional set of having' the emotion? Changing one's outward emotional behaviour, the way in which one acts in response to an occurrent emotion, may be difficult, but this difficulty seems to pale in comparison both to altering the emotion one experiences or to changing 'the habits or intentional set of having' the emotion.

Questions about which emotional responses to change are not, as Rorty (1988, p. 120) points out, straightforward. Emotions that are undesirable (Rorty says 'maladaptive') in particular cases may not be so generally. It may be better – highly beneficial – that our emotional responses are habitual instead of being dominated by rational considerations, 'and for them to be changed by rational considerations only with considerable difficulty. It is part of the discomforting character of our emotional life that the genetic programming and the social formation of emotional dispositions are not respecters of the rationality or the comfort of individual persons.'

This should be considered, and it should also be remembered that we might be mistaken as to whether discomforting and otherwise problematic emotions are maladaptive or fail to serve our well-being. Nevertheless, it leaves us with the question about the possibility of changing emotional responses where they are judged maladaptive (cf. Levine, 2000). The sought-after changes might involve getting rid of or moderating emotions that appear to do us no good, or perhaps substituting others in cases where we judge our responses inappropriate, maladaptive, harmful, and so on. But how can one change one's 'intentional habits of salience, organization, and interpretation' and associated and entrenched magnetising dispositions that largely explain not just the conservation of emotion but even ordinary emotional occurrences? Apart from one's earliest emotional episodes, the significant cause of an emotion is never in the immediate past. How could it be?

It is often possible, in varying degrees, to mask certain emotional responses by acting differently from the way one ordinarily would, for example by hiding one's anger. But consider what is involved in having a different emotion (not just acting differently), or no emotional response at all, in circumstances where one does ordinarily respond emotionally in a particular way. The dispositions and other factors that cause one to respond in particular ways in certain circumstances, not necessarily appropriate, reinforce those dispositions to respond similarly over time. All of this must somehow be forestalled or altered for different responses to occur.

In many cases the best chance of changing the way in which we emotionally respond is by displacing one emotional response with another (cf. Frijda et al., 2000). If so, then an entirely alternative 'significant cause' must somehow be invoked along with its distinctive set of magnetising dispositions. One must make the dispositions ordinarily operative in such emotionally invoking situations, inoperative – or at least weak enough so that they do not issue in the emotion they otherwise would. However, success in particular cases does little to suggest that one can alter a long-term pattern of response. It is this kind of patterned response that those who endeavour to change are after.

Rorty says (1980, p. 105) that the significant causes of our emotions, the events in their causal history that influence the way we habitually respond, also affect the way we conceive the objects of emotions. She cites three related strands in the causal history of an emotion (1980, p. 105): '(1) the formative events in a person's psychological past, the development of patterns of intentional focusing and salience, habits of thought and response; (2) the socially and culturally determined range of emotions and their characteristic behavioral and linguistic expressions; and (3) a person's constitutional inheritance, the set of genetically fixed threshold sensitivities and patterns of response.'

(2) and (3) are not reducible to (1). Although they are 'fixed background conditions' they are necessary to a complete account 'and often critical in explaining anomalies: their contribution to that explanation does not

simply reduce to a variant of individual psychological explanation' (Rorty, 1980, p. 105). Nevertheless (3), and to a lesser degree (2), do seem immune to change precisely because they do constitute *fixed* background conditions. Perhaps they may be overcome to a degree by the causal strength of (1) – even though they are the very things that in part determine (1).[8] At any rate, here is where the prospect for individual change rests. Of course, different background conditions – altering those conditions – will (no surprise) result in different sorts of people. But the context in which we are talking about people changing is focused on (1).

Given Rorty's explanation of emotions, both anomalous and ordinary, can we say emotions are *ever* wholly about what they seem to be about – what we usually take them to be about? If the significant cause of an emotion is historical and never wholly or even primarily occurrent, then emotions are never wholly or primarily caused by their immediate object. Nor are they directed at their immediate target. They are always partly caused by, and so about, something else – something that can only be explained by examining the significant cause. As we will see, much the same can be said given de Sousas's and Gardner's etiological account of emotions.

Gardner (1994) asks if the infantile phantasy that is the historical precursor to an occurrent emotion is in some way re-enacted in each occurrent case of emotion or merely remains part of its history having no immediate causal effect in producing an occurrent emotion. He remains undecided on this. Either way, a case can be made that an occurrent emotion is never wholly about its immediate target or cause.[9] It could be argued that if the phantasy is not present with each instance of an occurrent emotion, then on Gardner's scheme there would be a failure to account for the specific phenomenology of the emotion. But I do not think that is right. The phenomenology of the specific emotion would still be accounted for, albeit obliquely, in terms of its ancestor state in phantasy. There is an important sense in which even if the phantasy is not present the emotion would still not be about, or not wholly about, its immediate target, but about its historical (phantastic) precursor. This relation of historical ancestry needs to be cited in any meaningful, although not necessarily complete, explanation.

Is this like saying that if you want to fully explain walking, you have to bring in toddling and crawling and that walking is about them too? While I accept that for certain purposes a full explanation of walking may well require that one bring in toddling and crawling, I don't think that one can say that 'walking is about them too', in the same way that on Gardner's account, an occurrent emotion is never wholly about what it may seem to be about. The difference has to do with the intentionality or meaning of an occurrent emotion that is determined, in some degree, by its relation to its historical ancestor state in infantile phantasy. The same is not true or relevant when we seek to explain walking.

Occurrent emotions are as much if not more about significant emotion producing events earlier in one's life than they are about their immediate target. This suggests that we mistake or conflate an emotion's 'appropriateness' with the idea that the current situation explains why one is having the emotion. It suggests that we are utterly confused as to why we are emotionally responding as we do, and what the real target of emotion often is. The immediate target can never *wholly* be the real (historical) target. Another way of putting this, as we will see in discussing de Sousa's views, is that all emotions are, to a significant degree, 'transference' emotions.

In some ways Rorty's explanation of anomalous and ordinary emotions is a common-sense explanation. Yet in so far as Rorty's explanation implies the above, it conflicts deeply with a commonsense account of the causes and objects of our emotions.

Some important questions concerning Rorty's account remain. For example, given her explanation of the significant cause of an emotion, to what extent are we responsible for our emotions? If there is not even a significant cause present (or past) to be acted on, then not only are prospects for altering one's emotions dim, but responsibility for emotion becomes even more problematic.[10] If we cannot change our emotions, can we be responsible for them? And if we are not responsible for our emotions, can we nevertheless be responsible for changing them?

What Rorty's account does, like De Sousa's and Gardner's to follow, is to point in the direction of the fixity of emotional dispositions. One difference among them is in terms of how far back they think it necessary to go in order to trace the source of that fixity. Gardner most explicitly traces emotional disposition back to infantile phantasy. But there is nothing in the other accounts that prevents tracing it to infancy in at least some cases. Rorty leaves it open as to how far back in the casual history of an emotion one may have to go for an adequate explanation.[11] She suggests that what constitutes an explanation in a particular circumstance depends on how complete or thorough an explanation is sought. There is nothing in principle to suggest that the significant cause of an emotion does not have features that go back to early infancy – and in fact her account suggests it sometimes may. This is consonant with Gardner's allegedly Kleinian view that emotions are causally related to infantile phantasy.

3. Ronald de Sousa: learning and unlearning emotions

The central feature of De Sousa's account of the etiology of emotion is the 'paradigm scenario'. He says (1980b, pp. 286–90) that we learn our 'emotional repertoire' is in these scenarios. They take place for the most part in infancy but usually are, or can be, modified and some even rejected later in life. It is in these scenarios that instinctual responses are associated with – 'indeed sometimes acquire the name' of – an emotion. It is in paradigm scenarios that an infant's instinctive responses become expression of emotion. 'Otherwise, it lacks the property of being embedded in the complex structure characteristic of emotions.' The structure that he describes is similar to Rorty's. The emotion ordinarily involves a target that is the 'ostensible factual focus' of the emotion (for example, the object of anger). The structure will also involve a property, or 'formal object' that the current situation must share with the paradigm scenario if the emotion is appropriate. It is in the complex paradigm scenario that the infant learns the structural features integral to an emotion, and the appropriateness of an occurrent emotion is always determined, in part, with reference to the structure of such complex paradigm scenarios. When an emotion is learned it can then be applied to situations that are relevantly similar to those in which it instinctually originated. But in the paradigm scenario, an emotion is, 'by definition', appropriate. 'The origin of emotions in paradigm scenarios implies that each person's emotional "dialect" will be subtly different. For the content of emotions for which two people have the same name will depend on their individual temperaments and the specific details of their learning experience.'

De Sousa appears to regard paradigm scenarios as unique historical events that go back to infancy.[12] However, it is implausible to suppose that emotions are learned in a singular event. It is impossible that any singular situation can be sufficiently nuanced in the ways necessary for learning emotions in context. Little is lost from De Sousa's account if we think of paradigm scenarios not as unique historical events, but as a compendium or synthesis of many such contextualised emotion-type learning experiences over time. Sadness, anger and fear, for example, are all learned and refined in the context of numerous paradigm scenarios over a period of time. This process involves a change and refining of one's emotional repertoire to make them appropriate to situations in which those specific emotions are evoked.

As with Rorty's account, the implications of de Sousa's view for the ability to change emotionally are not good. We can learn to change our outward emotional behaviour to a degree, but this is distinct (or distinguishable) from changing the emotions we have. If emotions are learned in paradigm scenarios, then it is these scenarios that must be changed in order to change emotionally. However, one has no control over the emotion evoking paradigm scenario. Furthermore, time would merely reinforce one's initial responses – much like Rorty's magnetising dispositions do.

The case against the difficulty of self-induced change can be strengthened if we consider what de Sousa says about transference emotions. Given de Sousa's description of transference emotions and paradigm scenarios it seems, arguably, that all emotions are transference emotions. A situation or target will sometimes trigger an emotional response that is only partly appropriate because it is evoked by only an aspect of the paradigm scenario. De Sousa (1980b, pp. 287–9) says:

> The response has been associated with a paradigm scenario, defining an emotion which is then *read into* the present situation. This is what psychoanalysts call *transference*. The classic case of transference . . . takes place in the analytic situation, where the patient characteristically 'falls in love' with the doctor[13] . . . transference is not merely mechanical repetition triggered by a stimulus, but has a semantic structure of its own . . . Its defining feature is that it lacks *detachability* . . . from the paradigm scenario . . . As Freud put it, transference consists of new editions of old traits and . . . repeats infantile reactions. But this is the essential character of every state of being in love. There is no such state which does not reproduce infantile prototypes.[14]

Given that emotions originate as infantile instinctual reactions in paradigm scenarios, then Freud's observation about love can, as de Sousa observes, be extended to other emotions. If it is true that transference emotions reproduce infantile states and that it is a widespread phenomenon, then it follows that emotions commonly reproduce such states. Transference may not be 'merely mechanical', but it is mechanical. The extent to which the mechanism cannot be interfered with is a measure of the extent to which our emotional lives cannot be fundamentally altered.

Perhaps not all emotions are transference emotions. Maybe not all emotions – reproductions, projections and displacements – in or out of the clinic are transference emotions. Maybe the first editions of emotions in infant (and perhaps child) cannot be transfer emotions. But then they might not even be full-blown emotions. However, this qualification is minor.

If an emotion is to be rational, in the sense of being about what it purports to be about (that is, its ostensible target), then 'targets of emotions ought to become *fungible* in the manner of the referents of ordinary predicates . . . [I]n the economy of emotions and their objects a transference emotion is a mere substitute; fungibility is an achievement' (de Sousa, 1980b, p. 293). But, given the prevalence of transference, to what extent can we say that fungibility or emotional 'detachability' is ever achieved?

De Sousa questions whether transference emotions are authentic emotions, and baulks at the idea because of its untoward implications. He says (1980b, p. 289), 'If this is so [i.e. if transference emotions are authentic], then the "genuineness" even of normal emotions is bought at the price of systematic inappropriateness – an unwelcome implausibility.' What can de Sousa means by 'systematic inappropriateness', unless it means that emotions are not wholly – perhaps not even largely – about their ostensible objects? The causes of emotions are not primarily what we take them to be. But why is this implausible or, even if it is, why is it unacceptable? Much of what Freud has to say is, after all, *prima facie* implausible – even *wild*.

'We have no right to dispute [that transference love] has the character of "genuine love"' (de Sousa, 1980b, p. 289, quoting Freud). But de Sousa rejects this view. Apparently, he thinks that transference love and other transference emotions are not genuine instances of emotion types. He seems to think his position is dictated by the semantics of love and other emotions. However, once one understands the etiology of transference love and other emotions, then even in terms of de Sousa's own account, there is no reason why the semantics of emotion should prevent us from regarding, with Freud, such emotions as genuine.

In view of the fact that the origin of emotions in paradigm scenarios suggests that Freud's observation concerning love (above) can be applied to emotions in addition to love, de Sousa (1980b, p. 289) raises two questions: '[F]irst, whether transference emotions are *authentic* – whether they are the emotions they advertise themselves to be – and second, whether their real object and target are their ostensible ones.' But these are not, as de Sousa seems to think, distinct questions. If such emotions are in a sense 'inauthentic', this may be because their real objects are not their ostensible ones. But it is less contrived to maintain that the fact that their real objects and targets are not their ostensible ones does not imply that transference emotions are not genuine. At any rate, de Sousa's account of the etiology of emotion suggests that all emotions are transference emotions, to be regarded as all equally authentic or inauthentic. Take your pick.

De Sousa (1980b, p. 293) says:

> [T]he properties on which human attachment is based are not qualitative, but *historical*. Must we conclude that attachment emotions are not emotions at all? Perhaps. But we could say instead that they are always transference emotions in a sense different from the one Freud intended: their ideology requires that we generalize not from a fungible scenario, but from an individual *target* as the essential component of a succession of constitutive scenarios.

But how different is this notion of transference from Freud's? Freud (1912, 1914) distinguishes various kinds of transference, but basically transference is a defensive manoeuvre and there is no reason to suppose it takes place only in a clinical setting. Freud focuses on transference in the clinical setting because it is essential to psychoanalytic practice. The same kind of defensive strategies useful in a clinical setting will be useful outside it as well. Many emotions may have a defensive function. Gardner's (1994) Kleinian account of envy and gratitude (discussed below) as rooted in infantile phantasy suggests that both have a protective function. Much of what Freud says in connection with transference love can be extrapolated to other emotions. Heterosexuality is anaclitic (that is, 'leaning on') for Freud. Anaclitic object-choice occurs when the choice of subsequent love objects is based on the first love object. In emotions associated with the anaclitic object-choice one is generalising, as de Sousa says above, 'not from a fungible scenario, but from an individual *target* as the essential component of a succession of constitutive scenarios'.

However, de Sousa (1980b, p. 289) appears to reject these apparently profound implications. 'It is tempting . . . to take a hard line . . . emotions are always what they seem, and their objects are always the ostensible ones. And if this means that some emotions are inappropriate, then things are just as we know them.' But it is odd that de Sousa calls *this* the 'hard line'. Rather, the hard line, and the problematic one, would be the view that emotions are never what they seem to be about – that the ostensible objects of an emotions are never the real objects. It is these conclusions that, like Rorty's, de Sousa's account of the etiology of emotion, point to.

Elaborating on what seems to me to be mistaken conclusions, De Sousa (1980b, p. 289) says we must 'remember that in some cases the *content* of the emotion must be interpreted in terms of a reference to an object or target other than the ostensible one. This is preferable to talking of the paradigm as the "real object", for it allows judgements of degree in respect of the relative role of the present and the past in shaping present content.' However, contrary to de Sousa, it seems not all preferable to talk of the paradigm as the 'real object' if, as an analysis of transference emotions appears to show, the paradigm is the real object. Such talk would, a theoretical context, merely be obfuscating. There is no reason why 'the relative role of the present and the past in shaping present content' cannot be preserved if the paradigm is taken as the real object. On such an account the paradigm or 'real object' may be more or less wholly what an occurrent emotion is directed at, or really about, while in others it may be less so.

As with Rorty, there is a clear emphasis in de Sousa's account on the causal significance of past experience (paradigm scenarios) to occurrent emotion. Given the forward direction of the causal and semantic influence of paradigm scenarios, it seems one would have to go back and reconfigure (re-gestalt) paradigm scenarios in some way in order to change emotion. This is just how de Sousa thinks emotional response can be changed. Nevertheless, even if de Sousa is right that such change can occur, his account of the etiology of emotion suggests that the task of re-gestalting paradigm scenarios is daunting.[15] Things are looking bleak for change.

De Sousa claims that the distinction between neurotic emotions and normal ones is a matter of convention, and he says 'up to a point' this is the way it should be. '[F]or intuitively the difference between mere transference and authentic emotion is in whether the ostensible object is actually, in its present relation to the subject, fitting for the emotion that it occasions. Otherwise it is merely acting as a trigger for some thing to which it is only accidentally connected' (de Sousa, 1980b, p. 290).

I have endeavoured to show that the intuitive position is mistaken, in part by showing that on de Sousa's own account virtually all emotions are, in effect, transference emotions. However, de Sousa is wrong in thinking that this view has any implication for drawing the line between neurotic and normal emotions. The distinction will still be drawn along conventional lines. For the real difference between the normal and neurotic or appropriate and inappropriate does not rest in the latter being transference emotions and the former not. It rests instead with how the notion of appropriateness with regard to emotion is engendered. Furthermore, it is a mistake to regard the line between the two as merely conventional. The line is made evident by genuine patterns of discernment that are in turn dictated by complex social facts. These are not merely fortuitous but come about as a result of natural constraints on human response and interaction. These lines of demarcation are rooted in our natures.

4. Sebastian Gardner: emotion, irrationality and phantasy

On a psychoanalytic view, 'appropriateness in circumstances' is not even a *prima facie* reason to suppose that instances of emotion are rational – at least not fundamentally rational.[16] The psychoanalytic view rejects what Sebastian Gardner (1994, p. 36) calls the 'rationalistic account', which 'holds that emotions are direct and sufficient outcomes of complexes of belief'.[17] These beliefs typically identify the kind of emotion it is along with its cause and object and 'reflect its normative framework'. Psychoanalysis, says Gardner (1994, p. 44), holds that emotional states we recognise and ascribe to ourselves are '*historical descendants*' of infantile phantasies. Such states of phantasy are quite different and historically earlier kinds of states than those of emotion. He says (1994, p. 44):

> The philosophical claim is that a state of emotion is fully intelligible only in terms of such an ancestor state. So, even when an emotion occurs in adult life and is adjudged appropriate, appearing not to indicate any kind of unconscious activity, it remains true that it is at least a derivative of an infantile and phantastic prototype . . . an emotion is a thought-like power to determine phenomenological properties . . . the thought from which this power is derived is an unconscious, phantastic thought . . . [and] to each emotion-kind there corresponds a particular kind of phantastic thought.

Psychoanalysis, therefore, gives us reason to believe emotions are irrational in significant respects, no matter how appropriate they appear to be in the circumstance and irrespective of whether they serve our thriving.

What I have just said needs to be qualified. There is no one psychoanalytic view of emotion (or even of phantasy), there are many. There are also various views about Klein on the emotions and phantasy. Thus, Gardner's account should be taken as one among several interpretations. For the present purposes I am accepting Gardner's account, but there are grounds for challenging it. Is it really plausible to suppose that phantasy in every case antecedes the baby's emotional repertoire? In at least some cases, isn't the opposite the case? Do not rage, joy and satisfaction historically precede related phantasies – unless phantasy catches everything that passes through the baby's mind? And babies react emotionally to perceptions too. Does phantasy play a role here as well? Isn't it improbable that phantasy underlies every emotion given the huge disparity of types. An infant has a very restricted complement of emotions and phantasies: how could infantile phantasy underlie, be a progenitor of, all emotion?[18]

The reasons why emotions are irrational are also reasons why emotion is difficult to change. The fundamental irrationality of emotions also helps explain why they are typically experienced passively, and this provides additional grounds for understanding their resistance to change. Gardner (1994, pp. 44–5) says: 'The reason why emotion appears passively is that it derives from phantasy, at which level events are neither given to consciousness nor voluntary.' Given that the events causing emotion are beyond our reach, and neither conscious nor voluntary, it should come as no surprise that emotional response is difficult to alter – even when emotions are connected to belief in quite ordinary ways.[19]

An instance of an emotion is *prima facie* rational because it fits paradigm scenarios in which the emotion was learned. It is appropriate to those relevantly similar situations. But if the reasons we have the emotions we do, when we do, are fundamentally irrational, then this undermines grounds for believing emotions are overall rational. If the reason you have emotion *x* in situations like *y* is because of infantile phantasies arising out of desires or frustrations relating to one's body along with (as background conditions) genetic disposition and socio-cultural conditioning, then *x* is fundamentally irrational. It does not matter if it corresponds to learned scenarios or serves one's well-being. The emotion's etiology undermines its rationality. The fact that often particular emotional responses change with a change in belief does not affect the claim that the way we respond emotionally, given what we do believe at a certain time, does not change or is difficult to change over time.

We are not, if Freud is anywhere near the truth, the rational creatures, emotionally or otherwise, we take ourselves to be. That emotions are fundamentally irrational is perfectly compatible with David Sachs' claim (1982, p. 93) that Freud maintained a 'persistent adherence . . . to the idea that, between any person's emotions or affects and the causes or objects thereof, there always obtains an actual proportionality or real appropriateness, no matter how discrepant or incongruous those relations may appear to be, and regardless of the person's mental condition . . . [whether] psychotic, neurotic, or normal'. Once the etiology of emotion is psychoanalytically understood, 'actual proportionality or real appropriateness' between an emotion and its cause does not underwrite the emotion's rationality, but its irrationality.

Describing Klein's account of the emotions, Gardner (1994, pp. 42, 44) says that the formation of phantasy is governed by a 'general law' which causes or 'directs' phantasy to produce 'an ideal situation in which the distribution of badness and goodness on the "map" of self and world is such that all goodness is coincident with the ego and all badness external to it'. He calls this an a priori of phantasy. Is this law governing phantasy formation that determines which psychological states 'call for phantastic solutions and what formations of the inner world phantasy should and should not aim to produce'(1994, p. 42).

As described above, phantasy seems to be a product of wish-fulfilment. And if basic emotions such as envy and gratitude are derivative in the manner Klein describes, then how can they be basically rational?[20] Given that infantile phantasy appears to be well beyond our control, emotions are also going to be resistant to change. Whether phantasies are the historical ancestors of current emotions, or instead transiently invoked each time we have an emotion, makes little difference in terms of the likelihood of being able to alter occurrent emotions.

If one takes emotion to be rooted in phantasy and so fundamentally irrational, then there is a sense in which emotions are always the result of muddled emotion provoking scenarios, confused desires, and the like. This is so even if Freud was right in maintaining, as Sachs (1982, p. 93) claimed he did, that there was (almost) always an appropriateness between a person's emotions and the causes or objects thereof.[21] Of course, the 'actual proportionality or real appropriateness' between an emotion and its cause or object does not underwrite the emotion's rationality. It does not show that emotions are not in part the result of, or do not stand in an historical relation to, infantile phantasy. It is these features of the etiology of emotion that highlight the difficulty of change.

However, doesn't psychoanalysis require that we manipulate and change our non-rational emotional responses to certain beliefs and perceptions? The question of manipulating emotion is central to psychoanalysis. It arises when psychoanalytic theory meets practice. On the one hand, psychoanalytic theory provides us with solid grounds for supposing that the kind of change sought for in psychoanalytic practice is virtually beyond our reach. Yet on the other, its clinical *raison d'être* supposes such change is possible. Of course, there is no contradiction between supposing change to be both (very) difficult and possible.

Despite their fundamental irrationality, Gardner (1994, p. 48) suggests that emotions serve our well-being, and that even if they do not, it makes no sense to suppose we can excise them. 'If emotion does have a profoundly irrational aspect, ought we not try to excise it from our lives? This would make sense only if it were thought that people should aspire to live in a world stripped of emotional qualities and that they could prise themselves apart from their deepest sources of motivation. We would not know how to begin to act on either of these assumptions.' But this begs several questions and his assertion appears to be independent of psychoanalytic considerations. After all, one central task of psychoanalysis is to manipulate or realign emotions – which in some cases amounts to excision. Why shouldn't we try to excise at least some emotion from our lives?[22] Not all sources of motivation, even if deep, appear to be good. Is it really impossible for people to 'prise themselves apart from [some of] their deepest sources of motivation?' Would it not be desirable, even morally desirable, if they could? Doesn't psychoanalytic practice demand this in some cases? Perhaps Gardner's claim that it makes no sense to talk about excising emotion reflects not so much the belief that one would not know how to act on either of his stated assumptions, but rather the view that it is not possible to do so. Occasional relief from a particularly problematic sort of emotional response is perhaps all that one can hope for and in many cases all that psychoanalysis aims for.

Gardner talks about excising all emotion from our lives, but there are a number of middle positions. One can maintain that excising only emotions with particularly deleterious effects is desirable. Some psychoanalytic theory might regard it as possible to replace phantasies from which certain emotion-kinds are derived with more desirable and beneficial fantasies from which other, maybe even unknown, emotion-kinds might be derived. Perhaps this can be done by changing child-rearing arrangements or abandoning the nuclear family as some feminist psychoanalytic theory suggests. None of these methods however suggests that individuals can actually change their emotional makeup. On the contrary, they suggest that only by changing the early or the earliest childhood rearing practices can the psychosexual developmental process, including emotional makeup, be altered.

As Gardner (1994, p. 49) notes, Kleinian theory 'does not entail the undesirability of emotion. Rather it suggests the desirability of one's emotional life being structured by, and characteristically manifesting attainment of, the depressive position' instead of being 'structured by the paranoid-schizoid position' which is responsible for the 'undesirable emotional states that constitute human bondage'.[23] He says, 'given that we live in, and cannot want not to live in, an emotionally characterized world, what should be aspired to is a condition in which emotion contributes maximally to psychological integration and malforms belief as little as possible'. This is compatible with holding that some emotions should be excised or altered. Psychoanalysis supposes that some change is possible. Yet the psychoanalytic account of the etiology of emotion seems to stand in opposition to this.

I think there is a conflict or opposition, but just what it is needs to be elaborated. Psychoanalysis says that change of certain sorts may be brought about by therapy, or indeed taking drugs. But one needs to be specific. Getting rid of symptoms may, depending on the circumstances, be reasonably easy. Dealing with the perversions and character disorders may be much harder, and dealing with narcissistic disorders and psychoses harder still. Psychoanalysis can do this in various ways, for example, through realignment of internal object relations, and some of this may lead to change in emotional dispositions. It is not that unconscious phantasies are untouchable via the agency of the therapist. Rather, the question is just how malleable are they and what kind of effect on character and emotional makeup can one hope for? Self-change is, of course, another thing. One may want to consider Freud's 'self-analysis', but how many people are capable of that? It isn't even clear that Freud was capable of it. So there is no real inconsistency marked by the 'seems to be in opposition'. It also needs to be reiterated that there is no univocal psychoanalytic view. Nevertheless, it seems to me that while psychoanalytic practice, which is after all for the very, very few, may, for both good and not so good reasons, talks up the prospects of change via psychoanalytic intervention, a great deal of psychoanalytic theory, including classic Freud, suggests a far less positive story.

The idea that emotions are interrelated in ways that prevent strict individuation of emotion-kinds, or instances of particular emotions, in terms of commonsense or folk-psychological classification, can be found in psychoanalytic theory's emphasis on (1) the source of emotion in phantasy, and (2) its narrative understanding of emotions. Gardner (1994, pp. 45–6) says:

> [A]lthough psychoanalytic individuation of emotion-kinds must . . . remain *roughly* within . . . our ordinary classification, the important possibility is created that two different instances of emotion may be regarded as exemplifying different emotion-kinds despite an identity of feeling and conscious belief across cases, since this remains compatible with a difference in content at the level of phantasy.

On the Kleinian view, it is on the level of phantasy that emotion-kinds are primarily to be individuated – which is not to say (Gardner, 1994, p. 46) that psychoanalytic theory claims that our ordinary psychological distinctions are not real. The possibility Gardner cites is important, not just theoretically, but for psychoanalytic practice, where locating an emotion vis-à-vis the correct emotion-kind, as psychoanalytically determined, may be crucial in endeavouring to change. At any rate, the origin of emotion in phantasy suggests numerous reasons why voluntary change, if possible, is, as we know, difficult.

There are also less direct psychoanalytic reasons which suggest why change is difficult. For example, on Kleinian grounds, different criteria for the identity of emotions – ones based on their causal roles – become significant. Emotions may then be identified by criteria relating them to concepts of phantasy. Such concepts are not available in ordinary terms outside the realm of psychoanalytic discourse.

If this is so, there will be instances in which our efforts to change are altogether misdirected. The problematic emotions may be misidentified as those in ordinary thought instead of at the level of phantasy.[24] Gardner (1994, pp. 46–7) continues:

> [E]motion-kinds occupy roles in typical sequences, and this permits a relational identification of an emotion in terms of what precedes and what follows it in the model narrative set out in psychoanalytic theory. This contrasts with our pre-psychoanalytic 'atomism' about emotions: we do not ordinarily . . . suppose that emotions have a deep organization which interrelates them . . . we ordinarily take emotions on a one-off basis . . . Psychoanalytic theory improves on this 'shallow' view' [p. 46] . . . Emotion is formed out of phantasy in such a way that it carries over . . . the imprint of, phantastic thoughts.

These thoughts are different from those resulting form beliefs that rationalise emotion. Gardner calls them 'emotion's *constitutive psychological substrate*'. They are not conscious and so play no direct role in conscious inferences. Nevertheless, 'they have the power to determine important aspects of experience, thought, and action in a thought-like way' (Gardner, 1994, p. 47).

The implication is that in seeking change, it is the emotions' deep organisation, its location in a narrative that has to be taken account of. A piecemeal approach cannot suffice. And yet the requisite knowledge concerning emotions' deep organisation, their origin in phantasy and narrative location, let alone what to *do* about them, seems well beyond anyone not psychoanalytically trained – and even that may not help.

Notes

1. See Rorty (1985); Gardner (1994). My thanks to Tamas Pataki whose careful comments helped me to improve this chapter.
2. Correspondence, October 2001.
3. Sher (1998, pp. 7–8) says, 'Some philosophers . . . believe that "it is at least intuitively plausible that people can change or revise their characters, or . . . character traits." . . . [O]thers . . . believe instead that it is rarely if ever plausible to say that a person is energetic or lazy, kind or mean-spirited, and so on, as a result of conscious control over her or his character; and it is far from clear that most people *could* have sharply different characters as a result of conscious control on their part.' Sher (1998, p. 9) is inclined to the latter view. Also see Nagel (1979, pp. 25, 33).
4. See Rorty (1980, p. 107). The immediate object of an emotion is intentional. It is the focus of the emotion and seen by the person having the emotion as the

grounds for the emotion. Rorty calls the person's description of the focus of the emotion the '*the intentional component of the emotion*'.

5. Rorty (1980, p. 104) claims that it is not always appropriate to explain 'inappropriate' emotions by beliefs and desires that would ground it in some rational way. 'It is not the belief or emotion that is rationalized, but a person's coming to have it.'
6. Rorty notes (1980, p. 124 n10) that the kinds of beliefs and desires we are prone to have is a result of the traits we possess. Furthermore, theories of perception and motivation must be linked to any throughgoing account of the etiology of emotional dispositions (Rorty, 1988, p. 111).
7. On Rorty's account (1980, p. 110), the significant cause of an emotion is likely, but need not, involve 'events "fused and formed the person's magnetized dispositions, the patterns of salience and attention." It may also involve "idiosyncratic beliefs and associations . . . When in doubt about the rationale of an emotion, look for the intentional component of the significant cause of the dispositional set that forms the intentional component of the emotion".'
8. Rorty (1980, p. 119) says, 'The conservation of emotions has its explanation in the conservation of habit . . . [S]ocial and genetic factors also contribute to the causal story.'
9. There are other interesting similarities between Rorty and Gardner. They are both concerned with how the etiology of emotion impacts on our classification of emotion types and their views have much in common. Rorty (1980, pp. 120–1) says, 'Differences in the characteristic causal histories of their intentional components helps to explain why different instances of the same emotion-type often have different tonal and behavioral expressions.'
10. Rorty (1980, p. 116) says, 'In some cases, it might be said, the significant cause isn't significant at all. It casts no light on the rationale of the intentional component of an emotion because there is no rationale . . . Tolstoi remarks that in infancy and old age (and we might add: in adolescence) the apparent reasonableness that we believe really conditions our adult emotional life wears thin, and emotions reveal a rhythm and pattern of their own.' And she goes on to ask whether or not what Tolstoi claims to be the case in old age is not likewise during the whole of our lives.
11. Rorty (1980, p. 112) asks, '[H]ave we come to the end of an account of how we explain emotions. . . . Or do significant causes of magnetizing dispositions sometimes have no intentional component of their own?'
12. De Sousa (1980b, p. 295) claims that aesthetic emotions are probably an exception to this rule.
13. De Sousa (1980b, p. 288) claims that the patient unconsciously sees the doctor as one's parent. Generally, when the neurotic is made fully conscious of the identification they will reject it.
14. Cf. Freud (1912, 1914).
15. De Sousa claims (1980b, p. 295) that we can sometimes alter these early and influential paradigms. The process amounts to conscious raising. We describe and then redescribe propositions. He cautions that this process has its limitations. 'Verbal argument is not a powerful tool at the level of the immediate content of emotions. It doesn't help much to repeat, like incantations, "this isn't really frightening," . . . [T]he level at which the effort of rational redescription is most useful is . . . at the meta-level of ideology. It is in searching out assumptions about our emotions . . . that we are most likely to transform . . . their experienced content and emerge from self-deception.'

16. Gardner (1994, p. 49) says: 'The rationalistic account holds that the logically primary matrix of emotion is belief, and that emotions which are not warranted by beliefs are deviant phenomena and logically secondary; thus emotion *per se is* a rational kind or state. The psychoanalytic account holds, by contrast, that the logically primary matrix of emotion in adult life is not belief but phantasy; thus emotions which fail to be warranted by beliefs are not deviant phenomena and not logically secondary, and emotion *per se is* not a rational kind of state.'
17. See Gardner's essay for a critique of the rationalistic account of emotion in favour of the psychoanalytic theory that sees emotion as 'a kind of mental state which cannot be understood apart from – for the reason that it is derived from – the kind of mental state that psychoanalytic theory refers to as phantasy.' Some issues require clarification. If some emotions develop from phantasy but now operate independently of it (that is, the relation is developmental and historical but not current), then is the rationality of such emotion undermined by its relation to phantasy? It seems to me that the rationality of an emotion is undermined whether its relation to phantasy is (1) developmental and historical or (2) current – though it is more seriously challenged in the latter case than in the former. It also seems to me that (1) and (2) are integrally related. If an emotion's relation to phantasy is historical and developmental then it must also be current. However, even if an emotion is not rooted in phantasy, there remain the kinds of reasons cited by Rorty and de Sousa that support the view that the relation between past and current emotion is historical and developmental in such a way that makes it difficult to modify emotion.

    As Rorty (1985) has pointed out, 'rationality' has a variety of meanings. However, in the current context no particular specialised definition of rationality is needed. Gardner (1994, p. 49) says, 'What the rationalistic account [of emotion] is right about is not the causal explanation of emotion . . . [W]hat it correctly models is the non-causal, normative relations that constitute the concept of appropriate emotions.'
18. My thanks to Tamas Pataki for raising these issues.
19. Gardner (1994, p. 45) says, 'The discussion . . . [leaves] undecided the exact degree to which the descendant-state, both as a kind and in its individual instances, is in its actual operation either causally independent of or dependent on the present existence or operation of any of its ancestor-states.' He goes on to describe the options. On what he terms a 'weak view', emotions are independent of phantasy and autonomous once, as a kind, they have evolved as mental states. On such a weak view emotions could occur in subjects no longer capable of phantasy. The strong view maintains that emotional responses are all causally related to the actual occurrence of a phantasy. The 'mid-way position' claims that some kind of casual relation between phantasy and emotion must exist without which 'the capacity for emotional response would wither'.
20. See Melanie Klein (1957), or, for a brief account of Klein's theory of envy and gratitude, see Gardner (1994, pp. 42–3). Gardner (1994, pp. 43–4) claims that what Klein say of envy and gratitude can be applied or generalised to other emotions as well.
21. Cf. Lear (1990, p. 131). 'In his [Freud's] discussion of dreams, he says that an idea and the emotion attaching to it are merely soldered together . . . What he meant was that an emotion can be detached from the idea to which it is appropriate and then be attached to any idea whatever . . . this detachment only occurs at the manifest level of consciousness. Once we consider the deeper, latent content of

a dream, it emerges that an emotion is indissolubly attached to its appropriate idea. Similarly with the sexual drive and the sexual object.'

22. Which emotions, if any, generally impede our thriving so that it would be better to wean ourselves from them if we could? Even emotions people think they could better do without, and could often do better without (for example, envy, rage and jealousy), may overall enhance well being. Given the way they may relate to one's overall complement of emotions, it is far from clear that excising envy, greed and malice from one's psychic economy – rather than bringing them to consciousness, recognising them in their disguises, containing and mitigating them – would be a good thing. Psychoanalysis aims only at the latter, but its account of the etiology of emotion also highlights the difficulty of doing so.
23. Charles Rycroft (1970, pp. 32, 111–12) describes these positions: 'The "Depressive Position" "describes the position reached . . . by the infant . . . when he realises that both his LOVE and Hate are directed towards the same object – the MOTHER." The "Paranoid-Schizoid Position" is "a psychic configuration . . . in which the individual deals with his innate destructive impulses by (a) SPLITTING both his EGO and his Object-Representations into Good and Bad parts, and (b) projecting his destructive impulses onto the bad object by whom he feels persecuted".'
24. See Gardner (1994, pp. 49–50) for an account of how, in his view, the psychoanalytic account of emotion is able to resolve the difficulty inherent in the rationalistic account. 'What the rationalistic account is right about is not the causal explanation of emotion, since this is not in fact a process of syllogistic practical reasoning; what it correctly models is the non-causal, normative relations that constitute the concept of appropriate emotion.' Gardner goes on to give an account of Sartre's view of emotion as magical thinking. The role played by infantile phantasy in emotion can only be rationalised by believing in magic.

References

De Sousa, R. (1987). *The Rationality of Emotions*. Cambridge, MA: MIT Press.

De Sousa, R. (1980a). The rationality of emotions. In A. O. Rorty (Ed.) *Explaining Emotions*. Berkeley: University of California Press.

De Sousa, R. (1980b). Self-deceptive emotions. In A. O. Rorty (Ed.) *Explaining Emotions*. Berkeley: University of California Press.

Freud, S. (1912). *The Dynamics of Transference*. The standard edition of the complete works of Sigmund Freud, Vol. 12. London: Hogarth Press.

Freud, S. (1914). *Observations on Transference Love*. The standard edition of the complete works of Sigmund Freud, Vol. 12. London: Hogarth Press.

Freud, S. (1953–73). *The Standard Edition of the Complete Works of Sigmund Freud*. London: Hogarth Press.

Frijda, N. H., Manstead, S. R. and Ben, S. (Eds.) (2000). *Emotions and Beliefs: How Feelings Influence Thoughts*. Cambridge: Cambridge University Press.

Gardner, S. (1994). The nature and source of emotion. In J. Hopkins and A. Savile (Eds.) *Psychoanalysis, Mind and Art: Perspectives on Richard Wollheim*. Oxford: Blackwell.

Klein, M. (1957). Envy and gratitude. In R. E. Money-Kyrle (Ed.) *Envy and Gratitude and Other Works 1946–1963. The Writings of Melanie Klein*, Vol. 3. London: Hogarth Press.

Kupperman, J. (1991). *Character*. Oxford: Oxford University Press.

Lear, J. (1990). *Love and its Place in Nature: A Philosophical Interpretation of Freudian Psychoanalysis.* New York: Noonday Press.
Levine, M. P. (2000). Lucky in love: love and emotion. In M. P. Levine (Ed.) *The Analytic Freud: Philosophy and Psychoanalysis.* London and New York: Routledge.
Moody-Adams, M. (1990). On the old saw that character is destiny. In O. Flanagan and A. Rorty (Eds.) *Identity, Character, and Morality: Essays in Moral Psychology.* Cambridge, MA: Bradford.
Nagel, T. (1979). Moral luck. In T. Nagel, *Mortal Questions.* Cambridge: Cambridge University Press.
Rorty, A. O. (1980). Explaining emotions. In A. O. Rorty (Ed.) *Explaining Emotions.* Berkeley: University of California Press.
Rorty, A. O. (1985). Varieties of rationality, varieties of emotion. *Social Science Information,* 24, 343–53.
Rorty, A. O. (1988). The historicity of psychological attitudes: love is not love which alters not when it alteration finds. In A. O. Rorty (Ed.) *Mind in Action: Essays in the Philosophy of Mind.* Boston: Beacon Press.
Rycroft, C. (1970). *A Critical Dictionary of Psychoanalysis.* London: Penguin.
Sachs, D. (1982). On Freud's theory of the emotions. In J. Hopkins and R. Wollheim (Eds.) *Philosophical Essays on Freud.* Cambridge: Cambridge University Press.
Sher, G. (1998). Ethics, character, and action. *Social Philosophy and Policy,* 15, 1–17.

7

The Illusion of a Future

W. D. Hart

1. A fear of death is wired in, and unappeasable

All men are mortal, but sex is no prophylactic. All women are mortal too. Everyone dies. Nor is this a fluke; it is a matter of natural law that we will all perish. One such law is surely the second law of thermodynamics. Sometimes this law is put as a proscription of perpetual motion machines, and with them, immortal people. Another way to put it is by saying natural processes move from states realised in relatively few ways to states realised in more ways. There are many more ways that the stuff of life can be degraded into death than survive. As every tidy formation breaks up eventually, so we all die. The thousand natural shocks that flesh is heir to always end in death.

How might an environment where death looms select among creatures with minds? It stands to reason that creatures afraid to die will be more likely to take what steps they can to avoid or postpone death than creatures indifferent to dying. Assuming such steps are not always and utterly futile, taking them will increase their chances of lasting a bit longer and thus their opportunities to reproduce or nurture their offspring. So, since we are still here, at least for a while, it seems natural to think we have evolved as creatures afraid of death.

The roots of this fear in us are presumably genetic. Here one might recall those adrenaline spurts of terror and panic when the car suddenly starts to veer out of control or the floor one expected is missing and there is another step. But in social creatures with minds in whom it is natural to care for, and about, their children, culture is at least as efficient a carrier of the fear of death as chromosomes. It would be only natural for creatures with cultures to store in them devices for putting off death and to bequeath them to posterity.

Someone who has utterly no idea of scorpions or snakes will not fear them. He might be startled by his first scorpion, but until he recognises scorpions for what they are, he does not yet have a fear whose content is properly scorpions. If fear of death is built into us, then so too must acknowledgement of it be our birthright. Here one might wonder whether death is not too specific an idea to be innate. Perhaps we are born only with some much more general idea of harm or injury. Nevertheless, the strategy of opting for the least of several evils seems pretty basic. To apply it we need to be able to sort impending dangers not only as to likelihood but also as to seriousness; creatures deficient in such strategic skills would be at a competitive disadvantage. It is then only a baby step to the idea of the most serious dangers, which marks out a very short route to an idea of death.

But even if the idea and fear of death are not innate to us, in the midst of life we are in death. Its presence will inform the culture our parents impart to us. The idea and fear of death will be so deep in all human culture that it will be quite as if they were in our genes. If we were noble animals, the fact that we are fated to die, to know it and to fear it, might qualify as tragic; as we are, we might get away with calling it a predicament or a tearjerker. We are cast in an ineluctable and ubiquitous melodrama. It is natural to struggle against or scramble to avoid what we fear, and the more so the more we fear it. So we have pretty much no choice but to struggle against or scramble to avoid death, while at the same time we know we are going to lose after a while. It is as if Sisyphus not only knew how often he had pushed that rock up that hill, but also that it would eventually obliterate him.

A known, unavoidable, scary annihilation would seem fertile ground for psychopathology. Repression is the general form of defence mechanisms. But simply to sink the knowledge of death into wilful ignorance would presumably put at risk the techniques for postponing death that confer adaptive advantages on creatures with minds; it is harder to duck the arrow coming at you if you turn your back on it. So it seems more likely that clever creatures still around might have tended to distort their knowledge of death. Perhaps they might struggle to rethink death not as obliteration but rather as some sort of transition, the new idea being an afterlife for the creature in transit. The later phase might even come to be conceived as preferable to the earlier. An afterlife in which those who did wrong and got away with it in life get their comeuppance, and in which those who did right but suffered will profit, might seem desirable. Here the wishful thinking over the fear of death would do well not to encourage jumping the gun. Life could be thought of not as one's own but instead as a gift from someone it would be imprudent to offend, so one is smart not to toss it away but to live it as well as one can in hopes of that better life that someone may provide. Celebrating this someone for his gifts and promises would be a way to bleed off some of the passion animating the fear of death. Wishful thinking is the natural history of religion.

2. Freud's views on religion and immortality

The scheme sketched in the preceding paragraphs has some affinities with Freud's views on religion and death, but it is also more rationalistic and

Darwinian. Writing about the origins of animism in *Totem and Taboo*, Freud says, 'The chief starting-point of this theorizing must have been the problem of death. What primitive man regarded as the natural thing was the indefinite prolongation of life – immortality. The idea of death was only accepted late, and with hesitancy. Even for us it is lacking in content and has no clear connotation' (Freud, 1950, p. 96). (Freud cites with approval Schopenhauer's remark that the problem of death stands at the outset of every philosophy (Freud, 1950).) Animism responds to the problem of death by peopling all the world with spirits and demons, and among these demons are the souls of the dear departed whose departure was inadmissibly desired. A world so peopled can be dealt with as one already deals with other people; sorcery is a social skill (Freud, 1950). More generally, 'Animism is a system of thought. It does not merely give an explanation of a particular phenomenon, but allows us to grasp the whole universe as a single unity from a single point of view. The human race, if we are to follow the authorities, have in the course of ages developed three such systems of thought – three great pictures of the universe: animistic (or mythological), religious and scientific' (Freud, 1950, p. 97). While Freud distinguishes between animism and religion, he also says, 'With these three stages in mind, it may be said that animism itself is not yet a religion but contains the foundations on which religions are later built' (Freud, 1950, p. 97). These phases follow the vicissitudes of the omnipotence of thought. 'At the animistic stage men ascribe omnipotence to *themselves*. At the religious stage they transfer it to the gods but do not seriously abandon it themselves, for they reserve the power of influencing the gods in a variety of ways according to their wishes. The scientific view of the universe no longer affords any room for human omnipotence; men have acknowledged their smallness and submitted resignedly to death and to the other necessities of nature' (Freud, 1950, p. 110). Freud connects this struggle with the omnipotence of thought to our libidinal development from narcissism. 'The animistic phase would correspond to narcissism both chronologically and in its content; the religious phase would correspond to the stage of object-choice of which the characteristic is a child's attachment to his parents; while the scientific phase would have an exact counterpart in the stage at which an individual has reached maturity, has renounced the pleasure principle, adjusted himself to reality and turned to the external world for the object of his desires' (Freud, 1950, pp. 112–13). Science is what there is for those who have grown up and put away childish things like religion; there is no hope here of an honest accommodation between science and religion, and the salient sticking point is death.

Freud's attitude towards religion and the promise of immortality is unmistakable in these passages. But he was much too careful a thinker to oversimplify. 'There are no grounds for fearing that psycho-analysis, which first discovered that psychical acts and structures are invariably over-determined, will be tempted to trace the origin of anything so complicated as religion to a single source' (Freud, 1950, p. 125). Here it is as well to remember the variety of religions on offer. Christianity and Islam certainly stress immortality and an afterlife. Buddhism prolongs life enormously through cycles of reincarnation, but the wheel of karma (destiny) may eventually bring one to Nirvana (the desired ultimate state), and on some descriptions that sounds rather like obliteration. The difference between Christianity and Islam on the one hand, and Buddhism on the other, might be a difference in maturity.

Judaism is an example in which Freud took particular interest. Early in *Moses and Monotheism*, Freud remarks, 'The early Jewish religion, on the other hand, had entirely relinquished immortality; the possibility of an existence after death was never mentioned in any place' (Freud, 1939, p. 20). 'The contrast here is with the Egyptians. 'No other people of antiquity has done so much to deny death, has made such careful provision for an afterlife; in accordance with this the death-god Osiris, the ruler of that other world, was the most popular and indisputable of all Egyptian gods' (Freud, 1939, p. 20). Freud's account of early Judaism's silence on immortality is spellbinding. Moses, Freud says, was an Egyptian. The etymology of his name is a giveaway. Freud dates Moses to the reign of the Pharaoh Ikhnaton or soon after. The conquests of Thothmes III (before Ikhnaton) had made Egypt an imperial power in which a unifying religion would have political advantages. A unique god could tolerate no rivals for his worship. The stage is thus set for the monotheism for which Ikhnaton is famous. In his struggle to supplant the popular polytheistic religion in which Osiris and immortality have pride of place, Ikhnaton surrenders immortality; this is like a sort of branding of his monotheism. Ikhnaton enforces his new religion but it is never genuinely popular, and after his death there is a general reversion to the old death cults. But among some of the elite his new vision survives, and Moses is of the Egyptian elite. This prestigious nobleman converts the downtrodden Jews on the fringes of the Egyptian empire to the religion of Ikhnaton and leads them off into the wilderness. There is a great deal more to Freud's story, but the important thing for us is that he traced early Judaism's silence on immortality back to Ikhnaton's distinguishing his new monotheism from the popular polytheism of Egypt (Freud, 1939). It must have been a hard sell.

Freud assembled *Totem and Taboo* from four papers he wrote during 1912–13, while *Moses and Monotheism* is made up of two essays from 1937 and a third with a second preface dated 1938. There is thus a longish gap between the two books and so time for Freud to have changed his mind. He does say, for example, that 'this totemism, I conclude, may be regarded as the earliest appearance of religion in the history of mankind' (Freud, 1939, p. 105). So by the late 1930s he was more willing to blur the line between infantile totemism and childish religion than he had been back in the teens. But comparing Christianity and Judaism, he says:

> In certain respects the new religion was a cultural regression as compared with the older Jewish religion; this happens regularly when a new mass of people of a lower cultural level effects an invasion or is admitted into an older culture. The Christian religion did not keep to the lofty heights of spirituality to which the Jewish religion had soared. The former was no longer strictly monotheistic; it took over from the surrounding peoples numerous symbolical rites, re-established the great mother goddess, and found room for many deities of polytheism in an easily recognizable disguise, though in subordinate positions. Above all it was not inaccessible, as the Aton religion [of Ikhnaton] and the subsequent Mosaic religion had been, to the penetration of superstitions, magical and mystical elements which proved a great hindrance to the spiritual development of two following millennia. (Freud, 1939, p. 112)

It is hard not to think that Freud also thought the Christian promise of immortality to be another large step backward from Moses. It is easier for maturity to be lost socially.

These views about religion and death are, of course, also present in Freud between *Totem and Taboo* and *Moses and Monotheism*. Early in Chapter III of *The Future of an Illusion*, Freud mentions 'the painful riddle of death, against which no medicine has yet been found, nor probably will be' (Freud, 1961a, p. 19). A few pages later we learn that 'the gods . . . must reconcile men to the cruelty of Fate, particularly as it is shown in death' (Freud, 1961a, p. 22). Quickly, 'Death itself is not extinction, is not a return to inorganic lifelessness, but the beginning of a new kind of existence which lies on the path of development to something higher' (Freud, 1961a, p. 23) and then, 'life after death, which continues life on earth just as the invisible part of the spectrum joins on to the visible part, brings us all the perfection that we may perhaps have missed here' (Freud, 1961a, p. 24). One unfamiliar with Freud might miss the irony in these remarks taken out of context. Three years later, in *Civilization and its Discontents*, he is blunt. Toward the end of Chapter I he writes, 'The derivation of religious needs from the infant's helplessness and the longing for the father aroused by it seems to me incontrovertible, especially since the feeling is not simply prolonged from childhood days, but is permanently sustained by fear of the superior power of Fate' (Freud, 1961b, p. 20). In *The Future of an Illusion* we were told that Fate shows itself particularly in death; it is natural to remember this with a smile when Freud later mentions 'Fate (as it is best to call it)' (Freud, 1961b, p. 32). Freud's reference to the infant's longing for the father may sound oddly chauvinist in contemporary ears. But father or mother, it is only a page later in *Civilization and its Discontents* that he returns to the assurance to the common man 'that a careful Providence will watch over his life and will compensate him in a future existence for any frustrations he suffers here' and says it 'is so patently infantile, so foreign to reality, that to anyone with a friendly attitude to humanity it is painful to think that the great majority of mortals will never be able to rise above this view of life' (Freud, 1961b, p. 22). There is no mistaking Freud's attitude here.

3. Freud's views on unconscious knowledge and fear of death

So however overdetermined religion may be, wishful thinking about death is one of its driving engines. But where our Darwinian scheme traced religion back to a fear of death wired into thinking creatures by natural selection, Freud's understanding of our wishful thinking about death is intricate. This diagnosis has two aspects, a conceptual part about our deepest or most primitive ideas of death, and a conative part about our desires to survive. These two aspects cannot be entirely separated, but let us begin with the conceptual.

In the spring of 1915, about six months after the outbreak of World War I, Freud wrote two essays printed jointly in volume 14 of the Standard Edition under the title 'Thoughts for the Times on War and Death'. The first is called 'The Disillusionment of the War' and is about the naïveté of those disheartened by the barbarity manifest even so early in that portentous twentieth-century war. The second is called 'Our Attitude Towards Death' and is about our most basic notions of death. The news is that we have none. Freud writes:

> It is indeed impossible to imagine our own death; and whenever we attempt to do so we can perceive that we are in fact still present as spectators. Hence the psycho-analytic school could venture on the assertion that at bottom no one believes in his own death, or, to put the same thing in another way, that in the unconscious every one of us is convinced of his own immortality. (Freud, 1957, p. 289)[1]

Later in the same paper, he says:

> Our unconscious, then, does not believe in its own death; it behaves as if it were immortal. What we call our 'unconscious' – the deepest strata of our minds, made up of instinctual impulses – knows nothing that is negative, and no negation; in it contradictories coincide. For that reason it does not know its own death, for to that we can give only a negative content. Thus there is nothing instinctual in us which responds to a belief in death. (Freud, 1957, p. 296)

So much for the idea of death.

But what about the fear of death? In that same essay from 1915, Freud writes, 'The fear of death, which dominates us oftener than we know, is on the other hand something secondary, and is usually the outcome of a sense of guilt' (Freud, 1957, p. 297). He returned to this theme after the war. Some had objected to psychoanalysis that traumatic war neuroses (shell-shock, post-traumatic stress disorder) showed that 'a threat to the instinct for self-preservation could by itself produce a neurosis without any admixture of sexual factors and without requiring any of the complicated hypotheses of psychoanalysis' (Freud, 1979, p. 285). It was important to Freud that there be no instinct for self-preservation independent of libido. He said that no case of shell-shock had been analysed adequately. To cut a long story on the theoretical side desperately short, he held that in the basic narcissism of the infant the ego is cathected with its own libido; this is the narcissism we met earlier in animism. In the typical development from infant to child, the child manages to turn some of its libido outward, eventually in the typical case on to its parents. This is the phase of object choice we met earlier in religion. It also includes the Oedipus complex, which in turn includes a sense of guilt underlain by castration anxiety. In Freud's view, the fear of death is an elaboration of castration anxiety. He writes:

> But the unconscious seems to contain nothing that could give any content to our concept of the annihilation of life. Castration can be pictured on the basis of the daily experience of the faeces being separated from body or on the basis of losing the mother's breast at weaning. But nothing resembling death can ever have been experienced; or if it has, as in fainting, it has left no visible traces behind. I am therefore inclined to adhere to the view that the fear of death should be regarded as analogous to the fear of castration and that the situation to which the ego is reacting is one of being abandoned by the protecting super-ego – the powers of destiny – so that it has no longer any safeguard against all the dangers that surround it. (Freud, 1979, pp. 285–6)

Three years earlier he wrote:

> The fear of death in melancholia only admits of one explanation: that the ego gives itself up because it feels itself hated and persecuted by the super-ego, instead of loved. To the ego, therefore, living means the same as being loved – being loved by the super-ego, which here again appears as the representative of the id. The super-ego fulfills the same function of protecting and saving that was fulfilled in earlier days by the father and later by Providence or Destiny. . . . These considerations make it possible to regard the fear of death, like the fear of conscience, as a development of the fear of castration. (Freud, 1984, p. 400)

The fear of death is a synecdoche (whole for part rather than part for whole) for the fear of castration.

The fact that Freud did not want to admit an instinct for self-preservation separate from libido should not be taken to mean that he thought libido exhausts our instinctual endowment. On the contrary, alongside libido Freud came to discern an instinct of death (see, for example, *Civilization and its Discontents*, 1961b, pp. 77ff). Here the idea is that we start with a death wish, with aggression directed towards ourselves, and in the typical course of events turn at least some of it outward. Even if the fear of death is derivative from castration anxiety and thus ultimately from libido, none the less it is present; we do fear death. The obvious conflict between the primitive death wish and the elaborated fear of death is utterly no objection to the adumbration of either or both. After all, conflict is the very stuff of psychodynamics. On the other hand, if at the root of our mind deep in our unconscious there lies a wish to die, it is hard to make out how this wish could have its distinctive aim unless there were also some idea of our own death in the unconscious.

In 1915 Freud gave more than one argument against the presence of an idea of our own deaths in the unconscious. One was that 'It is indeed impossible to imagine our own death; and whenever we attempt to do so we can perceive that we are in fact still present as spectators' (Freud, 1957, p. 297). This argument seems to be a psychological version of what logicians call a use–mention confusion. Suppose Tom says, 'The Earth is round.' Then he has mentioned our planet and its shape by using the words he did. He certainly was not talking about words, let alone himself. Talking geography, he might say that England is larger than Russia, and he would be wrong because the island nation covers less ground than the bicontinental country; talking spelling, he might say that 'England' is larger than 'Russia', and he would be right because the first name includes one more letter than the second. In the first case, he mentioned two countries by using their names, while in the second, he mentioned their names by using quotation marks. In neither case did he mention himself even though he did the talking. Turning from speech to psychology, if Tom thinks to himself that Saturn has rings, then he is thinking about a planet rather than himself even though he is doing the thinking. If now Tom imagines Jupiter colliding with Saturn, then the two planets figure in his image but he does not, even though he made and introspects that image. Of course, he could put himself in the picture too by imaging himself in a rocket out in space watching the two planets collide. Then the image would be of him as well as inspected by him. But he need not include himself among the subject matter of his imaginings. To imagine the absence of an object is typically to imagine the habitat of that object without it. So to imagine the absence of the planet Venus, one might begin by imagining the solar system but with a gap from Mercury to the Earth. To imagine your own death then, you could imagine how life around you might go on without you. You could even include your decaying corpse in the image you make. But though you inspect your image, and maybe have strong emotions about what you envisage, if you are to imagine your own death, then you should include none of your thoughts, experiences or emotions in your cast of characters. But there is no more problem leaving them out than there is for Goethe to omit himself in the cast of *Faust* or for Leonardo not to have flanked Mona Lisa on the canvas with a portrait of himself. Freud notwithstanding, one can imagine one's own death, and even if one inspects the images one thus constructs, none of these images need depict oneself (whether inspecting those images or not).

Given the centrality of visualising to the imagination, we might think through the example of pictures a little more carefully. To depict a volume, like the contents of half a room, pick a point P in the other half of the room. Take each unobstructed segment starting at a point on the surface of an opaque object in the half of the room to be depicted and ending at P. Fix a rectangle parallel to the plane dividing the room in two, between P and the half of the room to be depicted, and on the same side of the plane dividing the room as P. For each point A in the rectangle there is a unique point B at which the ray from P through A first meets an opaque object in the half of the room to be depicted; give A the same colour as B. This will fill your rectangle with a picture of the other side of the room. To see what is going on here, look at Dürer's woodcut *Demonstration of Perspective*. Note that your chosen point P will not be among those represented in your picture. Of course, it is you who do your imagining, but it is not true that imagining a scene is imagining yourself perceiving a scene.

Freud's other argument against an idea of one's own death in one's unconscious is that there is no negation in the unconscious (or, as he also puts it, contradictories coincide there) and that we can give only a negative content to the idea of our own deaths. First, the two versions of the first premiss seem incompatible, for if there is no negation in the unconscious, then there will be no negation of (the surrogate for) a predicate there, and thus no contradictory for the predicate to coincide with. Second, it is unclear whether the absence of negation from the unconscious is peculiar to negation or extends to other logical operators. If it is peculiar to negation, one is curious as to why this operator is so distinguished. If the exclusion extends to other operators, then one wonders whether all conceptual compounds coincide with their components. In that case, for example, any (surrogate for) a predicate in the unconscious would coincide with its conjunction with any other predicate, and so with the other conjunct, and most conceptual differences would be lost; it would then seem very difficult to attribute any distinctive content to the unconscious. Third, many predicates belong to a range of alternatives; they are said to be determinants of a determinable. For example, each of the colours, like red or blue or green, is one of a range; red is a determinant of the determinable colour. Beyond this, most predicates inform partly by what they exclude; to say that an animal is an armadillo excludes its being an aardvark. If the psychoanalyst tells us that his analysand has deep in his unconscious the thought that he has property P, but that this attribution of property P excludes nothing because it coincides with anything we might think contradicts it, then it is quite unclear what if anything the analyst has attributed to the analysand. Fourth, if there is no negation in the unconscious and contradictories coincide there, then the prospect looms of an absence of conflicts from the unconscious, and in that case any psychodynamics rooted in conflicts would be at risk. Fifth, it is odd that so scrupulous a clinician as Freud describes none of the clinical experience that seemed best interpreted by denying that there is negation in the unconscious; one would like a chance to try out other interpretations, if only to see why a denial of negation becomes appealing. Sixth, Freud said each of us is convinced in the unconscious of his own immortality. The prefix 'im' makes this predicate the negation of mortality, which would seem to put negation in the unconscious. Part of the difficulty here is that it is easier to recognise a pair of predicates as contradictories (exclusive and exhaustive) than to tell which is the negative and which the positive. (Nowadays one often starts by defining infinite sets as those the same size as one of their proper subsets, and then defining finite sets as the rest, but the reverse order is possible too.) If we do not know which is the negative, we do not know which is excluded from the unconscious. (But if they coincide, 'both' are present, if either.) Seventh, Freud derives the fear of death as an elaboration of the fear of castration, so the idea of castration must be positive enough to occur in the unconscious. He says we can picture it on the basis of losing the mother's breast at weaning, so the idea of loss must be positive enough to occur in the unconscious. To picture one thing losing another, all we need do is picture the first without the second. To picture one's own death, all one need do is picture the world without one. It is as if somehow Freud thought we could not widen our imaginative panorama to include the world around us, and then erase ourselves from the vista. Eighth, a fade to black is a staying enough image of what it is like from the inside to die for it to have become conventional in the movies, and so left visible traces. Freud's second argument against an idea of one's own death in one's unconscious seems too problematic to carry conviction.

4. The illusion of a future

In the ancient world, wars seem to have been fought for glory, for spoils or for power. Alexander and Augustus may not have been nice guys, but neither do their motives seem to have been supernatural. The Moslems often went to war to convert their neighbours or, if their neighbour's religion was too robust, to exterminate them (Lewis, 2001). Christians returned the favour in the Crusades, and we were off and running towards the wars of religion such as the Thirty Years' War. This is not the pattern of all modern wars, but, pious nonsense notwithstanding, there is religious war today in Kashmir between Hindus and Moslems, in Ulster between Catholics and Protestants and in Israel/Palestine between Moslems and Jews.

But the struggle between rigid traditional thinking (loosely, fundamentalism) and pragmatic secular empirical thinking (roughly, science and liberal democracy) is even more ominous. Whether the issue is prayer in schools, abortion, evolution, American soldiers in Saudi Arabia, homosexuality, beards, burkas, or equal rights for women, we seem to inhabit a planet in which the hostility between the two sides (pretty much the ignorant masses and those who exploit them versus the educated elites) has deepened and sharpened over the last two centuries since the Enlightenment. It seems only a matter of time until the forces of reaction, in one or another of their incarnations, get hold of the weapons of mass destruction devised by the elite. Religion is God's plan for the extinction of Homo sapiens.

Freud worshipped at the altar of nineteenth-century science. He prized the gimlet eye; his observation and his thought, whether of his patients or anything else, were to be uncontaminated by wishful thinking. This dispassion leaps from his pages. It is not an impish wish to *épater les bourgeois* or stick it to the stuffy. He wants to get it right, even if this means thinking things all the way through to the bitter end. What really leaps from Freud's pages is intellectual courage.

What is Victorian, or even quaint, about Freud's faith is his hope. Towards the end of *The Future of an Illusion*, addressing the religious directly, Freud says:

> We desire the same things, but you are more impatient, more exacting, and – why should I not say it? – more self-seeking than I and those on my side. You would have that state of bliss begin directly after death; you expect the impossible from it and you will not surrender the claims of the individual. Our god, Λόγος, will fulfil whichever of these wishes nature outside us allows, but he will do it very gradually, only in the unforeseeable future, and for a new generation of men. He promises no compensation for us, who suffer grievously in life. On the way to this distant goal your religious doctrines will have to be discarded, no matter whether the first attempts fail, or whether the final substitutes prove to be untenable. You know why: in the long run nothing can withstand reason and experience, and the contradiction which religion offers to both is all too palpable. Even purified religious ideas cannot escape this fate, so long as they try to preserve anything of the consolation of religion. No doubt if they confine themselves to a belief in a higher spiritual being, whose qualities are indefinable and whose purpose cannot be discerned, they will be proof against the challenge of science; but then they will also lose their hold on human interest. (Freud, 1961a, p. 69)

The inevitable triumph of reason and experience over religion may be a consummation devoutly to be wished. But the withering away of religion seems no more likely than the withering away of the state. A religious faith in life after death is a defence mechanism against our inescapable knowledge and fear of death. The conflict at the root of this illusion is just plain insoluble. The illusion of immortality can withstand exposure to reason and experience for as long as our species lasts. Indeed the light of reason just makes the fear fight back all the harder. That is why, since the Enlightenment, religion has presented us with an angrier and angrier face. The illusion of a future probably has a future as long as ours.

Note

1. This view became orthodox in psychoanalysis; see Fenichel (1945, pp. 208ff). Just before the remarks cited in the text Freud mentions a charming German idiom, to think of something as though it were death, for wilfully ignoring that thing. La Rochefoucauld's twenty-sixth maxim says we can stare fixedly at neither the sun nor death.

References

Fenichel, O. (1945). *The Psychoanalytic Theory of Neurosis*. New York: Norton.
Freud, S. (1939/1967). *Moses and Monotheism*. New York: Vintage.
Freud, S. (1950). *Totem and Taboo*. New York: Norton.
Freud, S. (1957). *The Standard Edition of the Complete Works of Sigmund Freud*, Vol. 14. London: Hogarth Press.
Freud, S. (1961a). *The Future of an Illusion*. New York: Norton.
Freud, S. (1961b). *Civilization and its Discontents*. New York: Norton.
Freud, S. (1979). *Inhibitions, Symptoms and Anxiety*. Vol. 10. London: Penguin.
Freud, S. (1984). *The Ego and the Id*. Vol. 11. London: Penguin.
Lewis, B. (2001). The revolt of Islam. *New Yorker*, 19 November, 50–63.

8

Emotion, Evolution and Conflict

James Hopkins

If psychoanalytic claims about motivation are correct, we should be able to relate them to those of other disciplines, such as social psychology, developmental psychology, evolutionary psychology and neuroscience. In what follows I try to indicate some interdisciplinary links, by relating evolutionary and psychoanalytic discussions of emotion and infancy. The theory of natural selection gives us some idea of the main forces which have shaped basic aspects of the human mind (or brain). In so far as we can align these with psychoanalytic understanding, we may hope to triangulate more accurately on the points of connection between.

1. Evolution, morality, and conflict between groups

Human beings are particularly notable for their ability to organise themselves in co-operating groups and also for the violent conflicts in which such groups engage. Darwin sought to understand these phenomena by linking them with altruism and morality. He suggested that human beings have evolved altruistic moral tendencies via the selective advantages these gave to competing groups. Thus a tribe possessing 'a high standard of morality' would be 'victorious over most other tribes'. This might be a powerful evolutionary force, since 'At all times throughout the world tribes have supplanted other tribes; and this would be natural selection'. Darwin's enthusiasm for morality remained unqualified by its relation to group conflict, and his argument has recently been carried forward by Sober and Wilson (1998), who dedicate their account of the selection of altruism 'to altruists everywhere', while citing as an example the conquest of the Dinka by the Nuer.

As articulated by Sober and Wilson, Darwin's idea was that selection can act at different levels, and hence on tribes or other groups as well as individual creatures. In acting on either individuals or groups, selection also acts on genes; but in such cases the mechanism of selection involves not just the fate of genes, but also that of individuals or groups (and complex individual creatures can themselves be regarded as groups of cells containing genes who share a common fate in a common reproductive enterprise). Thus a gene can replicate at the expense of other genes in the same creature, by fostering a tumour, or alternatively in co-operation with them, in enabling that creature to reproduce. Likewise individuals (or their genomes) may reproduce at the expense of others in a group, or in co-operation with them, by helping that group to supplant others. By attending to different processes of selection in this way we can divide relations of reproductive co-operation and competition into distinct levels: among genes within individuals; among individuals (and hence their genes) within families and larger groups; and among groups (and hence individuals and their genes) in a larger population.

The features which enable groups to supplant one another seem cultural rather than genetic.[1] So intergroup competition involves both the transmission of culture within competing groups, and the use of cultural symbols to mark their boundaries. Thus as Boyd and Richerson describe matters:

> The propensity to cooperate with sympathy-inspiring ingroup members, and to use symbolic markers to define ingroups, is like the innate principles of language. The specific markers, size of group(s), and internal structure of the group(s) to which individuals belong are culturally variable parameters that generate a specific functioning instance of the innate propensities. Like innate language structures and adult lactose absorption, the social decision-making principles most likely coevolved as adaptations to an emerging cultural environment in which cooperation within culturally marked groups was becoming important. Success in intergroup competition came to depend upon within-group cooperation; an evolutionary arms race arose. The scale of cooperation-to-compete might escalate until ecological rather than evolutionary constraints bring a halt. (Richerson and Boyd, 1998)

Such work has also focused upon the darker side of morality and conscience. Thus Gil-White and Richerson stress the role of both punishment and moral anger.

> If much group competition is active rather than passive (e.g. violent combat for land), then within-group altruistic norms maintained by punishment will confer dramatic advantages. This could make the production of new altruistic groups faster than the processes which dilute altruism within the group . . . The result would be a panhuman selection pressure for cognitive adaptations reducing the likelihood of 'mistakes' in order to avoid costly punishment (prosocial emotions such as duty,

patriotism, moral outrage, etc. that commit us to predominant social norms even in the absence of coercion).

Clearly, the other side of the coin of group co-operation is group conflict. Groups that develop norms that channel their within-group co-operation towards outward bellicosity will force other groups to develop the same (or better) or go extinct. This process selects for ever-stronger forms of within-group co-operation and outward aggression and is likely an important force responsible for the creation of ever larger and more complex social human groups . . .

(Gil-White and Richerson, in press; see also Boyd and Richerson, 1992)

2. Parental investment and conflict within the family

The family seems to be one of the most basic of competing human groups, and family co-operation is underlain by genetic relatedness. Parents share half their genes with each child, so that full siblings share half their genes as well. From the perspective of the genome of a parent each child constitutes an instance of reproductive success; and from that of each child the reproductive value of two siblings or four half-siblings approaches one's own. This genetic overlap provides a basis for the unity of purpose shown by members of the same family, but also underwrites divergences. These can be investigated via the notion of *parental investment*, which encompasses any benefit provided by a parent towards the reproductive success of one offspring as opposed to that of others.[2] This includes the efforts of a mother's carrying a child in her body, those of providing food, shelter, protection, and so on – all aspects of parental care which make for the success of one child rather than another.

As Robert Trivers (1972, 2002) has argued, parental investment is an intrinsic source of conflict within the family. For roughly, whereas parents are selected to allocate investment to a number of offspring over the course of their reproductive lives, offspring are selected to seek benefits immediately and to the full extent of their individual (genetic) interests. Accordingly, each infant seeks more from its parents – particularly the mother – than they are inclined to give, and at the expense of its own siblings, whether actual or potential. These conflicts may in turn be exacerbated by those between the parents themselves, for as the modes of investment of men and women differ so do their reproductive strategies. For example, it may be to the advantage of either parent to shift burdens of investment to the other, or again to reproduce elsewhere. In consequence the means by which men and women allocate parental investment seem to include not only promiscuity, infidelity and the desertion of partners, but also abortion, infanticide, abandoning children (for example, to foundling homes) and varieties of selective neglect.[3]

These conflicts are interwoven, and can be observed from conception in the invasion of the mother's body by the placenta. The placenta is constructed by the activity of the father's genome to extract maternal investment on behalf of the foetus, discounting other children the mother might have. The placenta thus develops as 'a ruthless parasitic organ existing solely for the maintenance and protection of the foetus, perhaps too often to the disregard of the maternal organism' (Hrdy, 2000, p. 433).[4] For example, the placenta bores into the mother's blood vessels, secreting hormones which raise her blood pressure and blood sugars in ways that may injure her but benefit the foetus; her body responds by producing hormones which counteract these; and so on. Here conflict between the parents becomes conflict between mother and child; and the placenta may be involved in sibling rivalry more directly, as when one of a potentially multiple birth aborts others.

Conflict continues after birth, for obtaining maternal care – at whatever cost to others – is a matter of life or death for the infant. It may be in the interest of either parent to time reproduction by abandoning a child from the start, as often happens with babies deemed defective. Feeding one child may entail neglecting another, and nursing tends to space conception and so to delay the emergence of younger rivals, as would suit the interests of the mother as opposed to the father. So in sucking at the breast a baby may already be enforcing its own entitlements against the interests of its father and siblings; and if it stays long there it will conflict with those of its mother as well. By the time a baby is weaned its genetic interests are liable to have been opposed to those of every other member of the family, in conflict concerning the uses of the mother's body and potential rivals inside her.

In the first instance these conflicts concern only the prospects of replication of the genes of various members of the family. As we have seen, however, these prospects are translated into physiological and chemical conflict in the case of the placenta, and they seem translated into psychological and physical conflict in others. Sibling rivalry over parental care is often vicious or lethal: some piglets are born with teeth for slashing siblings in fighting for the best teats, and in other species litter mates or nest mates regularly kill one another. So it is not beyond possibility that in the service of comparable genetic interests human babies should instinctively desire to control the breast and resist weaning, should feel jealousy and anger about their parents' sexuality, and should be hostile to siblings or other potential users or occupants of their mother's bodies.

Even prior to considering any particular psychological mechanisms, we can see that these conflicts partly coincide with those described in psychoanalytic theory. Freud stressed rivalries between siblings, and also between parents and children; and Melanie Klein traced these into infancy. For example, she described the baby as desiring an invasive and placenta-like control of the breast and the inside of the mother's body; as having phantasies of attacking rival babies or the sexual presence of the father inside the mother; as angered and disappointed by weaning; and as feeling surrounded by potential enemies. Despite an unwavering scepticism about psychoanalysis, Trivers' exploration of parent-offspring conflict led him to hold that 'all the machinations Freud imagined going on in early life had a reality . . . which I had formerly disbelieved . . .' (Trivers, quoted in Hrdy, 2002, p. 430). The prospect of such innate readiness for conflict is not easy to accept; but if evolution can set the newly hatched cuckoo to destroy rival eggs so as to exploit the parental care of birds it has never seen, we cannot dismiss the possibility that it might also set the minds or brains of human babies to seek control of their mother's bodies against rivals outside, in order to protect their own interests against rivals within.

3. Co-operation, conflict and emotional development

We can thus think of human emotion as shaped by the requirements of at least three kinds of reproductive co-operation and conflict. Among adults actually reproducing we find the conflicts and co-operations involved in securing partners and resources for starting and maintaining children; within families we find those between parent and parent, parent and child, and the children themselves, as considered above. Then among families and larger groups we find ingroup co-operation and outgroup conflict which may turn on the operations of conscience and punishment.

We can readily see emotions such as love and affection as involved in human relations of reproductive co-operation, and hatred and aggression in human relations of conflict; and we can take these in a neuroscientific and developmental perspective as well. We can regard the emotions, in Damasio's phrase, as 'part of a multi-tiered and evolutionarily set neural mechanism aimed at maintaining organismic homeostasis' (Damasio et al., 2000, p. 1049). This is roughly the role Freud assigned to the drives; and the tiers, which we share with other mammals, include subcortical mechanisms which prompt distress at hunger, thirst and other forms of bodily disequilibrium, and also 'emotional command systems', which direct manifestations of rage and fear (and hence hatred), sexuality, maternal and paternal nurturance (and hence parental love), separation distress and social bonding, and play and social affection. These mechanisms are integrated with a general motivational 'seeking system', the nocturnal activation of which (as Freudian theory would predict) seems a content-specific cause of dreaming (Panksepp, 1998).[5]

The basic subcortical mechanisms of motivation are operative at birth. They enjoy inbuilt relations of excitation and inhibition, and come connected for expression through the baby's face, voice and movements. During the first year they attain further co-ordination and integration as the cortex develops through critical phases of synaptic growth, myelination and experience-dependent neural pruning, which coincides with the infant's using its experience of relating with others – and particularly the investing mother[6] – to build increasingly articulate representations of the self and other objects of emotion. So it appears (1) that complex human feelings result from the orchestration of the subcortical mechanisms of emotion and motivation, and (2) that this orchestration is accomplished via the cortical representations of the persons and situations which are the objects of emotion – those which arouse emotion, and at which it is directed.

4. Emotional development and parental investment

In so far as this is so, we should expect emotional development to show certain continuities and discontinuities. Roughly, we should expect continuities which reflect the constant working of the basic mechanisms of emotion, and discontinuities which reflect changes in the objects of emotion and the way these objects are represented.

We can trace these in terms of the notion of parental investment. Thus as regards the beginnings of post-natal life we should expect the infant's emotions to be shaped by selection to extract maternal investment. The infant's period as a selfish consumer of parental investment is however by nature preparation for a later role as an altruistic provider, and this transition is mediated by experience in a family in which parents allocate benefits to children (and encourage them to act towards others) in a way which is fairer than the infant's own genome would dictate. In consequence emotional development should have an overall structure which psychoanalysis has long stressed. It should involve a transition, facilitated by parental care and family life, from something like infantile egotism or narcissism, towards a capacity for non-self-regarding love (or altruistic reproductive co-operation) in relation to others. Accordingly, the kinds of love or other emotions of co-operation which are started in infancy with parents, siblings and other relatives or carers, should develop, with changes in representations and objects, from early self-regarding forms towards others which are more altruistic, and in which reproduction comes to play an increasingly dominant role. Likewise, early aggressions should become focused on family and later reproductive rivalries, and, as we shall consider below, on members of competing outgroups.

Speaking broadly, we can say that the infant has two ways of securing what it needs from the mother: either co-operatively, by eliciting affection and love; or coercively, by inflicting fear, anxiety and guilt. Accordingly, the mother is the first focus both for the positive emotions which will figure in later relations of co-operation, and for the negative emotions which will figure in later relations of conflict: both for the newborn's first expressions of affection and gratitude, and also for its uniquely arresting and motivating expressions of rage, hunger, pain and fear. Since nothing in the infant's life will be more important than getting what its mother can provide – and since its rage, fear, and so on, can produce no harm to others, and may provide benefit to itself – we should expect both sets of emotions to be engaged to the fullest possible extent. So, for example, a baby can be stimulated to rage just by the prolonged immobility of its mother's face.[7] (And on reflection this is scarcely surprising, since an unresponsive mother constitutes one of the most important early dangers an infant can encounter.)

From an evolutionary perspective the distress caused by the infant's expressions of such negative emotions as rage and fear is part of their efficacy as instruments of duress on the infant's behalf. Wittgenstein remarked that in an infant's cry one could discern 'terrible forces different from anything commonly assumed. Profound rage, pain and lust for destruction' (Wittgenstein, 1977, p. 2e). But in so far as such forces have enabled their possessors to thrive by coercing mothers (or others) to provide more than they otherwise would, we should not be surprised at their existence even in the adorable baby. (Preliminary findings, moreover, suggest that the father's genome may take a dominant role in constructing not only the placenta but also the subcortical mechanisms of emotion, whereas the mother's is dominant for the cortex.[8] If so, then we might view the infant's emotions as more specifically taking up the egotistic extractive role of the discarded placenta at birth, and thereafter being modified, as the cortex, under the influence of the mother's care, takes forward the task of directing co-operation with the mother and other members of the family.)

We may be inclined to think of parental investment as serving only to enable the infant to survive; but parental efforts make a difference only by assisting adult reproductive success. In light of this we might expect early experience and cortical modification to be relevant to forming the representations which actually guide later reproductive activity, and this would exemplify the kind of emotional continuity-in-difference considered above. Such continuity holds, for example, among birds who use the imprinted image of their parents to learn to choose mates which both resemble their parents and differ from them (Trivers, 1985).[9] By this they achieve a balance between inbreeding and outbreeding. On Freud's account we use the early imagoes of parents and siblings in an analogous way: they both provide prototypes for later relations of reproductive affection (or at least for one strategy or another in this matter), and mark their originals as unsuitable for this purpose.

In this perspective we can regard Freud's account of the Oedipus complex as describing the way early experience provides emotional preparation for later reproductive competition. The boy's rivalry and identification with his father, for example, yields patterns for later competition and co-operation with other males, while early images of his mother contribute, as noted, directly to choice. (Freud's actual analyses of the Oedipal aspect of adult motives, moreover, often display the early relationship as involving a precursor of one or another adult reproductive strategy.) Freud's claims that early relationships engage what are to develop into full-fledged sexual motives, like his views regarding infantile aggression, remain so rebarbative that even evolutionary psychologists generally avoid contemplating them. Still, connections between early experience and later reproductive behaviour are found in animals who have far less protracted childhoods,[10] and we should not expect evolution to be squeamish in using early nurturing relations as preparation for later reproductive ones.

5. Identification, projection and images of self and others

Freud (1933) understood our images of self and other as products of both *identification* and *projection*. Identification effects 'the assimilation of one ego to another' (Vol. 22, p. 63). In this it forms an image of the self as *like* the other, that so that the two share traits and perspectives. We can envisage this as effected by systems like the 'mirror neurons', which respond to the behaviour of others by producing a first-person image of their activities in one's own motor system.[11] Thus, as Meltzoff (1999) and others report, newborn babies can imitate adults who open their mouths, stick out their tongues, and so on. In a psychoanalytic perspective this shows the early working of an ability to assume an image presented by the other, which is involved in many forms of socialisation and learning, and which is basic to the formation of our self-image. Projection, by contrast, forms an image of the self as *unlike* the other, by dissociating motives, traits, or perspectives from the self. It represents the self as lacking, and the other as having, the trait or aspect in question, so that the other seems different from the self and alien to it.

These mechanisms work together to implement a division which we constantly impose in our psychological and social worlds, as between a self or *us* which we regard with favour, and an *other* or *them* which we take as correspondingly bad.[12] Social psychologists have described the remarkable readiness with which we form such divisions, and the tendency to ingroup cohesion and outgroup aggression which accompanies even apparently trivial examples. Also they study the many psychological misrepresentations – including self- and group-serving biases, mirror-image misperceptions of others, and systematic errors in psychological attribution – by which the *us* is preferred, flattered, and exalted, and the *them* correspondingly denigrated.[13] Schematically, we identify with aspects of others we regard as desirable, so identification creates images of a good self as allied in perspective with good others. We project aspects which we feel undesirable, so projection creates images of a good self as opposed in perspective to bad others. Since the badness seen in others is often that of aspects dissociated from the self, the good self (or us) and bad other (or them) seem to confront one another with mirroring directness; and since the projections on each part lend predictive value to those on the other, these mechanisms tend to lock us in step in our perpetual dance of group suspicion and hostility.

The Darwinian suggestion with which we began is that our tendency to ingroup cohesion and outgroup conflict has arisen from the co-evolution of two forms of aggressivity. Aggression which subserves ingroup cohesion (involving punishment and moral rage) has evolved in the service of outgroup aggression (involving potentially violent conflict). If so these two forms of aggression should appear in the individual as two sides of the same evolutionary coinage, in mechanisms which connect moral anger and punishment within the group with violence directed outside it. The mechanisms of identification and projection, and the phenomena of conscience to which they give rise, provide just such a connection.

6. Projection and self-esteem

To see this we start with some observations as to how maintenance of self-esteem relates to images of in- and outgroups. In several experiments, subjects are given a small setback – they are made to look clumsy, told that have failed a 'creativity test', or the like. After this they are probed for attitudes towards groups with whom they identify, or again from which they dissociate themselves (members of fraternities and sororities may be asked to compare their own with others, people may be asked about their attitudes to foreigners, and so on). People characteristically respond to such setbacks by thinking more favourably of their ingroups, and less favourably of the corresponding outgroups, than they otherwise would (Meyers, 1999 pp. 65.6, 361). It is as if the individual seeks to represent the self more favourably, by simultaneously magnifying the virtues of those it regards as *us* and denigrating those it regards as *them*.

Such fluctuations in the system of representation of *us* as opposed to *them* are unconscious; but we can compare them with phenomena described in full psychological detail by Freud. Thus consider the events which preceded the first specimen of Freud's *Interpretation of Dreams*, his dream of Irma's Injection (Freud, 1958, Vol. 4, pp. 104ff). The afternoon before the dream Freud met Otto, his family doctor, who had visited the household of Freud's former patient Irma. Freud had treated Irma for hysteria by an early form of psychoanalysis and thought he had done enough for her by explaining the causes of her illness, which he took to include the sexual frustrations of widowhood. Otto mentioned that he had been called away to give an injection, and this reminded Freud that another patient had recently been given injections by *another* doctor, apparently with an unsterile syringe. Freud himself, as he had reflected, was always careful to keep his syringes clean.

Also, Otto said something which threatened Freud's self-esteem. He remarked that Irma looked 'better, but not yet well', and Freud thought he detected a reproof. Consequently, he spent that evening writing up Irma's case history, so as to justify himself by discussing it with their senior colleague M. That night Freud dreamt that he and his wife were receiving guests, including Irma. On meeting Irma he said to her that if she still got pains, it was her own fault for not sufficiently attending to his 'solution'. She replied that her pains were bad, and Freud, worried that he had failed to diagnose a physical illness, conducted an examination. They were joined by a number of colleagues from Freud's medical circle, including M; and it emerged that Irma was indeed suffering from a physical illness. Otto had given her an injection of the toxic chemical trimethylamin. At the close of the dream Freud censured Otto, stressing that 'Injections of that kind ought not be made so thoughtlessly. And probably the syringe had not been clean.'[14]

Now this dream dealt with topics – the illness of a friend and patient, Freud's own misdiagnosis, bad practice by his family doctor, and so on – which were sources of anxiety to him. Still, by considering it in the context provided by Freud's memories and associations, we can see that it was wishful, in the sense that it actually represented things as Freud would partly have wished them to be. Freud had gone to sleep wanting to justify himself to M in respect of what he felt to be Otto's accusation of bad medical practice, and in the dream he received the most thorough justification, and in the presence of M and other medical colleagues. The psychotherapy about which Freud was now so enthusiastic could not be blamed for Irma's continued suffering, nor could Freud himself: for Irma had a physical illness which Freud could not have hoped to cure. Moreover this illness had been given her by Otto's toxic injection. Freud had felt guilty and reproached by Otto during the day; but by the end of his dream he was in a position to reproach Otto.

Further analysis showed that Freud's favourable representation of himself as opposed to Otto also touched on guilts which were older, deeper and far more serious. For Irma was linked in his mind with another friend and another patient from years before. The patient was a woman he had killed by repeatedly giving her what he took to be a routine injection; and in that case, as details of the dream reminded him, he had consulted with M as well. The friend had suffered from incurable nerve pain, as well as addiction to the morphine he used to treat it. Freud was an enthusiastic advocate of the medical use of cocaine (and was a user himself) and he had urged on the basis of his own experience that cocaine was not addictive. This was a serious dereliction, which, as he remembered, had brought 'serious reproaches down upon me'. Also, he had persuaded his friend to use cocaine instead of morphine, and his friend had become addicted and died a lingering and miserable death from cocaine injections. So, by ending his dream with 'Injections of that kind ought not be made so thoughtlessly', Freud was turning towards Otto a reproach which, as he could realise on analysing the dream, he might well have directed against himself.

Finally, the misrepresentation of Otto went further still, and in a way that touched on sexual motivation and the boundaries of the self and body. Freud had placed particular emphasis in the dream on the chemical trimethylamin, and noted that it was connected with sexual metabolism. (It was thought to be a decomposition product of semen.) Sexuality, as he noted, was also linked with Irma's illness, which he took to be partly due to her widowhood. But as he later confided to Abraham, further analysis of the dream revealed his own 'sexual megalomania'. The women in the dream, including Irma, were widows, and Freud had them all. As he said, echoing a physicians' joke common at the time, 'There would be one therapy for widowhood of course. All sorts of intimate things, naturally.'[15] Freud never seems to have acted inappropriately on sexual desire for a patient; but in the dream it was Otto rather than himself who harboured such desire, and Otto was depicted as satisfying it symbolically by injecting Irma with a product of decomposed semen.[16]

7. The social externalisation of internal conflict

Taking this in relation to our present theme, we can say that Otto's remark pricked Freud's self-esteem, by reminding him of traits and actions which he was liable to condemn in himself. In waking life Freud dealt with this in an ostensibly realistic and rational way, by writing a case report which would justify his present behaviour. In his dream, by contrast, he reacted in a way which was less reasonable, but simpler and more comprehensive. He projected the characteristics in question into Otto, and righteously censured them there. This use of projection thus transformed an internal and moral conflict (Freud's knowledge of his own unthinking and sometimes lethal medical behaviour vs. his own standards on the matter) into a social conflict concerning the conduct of another (Doctor Freud vs. Doctor Otto, as witnessed by their medical colleagues).

We can see clearly how this way of thinking leads to an image of a good self as opposed to another who may be censured or denigrated. Such thinking may also be co-ordinated within a group, as was that depicted in Freud's dream. Freud and Otto belonged to the same medical ingroup whose members were identified with one another and formed an *us* in respect of shared values relating to medical practice and Jewish and Viennese culture more generally. Such within-group projection as is portrayed in this dream works to balance each individual's liability to personal condemnation, guilt, shame and loss of self-esteem, by directing moral aggression away from the self and towards others in the group, and in accord with the individual's personal version of the norms of that group. Where group identification dominates and contains individual projection in this way, identification and projection work together to create a morally cohesive group: one whose members are ready to feel guilt and shame in relation to one another, and also to subject one another to censure or punishment, by reference to motives and standards which are psychologically shared as obtaining among them.

We can also readily see how projection might dominate indentification so as to yield a denigrated outgroup. Thus Trivers – who takes projection as one of a series of mechanisms which have evolved in the service of the unconscious deception of others – cites the example of homophobic men. Experiments indicate that heterosexual men who most energetically dissociate themselves from homosexuals, and who regard homosexual traits with particular discomfort and disgust – that is, heterosexuals for whom homosexuals are a bad *them*, as opposed to a good *us* – are in fact more likely than others to experience erections while watching homosexual pornography and also to deny that they have done so (Trivers, 2000, 2002).[17] This is consistent with the idea that in condemning homosexuality in others these men, like Freud in his dream, are censuring in others traits which they are dissociating from their own selves.

In this case projection concerning a single aspect of the self can create at once a potentially cohesive ingroup and a relatively well-marked outgroup; and the tendency to condemnation and punishment related to the projected aspect may be magnified rather than restrained by the identificatory ties which bind the projecting group.[18] So we find group phenomena such as queer-bashing, the legal persecution of homosexuals, their organised murder by Nazis and Falangists, and so on. Also, it is clear that the projective defining of an outgroup need not rest on any particular internal conflict such as we find in homophobia. For since projection can always enhance the self-esteem of the projector, a group or individual marked out for hostility is liable to be targeted by a wide range of projections which have little in common besides conflict in the individuals from whom they emanate.

8. The individual, the family and groups outside

On the account we are considering the motives which govern outgroup violence are to be seen as part of our evolutionary heritage. They will therefore be present in some form from early in life, and are likely to be expressed and modified by developmental processes which are sensitive to local environmental conditions, as are those by which the infant builds up its images of self and other. The baby receiving parental care is thus at the same time identifying with the adult who provides it, and so laying down images of itself as closely related to another whose ways of being and modes of caring and relating it will later be able to assume as its own. At the same time, particularly in anger and frustration, it creates projective images of others who are radically dissociated from this good *us* and are potentially bad.

As this dialectic proceeds the infant repeatedly identifies with others, including those previously taken as targets of projection, and thus comes to represent itself in more morally and motivationally complex ways. The child is thus bound by identification to members of its own family and a series of related ingroups, whose norms are woven into the fabric of the self. At the same time, projection operates to create a complementary series of others and outgroups, who are perforce different and alien. The same processes as maintain self-esteem and cohesion within the individual (as illustrated in Freud's dream) thus perform a comparable function within the family and larger groups. (In the case of the family the final binding identifications were those which effected the dissolution of the Oedipus complex, and hence also marked the path to a reproductive place in adult society.) Inherent in this, however, is a tendency to represent others and outgroups as liable to condemnation by the standards which unite the self and ingroups. As Freud (1930) observed, 'It is always possible to bind together a considerable number of people in love, so long as there are other people left over to receive the manifestations of their aggressiveness' (Freud, 1930, p. 114). So the family appears as the first of a series of social units which, like the individual, tend to maintain an idealised and co-operative image of things within, and a corresponding denigratory and conflict-inducing image of those without.

> Every time two families become connected by marriage, each of them thinks itself superior to or of better birth than the other. Of two neighbouring towns each is the other's most jealous rival; every little canton looks down upon the others with contempt. Closely related races keep one another at arm's length. We are no longer astonished that greater differences should lead to an almost insuperable repugnance, such as the Gallic people feel for the Germans, the Aryan for the Semite, and the white races for the coloured. (Freud, 1921, p. 101; cf. also p. 102)

And in accord with the role of projection he stresses that

> When once the Apostle Paul had posited universal love between men as the foundation of his Christian community, extreme intolerance on the part of Christendom towards those who remained outside it became the inevitable consequence . . . Neither was it an unaccountable chance that the dream of a Germanic world-dominion called for anti-Semitism as its complement; and it is intelligible that the attempt to establish a new, communist civilisation in Russia should find its psychological support in the persecution of the bourgeois. (Freud, 1930, pp. 114–15)

Freud (1921) was able to develop his thinking about this matter only in a schematic way. He urged that the cohesiveness of many groups results from the way their members identify with one another by taking a common figure – such as a charismatic leader (or in the case of groups which are not led by individuals a common creed or set of norms) – as representing what they regard as good, thereby reconstructing their egos in a common way (Freud, 1921, pp. 67ff). This serves to ensure that the individual's self-esteem is regulated by reference to the idealised persons, creed or norms which bind the group, so that aggression in service of these is a source of pride rather than guilt or shame. Individuals may also be identified by other means, such as the projection of their bad aspects – and in particular their hostile and aggressive motives – into some common locus, which therefore becomes a focus of legitimated and collective hate. In finding or creating such internal good or external bad objects members of a group feel at once unified, purified and able to focus aggression in a way which is validated by common ideals. Thus the same formations of conscience which regulate aggression within the group also provide for its unbridled expression against others outside. And although these rough ideas have been greatly refined by Freud's successors,[19] we can see that they complement the evolutionary considerations noted at the beginning.

9. Infantile roots in more detail

The individual conscience or superego serves to specify what is desirable or otherwise to the individual and so to determine what he or she is liable to identify with, or again to project. But this conscience is itself built up by these same mechanisms: it is formed by the individual identifying with, and so taking its own, images of condemnation, criticism or punishment which come from others, and which may have been influenced by prior projections. We have been hypothesising that these mechanisms operate from very early in life, and during the period when the infant's emotions are being co-ordinated in the co-operative and coercive modes of obtaining maternal investment discussed above. In consequence we should expect the early images of *self-and-us* involving identification, assimilation, and co-operation, to be very different from those of *self-and-them* involving projection, differentiation, and coercive conflict.

Freud described the basic representations of self and other built up in the first year as 'the earliest parental *imagoes*' (1993, p. 64), and he noted that they show a particularly radical opposition. The affectionate and co-operative aspect of the infant's relationship with its mother apparently began with satisfaction at the breast and was extended to the caring mother as a whole. This was 'laid down unalterably for a whole lifetime, as the first and strongest love-object and as the prototype of all later love relations – for both sexes' (Freud, 1940, p. 188). By contrast the conflictual relation was represented as particularly harsh, punitive and cruel. These coercive images made up the most primitive aspects of the superego, and Freud regarded them as so suffused with 'merciless violence' (Freud, 1923, p. 53) as to suggest that they were formed under the influence of an innate capacity for lethal aggression.

In section 4 above we stressed that the development of emotion should show a particular kind of continuity-in-difference: continuity owed to the repeated engagement of the same subcortical systems of motivation and difference owed to changes in the objects and situations in relation to which the emotions were directed and co-ordinated. In a Freudian perspective this continuity takes a particular form. The basic mechanisms of emotion tend to operate throughout life in patterns which are begun during the organisation of the cortex in the first year. The earliest representations of self and other, as formed by assimilating identification and differentiating projection in the context of maternal investment, are the first to organise the engagement and expression of emotion. These are overlain by later images, but they nonetheless influence our representation of self and other as identification and projection proceed into childhood and beyond.

10. Another clinical example

This kind of continuity often emerges in striking detail in child analysis. Thus to take an example from the play of a little female patient who suffered from depression.

> Erna often made me [Melanie Klein] be a child while she was a mother or teacher. I then had to undergo fantastic tortures and humiliations. If in the game anyone treated me kindly, it generally turned out that the kindness was only simulated. The paranoic traits showed in the fact that I was constantly spied upon, people divined my thoughts, and the father or teacher allied with the mother against me – in fact, I was always surrounded by persecutors. I myself, in the role of the child, had constantly to spy on and torment the others. Often Erna herself played the child. Then the game generally ended in her escaping the persecutions (on these occasions the 'child' was good), becoming rich and powerful, being made a queen and taking a cruel revenge on her persecutors.
>
> (Klein, 1975, p. 200)

Again, in her role as Queen, the same little girl played at getting married:

> [When she] had celebrated her marriage to the king, she lay down on the sofa and wanted me, as the king, to lie down beside her. As I refused to do this I had to sit on a little chair by her side, and knock at the sofa with my fist. This she called 'churning' . . . immediately after this she announced that a child was creeping out of her, and she represented the scene in a quite realistic way, writhing about and groaning. Her imagi-

> nary child then had to share its parents' bedroom and had to be a spectator of sexual intercourse between them. If it interrupted, it was beaten . . . If she, as the mother, put the child to bed, it was only in order to get rid of it and to be able to be united with the father all the sooner.

Freud had noted that adults frequently symbolise their parents in dreams by the figures of king and queen. This little girl's play used the same symbolism in representing her relations with her parents. In real life she expressed great fondness for her parents and did not want to be separated from her mother. In her play, by contrast, she depicted parental figures as tormenting, cruel and punishing (if the child interrupted it was beaten); and in her depictions the same emotions of conflict appeared and reappeared, now in one locus and now in another, as in accord with the dialectic of identification and projection described above. These depictions thus reflected 'the earliest parental imagoes', which informed the punitive conscience in which her depression was rooted.

11. Empirical developmental psychology

We can also go some way towards tracing these developments in other and more empirically accessible ways. Let us begin by attending to a particularly striking series of changes which occur towards the end of the first year. These are the interrelated appearances of *separation distress, stranger anxiety* and *social referencing*. As Schaffer observed:

> crying or some other form of protest on termination of contact with an adult was apparent from the early months on . . . in the first half-year infants were found to cry for attention from anyone, familiar or strange, and though responsiveness to strangers tended to be less immediate and less intense than to the mother, both could quieten the infant and the departure of both could evoke protest. At the age of approximately seven months, however, a change took place. The infants still protested at the same situations, but now their protests were directed solely at certain *specific* individuals. The departure of these alone elicited crying and only their renewed attention terminated the infants' distress. Strangers, quite on the contrary, upset the infant by *approaching* him.
>
> (Schaffer, 1971, p. 117)[20]

At this time infants also begin to rely on their mothers as trusted sources of information about what is safe as opposed to dangerous, and hence about strangers. As Campos reports,

> the communication between mother and infant becomes extended to include a whole event in the environment. During this period the infant

> can appreciate what in the environment is the target of the other person's emotional reaction, much as the infant at this age can appreciate the referent of the mother's pointing or gaze behaviour . . . Accordingly, during this period social referencing begins . . . the deliberate search for emotional information in another person's face, voice, and gesture, to help disambiguate uncertainties in the environment . . . a two-person communication about a third event . . . (Campos et al., 1983, p. 825)

12. Attachment: consolidation and continuity

These developments mark the consolidation of *attachment*, as studied in recent developmental psychology. For shortly after their emergence infants start to show regular and enduring patterns in the way they respond to being separated from their mother and left with a stranger, as measured in the experimental paradigm of Ainsworth's 'strange situation'. The ways infants cope with the mother's absence and the stranger's presence, and the varying attitudes with which they meet the mother on return (for example, forgiving and greeting; with hidden or overt unforgiving anger; with confusion and so on), can be classified in empirically reliable ways.[21] These responses yield well-defined and predictive categories of secure, avoidant, ambivalent and disorganised attachment, and they can in turn be seen to reflect the infants' differing initial resolutions of their own internal emotional conflicts, and hence the way they project these conflicts into social life.[22] As a wide range of empirical studies are beginning to demonstrate, they apparently mark the inception of basic and potentially enduring patterns of relationship to others.

We have seen in sections 9 and 10 how psychoanalysis describes some of the continuities and differences in emotional engagement discussed in section 4. Such continuities are also made visible by the tracing of patterns of attachment. The differing emotional responses to losing and regaining contact towards the end of the first year can be found in later losses and reunions as life progresses; and they also show in phantasy and art, in relations to teachers and other children, in adolescent social behaviour, in courting and reproductive strategy; in parenting; and in mourning and grieving. As regards aggression, for example, we can note that children who are securely attached – and therefore relatively free of emotional conflict within themselves – do not seem prone to aggressive conflict with others. When secure children play in pairs with others of any category, they neither victimise their playmates nor become victims themselves. By contrast, pairs of insecurely attached children almost always fall into such patterns; and those whose initial relation to the mother is so conflicted as to be disorganised tend to become coercive and controlling as childhood unfolds. The connections found in studies of attachment are, of course, not as precise or detailed as those which can be traced in the kinds of psychoanalytic examples we have considered. Still they are of the same general kind, and the fact that they can be detected by other than psychoanalytic means gives good reason to regard such continuities as real and significant.

Also these patterns pass from parent to infant. The categories of secure and insecure attachment observed for year-old babies map to counterparts discernible in the ways adults talk and think about their own childhoods. The category of an infant's attachment can be predicted with impressive regularity from the counterpart category assigned to its mother (or adoptive mother), even before the infant is born. The best explanation for this would seem to be that infants start to acquire basic patterns of emotional expression and relationship by identification (and perhaps projection) as between parent and child, as described above.

13. First representations: self and other and us and them

The correlation between the seven-month-old infant's new affectionate and communicative relation with mother and new fear of strangers indicates that the infant has now imposed upon its experience both a form of distinction between self and other, and a related distinction between a good *us* and a potentially bad *them*. These are linked; for as the emerging *I* of the infant self is a locus of individual feeling and will, so the emerging *we* of the mother/infant pair is a locus of shared feeling and collective will, particularly in relation to threats from outside, such as strangers apparently represent. The infant's emerging distinction between self and other thus resolves out of a prior but less focused sense of contrasting relationships, with the self already anchored in affectionate and information-gathering relations with carers, kin and other local familiars.

Together with the material noted above, this strongly suggests that the innate propensity which Boyd and Richerson (1992) describe – 'to cooperate with sympathy-inspiring ingroup members, and to use symbolic markers to define ingroups' – begins with relations of identification with the mother, and has its initial parameters set before the end of the first year. The same applies to the other side of the coin, the infant's projective distrust of the alien. But although this development seems clearly marked in the infant's behaviour, we should note that there is something paradoxical about it. The infant distinguishes its mother from other people from birth, and by the fourth month has developed many special ways of relating to her, including elaborate and affectionate 'proto-conversations', which it conducts only with her.[23] So the question arises: if the seven-month-old infant already has a longstanding specific relationship with its mother, why does it now so sharply distinguish between mother (and other familiars) and strangers?

And why does it so vigorously protest the departure of the one, and so readily fear the approach of the other?

The best explanation of this seems to be that the infant's prior sense of relationship includes its directing both its strongest affections and fiercest hostilities towards the mother herself, *but without yet grasping that these emotions are directed towards one and the same enduring individual, or indeed towards a person at all.* The change observable at seven months would thus result from the infant's working out that its mother was a single continuing communicating being, and thus unique and irreplaceable, so that her presence became uniquely valuable and her absence likewise threatening. This is in effect the hypothesis advanced by Melanie Klein, in her account of the paranoid/schizoid and depressive positions.[24] Thus the infant's initial consolidation of an image of itself as in a co-operative (as opposed to a conflictual) relation with its mother, which we see in separation distress and social referencing, would have as its projective corollary the initial consolidation of an image of others who were bad and threatening, which we see in fear of strangers. The opposition between good us and bad them would thus lie near the core of human individuality. It would be a consequence of the interaction of identification and projection with the infant's attainment of the ability to represent itself and others as single and continuously existing.

Specific behavioural manifestations of this development may be observable in experiments conducted by Bower (1982) and Bell (1970). Bower describes

> A simple optical arrangement that allows one to present infants with multiple images of a single object . . . If one presents the infant with multiple images of its mother – say three 'mothers' – the infant of less than five months is not disturbed at all but will in fact interact with all three 'mothers' in turn. If the setup provides one mother and two strangers, the infant will preferentially interact with its mother and still show no signs of disturbance. However, past the age of five months (after the co-ordination of place and movement) the sight of three 'mothers' becomes very disturbing to the infant. At this same age a setup of one mother and two strangers has no effect. I would contend that this in facts shows that the young infant (less than five months old) thinks it has a multiplicity of mothers, whereas the older infant knows it has only one.
> (Bower, 1982, p. 217)

This admits interpretation as showing that while at four months the infant takes its mother as a psychological other to whom it relates, it does not yet regard her as a single enduring person, as opposed to a potential multiplicity of presences whose spatio-temporal dimensions are as yet indeterminate. By five months, however, the baby opposes uniqueness to episodic multiplicity and starts to view the mother (and by implication/identification its own self) as individual, continuous and lasting.

We can also observe related changes in the infant's expressions of emotion. Thus when someone makes a four-month-old baby angry by impeding its movements, the baby directs its anger at the impeding hand. The four-month-old seems not to have worked out that the hand is part of, and so animated by, another person.[25] A seven-month-old, by contrast, directs its anger at the impeding agent's face. By this age the baby is capable of monitoring others' expressions and responding in complex ways to the feelings they show; and the identity of the frustrating person now apparently matters as well. The seven-month-old protests at being impeded by either its mother or a stranger; but it apparently expects its mother to comfort it after frustration by the stranger, and so is especially upset when she does not do this.[26] So by seven months the infant's anger towards its mother has been modified by the representation of itself as requiring, and her as providing, comfort and protection where strangers are concerned. Such representationally and cortically modified anger thus already differs from the newborn's initial subcortical rage.

Before the infant represents itself and its mother in these ways, however, it evidently makes her the target of anger and fear. As noted at the outset the young infant seems particularly prone to experience anger or fear whenever its mother is unresponsive or alien. Carpenter describes how infants presented with their mother's face in strange circumstances 'would tense as they averted their gaze appearing to keep the target in peripheral view. From this position they would frequently take furtive glances. Sometimes they would turn ninety degrees away.' She noted that looking right away, as if trying to end the episode, was particularly frequent when infants were shown their mother's face speaking with a different voice. Again, Cohn and Tronick observed babies of just over three months, comparing the ways they related to their mothers in normal circumstances with their responses when the mother's deliberately behaved in an expressionless way. Normally, the babies alternated between watching the mother, showing positive feeling and playing interactively with her. In the abnormal circumstances, by contrast, they were fearful and suspicious, and alternated between attending warily, protesting, and turning away (Cohn and Tronick, 1983).[27]

This is how infants later act with strangers while consolidating their images of self and other as unique lasting beings. So these observations are consistent with the idea that strangers – and by extension members of outgroups generally – inherit the fear and rage directed at mothers who seems strange or unresponsive in the first months of life. This provides a continuity between the 'merciless violence' which Freud ascribed to the earliest parental imagoes at the basis of conscience, and the violent outgroup aggression characteristic of our species life. We noted earlier that Darwin and his successors have indicated how the formations of conscience might have evolved by binding humans in internally cohesive and externally rivalrous groups. We can now see that Freud and his successors have complemented this, by describing in detail how these same formations create a moral unity encompassing punishment within groups who co-operate by identification, and also set these groups against one another in projection-driven conflict.

According to the discussion above psychoanalysis has also traced these conflicts to their individual psychological roots. These lie in the infant's early pre-personal and fragmentary projective images of the other, and hence in its first confused unknowing fears and desperate primitive extractive rage. If this is correct, then work in psychoanalysis and attachment has a particularly central place. For these disciplines are unique in addressing the task of moderating these emotions in infancy, overseeing their continuities during development, and altering the images that channel them into destructive conflict as life unfolds.

Notes

1. This does not entail that genetic influences have played no role. Provided that genetic relatedness among members of family-composed ingroups sufficiently exceeded that among members of competing outgroups, spiteful aggression might have evolved in accord with the rules specified by Hamilton. See Hamilton (1995), 'Spite and Price', 'Selfish and spiteful behaviour in an evolutionary model', and 'Innate Social Aptitudes of Man' in *The Narrow Roads of Gene Land*. Like Darwin, Hamilton stressed the selective value of conscience; and he linked conscience-related phenomena with racism, xenophobia, and the potential for ecological disaster.
2. The term 'parental investment' was introduced by Trivers (1972). For this paper as well as 'Parent–offspring conflict' (1974) and others discussed below, see Trivers (2002). Trivers also provides overviews in *Social Evolution* (1985). For recent discussion see Mock and Parker (1997).
3. For basic theory see Trivers (1972, 2002). For a wealth of related biological social and psychological detail see Hrdy (2000).
4. Quoted in Hrdy (2000, p. 433). For discussion see Haig (1993).
5. Panksepp (1998); see also Watt (2000). Sexual motivation is discussed in detail in Pfaff (1999). On the dreaming brain, see Solms and Turnbull (2002).
6. For accounts of infancy highlighting maternal investment in cortical development see Schore (2001); and the essays by Trevarthan and others in Braten (1998).
7. Personal communication, Professor Peter Molnar.
8. On genomic imprinting see Reik and Surani (1997); Ohlsson (1998); and Reik and Walter (2001). As Badcock in particular has urged, this suggests that psychological conflict within individuals can be seen as a continuation of that between maternal and paternal genes. See Badcock (2000). For a discussion of male–female genomic conflict, see Rice and Holland (1997).
9. See Trivers (1985) and the work by Bateson cited there.
10. Thus maternal deprivation may render monkeys sexually incompetent; and the reproductive development of male rat pups requires maternal licking of their anal and genital areas.

11. On mirror neurons, see Rizzolati et al. (2001); and Blakemore and Decity (2001). On the role of imitation, see Meltzoff (1999). For discussion of the development of the infant's awareness of itself and others, see the essays in Braten (1998).
12. Thus, as President Bush reminded the American electorate: 'When I was coming up, with what was a dangerous world . . . it was us versus them, and it was clear who the them were. Today we're not so sure who they are, but we know they're out there.' Unfortunately he was right. The problem is not just the blindness of these mechanisms but also their ubiquity.
13. For discussions and references to empirical work on groups, see, for example, Meyers (1999). For the relation of individual and group identify see 41ff, and for the readiness for group formation and subsequent ingroup bias see the work by Tajfel at 353ff. For the readiness with such divisions can become violent see the experiments by Sherif and Zimbardo at 576 and 138. For the self-serving bias and the accompanying false consensus and false uniqueness effects 51ff; and for the related group-serving bias and the manipulation of the fundamental attribution error in service of it 371–3, and for the outgroup homogeneity effect and mirror-image misperceptions 365 and 529–31. These and many other of the group phenomena described by Meyers and other social psychologists can be related to the working of identification and projection, as discussed here.
14. For a fuller account of this dream, and of Freud's method of analysis and the kind of support it can be taken to enjoy, see Hopkins (1999).
15. For this aspect of Freud's dream, see Abraham and Freud (1965). This also indicates how the dream is constructed around a pun on 'solution', which is a crossing point for a conceptual metaphor which maps mind to body. For discussion of the relation between psychoanalytic symbolism and conceptual metaphor, see Hopkins (2000).
16. In discussing this dream I have made tacit use of the notion of projective identification introduced by Melanie Klein. For discussion of this see Segal (1972).
17. See Trivers (2002) and Adams et al. (1996).
18. Compare the polarising effect of group thinking in Meyers (1999: 311) and deindividuation (1999: 304).
19. For some more recent views on this matter, see Segal (1995).
20. On stranger anxiety and its relation to men and beards, see Hrdy (2000: 414 ff).
21. For recent surveys which support the claims made in this section, see Cassidy and Shaver (1999) and Goldberg (2002).

    For introduction to the Strange Situation procedure and the linked categories, see the *Handbook* Ch. 14 and the summary tables 14.1 and 14.2; for relations to teachers and childhood bullying and so on, see Ch. 4; for the development of disorganisation into coercion, and some examples of phantasy see Ch. 23; for the adult attachment interview and correlations between adult and infant categories see Ch. 19 and the summary table 19.2; and for further discussion of attachment and evolution see Chs. 6 and 7. Goldberg's presentation covers most of the same topics, and her table 3.1 displays some of the work on continuity of attachment patterns.
22. This last claim in particular needs more explication and justification than I can provide here. Still the connection between avoidant/dismissing and conflict about the mother's significance has long been noted, and those for ambivalent/preoccupied and disorganised/unresolved are explicit in the descriptions of the categories themselves (see Chs. 14, 19 and 23 in the *Handbook*).

23. For details see Braten (1998).
24. For more detailed discussion, see Segal (1995), and Hopkins (1987).
25. Compare the psychoanalytic notion of an emotional relation to a part-object.
26. See Campos et al. (1983: 824) and Sternberg et al. (1983: 181).
27. Trevarthan cites a number of related experiments in Braten (1998: 31).

References

Abraham, H. and Freud, E. (Eds.) (1965). *A Psychoanalytic Dialogue: The Letters of Sigmund Freud and Karl Abraham, 1907–1926.* London: Hogarth Press.

Adams, H. E., Wright, L. W. and Lohr, B. A. (1996). Is homophobia associated with homosexual arousal? *Journal of Abnormal Psychology*, 105, 440–5.

Badcock, C. B. (2000). *Evolutionary Psychololgy: A Critical Introduction.* Oxford: Blackwell.

Bell, S. M. (1970). The development of the concept of the object as related to infant-mother attachment. *Child Development*, 41(2), 292–311.

Blakemore, S. J. and Decity, J. (2001). From the perception of action to the understanding of intentionality. *Nature Reviews Neuroscience*, 2(8), 561–7.

Bower, T. G. R. (1982). *Development in Infancy.* San Francisco: W. H. Freeman.

Boyd, R. and Richerson, P. (1992). Punishment allows the evolution of cooperation (or anything else) in sizable groups. Ethology and Sociobiology, 13(3), 171–95.

Braten, S. (Ed.). (1998). *Intersubjective Communication and Emotion in Early Ontogeny.* Cambridge: Cambridge University Press.

Campos, J. J. et al. (1983). Socioemotional development. In P. Mussen (Ed.) *Handbook of Child Psychology.* Vol. 3. New York: John Wiley.

Carpenter G. (1975). Mother's face and the newborn. In R. Lewin, ed., *Child Alive.* London: Maurice Temple Smith.

Cassidy, J. and Shaver, P. R. (1999). *Handbook of Attachment.* New York and London: Guilford Press.

Cohn, J. and Tronick, E. (1983). Three-month-old infants' reaction to simulated maternal depression. *Child Development*, 54, 185–93.

Damasio, A. R., Grabowski, T. J., Bechara, A., Damasio, H., Ponto, L. L. B., Parrizi, J. and Hichwa, R. D. (2000). Sub-cortical and cortical brain activity during the feeling of self-generated emotions. *Nature Neuroscience*, 3(10), 1049–56.

Freud, S. (1921). *Group Psychology and the Analysis of the Ego.* The standard edition of the complete works of Sigmund Freud, Vol. 18. London: Hogarth Press.

Freud, S. (1923). *The Ego and the Id.* The standard edition of the complete works of Sigmund Freud, Vol. 19. London: Hogarth Press.

Freud, S. (1930). *Civilization and its Discontents.* The standard edition of the complete works of Sigmund Freud, Vol. 21. London: Hogarth Press.

Freud, S. (1933). *New Introductory Lectures on Psychoanalysis.* The standard edition of the complete works of Sigmund Freud, Vol. 22. London: Hogarth Press.

Freud, S. (1940). *An Outline of Psychoanalysis.* The standard edition of the complete works of Sigmund Freud, Vol. 23. London: Hogarth Press.

Freud, S. (1958). *The Interpretation of Dreams.* The standard edition of the complete works of Sigmund Freud, Vol. 4. London: Hogarth Press.

Gil-White, F. and Richerson, P. (in press). Cooperation and conflict, large-scale human. In *Encyclopaedia of Cognitive Science.* London: Macmillan.

Goldberg, S. (2002). *Attachment and Development.* London: Hodder.

Hamilton, W. D. (1995). *The Narrow Roads of Gene Land.* Oxford: Stockton and Freeman publishers.

Haig, D. (1993). Genetic conflicts in human pregnancy. *Quartery Review of Biology*, 68, 495–532.

Hopkins, J. (1987). Synthesis in the imagination: Psychoanalysis, infantile experience and the concept of an object. In J. Russell (Ed.) *Philosophical Perspectives on Developmental Psychology.* Oxford: Blackwell.

Hopkins, J. (1999). Patterns of interpretation: Speech, action and dream. In L. Marcus (Ed.) *Cultural Documents: The Interpretation of Dreams.* Manchester: Manchester University Press.

Hopkins, J. (2000). Psychoanalysis, metaphor and the concept of mind. In M. Levine (Ed.) *The Analytic Freud.* London: Routledge.

Hrdy, S. B. (2000). *Mother Nature.* London, Vintage.

Klein, M. (1975). *The Collected Works of Melanie Klein.* Vols I and II. London: Hogarth Press.

Meltzoff, A. (1999). Born to learn. In N. Fox and J. G. Worhol (Eds.) *The Role of Early Experience in Infant Development.* Skillman, NJ: Pediatric Institute Publications.

Meyers, D. (1999). *Social Psychology.* Boston: McGraw Hill.

Mock, D. and Parker, G. (1997). *The Evolution of Sibling Rivalry.* Oxford: Oxford University Press.

Ohlsson, R. (Ed.) (1998). *Genomic Imprinting.* Heidelberg: Springer.

Panksepp, J. (1998). *Affective Neuroscience.* Oxford: Oxford University Press.

Pfaff, D. W. (1999). *Drive.* Cambridge, MA: MIT Press.

Reik, W. and Surani, A. (Eds.) (1997). *Genomic Imprinting.* Oxford: Oxford University Press.

Reik, W. and Walter, J. (2001). Genomic imprinting: Parental influence on the genome. *Nature Reviews Genetics*, 2(1), 21–32.

Rice, W. R. and Holland, B. (1997). The enemies within: Intergenomic conflict, interlocus contest evolution (ICE) and the intraspecific Red Queen. *Behavioral Ecology and Sociobiology*, 41(1), 1–10.

Richerson, P. and Boyd, R. (1998). The evolution of human ultra-sociality. In I. Eibl-Eibisfeldt and F. Salter (Eds.) *Ideology, Warfare and Indoctrinability.* New York: Berghahn Books.

Rizzolati, G., Fogassi, L. and Gallese, V. (2001). Neurophysiological mechanisms underlying the understanding and imitation of action. *Nature Reviews Neuroscience*, 2(9), 661–70.

Schaffer, H. R. (1971). *The Growth of Sociability.* Harmondsworth, Middlesex: Penguin.

Schore, A. N. (2001). Effects of a secure attachment relationship on right brain development, affect regulation and infant mental health. *Infant Mental Health Journal*, 22(1–2), 7–66.

Segal, H. (1972). *Introduction to the Work of Melanie Klein.* London: Hogarth Press.

Segal, H. (1995). From Hiroshima to the Gulf War and after: A psychoanalytic perspective. In A. Elliott and J. Frosch (Eds.) *Psychoanalysis in Contexts.* London: Routledge.

Sober, E. and Wilson, D. S. (1998). *Unto Others.* London: Harvard University Press.

Solms, M. and Turnbull, O. (2002). *The Brain and the Inner World.* London: Karnac.

Sternberg, C. R. et al. (1983). In P. Mussen (Ed.) *Handbook of Child Psychology.* Vol. 3. New York: John Wiley.

Trivers, R. (1972). Parental investment and sexual selection. In B. Campbell (Ed.) *Sexual Selection and the Descent of Man.* Chicago: Aldine de Gruyter.

Trivers, R. (1974). Parent–offspring conflict. *American Zoologist*, 14, 249–64.
Trivers, R. (1985). *Social Evolution*. California: Benjamin/Cummings.
Trivers, R. (2002). *Evolution and Social Theory*. Oxford: Oxford University Press.
Watt, D. (2000). The dialogue between psychoanalysis and neuroscience: alienation and reparation. *Neuro-Psychoanalysis*, 2(2), 183–92.
Wittgenstein, L. (1977). *Remarks on Culture and Value*. Oxford: Blackwell.

9

Freud, Object Relations, Agency and the Self[1]

Tamas Pataki

I

In the background to this chapter is a view about what is most significant and novel in the psychoanalytic understanding of mind. It could be summarised under these heads: (1) the developmental perspective in understanding mental functioning; (2) the unrivalled significance of object relations (relations to people and their parts in 'outer' and 'inner' worlds, including relations to one's self) in the life of the mind; (3) the systemic or structural conceptions of mind which evolved in and from Freud's later work;[2] and (4) the insistently orectic and wishfulfilling character of mind. The view is not only that these things are *clinically* most significant, but that they are also *philosophically* most significant. The latter claim is unlikely to attract the same level of agreement as the former, at least among philosophers working in the Analytic tradition. From that tradition's current redoubts this selection of psychoanalytic themes is likely to appear eccentric.

This claim about what is central and what by implication peripheral is, of course, very large and here my focus will be limited to some aspects of the relations between (2) and (3), the role of object relations in structuring mind and its bearing on a number of prominent philosophical problems. To my knowledge there is little that is directly relevant to this issue in the philosophical literature, but it turns out that all four themes hang together in various ways and there is some useful work bearing on (3) and (4). So one possible point of entry, which links all four themes, is a consideration of some of the recent work on wishfulfilment and partitive conceptions of mind.

It may be helpful to have at the outset a sketch of the discursive track my argument takes. Since Plato, philosophers have considered various partitive conceptions of mind. They have done so largely because the idea of a division or dissociation of mental contents and activities appears to offer a way of understanding some problematic forms of mental conflict and incoherence of belief, especially those which characterise the so-called paradoxes of irrationality, weakness of the will (akrasia) and self-deception. Some of these conceptions are *strongly* partitive, in the sense, roughly, that the mind or self is conceived to be divided into independent centres of agency (sections III and IV). In the main, these latter conceptions have been rejected (for example, Thalberg, 1974; de Sousa, 1976; Davidson, 1982; Moore, 1984; Johnston, 1988; Gardner, 1993; cf. Pears, 1984; Rorty, 1988). Where Freudian notions of partition, or something like Freudian notions, have been considered, they have usually been interpreted as being either incoherent or as non-partitive in the strong sense. Philosophical consideration has also been given to the important Freudian conception of *wish-fulfilment* but, to my knowledge, partitive conceptions of mind have not been employed in the attempt to illuminate it (section III). Taking a lead from Freud, I argue that conflict of desire and incoherence of belief are not the only phenomena which press towards strongly partitive conceptions of mind. The consolidation of certain kinds of internalised object relations involving a range of, broadly speaking, narcissistic attitudes, which are not in the usual sense conflictual and do not necessarily involve irrationality, produce forms of dissociation into agencies or self-like parts which, on most of the germane criteria, appear to be strongly partitive. Moreover, this development, which is itself the consequence of the ineluctable need for maintaining secure object relations, largely explains our capacity for a range of reflexive, self-solicitous attitudes of which some forms of wishfulfilment, self-deception, akrasia and their congeners are important compartments.

II

That is the outline of the argument. Before turning to it I want to make a few historical and polemical observations on the significance of the clinical dimensions of Freud's work and on some of the consequences of psychoanalytic phenomenology for a philosophical theory of mind.

Freud is by no means the whole of psychoanalysis but it remains a valuable exercise to follow the spoor of earlier thinkers in his work and to examine the similarities between his conceptions and those of his scientific and philosophical predecessors. It is important in such exercises to distinguish direct influence from mere thematic affinity, and to locate the significance of Freudian conceptions in their clinical as well as in their historical and philosophical contexts. Freud wrote on a range of issues – morality, civilisation, religion – that were in his time, as now, patently philosophical and his speculative and analytical work in metapsychology has pretty clearly a philosophical complexion. There is no harm in approaching Freud as if he were a philosopher (for example, Kitcher, 1992; Smith, chapter 4; Alford, chapter 3; Brook, chapter 2: this volume); but it is important to understand that that is not all he was. The most important fact about Freud as a theoretician is that he was a clinician and an unusually acute observer who, as Michael Levine has aptly noted, carried his couch around with him (Levine, 2000, p. 4). It is a gross error to maintain that all or most of the principal doctrines of psychoanalysis were borrowed, or educed *a priori*, from antecedent philosophical and scientific conceptions. The most egregious example of this widespread error known to me is P. Kitcher's *Freud's Dream*. To consider one specific theme amongst many, Kitcher argues (1992, pp. 102–11) that the superego concept was derived essentially from Freud's covert commitments in biology and anthropology; but Freud tried to conceal that, according to Kitcher, and presented the superego as a clinical discovery. Entirely lacking in her book is any informed discussion of guilt, melancholia, the negative therapeutic reaction, masochism or persecutory delusions; that is, of all those conditions which would deeply impress a sensitive clinician and which cry out for a conceptualisation of intrapsychic relations of kinds like those of which the superego concept is an instance. Similarly, it seems likely that Schopenhauer's elevation of sexuality as a supreme expression of Will (Gardiner, 1963; Brook, chapter 2: this volume) was well known to Freud. But it is the most bookish of turns to suppose that sexuality acquired the significance it did for him because of the philosopher's influence, or even of the influence of contemporary sexologists, and not because day in and day out his patients presented him with sexual difficulties, perversions, infantilisms, fixations to incestuous objects, and so on. Freud wrote of critics, in a similar context: 'Since in their opinion analysis had nothing to do with observation or experience, they believed that they themselves were justified in rejecting it without experience' (1925, p. 74).

Freud's earliest approaches to mind (1895) naturally were influenced by the medical tradition in which he trained and its associated philosophical and scientific tenets. However, it seems to me that an unfashionable view is true, that his mature theoretical work owed less to these factors than to his accumulated clinical experience. As Holt (1989) has observed, Freud's most important teachers were his patients. Even when he borrowed terms or conceptions from predecessors in psychiatry, biology or other adjacent fields, Freud sought nearly always to relate the empirical significance of psychoanalytic propositions employing them to clinical and associated material.[3] An historical reading of the literature, which is sensitive to the clinical issues psychoanalysis confronted, makes it abundantly clear that the evolution of psychoanalysis in Freud's life-time and after owes far more to its susceptibility to its clinical and observational base than to the *a priori* unfolding of its extra-disciplinary presuppositions and commitments.

From a high altitude a critical line of development in Freud's thinking could be seen like this. The influential psychiatrist Griesinger had declared in mid-nineteenth century that mental illness was disease of the brain or central nervous system. That view rested on and reinforced the reductionistic tenets of the medical science which influenced Freud's early thinking. In the late 1890s and early 1900s Freud's focus shifted from the adventures of the patient's central nervous system to her relations to objects and events in the world and the manner, more or less distorted, in which these enter into her phantasies. He moved, roughly speaking, from a neurological perspective to a psychological and social one. In the course of that move Freud lighted upon something so conspicuous that it is likely to be overlooked altogether. He noticed that *the most significant objects in the patient's world were other people!* This realisation – of the primacy of (what are now called) *object relations* in psychopathology (and, later, in normal psychological development) – was a profound event in the human sciences.[4] The magnetists and Romantic psychiatrists of the early nineteenth century had acquired a considerable understanding of the role of the passions in psychopathology, not least the sexual ones, and had appreciated the influence of the rapport – the relationship between therapist and patient that today is called transference (Ellenberger, 1970, passim). The sexual passions and transference are, of course, major expressions of an orientation towards other people. But conventional psychiatry by Freud's time, with the exception of important pockets in France, had become largely sealed against those earlier insights, much as it is again in our time.

Parents loom large in the infant's life, eclipsing almost everything else, and we should be ever-struck by the fact that even in our adult lives other people are in one way or another the objects of nearly all our endeavours. Dependence on others and the need for loving attachment are the deepest facts about an human life. Those facts are ignored or obscured in much contemporary thinking in philosophy and the human sciences; much of which, indeed, seems to be unconsciously animated by the need to ignore and obscure them. Freud focused on them as no one had before. First, he established that object relations, with the intense drama of sex, love, jealousy, hatred which they compose extend back to early childhood. Second, that the nodal object-relational concerns send out their roots and tap into the seemingly remotest prospects of life – for example, art, religion, politics – though they may be disguised or more or less distorted. Third, that our relations to objects, to people and to aspects of people variously construed, may be 'introjected' or internalised into a kind of inner world of unconscious imagination or phantasy which is, however, not treated as imagination but as if it were on a plane with the real, as constituting a 'psychic reality'. Then, in a later phase, he showed that through psychic processes of internalisation objects can enter into the constitution of our selves and structure or partition the mind into separate agencies or self-like entities.

The idea that the mind is partitioned into something like separate selves or sub-personalities, some more brilliant or healthy than the conscious, dominant ones, or ill or demonic ones (as in possession), was no novelty in the nineteenth century. During its course, demonic possession as a clinical entity was gradually replaced by hysteria and multiple personality (Ellenberger, 1970, passim). The variety of hidden personalities which were manifested in certain conditions or evoked by therapeutic procedures eventually suggested to many researchers of the time that 'the human mind was rather like a matrix from which whole sets of subpersonalities could emerge and differentiate themselves' (ibid., p. 139). Charcot introduced the idea that 'small, split-off fragments of the personality could follow an invisible development of their own and manifest themselves through clinical disturbances' (ibid., p. 149). 'Janet contended that certain hysterical symptoms can be related to the existence of split parts of personality (subconscious fixed ideas) endowed with an autonomous life and development' (ibid., p. 361). Novels and tales about demonic possession, doubles and split personalities abounded; Dostoyevsky and Robert Louis Stevenson wrote the most enduring ones. Psychoanalysis evolved against this backdrop of polypsychic conceptions, including of course an array of conceptions of the Unconscious. *Freud's special achievement in this connection was not only to develop a particularly detailed and fruitful conception of the (topographical) Unconscious, but to develop and link a particular polypsychic conception incorporating the features of that Unconscious – the structural theory – to the developmental and object-relational perspectives: to indicate some of the ways in which the intense need for objects in the course of development fundamentally modifies the structure of the mind.*

With the focus on object relations, the ordinary language used to describe interpersonal relations – the so-called 'Intentional', 'common-sense' or 'folk-psychological' idiom – becomes the basic currency of psychoanalysis' medical psychology. The concepts of Intentional psychology – *belief, desire, anxiety* and so on – and its patterns of explanation are exploited and augmented. So, for example, fundamental psychoanalytic concepts like *unconscious phantasy* and *introjection* are assimilated to, but also used to deepen, our conception of imagination. The phenomenon of mourning for a lost object is used to illuminate some forms of depression, and the idea of infatuated love is used to illuminate some forms of mania. 'Megalomania,' Freud says, 'is in every way comparable to the familiar sexual overvaluation of the object in [normal] erotic life. In this way for the first time we learnt to understand a trait of a psychotic illness by relating it to normal erotic life' (1916–17, p. 415). It's a two-way street. The psychoanalytic notions extract their explanatory cogency from Intentional psychology, but they also extend and deepen it. The most radical and perhaps problematic extension occurs with the introduction of the structural theory, where some of the concepts used to describe interpersonal configurations are applied to the 'constituents' and intrapsychic relations of the self.

Although Freud developed psychoanalysis into a powerful Intentional psychology, he never relinquished the hope that some day pharmacology and neurobiology would come to the aid of psychoanalysis (Smith, chapter 4: this volume). The tension between the attractions of the neurobiological perspective and his progressive reliance upon Intentional description eventually forced a kind of scission in his thinking between the Intentional psychology and the project of Metapsychology, which was in large part the lingering ghost of his earlier approach. Psychoanalysis has since tried to straddle Intentional and neurobiological explanation and there is no reason why it should not continue to do so. It is evident, even at the clinical level, that the entire domain of psychoanalysis will not be tractable to Intentional understanding. Aspects of infant attachment behaviour, dream formation and psychoses, for example, require for their understanding concepts of a different order. But there are reasons why the body of psychoanalytic theory could only be constructed using Intentional materials: chief amongst them is that the notion of *self-understanding* is at the heart of psychoanalytic theory and therapy, and we cannot even imagine what that would be like using non-Intentional concepts. That kind of understanding can be achieved only within the richness of the Intentional idiom of a natural language. It is not only conditioned by the conceptual resources and practices available to a culture, it requires an understanding of the culture; the understanding of those concepts and practices is internally related to the understanding of the culture. Of course, there may come a time when self-understanding in psychiatry and elsewhere will become an unwanted commodity and some of the rich resources of Intentional psychology will wither from disuse. We may be at the threshold of such a time.

III

I mean by 'agency', in the first instance, the capacity for action; it is of course a characteristic of agents. Psychoanalysis does not have a systematic account or theory of agency. Analytic philosophy has a set of closely related Intentional theories of agency, of which the Davidsonian variety has been most influential.[5] Not too much stress should be placed here on the notion of *theory*, however. What we have is a relatively clear survey of a stretch of conceptual terrain in which can be located in a reasonably systematic way the causal and other relations between desire, belief, reasons for acting, choice, intention, rational action, and so on; some ideas about how irrationality enters the picture and of how some of these various elements may be physically realised. About the time classical metapsychology collapsed, a number of philosophers, most notably Jim Hopkins and Richard Wollheim, began showing how an essentially Davidsonian theory could be fruitfully extended to provide the agential-causal structure of much of the sort of material which constitutes the psychoanalytic domain. For this, the notion of wish-fulfilment, more or less as conceived by Freud, was taken to be central (Freud, 1900, 1917d; Sandler, 1976; Sandler and Sandler, 1978; Wollheim,

1991 [1971], 1979; Hopkins, 1982). The crucial philosophical contention was that the processes of wish-fulfilment are, by and large, non-intentional. The idea was this. When one normally desires to do something or desires that some state of affairs occur, then the occurrence of the action or state of affairs is a necessary, though not a sufficient, condition for the satisfaction of the desire. In wish-fulfilment, by contrast, the occurrence of the action or state of affairs is not necessary. Instead, the agent achieves a kind of attenuated satisfaction, a *substitutive satisfaction* Freud called it, by creating some sort of representation – a dream, a phantasy or neurotic symptom, a wish-fulfilling belief or quasi-belief, for example – which, in certain circumstances, temporarily terminates or, in Hopkins' term, pacifies, the desire (Hopkins 1995, p. 471). These items are not, on Hopkins' view, created intentionally or, at least, are not the result of practical reasoning. The agential-causal origins of (most) instances of wish-fulfilment are unconscious, and Hopkins was in part led to his view by a consideration of the difficulties involved in the conception of unconscious intentional agency, of unconsciously originated intentional action; more specifically, of the apparent impossibility of finding suitable schemas of practical reasoning for such action.[6] Wish-fulfilment, Hopkins concluded, is engendered by 'an exercise of will of a kind prior to that in intentional action' (1982, p. xxii).

It is clear why a successful extension along these lines would provide psychoanalysis with a distinctive compartment of a theory of agency. Very generally, much psychopathology is trouble in which people try to do what can't in fact be done, or not at any rate with the means they employ. They try to undo the past, search endlessly for mothers who don't (and perhaps never did) exist, attempt transforming the world using phantasy; and so on. Because they can't bring about the desired changes in the world, they tamper with their *representations* of it; or they manufacture new representations which provide bogus evidence for the attainment of their desired ends or, at least, the appearances of those ends. From one useful angle these endeavours can be seen as attempts at self-cure, at righting what seems wrong in the world (including oneself), using bootless shortcuts. A theory of wish-fulfilment explains the types of action or activities which are performed in pursuit of these unattainable, or seemingly unattainable, ends. It can thus provide explanatory models for much of the psychoanalytic domain.

Wish-fulfilment does occupy a central place in psychoanalytic explanation and desire acting subintentionally, as well as other forms of expression and acts of spontaneity, can be causes for some of its kind. But it seems to me that without reference to unconscious practical reason and intention the full range of wish-fulfilling processes, including the most important of them from a clinical perspective, cannot be made intelligible. In my view wish-fulfilment involves a variety of techniques and processes, with varying degrees of intentional agential involvement. The simplest forms, of which hallucinatory wish-fulfilment (Freud, 1900) and some types of dreaming are paradigms, involve only non-intentional mechanisms operating in primitive mental conditions. But at the other end of the spectrum there are complex, reflexive processes in which imaginal or plastic representations, manipulation of other people, or tendentious selections from the available evidence are used intentionally and unconsciously by the self for the purpose of fulfilling its desires and wishes. Some types of compensatory daydream and masturbatory phantasies are obvious examples of this, as are, much less obviously, many forms of wish-fulfilling symptom and action. The reflexive, intentional forms of wish-fulfilment may be viewed as members of a class of self-caring or self-solicitous activities which also include, amongst others, self-consolation, self-appeasement and, in some of its forms, self-deception. These, albeit sometimes distorted, modes of caring for oneself may enter into various auxiliary or superordinate relations with each other. For example, self-abasement can be an instrument of self-appeasement, and self-deception is *often* in the strategic service of some superordinate mode of self-solicitude such as self-consolation. In self-solicitude the self takes itself as an object to be cared for and that involves, amongst other things, a concern to satisfy its desires and wishes.

There are difficulties with the notion of unconscious intentional agency employed in this summary;[7] but I believe there are weightier difficulties in the attempt to explain clinical material without it. Elsewhere I have argued (Pataki, 1996, 2000), and wish to emphasise again, that non-intentional models fail to provide adequate explanations for much of the complex clinical material whose explanation is the touchstone of adequacy. Non-intentional mental mechanics may suffice for the agential-causal explanation of psychically primitive processes like dreams and some defence mechanisms, but in cases where there are complex symptoms or manoeuvres and where at least the surface behaviour is plausibly construed as intentional – action symptoms, character disorders, and so on – it fares poorly. So I contend.

But on the other side there are the difficulties. One of the most prominent of these is that unconscious intentional agency seems to lead to the kind of strong partition of the self noticed above. This can be seen from example. David Pears (1984, p. 79) describes a girl who 'persuaded herself that her lover was not unfaithful . . . [but avoided] . . . a particular café because she believed that she might find him there with her rival . . .'. Let's suppose that consciously she was convinced of her lover's fidelity and that her belief that she may find him in the café and its implicated belief that he was not faithful, were unconscious. In that case she harbours contradictory but segregated beliefs about her lover's fidelity. But the important point to notice here is that by intentionally avoiding the café she seems to be *actively protecting* herself against beliefs which she, unconsciously, already has. One inviting way of describing this paradoxical situation is that an unconscious, caretaking part of herself ensures, by intentionally avoiding the café, that another part of herself, its conscious client self, would not confront the painful reality of finding her lover with her rival in the café. For the manoeuvre to succeed it is critical that the client self remain unaware of the caretaker's protective activity: the intentions and activity of the caretaking part of the self must be veiled from the self which is the object of care. The right hand cannot know what the left hand is doing.

So the supposition of unconscious intentional agency in the girl's actively protecting her conscious self from a painful reality she has already unconsciously registered seems to lead quite naturally to the supposition of a dissociation of her self into at least two quasi-independent, self-like centres of agency. This, then, is an instance of what was earlier termed a *strongly partitive* conception of mind, and a dissociation of this kind, given sufficient mental distance or opacity between the parts, does appear to resolve the paradoxes of irrationality the case exemplifies: incompatible beliefs are segregated; acceptable schemas of practical reason setting out the intentions and actions of each part-agency could be articulated; self-solicitous or wish-fulfilling activity is veiled from its beneficiary. But such radical dissociation in the self may be considered a price too high. It may appear to resolve some difficulties but it looks suspiciously like an artificial stratagem introduced *deus ex machina* for the sole purpose of curing the paradoxes of irrationality. Moreover, it is far from clear that the conception of such disunity, when examined in closer detail, can be accommodated within an intelligible, coherent conception of the self. Gardner, for example, argues that this kind of partition offends the view of persons as substantial unities embedded in ordinary psychology. 'This explains,' he says, 'the importance of the issue of partition for the philosophy of psychoanalysis. At stake is the harmony between psychoanalysis and ordinary psychology: if psychoanalytic theory is partitive, its agreement with ordinary thought is questionable' (1993, p. 7). But, on the other hand, if we *can* make sense of such disunity, and if it could be shown that there are good reasons for believing that the self *does* divide along these lines, for reasons unconnected with irrationality and conflict, then that would provide some support by consilience for the account of self-solicitude I have sketched and the unconscious intentional agency which seems to entail it.

IV

So I turn now to another sense of 'unconscious agency', referring this time not to the capacity for action, but to the substantive self-like organisations which I allege are concomitant with strong partition and play essential parts in self-solicitude. I will consider two main aspects of this. First, whether there are grounds unconnected with conflict of motive or incoherence of belief for positing these agencies. Second, whether any types of such agencies are suitable for assuming the roles required for self-solicitude, particularly of intentional wish-fulfilment.

We need now to sharpen the conception of an *independent agency*. Gardner (1993), distilling some work of Pears (1984), has identified the following criteria for what he calls 'sub-systems', which are much the sort of thing Freud called 'agencies' or 'structures': (i) Sub-systems have their own points of view or subjectivity; in particular they can have the representation 'other sub-system' in a way that the agent as a whole cannot; (ii) they are autonomous 'rational centres of agency', that is they exercise strategic, intentional agency in pursuit of their own goals; and (iii) they are subjects of mental ascriptions which exclude such ascriptions to the whole person. Implied in these conditions is a fourth worth expressing separately (iv) that there is a degree of coherence within the agencies sufficient to support the attributes noted in (i)–(iii). And to approach closer to the conditions assumed in psychoanalytic discussion of these matters it is necessary to add a fifth, which may not be implied in the first four: (v) there is a degree of continuity in the agencies, they perdure as parts or personations of the self, can undergo change, and are not merely summoned into existence at critical moments, in the way for example that Pears' (1984) 'protective systems' seem to be.

Now, within psychoanalysis it is commonplace, though by no means universal, to hold that the mind is constituted of independent agencies with features like the ones just noted. To name names: Freud, Fairbairn, M. Klein, Winnicott, Bion, Ogden, S. Mitchell have explicitly enjoined partitive conceptions of the self. Of course, a roll-call doesn't settle anything about the adequacy of partitive conceptualisation, but it can suggest that the observed clinical phenomena do press strongly in its direction. It is not so with philosophers. Davidson has argued, influentially, for segregating constellations of propositional attitudes, but he did not hold that these constellations constitute independent centres of agency: 'such constellations,' as Hopkins (1995, p. 473) says, 'do not *have* motives; rather they *are* (groups of) motives'. Amongst philosophers, only David Pears has, to my knowledge, argued explicitly for a conception of mind whose (albeit transient) parts satisfy the conditions for independent agency as described.

Moreover, philosophical approaches to partition have been mainly confined to the consideration of conflict between motives and inconsistency in belief. Freud was also occupied with these types of conflicts and inconsistencies: between sexual and ego instincts, Eros and the death instinct, ego, id and superego aims, between split-off beliefs and consciously held beliefs, and so on. But we are likely to miss something important if we approach Freud entirely through conflict of desire and belief and ignore his contributions to understanding the structural consequences of internalised object relations. These consequences have been elaborated in recent work in object relations theory, but for present purposes a consideration of some of Freud's work will more than suffice. I am not, at present, trying to endorse, or adjudicate on, Freud's account of the macro-structures, ego, id and superego, though I think that there is much to be said for it: the model, rightly understood (see note 2), is the right *kind* of model. At this stage I am just trying to clarify what certain aspects of that account are.

Why did Freud introduce the structural division of the psychical apparatus? There were several reasons, all of them of great clinical and philosophical interest. Freud tells us in several places how forcibly he had been struck by the clinical picture of melancholia. In it

> the ego [is] divided, fallen apart into two pieces, one of which rages against the second. This second piece is the one which has been altered by introjection and which contains the lost object . . . [a critical] agency develops in our ego which may cut itself off from the rest of the ego and come into conflict with it. (1921, p. 109)

Notice that the conflict here is not substantially a conflict of desires or aims, it is more like a conflict of arms:

> during a melancholic attack [the] superego becomes over severe, abuses the poor ego, humiliates it and ill-treats it, threatens it with the direst punishments, reproaches it for actions in the remotest past . . . as though it had spent the whole interval collecting accusations . . . (1933, p. 61)

Delusions of self-observation in some patients also suggested partition: 'under the powerful impression of this clinical picture, I formed the idea that the separation of the observing agency from the rest of the ego might be a regular feature of the ego's structure . . .' (1933, p. 59). Freud must have been even more forcefully impressed by the negative therapeutic reaction encountered in clinical work, which he linked to an unconscious sense of guilt or need for punishment (and to moral masochism). In so doing he recognised that resistance emanated not only from the superego but also from the ego which had developed a masochistic attachment to the superego:

> The sense of guilt, the harshness of the superego, is . . . the same thing as the severity of the conscience . . . The fear of this critical agency (a fear which is at the bottom of the whole relationship), the need for punishment, is an instinctual manifestation on the part of the ego, which has become masochistic under the influence of a sadistic superego; it is a portion, that is to say, of the instinct towards internal destruction present in the ego, employed for forming an erotic attachment to the superego. (1930, p. 136)

These passages notice erotic, aversive and malevolent relations between the agencies ego and superego, but there are more transparently libidinal relations also:

> The fear of death in melancholia only admits of one explanation: that the ego gives itself up because it feels itself hated and persecuted by the superego, instead of loved. To the ego, therefore, living means the same as being loved – being loved by the superego, which here again appears as the representative of the id. The superego fulfils the same function of protecting and saving that was fulfilled in earlier days by the father and later by Providence or Destiny. But, when the ego finds itself in an excessive real danger which it believes itself unable to overcome with its own strength, it . . . sees itself deserted by all protecting forces and lets itself die. (1923, p. 58)

Freud also describes libidinal relations between id and ego:

> [the ego] is not only a helper to the id; it is also a submissive slave who courts his master's love. Whenever possible it tries to remain on good terms with the id; it clothes the id's Ucs. commands with its Pcs. rationalizations; it pretends that the id is showing obedience to the admonitions of reality, even when in fact it is remaining obstinate and unyielding; it disguises the id's conflicts with reality . . . (1923b, p. 56)

Further, the ego could take a component of the superego, the ego-ideal (or, as might be better put, the ideal self) as an erotic object: the ego-ideal becomes 'the target of the self-love which was enjoyed in childhood by the actual ego' (1914, p. 94). Loving the ego-ideal *recovers* the lost narcissism of childhood, which must imply at least a transient identification with the ego-ideal. Here we can in fact discern three distinct processes that Freud does not always clearly distinguish: the narcissistic rewards of living up to the ego-ideal or the ideals implicit in the superego; the reward of being loved by the superego; and loving the ego-ideal (ideal-self) with which one is identified and thus recovering the lost narcissism of childhood.

Now, on the Freudian account the agencies ego and superego, which enter into these libidinal and aversive relations with each other and the id, differentiate from the id largely as a result of identification with objects. Objects are first phantasised as being incorporated through a body orifice; then in some circumstances there may supervene a further vicissitude, introjection, in which they acquire a kind of permanence in the mind; beyond that, under favourable conditions, some introjects may be identified with: their features are appropriated into the self.[8] Identification is motivated by a variety of factors, but most significantly for Freud it is a consequence of the inability to relinquish libidinised objects; that is, of the intensity of object need. 'It may be,' Freud says, 'that . . . identification is the sole condition under which the id can give up its objects' (1923, p. 29). To retain a relationship to objects we modify our own characteristics upon their model and thereby achieve a kind of internalised, reflexive relationship between self and self-modelled-on-object. Freud puts this point colourfully: 'When the ego assumes the features of the object, it is forcing itself, so to speak, upon the id as a love object and is trying to make good the id's loss by saying: "Look, you can love me too – I am so like the object"' (1923, p. 30). In becoming like the object we adopt some of the repertoire, perspectives, perhaps physical characteristics (like gait) and, critically, the attitudes which the object had towards us or was perceived as having towards us. As well as new perspectives and attitudes, new aspects of the self are acquired, for aspects are what one perceives from particular perspectives. An example may make these matters clearer.

In his earliest discussion of constructive (as opposed to hysterical) identification, in the book on Leonardo da Vinci, Freud speculates on the sources of Leonardo's homosexuality. He suggests that for a while the young Leonardo had an intense and exclusive relationship with his mother, which was suddenly terminated. The boy then repressed his love for her and 'puts himself in her place, identifies himself with her and takes his own person as a model in whose likeness he chooses the new objects of his love . . .' (1910, p. 191). That seems to account for an aspect of Leonardo's narcissistic object choice, Freud's main theoretical concern in the paper. But Freud then continues:

> A man who has become a homosexual in this way remains fixated to the mnemic image of his mother. By repressing his love for his mother he preserves it in his unconscious and from now on remains faithful to her. While he seems to pursue boys he is in reality running away from other women, who might cause him to be unfaithful. (1910, p. 192)

In remaining faithful to his (deceased) mother Leonardo is perpetuating a relationship, but not just with a mnemic image or the memory of his mother: these things are possible – remaining faithful to memories as to ideals and vows is not unknown – but they would not account adequately for the features of Leonardo's narcissism discussed in Freud's book: his apparent self-love, self-sufficiency, love of boys of certain types, and so on. The underlying structure of that narcissism, which at this stage Freud cannot fully articulate, is that Leonardo is maintaining a relationship with himself-identified-with-mother; so his mother lives on in him (magically, so to speak) and retains a relationship with him; though for her love to be expressed *his* (probably ideal) self has to be projected on to other boys.

There is one more thread I want to draw out from this Freudian tapestry. The structural differentiation brought about by identification, which creates the macro-agencies ego and superego and defines the scope of the id, does *not*, in Freud's view, by itself imply disunity or conflict in the self. It creates only the preconditions for dissociation and conflict between agencies. Although the agencies are 'realms, regions, provinces, into which we divide the individuals mental apparatus' (1933, p. 79), the apparatus is – paradoxically perhaps – conceived as a unity, at least in health. Freud's insistence on this point is frequently overlooked:

> We were justified, I think, in dividing the ego from the id, for there are certain considerations which necessitate the step. On the other hand the ego is identical with the id, and is merely a specially differentiated part of it. If we think of this part by itself in contradistinction to the whole, *or if a real split has occurred between the two,* the weakness of the ego becomes evident. But if the ego remains bound up with the id and indistinguishable from it, then it displays its strength. The same is true of the relation between ego and superego. In many situations the two are merged; and as a rule we can only distinguish the one form the other when there is a tension or conflict between them. In repression the decisive fact is that the ego is an organization and the id is not. The ego is, indeed, the organized portion of the id. We should be quite wrong if we pictured the ego and the id as two opposing camps . . .
>
> (1926, p. 97; emphasis added)

Freud distinguishes here between structural differentiation and 'a real split' between the agencies; it will be convenient to give this kind of splitting a special name to distinguish it from other splitting processes: the slightly archaic 'diremption' will serve. And now this distinction invites questions about the circumstances in which structural differentiation (brought about largely by identification) graduates to diremption. (It also casts in deep relief our uncertainty about the precise way in which Freud's conception of the agencies should be understood.) Freud mentions 'tension or conflict' between the agencies but we have seen reason not to interpret these conditions too narrowly. If we review the examples of intrapsychic relations above, it appears that one common circumstance is that in each case one agency, or part or personation of the self, is treating another as if it were an external object, as something other than itself. Freud is explicit that the self can treat itself as it can external objects. When the ego 'enters into the relation of an object to the ego ideal which has been developed out of it . . . all the interplay between an external object and the ego as a whole, with which our study of the neuroses has made us acquainted, may possibly be repeated upon this new scene of action within the ego' (1921, p. 62).

> the ego is in its very essence a subject; how can it be made into an object? Well, there is no doubt that it can be. The ego can take itself as object, can treat itself like other objects, can observe itself, criticize itself, and do Heaven knows what with itself. In this, one part of the ego is setting itself over against the rest. So the ego can be split . . . (1933, p. 58)

But we do not have a firm grasp of this vicissitude. Is treating oneself as an object always to treat oneself as an external object? Is studying one's hand or reflecting on one's virtues to treat oneself as an external object? Does treating oneself as an object always involve diremption? Freud seems to suggest, implausibly, that it is so in both cases. However, it would seem more plausible to suppose that treating oneself as an object does not always involve treating oneself as an external object, as something other than oneself; that diremption is *sometimes* a consequence when the self treats itself as an object; and that whether it occurs depends on the nature of the particular relations between parts of the self, the personations with their assumed perspectives and aspects: perhaps those very relations which determine the attitudes involved in treating (parts of) oneself as an *external* object. (Diremption, it should be noted, may have other causes or conditions; conflict of agential aims, for example.) What some of those particular relations may be we'll consider in a moment, but first it seems in order to summarise our findings and consider some objections to them.

I think that this protracted citation and discussion supports the following propositions:

1. Freud conceived of the structures or agencies as capable of entering into a broad range of mutual 'personal' relations which can only be partially characterised as arising from conflict of motives and beliefs.
2. They are conceived as, at least episodically, independent centres of agency, satisfying the conditions for sub-systems or strong partition set out above (see discussions above, p. 166).
3. Freud believed that the self's taking (part of) itself as an object (sometimes) involved it's diremption into the kind of entities specified in (1) and (2).
4. Despite conditions (1) to (3), Freud enjoined some kind of underlying unity in the self.

There are two objections that threaten to undermine entirely the constructions I have placed on the cited passages. First, that in these passages Freud was merely indulging in metaphor; second, that he was hypostatising phantasy.

Heinz Hartmann and his colleagues long ago endeavoured to cleanse psychoanalytic metapsychology of metaphorical and anthropomorphic formulations and set its theory on a foundation of quasi-mechanical causes operating on and between subpersonal, functionally defined mental structures. Thus in their influential paper 'The formation of psychic structure' (Hartmann et al., 1964) they chide one of Franz Alexander's early books in which 'the id, ego, and superego have indeed become exalted actors on the psychic stage'. Their reaction to Freud's treatment of the phenomena instanced above is revealing:

> a more generalized penetration of the phenomena . . . becomes possible only at some distance from immediate experience. This was the function of Freud's structural concepts. If we use these concepts in a strict sense, the distance from experience grows. Freud's metaphorical usage of his own terms clearly intended to bridge this gap. It might thus be said that Freud's usage bears the imprint of the clinical source from which the concepts were originally derived, the imprint of the communication with patients. Requirements of communication may ever and again suggest richness of metaphor, but metaphors should not obscure the nature of the concepts and their function in psychoanalysis as a science.
>
> (1964, pp. 33–4)

Although they allege taint by metaphor, the authors recognise that the Freudian conceptualisation of the agencies was intended to capture certain kinds of clinical manifestation, the 'exalted actors on the psychic stage'. When, for example, the superego abuses, punishes, humiliates the ego, these things are manifested in the behaviour and discourse of the person whose superego it is; it is as if the person or self were acting in a certain register or personation. The cited passages from Freud convey the sense of the phenomena at issue. But the authors think that these clinical personations are not basic to Freud's thought and have no place in scientific explanation. They argue that Freudian agencies are best considered as underlying, subpersonal organisations of functions and associated contents interacting causally under determinable laws to yield the surface behaviour and experience of whole persons. In a recent treatment of the same issue, Hopkins (1995) also argues that the Freudian agencies, although distinct and autonomous, are meant to be understood, not as agents bearing propositional attitudes, but as subpersonal neural systems functionally defined. These systems can be described teleologically, that is in terms of goals and information which are in turn related to motives of actual persons (the parents), who are embodied as neural prototypes in the systems. Such descriptions of the agencies are useful and 'serve to generalize over clinical data' because, as Freud had importantly observed, the way people 'actually function depends upon the prototypes by which they represent themselves and their relations to others' (Hopkins, 1995, p. 475). But when we do so describe them we speak only metaphorically:

> We may describe such systems as if they had motives, in describing their goals and information on which we take them to operate; but we do not take these descriptions to have the same consequences as in the case of the desires and beliefs of persons. . . . Freud's distinct systems constitute one person, and the way these are ascribed motives, although metaphorical, is nonetheless genuinely explanatory, so far as it goes.
>
> (1995, pp. 474, 476)

It should be plain that neither of these accounts correspond to Freud's mature thought about mental structure. Freud did provide – incomplete and problematic – functional descriptions of the agencies (1923, 1940). But the passages cited above show that he was prepared to use a vocabulary of relationship to describe their mutual relations far richer than anything that can be cobbled together out of properties plausibly attributable to subpersonal systems, goals and information; indeed, richer than anything that can be cobbled together from the propositional attitudes *belief* and *desire*. He did so, I think, because he recognised that the complexity of the relations between the agencies as he characterised them required descriptive materials that far outran anything available in an idiom conceived as apposite to subpersonal systems, the language of his metapsychology, for example. The later attempts by theoreticians of ego-psychology to flesh out a subpersonal account of the structures highlights this limitation. Consider Hartmann's (1964) recommendation that 'tension' be used instead of such words as 'disapproval' to describe a relation between superego and ego. Suppose that *tension* was indeed the kind of relation that could intelligibly subsist between subpersonal systems. That is primitive, but the principle at issue would seem to remain unaltered even if more sophisticated substitutes drawn from neurobiology were available. It seems evident that the number of relations subsisting intrapsychically between agencies must still outrun those available for reference in any subpersonal or neuroscientific idiom. In the present case, we could not even begin to variegate *tension* to cover for disdain, contempt, hatred, reproach – the list is very long – each of which carries nuances essential to a clinical language adequate to the accurate description of intrapsychic relations. Freud's rich Intentional descriptions were born of fidelity to clinical reality. He may have considered them (wrongly) to be provisional, but they were not intended to be metaphorical.

Even if they were not intended by Freud to be metaphorical, in the sense that Hartmann wished to eschew, could they not be considered metaphorical as a matter of fact, in the sense that Hopkins enjoins? I think not, though the full argument would be arduous. It would have to show, at least, that the personal idiom necessary to an adequate description of intrapsychic relations is not reducible to, or eliminable in favour of, any conceivable neuroscientific replacement. That is so because it is a feature of metaphor that it is susceptible to paraphrase, and the idiom of paraphrase appropriate here is contended to be subpersonal. For our present purposes, however, it may suffice to indicate that the contention that teleological description of the agencies – *a fortiori* attributions of propositional attitude – *is* metaphorical rests on the prior supposition that the agencies *are* subpersonal; that bit of theory is what is supposed to render *prima facie* quite ordinary personal description metaphorical. And that supposition may be challenged. My contention is that, although there is tension here in Freud's thought, by and large his descriptions of the agencies in terms appropriate to selves or persons was not intended to be metaphorical because the agencies were not conceived as subpersonal entities; and, indeed, are not. They are, I think, better conceived of as kinds of protean expressions or personations of the self than as subpersonal functional systems or as mereologically constitutive self-like parts. If that is correct then it yields several satisfactory corollaries. The old question within psychoanalysis about how attributes of subpersonal structures can sum to yield personal attributes simply doesn't arise. The agencies being self-like or personal are therefore not in competition with cognitive modules, 'stupid' homunculi, functional organisations or other products of decomposition. And we seem to have the right kind of entity to answer to the clinical phenomenology. But now it must be admitted that the character of the agencies has become rather obscure and it becomes more pressing to ask whether what we have taken for substantial protean entities are not just the shadows of phantasies, as the second objection urges.

> [A patient] would rave against girl children and in fantasy would describe how she would crush a girl child if she had one, and would then fall to punching herself (which perpetuated the beatings her mother gave her). One day I said to her, 'You must be terrified being hit like that'. She stopped and stared and said, 'I'm not being hit. I'm the one that's doing the hitting.' (Guntrip, 1968, p. 191)

This person *seems* to be radically dissociated, much in the way denoted by 'diremption'. It may be urged, however, that all the appearances can be explained as the consequences of a unified agent acting out a complex phantasy or pantomime. I believe that approaches along these lines fail to accommodate essential details of this kind of case. It may be possible to demonstrate this failure without going into the specific contents of the proposed phantasies or the variations on these lines. First, these phantasies must have causes and reflect, in Gardner's phrase, 'a stretch of causally efficacious psychological reality' (1993, p. 180). Second, for a phantasy to be efficacious it must operate in conditions which enable it to be so. What are the psychological conditions which give rise to such a phantasy and enable it to be efficacious? Well, it would seem that this patient identifies with her mother (Guntrip elaborates on this feature later), who was experienced as hating her and, consequently, she now hates herself, or at least some of the childish aspects of herself: she phantasises destroying other children and acts out a similar phantasy by punching herself. Recalling the discussion of Leonardo we may conjecture that in these performances she is maintaining a wished-for dual relationship with her mother: on the one hand, by identifying with her and, on the other, by masochistically yielding to her. These, or some such, psychological configurations causally articulate her phantasy.

But now, for this putative phantastic scenario to express her various wishes and to be efficacious in pacifying some of them, *must there not already be in place* the kind of diremptions and mutual opacities between parts of the self which we entertained above? For, it may be asked, is it not precisely a dirempted psychological reality which gives rise to this particular phantasy? How *can* she phantasise that she is mother, or that she is strong like mother, when that phantasy is her own creature and the assumption of strength is defensively predicated on awareness of her weakness? How *can* she triumph over herself when she, the triumphant one, is her own victim? How could she be so unsympathetic and careless of her own pain and needs if it were not that she was profoundly dis-integrated? And so on. In sum, it would seem that diremption, whose assumption phantasising of the proposed kind is supposed to render superfluous, is in fact partly the cause of the phantasy and a condition of its efficaciousness. Phantasy can reflect and exploit psychological reality but cannot go counterfeit for it.

So these objections to the strongly partitive interpretation placed on the cited passages from Freud appear to founder. It does seem to be Freud's mature view, and it seems to be the correct view, that the self can split – dirempt – into parts or personations which satisfy the conditions for independence of agency outlined earlier. In some of these cases diremption may lead to internal conflict of motive and incoherence of belief of the sort that philosophers have traditionally considered, but the diremption is not *engendered* by that sort of conflict. Diremption occurs when (though not only when) one part or personation of the self treats another as if it were an external object, and in the cases discussed that vicissitude is intimately linked to the identification with external objects in the formation of the macro-structures or agencies.

Consider again Guntrip's patient. From an external perspective we see a person wracked by internal conflict punching herself. When she speaks she does not seem to speak for the whole of her. As the speaker sees it, the conflict seems to be with an external being. There appear to be at least two perspectives in this self: one from the self doing the punching and one from the self being punched. They appear to be mutually alienated: the speaker says she's not being punched, she's doing the punching. This situation is difficult to understand, but examining the patient's development and the way in which internalisation of her object relations has come to structure her self sheds some light on it. We know that this person has identified with and taken on (or in) the perspective of a punitive mother while retaining the aspect of the detested child she at bottom feels herself to be, a 'child within' who maintains a relationship with the internalised mother. One natural way of describing the situation, then, is that a part or personation of the self is being treated as a hated object by another punitive, salient part (the speaker). It is unconsciously perceived by the salient part under the aspect of a hated, childish object; while from the other perspective, from the masochistic child within, a part of the self unconsciously identified with the punitive mother is perceived under the aspect of that object. The speaker doesn't see her object as herself; she sees only a child she hates; and something similar applies from the other perspective. Perceiving each other as alien, the personations treat each other as if they really were external objects. The patient's self thus appears to be divided in perspective, subjectivity and agency. I suggest that the way to explain that appearance is to follow Freud and accept that the patient *is* so divided.

However, from the fact that the self can divide in the respects considered here it does not follow that there are *no* threads that bind its parts together. Although I have argued that Freud held a strongly partitive conception of mind and have suggested that such a view is, in essence, correct, further consideration of the relations between the agencies or personations may yield principles of self-unity which transcend division. This theme cannot be pursued here, nor can several other themes that have been left in the air: *personation* has been left precariously under-explicated; and the sketch of the path to self-dissociation engendered by the *self treating a part of itself as an external object,* though adumbrated in Freud's work and supported by a range of psychoanalytic considerations, is most incomplete and hemmed by paradox.[9]

Finally, if the conclusions reached here about self-partition are correct, then they provide indirect support for the account of self-solicitude outlined in earlier parts of the paper. The agencies or personations are candidates both for the objects of solicitude and caretaker. They possess precisely the kind of independence, opacity and relatedness required by that account. Several such self-solicitous relations are noted in the literature: the ego setting itself the tasks of self-preservation which the id neglects; the relation of loving superego to ego; the false-self's protection of the true-self; and others. It is evident that the internalisation of objects providing parental caring functions will be of primary interest to the investigation of these relationships.[10]

Notes

1. I thank Michael Levine and Agnes Petocz whose comments on an earlier draft have helped me clarify several themes in this essay and avoid many errors and exaggerations; and Man Cheung Chung for his editorial guidance.
2. Freud's account of the structural theory (1923, 1926, 1940), which conceives the mind as divided into quasi-independent agencies – ego, superego, id – is deeply equivocal. There is problematic tension in that account between (amongst other things) rival characterisations of the agencies. Freud seems sometimes to have conceived of them as subpersonal systems functionally defined and mereologically constituting the (mental) self. This characterisation has been elaborated by the ego-psychologists (for example, Hartmann, 1964; Hartmann et al., 1964). Sometimes Freud thought of the agencies as quasi-independent, self-like entities

bearing personal relations to each other, but still mereologically constitutive of the mental self. This view was developed by Fairbairn (1976), who conceives of the central ego, libidinal ego and anti-libidinal ego as having ego character but as being distinct compositional structures. In this view the self is conceived as, in Fairbairn's phrase, a multiplicity of egos. There is a third way of conceiving the agencies, which I will partially develop here, in which they are seen as particular manifestations or personations of the whole (psychophysical) self or person (cf. Guntrip, 1961, p. 138). Here 'personation' seems preferable to 'persona', since the latter suggests the notion of a mask or pretence, whereas the intended reference is to something like a transformation or radically altered condition of the self. The conception of the agencies, often attributed to Melanie Klein, as phantasy objects or as the Intentional objects of phantasy, is not, I think, a structural conception in the way Freud understood this notion: that is, as involving more or less coherent, enduring *organisations* of mental processes of which agency is a feature. Of course, such an account may prove explanatorily more successful than the Freudian one. It should perhaps be noted here that the *tripartite* division enjoined by Freud is not strictly an essential part of a structural conception. In this essay Freud's topographical account of the mind remains in the background.

'Self' is used here to cover sometimes for the 'whole' *mind* (equivalent to Freud's 'psychic apparatus' and its contents); sometimes for the whole creature with a mind; sometimes for particular manifestations, transforms or, in my favored usage, *personations* of the self, as in Section IV below; and sometimes, in the commonly used psychoanalytic sense, as the representation that a person has of themselves, as in 'ideal self'. The contexts will hopefully make clear which sense of 'self' is being employed.

3. My claim is not, of course, that Freud derived *everything* from the clinical phenomena or that he came to clinical material without theoretical preconceptions.
4. It is part of this chapter's contention that Freud's object relational concerns have been under-estimated. Cf. Freud (1921, p. 69): 'only rarely and under certain exceptional conditions is individual psychology in a position to disregard the relations of [the] individual to others. In the individual's mental life someone else is invariably involved, as a model, as an object, as an helper, as an opponent; and so from the very first individual psychology, in this extended but entirely justifiable sense of the words, is at the same time social psychology as well.'
5. I am thinking of the line of work which extends from Anscombe (1957), Davidson (1980) and Goldman (1970) through many others. For the application to psychoanalysis, see Wollheim (1979, 1984, 1991); Hopkins (1982, 1988, 1995); Moore (1984); Lear (1998); Gardner (1993); Cavell (1993).
6. For the difficulties in providing schemas of practical reason for unconsciously motivated behaviour, see Hopkins (1982), Moore (1984), Cavell (1993), Gardner (1993). Wollheim (1991) is the only philosopher I know who countenances action caused by unconscious practical reasoning or, at least, by the having of unconscious reasons understood as belief/desire pairs suitably conjoined; but he does so only for a very restricted range of cases. The non-intentional options have been more vigorously explored. The favourite motive is sub-intentional causation understood as the causal expression of desire without facilitation of instrumental beliefs or anything else (O'Shaugnessy, 1980). But there are other forms of expression, not involving desire: those, for example, which have an archaeology but no teleology, as when I clench my fists in (out of) anguish. Wollheim (1984) has iden-

tified a group of 'mental activities' which involve desire and, instead of belief, something he calls 'instinct'; Marshall (2000) has drawn attention to the role of action initiating mental activities – such as noticing, realising, recognising – which are neither subintentional nor forms of expression. The claim enjoined by Hopkins, Cavell, Lear, Gardner and others that subintentional explanation is paradigmatic of psychoanalytic explanation is criticised in Pataki (1996, 2000).

7. Freud was not concerned: 'All the categories which we employ to describe conscious mental acts, such as ideas, purposes, resolutions and so on, can be applied to them [unconscious mental acts]. Indeed, we are obliged to say of some of these latent states that the only respect in which they differ from conscious ones is precisely in the absence of consciousness' (1915, p. 168).
8. 'We have said repeatedly that the ego is formed to a great extent out of identifications which take the place of abandoned cathexis by the id; that the first of these identifications always behave as a special agency in the ego and stand apart from the ego in the form of a superego, while later on, as it grows stronger, the ego may become more resistant to the influences of such identifications' (1923, p. 48). It is evident that identification, as Freud himself came to see, is not the only source of structural differentiation.
9. Agnes Petocz (personal communication) has alerted me to several difficulties in the ontology of 'self' and 'personation' I deploy, some of which may have been apparent to other careful readers. These are, I think, resolved in my forthcoming *The Varieties of Wishfulfilment.*
10. Spitz (1965) and Winnicott (1965) made early contributions to this area. More recently Bollas (1987) and Kumin (1996) have taken up the theme of the self unconsciously taking itself as an object through maternal identifications.

References

Anscombe, G. E. M. (1957). *Intention*. Oxford: Basil Blackwell.

Bollas, C. (1987). *The Shadow of the Object*. New York: Columbia University Press.

Cavell, M. (1993). *The Psychoanalytic Mind*. Cambridge, MA: Harvard University Press.

Davidson, D. (1980). *Essays on Action and Events*. Oxford: Clarendon Press.

Davidson, D. (1982). Paradoxes of irrationality. In R. Wollheim and J. Hopkins (Eds.) *Philosophical Essays on Freud*. Cambridge: Cambridge University Press.

De Sousa, R. (1976). Rational homunculi. In A. Rorty (Ed.) *The Identities of Persons*. Berkeley: University of California Press.

Ellenberger, H. F. (1970). *The Discovery of the Unconscious*. New York: Basic Books.

Fairbairn, W. R. D. (1952/1976). *Psychoanalytic Studies of the Personality*. London: Routledge & Kegan Paul.

Freud, S. (1895). *Studies in Hysteria* (with Joseph Breuer). The standard edition of the complete works of Sigmund Freud, Vol. 2. London: Hogarth Press.

Freud, S. (1900). *The Interpretation of Dreams*. The standard edition of the complete works of Sigmund Freud, Vols 4 and 5. London: Hogarth Press.

Freud, S. (1910). *Leonardo DaVinci and a Memory of his Childhood*. The standard edition of the complete works of Sigmund Freud, Vol. 11. London: Hogarth Press.

Freud, S. (1914). *On Narcissism: An Introduction*. The standard edition of the complete works of Sigmund Freud, Vol. 14. London: Hogarth Press.

Freud, S. (1915). *The Unconscious*. The standard edition of the complete works of Sigmund Freud, Vol. 14. London: Hogarth Press.

Freud, S. (1916–17). *Introductory Lectures in Psychoanalysis*. The standard edition of the complete works of Sigmund Freud, Vols 15–16. London: Hogarth Press.

Freud, S. (1917). *A Metapsychological Supplement to the Theory of Dreams*, Standard edition of the complete works of Sigmund Freud, Vol. 14. London: Hogarth Press.

Freud, S. (1921). *Group Psychology and the Analysis of the Ego*. The standard edition of the complete works of Sigmund Freud, Vol. 18. London: Hogarth Press.

Freud, S. (1923). *The Ego and the Id*. The standard edition of the complete works of Sigmund Freud, Vol. 19. London: Hogarth Press.

Freud, S. (1925). *An Autobiographical Study*. The standard edition of the complete works of Sigmund Freud, Vol. 20. London: Hogarth Press.

Freud, S. (1926). *Inhibitions, Symptoms and Anxiety*. The standard edition of the complete works of Sigmund Freud, Vol. 20. London: Hogarth Press.

Freud, S. (1930). *Civilization and its Discontents*. The standard edition of the complete works of Sigmund Freud, Vol. 21. London: Hogarth Press.

Freud, S. (1933). *New Introductory Lectures on Psychoanalysis*. The standard edition of the complete works of Sigmund Freud, Vol. 22. London: Hogarth Press.

Freud, S. (1940). *An Outline of Psychoanalysis*. The standard edition of the complete works of Sigmund Freud, Vol. 23. London: Hogarth Press.

Freud, S. (1887–1902/1954). *The Origins of Psychoanalysis*. New York: Basic Books.

Gardiner, P. (1963). *Schopenhauer*. Harmondsworth: Penguin.

Gardner, S. (1993). *Irrationality and the Philosophy of Psychoanalysis*. Cambridge: Cambridge University Press.

Goldman, A. I. (1970). *A Theory of Human Action*. Englewood Cliffs, NJ: Prentice-Hall.

Guntrip, H. (1961/1973). *Personality Structure and Human Interaction*. London: Hogarth Press.

Guntrip, H. (1968/1977). *Schizoid Phenomena, Object Relations and the Self*. London: Hogarth Press.

Hartmann, H. (1964). *Essays in Ego Psychology*. New York: International Universities Press.

Hartmann, H., Kris, E. and Loewenstein, R. (Eds.) (1964). *Papers on Psychoanalytic Psychology*. New York: International Universities Press.

Holt, R. R. (1989). *Freud Reappraised*. New York: Guilford Press.

Hopkins, J. (1982). Introduction: philosophy and psychoanalysis. In R. Wollheim and J. Hopkins (Eds.) *Philosophical Essays on Freud*. Cambridge: Cambridge University Press.

Hopkins, J. (1988). Epistemology and depth psychology. In P. Clark and C. Wright (Eds.) *Mind, Psychoanalysis and Science*. Oxford: Blackwell.

Hopkins, J. (1995). Irrationality, interpretation and division. In C. Macdonald and G. Macdonald (Eds.) *Philosophy of Psychology*. Oxford: Blackwell.

Johnston, M. (1988). Self-deception and the nature of mind. In A. Rorty and B. P. McLaughlin (Eds.) *Perspectives on Self-deception*. Berkeley, CA: University of California.

Kitcher, P. (1992). *Freud's Dream*. Cambridge, MA: MIT.

Kumin, I. (1996). *Pre-object Relatedness*. New York: Guilford Press.

Lear, J. (1998). *Open Minded*. Cambridge, MA: Harvard University Press.

Levine, M. (2000). Introduction: how right does psychoanalysis have to be? In M. Levine (Ed.) *The Analytic Freud*. London and New York: Routledge.

Marshall, G. (2000). How far down does the will go? In M. Levine (Ed.) *The Analytic Freud*. London and New York: Routledge.

Mitchell, S. A. (1993). *Hope and Dread in Psychoanalysis*. New York: Basic Books.

Moore, M. (1984). *Law and Psychiatry*. Cambridge: Cambridge University Press.
Ogden, T. H. (1986/1993). *The Matrix of the Mind*. New Jersey: Jason Aronson.
O'Shaughnessy, B. (1980). *The Will: A Dual Aspect*. Cambridge: Cambridge University Press.
Pataki, T. (1996). Intention in wish-fulfilment. In *Australasian Journal of Philosophy*, 74, 1.
Pataki, T. (1998). Review of *Irrationality and the Philosophy of Psychoanalysis* (Gardner, 1993) and *The Psychoanalytic Mind: From Freud to Philosophy* (Cavell, 1993) in *Australasian Journal of Philosophy*, 76, 4.
Pataki, T. (2000). Freudian wishfulfilment and subintentional explanation. In M. Levine (Ed.) *The Analytic Freud*. London and New York: Routledge.
Pears, D. (1984). *Motivated Irrationality*. Oxford: Clarendon Press.
Petocz, A. (1999). *Freud, Psychoanalysis and Symbolism*. Cambidge: Cambridge University Press.
Rorty, A. (1988). The deceptive self: liars, layers and lairs. In B. P. McLaughlin and A. Rorty (Eds.) *Perspectives on Self-deception*. Berkeley: University of California Press.
Sandler, J. (1976). Dreams, unconscious fantasies and 'identity of perception'. *International Review of Psychoanalysis*, 3, 1.
Sandler, J. and Sandler, A. M. (1978). The development of object-relationships and affects. *International Journal of Psychoanalysis*, 59, 2.
Spitz, R. (1965). *The First Year of Life*. New York: International Universities Press.
Stern, D. N. (2000). *The Interpersonal World of the Infant*. New York: Basic Books.
Thalberg, I. (1974). Freud's anatomies of the self. In R. Wollheim (Ed.) *Freud: A Collection of Critical Essays*. New York: Anchor Books.
Winnicott, D. W. (1965). *The Maturational Process and the Facilitating Environment*. London: Hogarth Press.
Wollheim, R. (1971/1991). *Freud*. London: Fontana.
Wollheim, R. (1979). Wish-fulfilment. In R. Harrison (Ed.) *Rational Action: Studies in Philosophy and Social Science*. Cambridge: Cambridge University Press.
Wollheim, R. (1984). *The Thread of Life*. Cambridge: Cambridge University Press.
Wollheim, R. and Hopkins, J. (Eds.) (1982). *Freud: A Collection of Critical Essays*. 2nd edn. New York: Anchor.

10

Autonomy and the Problem of Suffering: Tragedy and Transcendence in Psychoanalytic Discourse

Suzanne R. Kirschner

Scholars have long attempted to place autonomy in context, demonstrating that the autonomous person has been produced in particular sociohistorical (Mauss, 1985; Taylor, 1989; Cushman, 1990) and cultural (Weber, 1958; Doi, 1973; Gaines, 1982; Bellah et al., 1985; Dumont, 1986; Kurtz, 1992) environments. Some theorists have also found him to be, to some degree, a gender specific type (Chodorow, 1979; Gilligan, 1982). Still other scholars go so far as to assert that the autonomous person may not even exist, that he is a modern European invention in an even more radical sense – that of being fabricated, a lie, an illusion (Gergen, 1991, 1994).

This chapter belongs to this rather heterogeneous family of projects. My aim is to explore some culturally constituted assumptions that inhere in the depictions of autonomy found in the writings of psychoanalytic developmental psychologists. I will argue that while the autonomous person of contemporary psychological discourse is indeed historically distinctive in many respects, psychoanalytic psychologists' depictions of autonomy, and of how it develops through the life course, are not devoid of older cultural influences. I will suggest that the meaning of autonomy as a modern psychoanalytic goal needs to be understood not simply in terms of how it embodies a radical break with older cultural and religious beliefs and values, but also in terms of how it perpetuates a distinctive Judaeo-Christian spiritual heritage. For all its genuine novelty as a modern secular construction, psychoanalytic discourse on autonomy also bears the imprint of a centuries-old family of spiritual traditions that address the problem of human suffering. It derives some of its continuing power from its linkage to this enduring soteriological vision.

In this chapter, I focus on depictions of autonomy found in the writings of an influential group of post-Freudians, psychoanalytic theorists of the development of the self. By psychoanalytic developmental psychology, I refer to three broad movements or schools – ego psychology, object relations theory and self psychology – that emerged during the mid- to late twentieth century. Prominent ego psychologists include Erik Erikson (1902–94), Margaret Mahler (1897–1985) and Otto Kernberg (1928–); the most influential object relations theorists were Donald Winnicott (1896–1971) and Ronald Fairbairn (1889–1964); and the architect of self psychology was Heinz Kohut (1913–81). These psychodynamic theories retain certain basic assumptions from 'classical' psychoanalysis, but also depart significantly from Freudian metapsychology. Perhaps the most important difference is that they de-emphasise the role of the instincts, instead focusing on the development of the self (or ego) and its modes of relating to others. These approaches have been developed most fully in the United States and Great Britain, though many of the most prominent post-Freudian theorists had immigrated to these countries from Central Europe. They have been particularly influential in clinical and educational practice in those Anglo-American countries, most of all in the United States. The fact that psychoanalysis went in this direction in these Anglo-American culture areas, whereas it went in rather different directions in France and South America, for example (see, for example, Turkle, 1981; Olinor, 1988), is not accidental, since the version of the autonomous person depicted in these theories strongly resembles the ideal person of American cultural ideology, and, to a lesser degree and with some variation, of English cultural values (Gaines, 1982; Kirschner, 1996).

Post-Freudian psychoanalytic theories vary in some of their particular features and emphases, but they all narrate the development of the self in terms of a distinctive developmental sequence. Out of an original subjective state in which the self is not distinguished from other persons and objects, the individual develops a sense of separate identity. This process of 'psychological birth' (Mahler et al., 1975) is depicted as both pleasurable and problematic. It is pleasurable in that the developing infant and child possess an intrinsic tendency towards individuation, towards a maturational unfolding of her cognitive and motor functions, and thus derive excitement and satisfaction from the exercise of their developing abilities. But it is problematic in that the birth of the self also entails a painful recognition of the realities of loss, disappointment and ambivalence. After a period in which the infant believes in the limitlessness of his own and his mother's powers, and in the identity of his own wishes and interests with those of other persons, he begins to recognise that limitation, disappointment and frustration are indeed the stuff of reality and relationships. This dawning awareness of rupture and division culminates in a sharp crisis, such as Mahler's 'rapprochement phase' (Mahler et al., 1975), or a more protracted negotiation of the disillusionment, necessary losses and painful tensions inherent in the developmental process, such as is depicted in Winnicott's 'transitional stage' (Winnicott, 1989, p. 3) and Kohut's depiction of the use of other people as progressively more differentiated 'self-objects' (Kohut, 1977). Thus, by the age of three, the child has begun to develop tolerance of the fact that others are separate and different from him, and that he is unable to have all his wishes fulfilled. The self that emerges out of these developmental travails not only begins to assert himself as separate and independent, but also starts to re-work his sense of connection to others. Although a provisionally individuated self has normally evolved by the age of three, the developmental process is seen to entail a great deal of additional maturation and development, with the era of adolescence being a period when the struggles and crises of early childhood are recapitulated and reworked at a higher level (A. Freud, 1954; Erikson, 1963; Blos, 1967). The developmental trajectory reaches its culmination when the individual attains both autonomy and a further capacity for which autonomy is considered a prerequisite: the ability to form lasting intimate relationships. Below I explore one of these developmental goals – autonomy – in greater detail.

As represented in these theories, autonomy has four different facets. These are self-assertion, self-reliance, rationality and authenticity. I will explicate each of them separately, and then explore several themes that inhere in the psychoanalytic narrative of the development towards autonomy. The first facet of autonomy is *self-assertion*. The achievement of autonomy is seen to be the culmination and realisation of an innate individuating thrust, a drive on the part of the human being to develop her own individuality and capacities and to use these to engage with and act upon the world. Winnicott, for example, wrote that 'the self is constituted in aggressive assertion' (Winnicott, 1989, p. 3), and that '[w]hen the Me and the Not-Me are being established' it is this 'aggressive' individuating thrust that propels the individual to differentiate himself and perceive all other 'objects' as external (Winnicott, 1989, p. 89). And Mahler asserted that the infant's gradual emergence, or 'hatching', from a sense of oneness with mother is motivated by the normal infant's '*drive for and toward individuation*', which she claims '*is an innate*, powerful *given* . . . [which manifests] itself all along the separation-individuation process' (Mahler et al., 1975, p. 19, emphasis in the original).

A second aspect of autonomy is *self-reliance*. The imperative of self-reliance dictates that one not be overly dependent upon the presence or actions of others in order to function or be comfortable. All of these post-Freudian developmental theorists emphasise that the person must develop the capacity to take over the functions of her caretakers. For Winnicott, one of the most important developmental lines is the individual's movement 'towards independence' (Grolnick, 1990, p. 62). Mahler describes the development of self-reliance in terms of the acquisition of capacities for 'internalisation' and 'constancy'. Beginning in toddlerhood, the child begins to internalise a representation of the 'good' mother which 'supplies comfort in the mother's absence . . . [This] permits the child to function separately despite moderate degrees of tension (longing) and discomfort' (Mahler et al., 1975, p. 109).

The capacity for self-reliance is further abetted by the development of 'constancy', in which the internalised image of the parent includes an integration of both 'good' (satisfying) and 'bad' (frustrating and disappointing) images of them (Mahler et al., 1975, p. 110). Kohut describes the development of self-reliance in terms of a similar dynamic which he calls 'transmuting internalisation', a mechanism by which functions such as self-soothing and self-esteem maintenance, initially performed by caretakers, are taken inside to form a part of the coalescing self. Thus the mature self, according to Kohut, is not compulsively or intensely dependent upon others to bolster self-esteem, contain anxiety, or mitigate frustrations and disappointments (Kohut, 1977, p. 87).

A third dimension of autonomy is *rationality*. The autonomous self has developed the capacity for rational reflection, enabling her to stand at a critical distance from both external influences and constraints, and the press of internal passions. Throughout the history of psychoanalytic thought, the question of the nature and limits of human rationality has been a complex and contentious one (Holt, 1989, pp. 199–252). To this day, psychoanalytic writings continue to embody the tension between Freud's essentially deterministic view of human action and his depiction of successful psychoanalytic treatment as engendering a strengthened ego which possesses the capacity for a more flexible and empowered relationship with its own wishes and desires as well as with society's conventions. Some ego psychologists have endeavoured to preserve a rigid determinism even while emphasising that the subjective experience of freedom of choice and self-mastery is essential to mental health. Such a 'weak' reading of the meaning of rational autonomy was offered by Robert Knight, who wrote that 'this kind of 'freedom' is experienced only by emotionally mature, well-integrated persons; it is the goal sought for one's patients in psychotherapy'. He immediately added that 'this freedom has nothing whatever to do with free will as a principle governing human behavior, but is a subjective experience which is itself causally determined' (Knight, 1946, p. 256, quoted in Holt, 1989, p. 220).

However, the majority of practising American psychoanalytic therapists – influenced by American cultural values, the ideas of less deterministic 'revisionist' analysts such as Karen Horney and Harry Stack Sullivan, and existential-humanistic psychologies – would advocate a stronger reading of humans' potential for rationality. They would concur with ego psychologist Robert Holt's assertion that Freud's dictum, '"where id was there shall ego be" makes no sense if we do not include under it the recognition that mature, non-neurotic people usually have the capacity to make free choices'. Holt continued:

> we should all of us shut up shop, we who try to teach, do therapy, or otherwise alter behavior by the use of words, if we really believed that

human beings were in fact incapable of making choices and in fact doing so on rational grounds. We *act* as if we believed Freud when he said, 'The voice of the intellect is a soft one, but it does not rest till it has gained a hearing. Finally . . . it succeeds . . . a point of no small importance.'
(Freud, 1927, p. 53, quoted in Holt, 1989, p. 247)

As with all aspects of psychoanalytic autonomy, the movement towards more fully rational capacities such as self-insight and adaptive self-control is viewed as never being complete or absolute. In the words of ego psychologist Ernst Kris, 'it is a goal never to be [fully] reached' (Kris, 1956, p. 452).

A final component of autonomy, one emphasised by many of the Anglo-American theorists but notably absent from both Freudian and Lacanian psychoanalysis (Olinor, 1988; Kirschner, 1996), is *authenticity*. Like rationality, authenticity entails the development of one's inner mental resources for the purposes of living a freer life. But what is realised in the case of authenticity is not some abstract and presumably universal capacity for critical reason and self-governance. Rather, the mark of the authentic self is that it is in touch with the truth of its own inner uniqueness, what Winnicott (1965, pp. 140–52) called the 'true self' and Erikson (1963) called 'identity'. The imperative of authenticity is that one should listen to one's 'inner voice' and thereby gain knowledge of what is in one's heart and mind, because to maximise one's attunement to one's inner essence is a good in itself. The concept of identity also entails a subjective sense of coherence, of 'inner sameness and continuity' (Erikson, 1963, p. 263). Some theorists, most notably Erikson in the United States, hold that it is a further, even greater good to assert and develop one's inner voice by expressing it in one's activities and relationships.

Underlying all four of these images of autonomy is a metaphysical assumption that human existence is best characterised in terms of splits and ruptures – in terms of unbridgeable gaps between wishes and reality, and between self and others. The growth of the self towards maturity, then, entails coming to terms with the reality of one's separateness and thus realising the potentials, as well as facing the limitations, inherent in that reality. This metaphysical picture of the self–world relationship as one of severance and estrangement has a dual message encoded in it: autonomy gives pleasure and power, but it develops partly in response to a tragedy over which it can triumph only incompletely. It is to that duality that I will now turn.

On the one hand, to develop one's separateness is a source of pleasure, pride, and, above all, freedom. As was discussed above, there is an assumption that each human being possesses an innate striving to individuate and assert her distinctive powers and qualities. In the case of self-assertion, then, autonomy means the full realisation of such individuality and abilities. The disentangling of the self from forces and relationships that would interfere with its individuation – a developmental movement that culminates in self-reliance, rationality and authenticity – also facilitates greater freedom to act upon and satisfy the self's needs and choices. Thus, from this angle, autonomy is the relatively unproblematic culmination of a positive movement.

On the other hand, however, psychoanalytic construals hold that autonomy also has a tragic underside. For these theories stress that the experience of loss and limitation that is concomitant to the fact of human separateness can never really be overcome. Thus the second message encoded in these images of the autonomous person is that separateness is ineradicable. In fact, separateness can be viewed here as a metaphor for much, if not all, that is painful about the human condition. The human being can never actually overcome that condition, but in following the developmental path in the direction of autonomy, we are told, the self can become edified and ennobled, and can thereby come to find reality more bearable and more navigable. Separateness and separation are thus seen to be awful and fortunate at the same time, for to face them and grow towards a more rational, self-reliant and authentic state is, quite simply, to become a better person, edified by virtue of the difficult passage one has endured. It is also, say these theories, to improve (though not to ensure) one's chances of being more successful and effective in the world. At the very least, such a person is considered better off for being able to tolerate life's vicissitudes and still appreciate its richness, so that maturity is seen to constitute its own reward.

But the rewards of separation-individuation – its hard-won benefits – can go beyond this. They can, in fact, include a kind of mitigation of the reality of separateness, a partial and transient transcendence of it, through various forms of reconnection or reintegration. The clearest example of such reconnection is found in intimate relationships. For, these developmental theorists tell us, only the firmly bounded, independent, authentic self can safely experience the transient ecstasy of falling in love, or achieve a more enduring and realistic integration of his life with another person's, without succumbing to the pull of regression and forfeiting the autonomy he has struggled to achieve (Bergmann, 1971, pp. 15–40; Kernberg, 1980, pp. 278–90). The same holds true for other forms of mature reconnection, such as the creative process (Kohut, 1977), play (Winnicott, 1989) and even a mother's immersion in relationship with her infant, which Winnicott called 'primary maternal preoccupation' (Winnicott, 1958, pp. 300–5). There is also a subtle form of reconnection evident in the achievement of authenticity. For what is the notion of identity but a depiction of a self that has found itself, has reached inside and rediscovered an inner voice with which it had lost touch? For some theorists, particularly in the United States, identity implies yet a further reconnection, of the inner self to the larger society. For

Erikson, attaining a sense of identity is not merely a function of looking inward to discern one's deepest inclinations. Rather, such a 'finding' of the self must occur in the context of the roles and activities that are available within one's social milieu (Erikson, 1963).[1]

Thus it is possible to identify several basic themes embodied in psychoanalytic construals of autonomy. First, autonomy grows out of an innate movement towards self-assertion and freedom. Second, autonomy has a tragic dimension, because it includes an awareness of the imperfect and painful nature of the human condition. Third, the development of autonomy is a movement of constructive estrangement: the necessity of having to come to terms with tragic separateness and limitation renders the autonomous person an improved person, precisely because she has had to develop a more constructive relationship to the limitations of existence. Finally, autonomy is, or can lead to, a mitigation or partial transcendence of the human tragedy, since the developed self is also, at least potentially, a reconnected self. Such reconnection occurs through the reintegration of the self with others in relationships, through a satisfying rejoining of the self to its own inner essence, and through a further reconnection of the authentic self to fulfilling work and meaningful social activities.

These meanings of autonomy, as well as the developmental narrative in which they are embedded, have emerged out of a long cultural history.[2] The relatively close ancestor of the psychoanalytic story of the development of the autonomous self is a nineteenth-century romantic narrative[3] which is detectable in a broad array of German and English philosophical and literary writings, including the philosophy of Fichte, Schelling and Hegel and in the poetry of Wordsworth, Blake, Coleridge, Hölderlin and others. Like the post-Freudian psychoanalytic developmental trajectory, the romantic narrative offers a vision of the human condition that is at once tragic and transcendent (Abrams, 1973; Bloom, 1971). But whereas psychodynamic theorists concerned themselves with the developmental progress of the individual human psyche, the romantic philosophers and men of letters told a story of the history and destiny of humankind. The parallel protagonists of this story were the human race and the individual mind that lives out the history of the race. In romantic accounts (for example, Schiller, 1986, 1981;[4] Wordsworth, 1988), this collective and individual mind, self or subject was originally at unity with the natural world but underwent an unavoidable estrangement from it. The mind or subject thus 'fell away' into a bitter but edifying consciousness of itself and of the cleavage between subject and object. Such division and fragmentation are the source and expression of the human tragedy, but have also made possible the achievements of modern civilisation, such as rationality, autonomous personhood, and scientific and political specialisation. The subject's deepening disillusionment and awareness of his alienated and divided state, and of all the painful and evil cleavages that characterise the human condition, culminate in a crisis.

Thus the severance of mind from nature was viewed by romantics as a necessary rupture, a progressive movement in the direction of increased knowledge, mastery and freedom – all these being central aspects of autonomy. But, according to these thinkers, the development of the mind or subject did not cease at that point of civilised, intellectually advanced estrangement. Rather, they held that various forms of reconnection are possible – higher integrations of mind and nature, subject and object, and reason and feeling which preserve but surpass the individuated self and the splits and distinctions that are concomitant to it. These configurations of what Coleridge called 'distinctions without division' most often take the form of extraordinary moments of artistic and imaginative transcendence, but they also characterise the mature philosophic mind in a more enduring way. The motif of higher integration is also present in the distinctively American romantic 'expressive individualist' ideal of authentic self-expression in various forms of worldly activity (Bellah et al., 1985), and even in the discourse of romantic love. Romantic treatments of autonomy thus evince many of the underlying themes and complexities found in psychoanalytic construals. Like post-Freudian accounts, they depict the movement towards autonomy as being at once necessary, tragic, constructive and ultimately transcendent (both in the sense that autonomy itself contains elements of transcendence, and in that autonomy is a necessary step on the way to transcendent reconnection, through a mitigation and overcoming of its own tragic elements).

The romantic narrative was very widely disseminated during the nineteenth and early twentieth centuries, and in both its original and post-romantic versions it continues to be diffused throughout Euro-American cultures and societies today. Psychoanalytic theorists – educated in the gymnasia, secondary schools and universities of Central Europe and Great Britain during the late nineteenth and early twentieth centuries – were immersed in this literature.[5] It is beyond the scope of this chapter to discuss why psychoanalytic theorists have drawn so heavily (usually reflexively and unselfconsciously) from romantic and post-romantic narratives (see Kirschner, 1996, pp. 177–8, 199–200). However, the affinity and connection between romanticism and psychoanalysis[6] (particularly Anglo-American psychoanalysis) may be accounted for at least partly by the fact that most psychoanalytic approaches expose and articulate points of tension and contradiction within a given sociocultural system. Introduced into Anglo-American societies, whose cultures uphold strong conventions and values concerning separate selfhood and autonomy, the psychodynamic system came to focus principally on the inevitable tension between the drive to individuate and the longing for oneness and connection. In thus emphasising the dark 'underside' and vicissitudes of the development towards autonomy, psychoanalytic theorists, apparently unselfconsciously, drew upon an existing cultural repertory of romantic and post-romantic formulations. Those formulations had similarly attempted to criticise and complement earlier modern celebrations of human individuation and progress.

Thus far I have discussed the romantic roots of the psychoanalytic narrative of the growth of autonomy. In order to more fully appreciate the complexity of this cultural genealogy, however, it is necessary to look not only to romanticism but also to still older narrative patterns upon which the romantic thinkers drew. For this story of unity, rupture and estrangement, and higher reconnection did not originate in the post-Enlightenment era. As numerous scholars have demonstrated (Nelson, 1965; Abrams, 1973; Brown, 1977; Benz, 1983; Walsh, 1983) and as many of the romantics themselves acknowledged, the romantic narrative is a secularised, naturalistic transmutation of the Christian mystical story of the history of humankind (both the race and the individual soul) and the sources of suffering. The nineteenth-century romantic poets and idealist philosophers were in revolt against certain dominant intellectual and social trends of the seventeenth and eighteenth centuries, many of which were connected to the emergence of autonomy as a modern ideal. They believed that those forms of autonomy most associated with modern bourgeois society and with Enlightenment and Kantian philosophy, forms I have called self-reliance and rationality,[7] were insufficient as human ideals, because they failed to take account of both humankind's tragic limitations and some of its triumphant possibilities. They were concerned that the emerging secular worldview, for all its glorification of autonomy and promise of human progress, offered an inadequate and impoverished way of making sense of the human condition as well as the potentials for its renovation. Therefore they looked backward, to renderings of the human condition found in religious doctrines, and attempted to translate them into secular form. The doctrines upon which they drew – radical Protestant traditions including the doctrines of Jacob Boehme and 'inner light' sects, as well as various older Christian and Jewish mystical texts and traditions – offered versions of the Biblical historical narrative which were heavily infused with Neoplatonic themes and motifs. Many romantic thinkers were drawn to these esoteric (but widely diffused) renderings of Biblical history because they felt they could use them to articulate a counter-discourse that would challenge or supplement the rationalist and materialist emphases of Enlightenment thinkers. Coleridge, for example, wrote that he looked to mystical traditions because he perceived them to embody 'deeper feeling and stronger imagination than belong to most of those to whom reasoning and fluent expression have been as a trade learnt in boyhood'. He found in radical Protestant mystics such as Jacob Boehme and George Fox (the founder of the Quaker movement) 'fulness [*sic*] of heart' as well as of intellect; 'they contributed', he wrote, 'to keep alive the *heart* in the *head'*. This was essential, he believed, because 'my opinion is that deep thinking is attainable only by a man of deep feeling' (Coleridge, 1973, p. 97; emphasis in the original).

The mystical narratives upon which the romantics drew were very heavily influenced by a Western pagan mystical tradition, Neoplatonism.[8] Neoplatonism posits a first principle, the One, which is synonymous with the Good. All existing entities emanate from or flow out of this primal undifferentiated unity, wilfully turning away from the One but also striving to return to it. The individual human soul also participates in this dynamic. Separation, division, selfhood and self-consciousness are viewed as the source of, and synonymous with, evil and suffering.

Neoplatonist themes began to show up in the writings of early Christian mystics beginning at least with the work of Augustine, and probably preceding him. Since then, elements of this Christian mystical narrative have appeared in a large and diverse group of theological writings, both orthodox (for example, Aquinas, Dante) and esoteric or dissenting (for example, Kabbalistic and Behmenist teachings). The intermingling of Biblical and Neoplatonic doctrines resulted in the integration of certain mystical themes into the Biblical narrative of humankind's creation, fall and redemption. The Biblical fall thus became associated with separation, division and self-consciousness. The fallen soul became a severed soul; its sin was selfhood and self-consciousness. At the same time, there persisted a tension in much Christian mysticism between the negative valence accorded to selfhood by Neoplatonism, and the relatively more 'world-affirming' and 'individualistic' character of Judaeo-Christianity (a tradition that tended to affirm the value, meaning and importance of individual selfhood and earthly life). Another tension within this Christian mystical theodicy concerned the shape and direction of the narrative: Biblical history is linear, progressive and finite while the Neoplatonist story is circular and cyclical.

Over many centuries, increasingly secularised versions of the narrative became prominent. The more 'worldly' and 'individualistic' Judaeo-Christian themes, which were in tension with Neoplatonic trends, gained ascendance and were taken even farther. Thus in keeping with the Judaeo-Christian positive valuation of individuation and earthly life, the soul's separation from the Divine (the Fall) came to take on a more positive, constructive significance, and to be regarded (albeit somewhat blasphemously) as a fortunate severance, while still retaining its tragic and evil connotations.[9] And the end of the narrative trajectory – Biblical salvation or redemption – was understood to be a higher reunion with the Divine, often described as a marriage or sexual union of the soul with God, and as a finding of one's true self through rejoining with God (both images are found in Neoplatonic depictions of salvation). In addition, linearity and circularity intermingled to yield a spiral narrative shape – a developmental story with an end that recapitulates, but is higher than, its beginning. These tendencies became very marked in later medieval and Protestant versions of this narrative, with their valorisation of worldly activities and relationships (Williams, 1967), and (in the case of Protestantism) their emphasis on the individual and his unmediated relationship with God. Also, the narrative came to be read as being primarily about the progress of the individual soul, rather than the collective history of humankind, though the dual reading (which literary critic M. H. Abrams called 'psychohistorical parallelism') continued to be evident in Protestant and romantic versions of the narrative (Abrams, 1973). Thus, by the late medieval and Protestant eras, this increasingly worldly version of the Neoplatonised Biblical narrative already evinced themes resembling those observed in the psychoanalytic developmental story: There is the idea that the soul intrinsically tends toward individuation; there is the fact that this tendency is considered to be tragic – the source of all evil and suffering – yet at the same time is hinted to be necessary and even constructive; and there is the notion of a redemptive goal towards which the soul strives, a goal that is framed in terms of a higher union, a re-connection of the soul to God.

I noted above that many romantic thinkers sought to transmute Christian mystical narratives into secular form in order to challenge or supplement the post-Enlightenment glorification of reason and autonomy, which they found to be morally and spiritually impoverished. In the romantic reworking, the soul's estrangement from God was recast by romantics as the mind's estrangement from nature, and many of the powers that had been ascribed to God were attributed to the mind. The developmental unfolding of creation (God's self-realisation) was reframed as the mind's developmental trajectory – the romantic story of unity, crisis of necessary rupture and estrangement, and higher reunion. Like the older, religious version, the secularised narrative remained a story that explained and offered some justification for why the human condition is characterised by suffering and moral evil. But instead of framing that explanation in theological and otherworldly terms, romantics turned the Biblical theodicy into a 'biodicy' (Abrams, 1973) – a secular, historical account which conceptualised the problems of existence, and the prospects for their mitigation, in entirely naturalistic, this-worldly terms.

During the twentieth century, post-Freudian theorists (even more fully than Freudians) absorbed and further transmuted the romantic biodicy, now shifting the setting of this narrative to the personal and interpersonal arena. They changed its protagonists yet again, from 'mind' and 'nature' to 'self' and 'objects' ('objects' being their preferred term for other persons). Without any of the ambiguity sometimes evinced by their romantic forebears, these psychodynamic theorists hold to a materialist metaphysic, and to a first premise that separateness is the ultimate reality. In keeping with these assumptions, most post-Freudians strongly valorise autonomy as an end in itself; and their images of redemptive reconnection are far more modest (even to the point of being ironic) than the romantic endpoints were. They do not consider intimacy, creativity or even authenticity to constitute a genuine remaking of the human condition, let alone of the world. But although the narrative has changed in these and other ways, certain older spiritual themes persist in this post-Freudian rendering of the movement towards autonomy and beyond. One such theme is present in the image of autonomy as a crucial telos of a movement that is at once tragic, necessary and fortuitous. According to this vision, the autonomous person actualises her humanity through the development of her relationship to loss, conflict, destructiveness and imperfection, evolving in a manner that does not eradicate these evils, but incorporates awareness of them into a higher form of personhood. Thus, like its predecessor religious and romantic tropes, post-Freudian discourse on the development of autonomy functions as a framework for making sense of human existence. As a latter-day 'biodicy', psychoanalytic developmental psychology constructs human development and its vicissitudes in terms of an inherited family of narratives about the meaning of suffering and the prospects for its mitigation.

There are, of course, multiple ways to interpret the genealogy I have sketched in this chapter. Some might suggest that the psychoanalytic account of the development and complexities of autonomy resembles its literary and religious 'precursors' because all of these narratives, with increasing precision, faithfully map a natural and universal reality of human ontogenesis. According to this view, psychoanalytic theory embodies a more refined, scientific version of what was intimated in cruder and more primitive form in romantic and religious texts.

However, one must be very cautious about uncritically accepting this interpretation. As Mauss (1985) implied, and Foucault (1971) suggested more recently, contemporary secular humanist categories such as 'self', 'ego', 'object' and 'other' are historically and culturally contingent discursive formations, rather than ontological essences. They argued that there is no way of knowing whether these particular current conceptualisations will endure or precisely what will take their place. Moreover, even if we accept that human and natural (as opposed to supernatural) phenomena should be accorded privileged ontological status, we cannot assume that distinctively Euro-American depictions of the desirable self and its development articulate the universal deep structure of human psychological evolution. For it seems to me that there is ample cause for scepticism when our 'scientific' psychology corresponds so conveniently to the narratives which are most widely diffused throughout our own Judaeo-Christian culture areas. Those narratives have a distinctive set of episodes, spiral shape, and forward-looking orientation, and they valorise individuation, individuality, and worldly activity. But non-Biblical renderings of the history and destiny of humankind – for example, Buddhist and Hindu doctrines – do not possess these features. Clearly, we risk a simplistic ethnocentrism when we conclude that the particular religious and philosophical doctrines with which we are most familiar anticipated the objective shape of the developmental process better than those of cultures that lie outside the Judaeo-Christian orbit. For this reason, I would argue it seems at least as plausible that what the foregoing genealogy demonstrates is that these current psychological models of the self and its development are structured in terms of an inherited cultural pattern or template that has traditionally been used to make sense of suffering. In other words, these modern psychologists have, for the most part unselfconsciously, drawn upon several generations of a pre-existing narrative template (most often a romantic or post-romantic version) and used them as generative metaphors (Danziger, 1990) in the construction of their theories.

In introducing this chapter, I noted that it belongs to a broad family of projects that seek to contextualise the discourse of autonomy and, in some cases, to criticise it as a moral, epistemological or psychological ideal. Thus one of my aims has been to make more explicit the ways in which ostensibly naturalistic and universal theories of the development towards autonomy are structured in terms of a culturally distinctive narrative pattern. A second aim has been to highlight the fact that while there is undeniably much that is radically modern about the autonomous person, there are also significant continuities between these modern theories of the autonomous self and older spiritual doctrines that endeavour to explain the meaning of human suffering.

Finally, I will make a third point about these theories. One of the qualities that has made this secular narrative so tenacious in cultural life – even now that psychoanalytic views of the person have been marginalised in psychiatry in the United States and elsewhere – is that it has what William James called a 'completeness' to it. In *The Varieties of Religious Experience*, James made a distinction between two different ways that religions deal with the problem of evil and suffering. One type of approach he called 'healthy mindedness': Healthy minded religions deal with evil and suffering by systematically extruding and excluding them – by 'systematically declining to lay them to heart or make much of them. . . . or even, on occasion, by denying outright that they exist' (James 1982, p. 127). By contrast, he argued, there are more 'complete' spiritual systems, which include evil – sorrow, misfortune, destructiveness, and death – among their formal elements. These more complete religions view spiritual advance as attained not through the eradication or denial of such evil, but rather through an incorporation of it in a way that can lead to a mitigation or transcendence of some of its sting.

It is a truism that for many persons in late modern societies, discourse on the self, both 'lay' and 'professional', has taken on some of the key functions and meanings of religious discourse. Among these are the 'meaning-making' and 'evil-mitigating' functions described above. In other words, modern psychological theories of the self function partly as symbolic systems used to make sense of, and in some measure transcend, the suffering and evil that characterise the human condition. This being the case, we might use James' framework for appraising spiritual systems to judge the value and adequacy of various psychological theories. Viewed in this light, the psychoanalytic model I have examined – which encodes evil and suffering in separateness, and views autonomy and intimacy as higher forms of selfhood and relationship which none the less preserve and integrate tragic and dangerous elements – would seem to possess more of this completeness than do many other modern psychological and psychiatric models of personhood and human nature. Certainly most of the models of personality that dominated psychology during the twentieth century did not possess this dialectical, tragic-transcendent quality that James termed 'completeness'. Some of these psychologies, including cognitive-developmental (for example, the stage theories of Piaget, Kohlberg and Lovinger) and humanistic theories, are 'incomplete' because they tend to champion autonomy as a relatively unproblematic and monolithic developmental goal.[10] Other models of human nature are healthy minded precisely because they go too far in the opposite direction. For example, both behaviourism and social constructionism maintain that autonomy is a chimera and attempt to dissolve individuality into situation and context. They likewise lack a tragic-transcendent vision. From this perspective, then, the psychoanalytic depiction of autonomy and its development is worthy of endorsement and perhaps even preservation, because it draws upon and perpetuates a relatively more 'complete' – deeper and more sophisticated – generative metaphor for grappling with issues of ultimate meaning.

We would also do well to apply this criterion of completeness to emerging or future discourses that may come to overtake the psychological worldview. Postmodernists (Foucault, 1971; Gergen, 1990, 1991, 1994) suggest that individualistic models of social life, and of the autonomous self, are on the wane. If indeed the face drawn in sand is being washed away by the sea (Foucault, 1971, p. 387) – if twentieth-century images of the autonomous self are coming increasingly to strike us as outmoded and inadequate – we will none the less not be able to leave all the elements of such images behind completely. To take hold, any post-humanistic discourse that accounts for human action and social life will, like its predecessor narratives, need to function as a construction of the problem of evil and suffering. I hope and expect that among these postmodern tropes, there will emerge some more 'complete' variations.

Acknowledgements

An earlier version of this chapter was delivered at the First Heidelberger Wissenschaftskolleg, 'The Autonomous Person – A Modern Invention', which was held at the Internationales Wissenschaftsforum Heidelberg in Heidelberg, Germany in July 1997.

I am grateful to Michael Welker for inviting me to participate in this conference. I also thank Leonard Evenchik, Kenneth J. Gergen, and the late Helen Kirschner Berke for their support of this work.

Notes

1. Erikson's very 'American' account of the formation of identity strikingly contrasts with that of the English Winnicott, who wrote of the 'true self' in the following terms: 'Although healthy persons communicate and enjoy communicating, the other fact is equally true, that *each individual is an isolate, permanently non-communicating, permanently unknown, in fact unfound*' (Winnicott, 1965, p. 187; emphasis in original). He claimed that it was essential to psychological health that this inner core be permitted to remain incommunicado. These differences reflect the fact that American ideals of personhood celebrate both authenticity and the need to live out one's authentic self in society (in personal relationships, work and other activities) more so than is the case in English ethnopsychologies (Gaines, 1982), even if class differences among the English are taken into account. However, as the saga of the late Princess Diana's life and its widespread resonance would seem to demonstrate, there are indications that the quest for authenticity and identity is becoming more widely diffused and 'globalised'.
2. For a fuller discussion of the genealogy discussed in the following section, see Kirschner (1996).
3. Following the literary critic M. H. Abrams (1973), I use the term 'romantic' somewhat broadly here. For a more detailed discussion of twentieth-century debates on the use of the term, see Kirschner (1996, pp. 153–8).
4. According to the 'broader' characterisation of romanticism, employed by Abrams (1973), Taylor (1989), Sass (1994) and others, Schiller, although not, by narrow definition, a 'romantic', is included in this category because in some of his important writings (for example, Schiller, 1981, 1986), he utilised the narrative pattern which Abrams and others denote as 'typically romantic'. In these writings he also expressed some characteristically 'romantic' responses to the limitations of Enlightenment thought and the 'failure' of the French revolution to successfully implement rationalistic ideals.
5. It would be extremely difficult to find Central European and British psychoanalytic theorists who were not exposed to romantic and post-romantic texts and themes. Although it is well beyond the scope of this paper to trace such influences on specific theorists, I will note that scrutiny of the intellectual backgrounds of Rank (Roazen, 1974; Klein, 1981), Mahler (Mahler, 1988), Winnicott (Phillips, 1988), and Jacobson and Fenichel (Jacoby, 1983) gives evidence of their exposure to and influence by romantic and post-romantic literary and philosophical motifs.
6. I am not suggesting that romanticism was the only influence on psychoanalysis. Freudian and post-Freudian theories were influenced by many different sources and factors of all kinds. Some of the systematic intellectual and cultural traditions that can be detected in psychoanalytic theories include Enlightenment rationalism, evolutionary theory, nineteenth-century neurology and psychophysics, and German Classicism.

7. These ideals have significant religious roots of their own, chiefly in Puritanism and Pietism. See Kirschner (1996); Lukes (1973); Schott (1989); Taylor (1989); Weber (1958).
8. Neoplatonism took shape in the writings of the pagan mystical philosopher, Plotinus, who was probably Greek and lived during the third century AD. This philosophical system, set forth in the *Enneads* (Plotinus, 1962), was an amalgam of Platonic, Aristotelian, Stoic and Eastern doctrines. On the centrality of Neoplatonist influence in both mainstream and 'marginal' Christian mystical traditions, see Wallis (1972), Abrams (1973), Louth (1981) and McGinn (1992).
9. The noted intellectual historical A. O. Lovejoy discussed this tension within Christian theology, and its development over time, in his essay on the idea of the *felix culpa* ('fortunate fall') (1948, pp. 277–95).
10. Existential psychology doesn't completely conform to this generalisation, because its vision of the human condition is both tragic and transcendent. But the developmental goal of autonomy that existentialism endorses lacks the dialectical and ironic quality that psychoanalytic models of autonomy possess.

References

Abrams, M. H. (1973). *Natural Supernaturalism.* New York: W. W. Norton.

Bellah, R., Masden, R., Sullivan, W. M., Tipson, S. M. and Swidler, A. (1985). *Habits of the Heart.* Berkeley: University of California Press.

Benz, E. (1983). *Mystical Sources of German Romantic Philosophy.* Allison Park, PA: Pickwick Publications.

Bergmann, M. S. (1971). Psychoanalytic observations on the capacity to love. In J. B. McDevitt and C. Settlage (Eds.) *Separation–Individuation: Essays in Honor of Margaret Mahler.* New York: International Universities Press.

Bloom, H. (Ed.) (1971). *Romanticism and Consciousness: Essays in Criticism.* New York: W. W. Norton.

Blos, P. (1967). The second individuation process in adolescence. In Various (Eds.), *The Psychoanalytic Study of the Child,* Vol. XXII. New York: International Universities Press.

Brown, R. F. (1977). *The Later Philosophy of Schelling: The Influence of Boehme on the Works of 1809–1815.* Lewisburg, PA: Bucknell University Press.

Chodorow, N. (1979). *The Reproduction of Mothering.* Berkeley: University of California Press.

Coleridge, S. T. (1973). *Biographia Literaria.* Oxford: Oxford University Press.

Cushman, P. (1990). Why the self is empty: toward a historically situated psychology. *American Psychologist,* 45(5), 599–611.

Danziger, K. (1990). Generative metaphor in the history of psychology. In D. E. Leary (Ed.) *Metaphors in the History of Psychology.* Cambridge: Cambridge University Press.

Doi, T. (1973). *The Anatomy of Dependence.* New York: Kodansha International.

Dumont, L. (1986). *Essays on Individualism: Modern Ideology in Anthropological Perspective.* Chicago: University of Chicago Press.

Erikson, E. (1963). *Childhood and Society.* New York: W. W. Norton.

Foucault, M. (1971). *The Order of Things.* New York: Pantheon.

Freud, A. (1954). *The Ego and the Mechanisms of Defence.* London: The Hogarth Press.

Freud, S. (1927/1961). *The Future of an Illusion.* The standard edition of the complete works of Sigmund Freud, Vol. 21. London: The Hogarth Press.

Gaines, A. D. (1982). Cultural definitions, behavior, and the person in American psychiatry. In A. J. Marsella and G. M. White (Eds.) *Cultural Conceptions of Mental Health and Therapy.* Dordrecht: D. Reidel.

Gergen, K. J. (1990). Social understanding and the inscription of self. In J. S. Stigler, R. A. Shweder and G. Herdt (Eds.) *Cultural Psychology: Essays in Comparative Human Development.* Cambridge: Cambridge University Press.

Gergen, K. J. (1991). *The Saturated Self.* New York: Basic Books.

Gergen, K. J. (1994). *Realities and Relationships.* Cambridge, MA: Harvard University Press.

Gilligan, C. (1982). *In a Different Voice.* Cambridge, MA: Harvard University Press.

Grolnick, S. (1990). *The Work and Play of Winnicott.* Northvale, NJ: Jason Aronson.

Holt, R. (1989). *Freud Reappraised.* New York: Guilford Press.

Jacoby, R. (1983). *The Repression of Psychoanalysis: Otto Fenichel and the Political Freudians.* New York: Basic Books..

James, W. (1982). *The Varieties of Religious Experience.* New York: Penguin Books.

Kernberg, O. (1980). *Internal World and External Reality.* New York: Jason Aronson.

Kirschner, S. (1996). *The Religious and Romantic Origins of Psychoanalysis.* Cambridge: Cambridge University Press.

Klein, D. (1981). *Jewish Origins of the Psychoanalytic Movement.* New York: Praeger.

Kohut, H. (1977). *The Restoration of the Self.* New York: International Universities Press.

Knight, R. (1946). Determinism, 'freedom,' and psychotherapy. *Psychiatry,* 9, 251–62.

Kris, E. (1956). On some vicissitudes of insight in psychoanalysis. *International Journal of Psycho-Analysis,* 37, 445–55.

Kurtz, S. (1992). *All the Mothers are One.* New York: Columbia University Press.

Louth, A. (1981). *The Origins of the Christian Mystical Tradition.* Oxford: Clarendon Press.

Lovejoy, A. O. (1948). *Essays in the History of Ideas.* Baltimore: Johns Hopkins University Press.

Lukes, S. (1973). *Individualism.* Oxford: Basil Blackwell.

Mahler, M. S. (1988). *The Memoirs of Margaret S. Mahler,* ed. P. Stepansky. New York: The Free Press.

Mahler, M. S., Pine, F. and Bergman, A. (1975). *The Psychological Birth of the Human Infant.* New York: Basic Books.

Mauss, M. (1985). A category of the human mind: the notion of person; the notion of self. In M. Carrithers, S. Collins and S. Lukes (Eds.) *The Category of the Person: Anthropology, Philosophy, History.* Cambridge: Cambridge University Press.

McGinn, B. (1992). *The Foundations of Mysticism. The Presence of God: A History of Western Christian Mysticism,* Vol. 1. New York: Crossroad.

Nelson, B. (1965). Self-images and systems of spiritual direction in the history of European civilization. In S. Z. Klausner (Ed.) *The Quest for Self-control.* New York: The Free Press.

Olinor, M. (1988). *Cultivating Freud's Garden in France.* New York: Jason Aronson.

Phillips, A. (1988). *Winnicott.* Cambridge, MA: Harvard University Press.

Plotinus (1962). *Enneads.* London: Faber and Faber.

Roazen, P. (1974). *Freud and his Followers.* New York: New American Library.

Sass, L. (1994). Psychoanalysis, romanticism, and the nature of aesthetic consciousness – with reflections on modernism and postmodernism. In M. B. Franklin and B. Kaplan (Eds.) *Development and the Arts.* Hillsdale, NJ: Lawrence Erlbaum Associates.

Schiller, F. (1981). *On the Naïve and Sentimental in Literature.* Manchester: Carcanet New Press.
Schiller, F. (1986). *On the Aesthetic Education of Man: In a Series of Letters.* Oxford: Oxford University Press.
Schott, R. (1989). *Cognition and Eros: A Critique of the Kantian Paradigm.* Boston: Beacon Press.
Taylor, C. (1989). *Sources of the Self.* Cambridge, MA: Harvard University Press.
Turkle, S. (1981). *Psychoanalytic Politics.* Cambridge, MA: MIT Press.
Wallis, R. T. (1972). *Neoplatonism.* New York: Charles Scribner's Sons.
Walsh, D. (1983). *The Mysticism of Worldly Fulfillment.* Gainesville, FL: University Presses of Florida.
Weber, M. (1958). *The Protestant Ethic and the Spirit of Capitalism.* New York: Charles Scribners' Sons.
Williams, G. (1967). Popularized German mysticism as a factor in the rise of anabaptist communism. In G. Muller and W. Zeller (Eds.) *Glaube, Geist, Geschichte: Zeitschrift für Ernst Benz.* Leiden: E. J. Brill.
Winnicott, D. W. (1965). *The Maturational Processes and the Facilitating Environment.* New York: International Universities Press.
Winnicott, D. W. (1989). *Playing and Reality.* New York: Routledge.
Wordsworth, W. (1988). *The Prelude.* London: Penguin Classics.

11
The Self in Psychoanalysis: Heinz Kohut and Narcissism – a Critique

İlham Dilman

1. Heinz Kohut: self-psychology and narcissism

Psychoanalysis began with Freud; it is his brain-child. But thankfully it has not remained static. Its ideas have developed and its focus has changed; or rather new foci were brought into the ambit of its ideas. This was due in part to the change in the cultural environment within which psychoanalysis was practised and its ideas developed, and also partly because the patients who came to analysis and the problems they brought to it changed. Still throughout this development it maintained a continuity in its loyalty to some of Freud's most basic ideas.

I have suggested elsewhere (Dilman, 2000a) that what Freud calls 'the ego' is what lies at the centre of a divided personality, a personality divided in itself. It is 'embattled' as Freud puts it, it has its hands full with the conflicts it tries to mediate, and so it is self-absorbed. If, in a successful psychotherapy these divisions are healed, the divided parts are transformed, including the ego itself. Indeed, we could say that the ego disappears in the sense that in this coming together the person finds himself. That is he can be himself instead of having to give in to, compromise with, conflicting voices in himself. In other words, if he can face his inner conflicts and engage in the inner work which dealing with such conflicts calls for, he can move towards autonomy so that he has a centre from which he acts and as such is his own person. Freud's ego is by its very nature embattled and self-absorbed since it is besieged with problems on the home front. It is only when these problems are eased that a person can turn outwards and in his interaction with the outer world, in his interests in and concerns for what goes on there, come to himself.

If, as Freud puts it, the ego is like the rider of a horse on which he is dependent for his mobility, if he presides over a divided self, then it should not be surprising that I find a certain affinity between it and the self which spiritual religions are enjoining us to turn away from. To be oneself, one's own person, and so to be able to give of oneself, be generous, one has to forget oneself, that is to lose one's ego, they tell us. Only then, they tell us, that is if one is genuinely disinterested, will one find spiritual growth in the sustenance one finds in what one receives, provided one has not sought it.

Now 'self-psychology', as I understand it, is a development in psychoanalysis which focuses on the development of the self from infancy onwards and its failures. But wasn't Freud interested in this development too? He was. So how is the focus of Kohut, and other analysts who engaged in the same debate, different from Freud's focus? Freud focused largely on the conflicts between what he called the id and the super-ego, that is between the demands of sexuality and those of morality, as he understood these. Kohut et al., on the other hand, go further back in a person's early life, past Freud's Oedipus complex, into the way the infant's relations with his mother and his relations with himself affect each other. They focus on the way the mother's treatment of her baby can damage the baby, sometimes for life, in himself or herself, that is in his or her ability to grow up to be himself or herself, to be authentic, not false, and autonomous and, therefore, whole. The damage is what Kohut calls 'disorders of the self' which result from 'miscarriages in the normal development of the self' – where 'normal' refers to the ideal situation which *may* be realised or at least approached. An example of such a 'disorder' is low self-esteem and, at an extreme, a feeling of worthlessness in which the person feels he hardly exists in other people's eyes and so in himself too.

If nothing that defines a person's identity is truly his, if nothing that he does comes from genuine conviction, if, for instance, he simply toes the line or does things so that others will accept him, then he has no life in which to be himself. Such a person has nothing he can call his own, not even his parents: he cannot be himself with them, he feels alienated from them. Originally the fault *may* be theirs. Perhaps as a child his mother treated him as an extension of herself, showed him off to her friends for her own satisfaction. Perhaps his father wanted to fulfil his own ambitions in him. Perhaps thus he was not given a chance to be himself – to be naughty for instance. He may as a result have felt he could not be himself and be accepted as such.

Often such a person tries to escape his feelings of worthlessness and unacceptability, their paralysing pain and feeling of emptiness, by denial. One way of doing so is by the pursuit of success and achievement. Such successes boost his ego and may indeed go to his head. He may feel important; he may even feel the satisfaction of putting down those in whose eyes he felt unacceptable. But though this may lull his sense of worthlessness and inconsequentiality, it does not make it go away. It cannot do so because he does not engage in the things which bring him success for their own sake. He does not really give himself to them and forget himself. He cannot lose himself in what he is doing and so he cannot find himself in them. His successes, therefore, are nothing more than a palliative. The self-esteem he thinks he has thus restored is a sham. The slightest failure has the effect of a bomb shell on him. It sends him into a depression which is incongruous with the failure taken at face value. But in this depression he is more in touch with himself and closer to redemption.

The truth is that such a person has made his achievements and successes and the qualities by means of which he has attained them into a measure of his worth. As Kafka put it so well in his *Diaries*, 1910–13: 'whoever appears as a complete citizen, that is, travels over the sea in a ship with foam before him and wake behind, that is with much effect round about, quite different from the man in the waves on a few planks of wood that even bump against and submerge each other – he, this gentleman and citizen, is in no lesser danger. For he and his property are not one, but two, and whoever destroys the connection destroys him at the same time' (Kafka, 1948, p. 25). What Kafka's complete citizen *has*, including his qualities, are external to him. They are not owned by him, they are used by him. They are used as a mirror in which his image shines and makes him feel great. They are no more part of him than are the clothes in which he appears before the dignitaries in the town hall who look up to him and pay him their respect. They are not part of what he *is* in himself. What this means is that he is not authentic in his mode of being.

We tend to think of the self, in other words, what a person *is* when he is himself, as something that exists in the way that his naked body exists behind the clothes which cover it. This is true in such cases as when we say, 'he is, or he is not, himself today', meaning his usual or everyday self. However in his everyday self he may not be authentic. Again, it is true in such cases as when we say 'he lost his cool and showed his true self, or his true face', meaning that he was hiding behind a mask. But it is not true in those cases which interest us here, such as those in which a psychoanalyst may say, 'after years of therapeutic work, he is at last beginning to come to himself'. Here the self to which he comes when he has the courage to discard the clothes, in a metaphorical sense, which make him feel great, face himself naked in his depression and feeling of insignificance, and after much inner work climb out of his depression and find his feet in life, is not something already there, waiting to be discovered. His clothes, to change the metaphor, were his crutches, they were the support of his self-esteem. A person who has walked with crutches all or most of his life has still to learn to walk when he throws them away.

Similarly, a man who can discard the attitudes behind which he feels safe or important has still to learn to be authentic, learn to come to a mode of being in which he is himself, learn to be himself. In the course of his individual, affective, spiritual development he was lured to take the wrong turning. He got trapped in a dead-end road, his development came to a standstill in certain respects. He has now to make up for the development he has missed; there are many lessons he has to learn. It is through such learning in which he changes that he moves towards finding himself. He thus comes to a mode of being in which, within the contingencies of his life – such as where and to what parents he was born, the education he has received, the capacities he has so far developed or failed to develop – he can be authentic, himself, whole. Coming to a mode of being is something very different from coming to something that exists independently of one's coming to it.

But in that case why is it that we describe what he comes to in this way as *being himself*? Why do we say that in coming to it he *comes to himself*? There are several connected reasons for this. One of these is that he can at last be *at home* in himself. He no longer has to justify himself, to defend himself, to seek compensation for what he feels he lacks. Nor does he have to shut himself off from the outer world, to restrict his contacts with it. At home in himself he does not have to live in a fortress. At peace with what gives him his individual identity, he does not have to feel ashamed for what he is, to apologise for it.

Another reason is that his actions *come from him*; he does not need external guidance, nor is he pushed into doing what he does. He has values and owns them. He cares for things, he gives himself to them, and in his responses to them he is genuine, as are the feelings which his responses carry. Others know where they are with him; they know that they can rely on him, trust him. He has a stable personality; he neither blows with the wind nor is he rigid, unable to give without breaking. What holds him together are his beliefs, his having things for which he cares and in which he is interested, things outside himself. It is in the things to which he gives himself and is loyal to that he finds his identity. This identity, that which makes him who he is, is thus not imposed on him. He owns it, he has made it his own.

I said that the mode of being to which a person comes, in coming to himself, is formed and takes shape through the changes and development to which he contributes. Does that mean that he fashions himself, that he makes himself the way he is when he is authentic? On the contrary, where a person comes anywhere near doing so he becomes inauthentic; what he is becomes something like an act. There is much in a person's life, in the life in which he has to learn to be himself, which he does not and cannot choose. As Sartre puts it in *L'Être et le néant*: 'I am thrown in the midst of certain brute existents, into a worker's world [for instance], French, from the Loire or the South, a world which offers me its significances even before I have had time to unseal them' (Sartre, 1943, p. 596). But although I am thrown there, I don't just happen to be there. I grow in it, I choose from it, I make it my home. In just this way I can make myself at home in what I am, for instance the son of a labourer, abandoned by my mother when I was young, and so on, and so on. I have to find a way of being in which I can accept myself, make peace with what I don't like or what pains me there. If I can then I would not need to try constantly to make myself acceptable to others, whether by conforming to their expectations or by trying to outshine them. This leaves me free to be myself, my own person.

I take this to be at the centre of 'self psychology', that is a psychology concerned to understand failures in the development of the self, to help those who suffer from 'disturbances of the self'. Its advocates call such disturbances also 'narcissistic disturbances'. But why 'narcissistic'? I take it that they are so called when the preoccupations of a person who is unable to be himself are preoccupations with himself. Whereas a person who is at home and at peace with himself is not so preoccupied, absorbed in himself. It is the same with a person who is in good physical health. He is not preoccupied with his health, he has no ailments to seek to find relief from – unless, of course, he is a hypochondriac. If he is, then his hypochondria is an expression of his not being at home with himself, constantly imagining that there is something physically wrong with him. In such a case the body is what the person identifies with and the trouble he feels there is an expression of his inability to accept himself in the body he has. His hypochondria is an expression of an unhappy love affair he has with himself. A narcissistic disturbance is just this: the expression of an unhappy love affair with oneself.

But is there such a thing as a happy love affair with oneself? Kohut, I believe, holds that there is. I shall argue that there is and can be no such thing.

2. Narcissism: healthy, unhealthy?

First, what is narcissism? I think it means self-love or love of oneself. In the story Narcissus is *in love* with himself. He is handsome, his mother is proud of his beauty and he is much loved by the nymphs. Echo who loves him most approaches him, only to be rejected. In her grief she dies, leaving behind the echo of her voice. To avenge her, the gods arrange for him to experience the feeling of unreciprocated love of which Echo died. They arrange for him to see his reflection in a clear pool and to fall in love with it. He is unable to evoke any response from it since it disappears, fragmenting each time Narcissus reaches out to embrace it. He pines away in melancholy. When the nymphs come to bury him they find a plant growing where his body had been. So like his image his body too disappears, leaving behind only a flower.

The narcissistic person is thus in love with himself. By its very nature such love is unrequited, without issue. In such a love the person may be self-satisfied. He may have been spoilt in his childhood, idolised by a mother who treated him as an extension of herself. So he will feel complete in himself and take no interest in anyone outside himself. He will treat others as pawns in a game he plays with himself. If they resist him he tries to crush them in his rage; if he fails, if they prove completely unmanipulable, his self-satisfaction slips away and he sinks into depression. He may even be totally shattered in the way that the reflection of Narcissus in the pool fragments when he tries to embrace it. The self-satisfaction thus protects the narcissistic person from the realisation of the unrequited character of his self-love. We shall see this further down in the example of Rosamond in George Eliot's (1956) novel *Middlemarch*.

On the other hand, the narcissistic person may not be smug or self-satisfied. No longer enjoying the symbiotic relationship he had with his mother long ago but still clinging to it, he feels incomplete. He seeks what he has failed to grow out of and still yearns for in his present love relations without ever being able to find it. In his novel *A la Recherche du Temps Perdu* Proust depicts such loves with great sensitivity and perception (Proust, 1954). Marcel has been unable to differentiate himself from his mother, and from his grandmother too: 'I, for whom my grandmother was still myself, I who had never seen her save in my soul.' In the kiss which his mother gives him every night before he goes to sleep, he tells us, he found 'that untroubled peace which no mistress, in later years, has ever been able to give me, since one doubts them even at the moment when one believes in them, and never can possess their hearts as I used to receive, in a kiss, my mother's heart, whole and entire, without qualm or reservation, without the smallest residue of an intention that was not for me alone'. He seeks what he found in that kiss in his later loves but can never find it. Freud would, therefore, talk of his later loves as Oedipal.

Marcel interacts with Albertine but he cannot touch her, cannot enter into contact with her. He finds her inaccessible and describes what he succeeds in touching as 'no more than the sealed envelope of a person'. His love is a yearning for what he had and lost in the past and cannot find in the present. What inspires it thus is not anything outside his soul. The beloved, he says, is 'a product of our temperament, an image, an inverted projection, a negative of our sensibility'. He describes it as 'not so much a love for her as a love in myself'. But it can also be characterised as 'narcissistic' because it seeks to exclude the beloved's independent existence as a person in her own right, longs for a relationship in which she is part of him so that in loving her he loves himself. In this way he hopes to relive the blissful existence he had in the past when he was loved by his mother from whom he remained undifferentiated. Thus the love he received came from him – from his mother who, like his grandmother 'was still himself'. As I put it: 'the magic of love depends on the separateness of the lovers; it is this which makes their response to one another a gift . . . Without it, where the other person becomes a mere shadow or extension of one, one only loves oneself in her' (Dilman, 1998, p. 106). Such a love, therefore, which is at once Oedipal and narcissistic, is without issue; it cannot attain what it craves for.

Narcissism and narcissistic love belong to an early stage of a person's affective development where the development has come to a standstill. This is certainly acknowledged by Freud. Kohut, however, holds that narcissism is originally a primitive concern that the self has for itself and, provided it is treated in the right way, is a help and not a hindrance in the development of a person. A person's love of himself, he believes, is surely something one would expect to make a positive contribution to his development towards greater autonomy. As Marjorie Taggart White puts it: Kohut holds that 'there are two lines of development . . . one arising from normal infantile narcissism, which leads to higher forms of healthy narcissism. The other line goes from infantile narcissism to object love, as Freud foresaw. He states that these two lines of development co-exist in every individual, that they produce different problems, and at last in pathological narcissism, they have to be treated separately' (White, 1986, pp. 148–9).

In the same collection of papers Arnold M. Cooper points out that 'few concepts in psychiatry have undergone as many changes in meaning as has "narcissism". Perhaps the single consistent element in these changes is the reference to some aspect of *concern with the self* and its disturbances' (Cooper, 1986, p. 112; emphasis added). In other words, 'being in love with oneself' has been changed to 'being concerned with oneself' – a significant change, as we shall see. This is revealing as is something that Karen Horney is paraphrased as saying: 'The narcissistic individual is someone whose emotional ties are tenuous, who suffers a loss of the capacity to love' (Cooper, 1986, p. 120). We shall see this to be the case in the example of Rosamond in George Eliot's *Middlemarch*. However it leads Karen Horney to say that 'narcissism, therefore, is not an expression of self-love, but of alienation from the self' (Cooper, 1986, p. 121). Like Kohut she thus takes 'self-love' to be something positive, something that involves care and concern directed to the self, oneself, and so would contribute to one's psychological welfare and development as an individual. So, given her correct view that narcissism is self-alienating, she dissociates it from self-love.

The truth, I believe, is that it is self-love that is alienating and that, as we shall see, it has little to do with self-esteem. Nor does it involve a concern *for* oneself in the way that love of another person, when it is mature and selfless, does so. It is a concern *with* oneself in the way that one may be concerned with a pain that absorbs all one's attention so that one cannot think of anything else. It would be more correct to describe it as self-absorption, the kind of absorption we find in a person in love. If so, clearly it would stand in the way of a person's development towards greater authenticity and autonomy. For it is by *giving* himself to others, taking an interest in things outside himself that a person comes to himself.

This is the misunderstanding behind Kohut's view of narcissism as something to be nurtured, something that would contribute to a person's development if it is not thwarted in early childhood. Even the words 'love your neighbour *as yourself*' have the potential of being misunderstood in this way. What is being said in these words is not that one should love one's neighbour in the way, or as much as, one loves oneself. Nor is there any suggestion in them that unless one loves oneself, or loves oneself properly, one cannot love one's neighbour. No, what is being said could be put as: 'do not do unto others what you do not want others to do unto you', in other words 'treat them with love and justice'. As for the idea that to be able to love your neighbour you have to love yourself first, this is a distortion of the truth that to have a love of others in your heart you have to be on good terms with yourself. But to be on good terms with oneself is very far from being in love with oneself, which I believe to be the true meaning of narcissism. The so-called change of meaning of that word is not a straight-forward change of meaning. It is a distortion of the concept of self-love rooted in conceptual confusion.

I should like to quote a few words from a Scottish lighthouse keeper I heard in an interview on a Sunday morning programme on the BBC, Radio 4, on 17 March 2001. The interviewer asked him whether he felt lonely during his work in the lighthouse. The lighthouse keeper replied: 'No . . . You have to like your own company [to do what I am doing] . . . You have to like yourself . . . Early in the morning you see the dawn. It is so beautiful . . . You really are devoted to your duty . . . Everything else comes second to it . . .' These are the words I jotted down from memory after the programme. 'You have to like yourself' meaning 'not dislike yourself', 'to have accepted yourself, to have come to terms with yourself', 'to have made peace with yourself'. The point is that if you are at peace with yourself you will be left free to be open to the outside world, to appreciate the dawn in the early morning, to be moved by its beauty. 'You really are devoted to your duty. Everything else comes second to it.' In other words, you forget yourself, you give yourself to serving others. But if you don't like yourself, you cannot forget yourself. It is like a pinching shoe; you cannot forget it.

Liking yourself, as the lighthouse keeper meant it, is the very opposite of narcissism as self-love. This is what Kohut and his followers wish to catch in their talk of 'a healthy narcissism', but fail. This is *not* a merely verbal matter at all. Liking yourself, as the lighthouse keeper meant it, sets one free to give, to appreciate, and in the giving to grow. The narcissist, by contrast, is taken up with himself. For instance, like Rosamond in *Middlemarch*, he pampers himself, wants others to pamper him. He likes to be adored, admired, caressed, spoiled, to be 'mirrored' as Kohut puts it.

Rosamond was such a character, narcissistic to a high degree. She thrived in being pampered; she knew how to use her charm to get it and she lapped it up. She thrived in having her way with others. She did not have to consider them; it is others who had to consider her, to indulge her. She thought of other people as there to please and gratify her because the sun shone from her. If, for any reason, they did not oblige, she thought of them as disagreeable. The fact that they had a life of their own, hopes, concerns and aspirations in their own right, never entered her head. Her affective life simply blocked all this off. In her narcissism she was safe; others could not hurt her, rouse any deep passions in her – hatred or compassion, longing or grief. They could only please or displease.

George Eliot describes an incident which pierces her narcissism and brings her a brief and terrifying flash of illumination in which other people lose the dream-like character they have for her: 'What another nature felt in opposition to her was being burnt and bitten into her consciousness' (Eliot, 1956, p. 571). She can no longer keep a caressing consciousness of herself. Will Ladislow who ceases to pander to her suddenly become real to her? She is so unused to this, so used to getting her own way with her husband, Dr Lydgate, that it threatens her with annihilation. As George Eliot puts it: she 'was almost losing the sense of her identity and seemed to be waking to some new terrible existence' (Eliot, 1956, p. 571). She tries to get up from her seat but falls back fainting.

Is Rosamond's narcissism healthy or unhealthy? According to Stolorow, 'the issue of whether a piece of narcissism is healthy or unhealthy reduces to the question whether or not it succeeds in maintaining a cohesive, stable and positively coloured self-representation' (Stolorow, 1986, p. 206). According to Alice Miller, '"healthy narcissism" can be characterized as the full access to the true self' and 'the narcissistic disturbance [by contrast] can be understood as a fixation on a "false" or incomplete self' (Miller, 1986, p. 346). The two definitions are more or less in accord. To put what they say in less jargon-ridden language: a narcissistic person's narcissism is healthy if it helps to give a person a good opinion of himself, a stable personality, and contributes to his wholeness in himself in which wholeness he is himself. How does Rosamond fare on this criterion?

Has she got a good opinion of herself? At least on the surface she does. Has she got a stable personality? This question is more difficult to answer. She hasn't got good relations with her husband, which is not surprising when she hardly ever considers him, ignores his wishes, is bent on having her own way, is intent on manipulating others to get what she wants, however much disinclined they may be to give it her. Their disinclination does not deflect her; she carries on with her schemes regardless. Her charm and good opinion of herself are largely responsible for her successes. It is true that in the end she cracks up and takes a long time to recover. But George Eliot makes it clear that she learns nothing from this experience and lives the rest of her life with the same 'equanimity' and good opinion of herself while her 'good luck' stands her in good stead.

Does this mean she has a stable personality? Well, what stability she has is due to her narcissism and her good luck. Is her narcissism to be praised or recommended for this? No more than if her stability was based on self-deception and the circumstances which helped to maintain it. What about her good opinion of herself? I would describe it as a 'concoction' and as 'arrogant'. In fact I do not see how a good opinion of oneself could be anything else. It can help a person to get on in life, but I do not see how it can advance self-honesty – that is being honest with oneself. Only in genuine humility can a person accept himself and find personal stability.

What about wholeness, 'cohesiveness of self'? Rosamond is clearly held together by the pleasing image which those who succumb to her charms reflect to her, thus supporting her good opinion of herself. She is held together by her ambition and her determination to have her own way. If her narcissism serves any function, as Kohut holds narcissism often does, then it is a purely pragmatic function. The psychological judgements made from the perspective of its ethos, like those made by Kohut, totally miss out an appreciation of what honesty and humility can bring into a human life. I do not see how narcissism, whatever form it takes, can bring that into a person's life.

So what is our judgement on Rosamond's narcissism: is it healthy or unhealthy? On Kohut's criteria we do not get a clear-cut answer. But it is the criteria themselves that are defective. I have in mind his making the distinction between healthy and unhealthy narcissism turn on the fulfilment of the function of narcissism. It is perfectly true that we speak of an organ as being in an unhealthy state when it cannot fulfil its function – for example, the pancreas when it cannot secrete the enzymes which help digestion. But there is no true analogy here between an organ and an affective orientation such as narcissism. Narcissism may play a particular role in a person's psychological economy. That, however, is not to say that we can attribute a function to it in general. A person becomes narcissistic because of his early experiences and the kind of early relationships he has with his parents as originally initiated by them.

In any case cohesiveness of self, and so on, are not products of narcissism. On the contrary a person comes to these things by turning outwards, by coming to care for others and developing an interest in things outside himself. Nor is narcissism a 'concern for self relations' (White, 1986, p. 150), if that means a concern to put them right when things go wrong in the way one treats oneself in certain kinds of situations.

If, as I quoted Miller to say, a narcissistic disturbance is a fixation on a false or incomplete self, then narcissism cannot be a 'healthy' mode of being by its very nature. For it is an early stage of development in which a person is stuck or to which he regresses under certain psychological pressures. A narcissistic person is someone who is in love with himself and as such someone ungiving, someone not concerned about others. Such narcissism, therefore, cannot contribute to his affective development. A person comes to a cohesive self, finds himself, by relinquishing his narcissism, by growing out of it.

There is a popular distinction made in everyday language when someone is referred to as a 'pathological liar'. Such a person is someone who cannot stop lying, someone to whom honesty means very little. The contrast is between such a person and someone who may lie on rare occasions, where lying is a lapse with him under pressure. What is in question is not merely a matter of degree, or one of how often he lies. It is difficult, if not impossible, to make a similar distinction in the case of narcissism. For the differences are only differences of degree. There is no such thing, for instance, as a lapse into narcissism. Regression is quite a different thing altogether. Or again there is nothing here to correspond to a white lie or a lie that a person tells to save someone needless pain. So no distinction in character can be made between two kinds of narcissism, one unhealthy, the other healthy.

3. Narcissism and self-esteem

We have already seen that it is easy to confuse narcissism with something else and attribute a positive character to it – for example, 'healthy', 'mature', 'constructive', and so on – for instance, a positive 'concern for self relations'. It is equally easy to confuse it with self-esteem. The very term in French for personal dignity which is an expression of self-esteem is *amour propre*. Literally translated this would give 'love of oneself'. Thus Annie Reich begins her essay on self-esteem by quoting its definition in Webster's dictionary as 'a high opinion of oneself'. She herself defines it as 'the expression of discrepancy or harmony between self-representation and the wishful concept of the self' (Reich, 1986, p. 45). In other words and in plain English, if our opinion of ourselves coincides with the way we wish to be, we have high self-esteem; if it falls below, we have low self-esteem. That is, on this view, we have a good opinion of ourselves in the first case and a poor one in the second, good or poor relative to our wishful conception of ourselves. Furthermore, on this view, in the latter case our narcissism comes to the rescue, compensates for our low self-esteem and raises it. It tops up, as it were, our low good opinion of ourselves. That is the voice of our love of ourselves reassures us: 'You are not as lacking in worth as you think.' Or it redirects our attention to our various qualities and successes, urges us to achieve even better results.

Many of the authors in the collection from which I quote refer to this as 'self-esteem regulation', and where a person's good opinion of himself fluctuates they speak of it as 'self-esteem stabilization'. Thus on this view self-esteem is seen as a product of our love of ourselves and as susceptible to self-manipulation. Where we fail we become disturbed in ourselves. As Stolorow points out, 'Reich clearly interpreted observed "narcissistic disturbances" as abortive attempts to restore and stabilize self-esteem' (Stolorow, 1986, p. 199).

Pulver points out that 'a good opinion of oneself – high-esteem – could exist as a realistic, non-defensive feeling' (Pulver, 1986, p. 106). Presumably, the implication is that this would make for a genuine form of self-esteem, since it would not involve any self-deception. Thus a distinction is made here, as Stolorow puts it, 'between pathological inflations of the self and a realistic good feeling about oneself' (Stolorow, 1986, p. 206). So, according to Pulver, genuine self-esteem is 'a realistic good feeling about oneself'. Kohut speaks in a way that falls between these two stools. He speaks of patients with 'narcissistic behaviour disorders' who, as their analysis progresses, are 'able to relinquish it (their symptomatic behaviour) and substitute for it more mature and realistic support for their self-esteem' (Kohut and Wolf, 1986, p. 180). Here it is the support that is realistic and, presumably, makes the self-esteem realistic. But supposing that self-esteem is a good opinion of oneself, does it need to be supported? Does one have to verify one's worth, as if one were a commodity, to have self-esteem?

It seems to me that this whole way of thinking about self-esteem or self-respect is psychologistic and confused. I said earlier that to have love for others in one's heart one has to be on good terms with oneself and that this is very different from loving oneself or narcissism. Being on good terms with oneself certainly involves self-respect. How can a person who does not respect himself be on good terms with himself? It is equally true that unless one respects oneself one cannot respect others. One anti-thesis of self-respect is servility, which should not be confused with humility. A servile person cringes before others, for he has a low self-esteem. He feels worthless in himself but his exaggerated sense of the worth of others is not genuine. He simply feels they are or stand above him, and so he lowers himself before them. But he resents it. He feels he has to lower himself because it is demanded of him by the hierarchical order of things, or in order to placate them and so avoid their displeasure. Fearing their displeasure, however, is not respecting them, except in a popular sense of respect, a corrupt form of respect. Nor does conformity to what is demanded of one amount to genuine respect. To repeat, a person who lacks a sense of inner worth, *that is* self-respect, does not find any genuine worth in others and so does not respect them.

A person can, of course, have a lower self-esteem; but a high self-esteem – if that means a high opinion of oneself – is suspect. Genuine self-esteem is silent and invisible. It hides from one and from others. The person himself is not aware of it, nor does it show itself to others. It is a mode of being, not an object of self-assessment. It is seen by others in the person's conduct if they have the discernment to see it. Self-esteem is thus humble.

The French term *amour propre*, I said, means personal dignity. In other words, a person who has self-esteem or respect for himself will not, for instance, sell himself or be bought for money. He will not lower himself morally in order to obtain something he wants. This is not because he is proud. There is a difference, of course, between being a proud person and being proud of something one has done well, between pride as a feature of a person's character and taking pride in something one does well. The former is an antithesis of humility and as such is in the same league with servility, although it is its opposite.

I said that the servile person feels unworthy in himself and when he lowers himself before others, this is not an expression of genuine respect. Nor does it add up to humility. Respect and humility belong together; fear, on the other hand, as I said, excludes genuine respect of others. As for self-respect, it requires humility and excludes both pride and servility. However, just as one can take pride in what one does well without being a proud person, likewise one can lower oneself in front of something one genuinely values and looks up to without servility. The lowering of oneself in such a case is an expression of one's humble and, therefore, genuine admiration and respect. It is as when one says: 'I am not worthy of your kindness, though I am grateful for it.' Here one feels indebted and not resentful. Such indebtedness confers a responsibility on one to try to be worthy of the goodness one has received. To feel indebted is to accept such responsibility. The recognition of this kind of indebtedness belongs to gratitude. It is in trying to be worthy of the goodness one receives that one builds up inner worth, the kind that is both invisible and inaudible.

Such inner worth and the self-respect or self-esteem with which it forms a part cannot, therefore, be an expression of narcissism. For in narcissism, as self-love, one accords oneself a high place in one's apprehension of oneself, whereas self-esteem, I argued, is humble. A narcissistic person's high esteem of himself is either a product of his love of himself, and as such not genuine, or it is an illusion which is meant to compensate for the low esteem he has of himself, and as such false. So until he can relinquish his narcissism he cannot come to have genuine self-esteem, he cannot find genuine self-respect. To do that he has to give up his interest in himself, turn outwards, learn to be grateful for what he receives, to appreciate beauty wherever it is to be found.

Freud makes the same mistake which I am trying to correct when, in his essay on narcissism (reprinted in Morrison, 1986), he writes that self-regard (if by that he means self-esteem) is 'an expression of the size of the ego'. But what is an expression of the size of a person's ego is a big head, in other words conceit or pride, and not self-esteem. When a person is insulted and he is vulnerable to the insult, his ego shrinks. To relieve the pain of its humiliation he seeks to inflate his ego. One way to do so is to return the insult to where it came from. What he thus regains may be his good opinion of himself, but it is not his self-esteem. His good opinion of himself, which is an expression of the size of his ego, and as such vulnerable to the insult, is a corrupt form of self-esteem. A person whose self-esteem is genuine and secure is not easily insulted.

I can illustrate what I am suggesting in the following example. I said that self-esteem is not a love of oneself which belongs to the ego, but personal dignity. Let us think of the dignity which one expects to find in or associates with a king or a high dignitary. If the king maintains his dignity in the way he behaves because he represents his country and its traditions which he loves, then the dignity with which he behaves is genuine. If, however, in identifying himself with the position he holds he receives food for his ego, then this dignity is a corrupt kind of dignity. In the one case he puts himself aside in the love he has for his country and its traditions and wants to represent them in a fitting way. He is genuine in the way he represents his post. In the other what he does is an act; it doesn't carry his heart; he puts it on for something he wants for himself.

It is the same with personal, moral dignity of which a person's self-esteem is an expression. So, for the same reason, when it is an expression of his narcissism – it is not genuine self-esteem. It is trumped up and has a psychological explanation. But when what is in question is a person's moral dignity, his self-esteem has no psychological explanation. It is not a product of his psychology but an expression of the moral convictions in which he is who he is. To think otherwise is to fall a prey to psychologism. This is the idea that psychology can provide an explanation for everything that a human being does (see Dilman, 2000a, 2000b).

4. Supposed higher forms of narcissism

I have argued that narcissism is an early stage in the individual's development in which a person's affective development could come to a standstill or to which he could later revert by regression. It has no positive contribution to make to such development. If the development is to continue, if the person is to grow affectively, he needs to relinquish his narcissism, turn away from himself and grow out of it. But, of course, to different degrees we can find remnants of it in most people.

Kohut, we have seen, takes a different view which, I have argued, rests on certain conceptual confusions or misunderstandings. He thinks that self-love has a positive contribution to make to a person's affective development and that what is needed is its transformation into a higher form much, I suppose, as a person's love for another can be transformed into a more mature love. But the two cases are by no means parallel; they are antithetical. For a person's love for another is thus transformed as it becomes more selfless. How can a person's narcissism or self-love become selfless? For this to happen he has to grow out of his narcissism. A selfless narcissism is clearly a contradiction in terms.

Kohut's idea of the transformation of narcissism in some ways reminds me of Freud's idea of the sublimation of sex – artistic creation, for instance, as the sublimation of sex. The respect in which the two parallel each other is the finding of a common root in diverse phenomena. This is not meant to be a criticism as such: sometimes diverse phenomena do have a common root, and sometimes finding a common source behind them is a form of reductionism. Certainly, Freud gave the Oedipus complex a prominent position in his analysis of certain forms of human behaviour. Kohut does the same with narcissism. Thus, as Cooper puts it: 'Disturbances of the self ["narcissistic disturbances"] are part of *all* psychological disturbances' (Cooper, 1986, p. 134; emphasis added). We have seen this to be the case with Marcel's loves in Proust's novel: they have an Oedipal and narcissistic character at one and the same time.

The parallel I made between Freud's conception of sexuality and its place in human life in its many forms and Kohut's conception of narcissism and its place in human life in its primitive and adult forms, I said, was meant as an observation and not a criticism. I now want to consider some areas where Kohut finds narcissism transformed into a mature form critically. Kohut mentions five such areas of human achievement: creativity, the ability to be empathic, the capacity to contemplate one's own impermanence and face death with equanimity, sense of humour and wisdom. I should like to examine some of these very briefly.

Is creativity narcissistic? My answer is that it *can* be; certainly sometimes it is. In writing a novel, for instance, the novelist is giving expression to something of himself, articulating his own experience of life. When others admire what he has written, which he hopes they will, they will be savouring and admitting something that belongs to him intimately. Indeed, he will himself relish it in the mirror of other people's enjoyment and admiration of it. Hence in the pleasure the author finds in this, there is a sense in which he will be loving himself. Even in exhibiting something intimate that he treasures, there is a sense in which he caresses himself.

In *A la Recherche du Temps Perdu* we can say that Proust (1954) relives his narcissism in the character of Marcel, his own first name. He is indulging in exhibitionism in a covert sort of way. But we can *also* say that he is trying to come to terms with what he exhibits, with his sufferings and disappointments. True, he is trying to immortalise what he has experienced and suffered; but he is also trying to surmount it, indeed to surmount his narcissism and find a peace which he never had while he was living what he has put in his novel. Further than this, is he not also giving us something from which we can learn? If he is, at least in this giving his creativity goes beyond narcissism.

In any case, what about different instances of creativity, for instance a scientist's creative work? He has to discipline himself to be objective, his interest is directed to the object of his research. He may identify himself with it, but he may not. He may come out of himself in that work. Must the fact that he finds pleasure in it make him a narcissist? Must it be the case that his pleasure engages his narcissism? My answer is, no. He doesn't have to do this work for the pleasure he finds in it. If he discovers something new he may not take a possessive attitude towards it, think of it as his, bask in its light. I do not think that many of the scientists involved in the war effort during the Second World War in Britain thought much about themselves. Yet some of them were very inventive, their work certainly engaged their creativity. I do not think there was anything narcissistic about that creativity.

Let us imagine Kohut protesting: 'But you are thinking of narcissism in its immature form.' My reply would be that as I have argued there is no such thing as mature narcissism. A mature person will have made peace with himself, be at home with himself, 'like his own company' as the lighthouse keeper put it. But this is not 'mature or transformed narcissism'; it is not narcissism at all.

What about a sense of humour? Kohut quotes Freud saying that 'humour has something liberating about it' (Kohut, 1986, p. 82). He refers to Freud's example of a criminal being led to the gallows on a Monday remarking: 'Well, the week's beginning nicely.' Freud comments that this has 'something of grandeur' and speaks of it as a 'triumph of narcissism', 'the victorious assertion of . . . invulnerability'. It is achieved, he says, by a person's withdrawing 'the psychical accent from his ego' and 'transposing it onto his super-ego'. Yes, the criminal in this example laughs at himself, thereby showing that he does not take himself seriously. But I think that he is ironic in the way he identifies himself with his executioner – his super-ego. A triumph of narcissism here could only mean: 'You see *I* am not afraid. You cannot harm me.' However, I doubt that the man led to the gallows was showing off in this way. He was withdrawing 'the psychical accent from his ego'. So he was triumphing *over* his narcissism.

Kohut comments that humour is a transformation of narcissism which aids a person in achieving mastery over the demands of the narcissistic self. I agree; but why a transformation of narcissism rather than a renouncement of it? A man obsessed by sex turns to writing, his life changes. Why is this a sublimation of sex rather than a coming free of his obsession? Is he not taken up by something else, though not in the same way? Why is this not a new though not different kind of passion?

We have a similar type of confusion in what Kohut writes about wisdom. He says that 'wisdom is achieved through man's ability to overcome his unmodified narcissism' by 'the renouncement of these narcissistic demands' – that is the demands of the person's *unmodified* narcissism (Kohut, 1986, p. 83). All right, but these demands are precisely those I have been referring to in this discussion. So where does modified or transformed narcissism come in? What is this 'creation of a higher form of narcissism' (Kohut, 1986, p. 81)? Kohut speaks of a person's 'acceptance of the limitations of his physical, intellectual, and emotional powers' (Kohut, 1986, p. 83), that is his relinquishment of his infantile delusions of omnipotence as Freud would put it. Kohut puts it as 'a maximal relinquishment of narcissistic delusions' (Kohut, 1986, p. 84). He also expresses this in terms of the Freudian metaphor:

> The final control of the rider [the ego] over the horse [the id], may after all have been decisively assisted by the fact that the horse, too, has grown old. And, lastly, we may recognize that what has been accomplished is not so much control but the acceptance of the ultimate insight that, as concerns the supreme powers of nature, we are all 'Sunday riders'.
>
> (Kohut, 1986, p. 85)

With reference to the horse Kohut speaks earlier of 'a decathexis of the narcissistic self through a rearrangement and transformation of the narcissistic libido' (Kohut, 1986, p. 83). Why is the libido described as narcissistic? Because in earlier youth as the adolescent awakes to adult sexuality he is primarily concerned to seek sexual gratification and in that discovery of his new capability find self-gratification. If later in life he can integrate his sexuality with love then his sexuality will lose its narcissistic character. But note that the transformation is in the person and in the character of his sexuality, and *not* in his narcissism. His narcissism simply decreases as he is able to renounce it in this way.

Earlier when Kohut speaks of the renouncement of the demands of unmodified narcissism he says that wisdom rests on a person's 'acceptance of the limitations of his physical, intellectual, and emotional powers' (Kohut, 1986, p. 83). All right, so this way the person gains in maturity and as he does so his narcissism decreases at the same time. What decreases here is the person's 'unmodified narcissism', that is his self-love. It is the *person* who changes, grows into maturity, *not* his narcissism. His narcissism is not modified or transformed, it simply decreases. There is nothing else it can do; the person grows out of it, if not completely, then at least to a certain degree.

Kohut rightly contrasts what in reality amounts to a relinquishment of narcissism with the case of a soldier in battle marching towards enemy fire together with other soldiers in his battalion, singing patriotic songs. Such a person has not really renounced the ego from which his narcissism flows. Rather, Kohut says, he is in 'a frenzied mental condition in which the ego is paralyzed, as if in a trance' (Kohut, 1986, p. 83). Hence, he says, his narcissism is denied, in other words it has not been renounced. Even this need not be the case. The soldier may not be in a frenzied condition in which his ego is paralysed. He may be facing enemy fire with courage, and thus fully aware of the danger to his life, a courage he finds in a genuine love for his country. Simone Weil (1948) refers to a case that bears a certain similarity to that of the soldier in our example: that of the Christian martyrs during the time of the Roman empire who were thrown to the lions in the

Coliseum. They linked arms and, singing hymns, faced the lions, knowing they would be torn apart. They found this courage in the faith in which they had given their love to God and in that love turned away from themselves. They found support in their solidarity with each other in their common fate. Still Weil contrasts their case with Christ on the cross, alone, believing he had been abandoned by his Father. She points out that even then he kept faith with his Father and calls this *fidélité à vide* – fidelity in the void. Here there is not a shred of narcissism and what we have is a supreme example of the contrast between a totally selfless love and self-love or narcissism.

In the *Phaedo* (Plato, 1973) Socrates speaks of the purification of the self. The self is purified from the ego, and so of narcissism since narcissism has its source in the ego. It is a form of ego-centricity, though not the only one. Socrates, for whom philosophy is 'a love of wisdom', in the *Phaedo* speaks of philosophy as learning to die: learning to die to the self in the sense of 'ego'. What is in question is the relinquishment of our egocentricity and narcissism. Only then can a person be wise and learn to face death, when it comes, with equanimity, as Socrates did when he was given hemlock.

The upshot of my argument is that wisdom involves the relinquishment of one's narcissism, not its transformation. It is the person who is transformed in coming to be wise. Kohut is right in saying that wisdom is not merely a matter of cognition, but involves affective growth, and so takes 'experience and work' and time. It cannot therefore 'be an attribute of youth' and is 'reserved for the later phases of life' (Kohut, 1986, p. 84). Here I agree with Kohut. Where I disagree is that this transformation of the person involves the shedding of his narcissism, not its transformation. There is no higher form of narcissism attained by its transformation. At the root of the idea that there is such a benign form of narcissism are certain conceptual confusions which I have tried to point out.

5. Summing up

There is no doubt that Kohut and the psychoanalysts who have contributed to the psychology debate with him have expanded the field of psychoanalytic therapy and have made a genuine contribution to psychoanalysis. But Kohut, on whose ideas I have concentrated, has been trapped in a number of conceptual confusions, which are not mere verbal confusions, and which have done harm to his contribution.

I have concentrated on his ideas about narcissism and his view that it can take a higher form in which it has a positive contribution to make to the affective development of a person. My main claim has been that narcissism, as self-love, can have no such contribution to make. I have no quarrel with Kohut and the others about what they call 'narcissistic disturbances' and the way early relationships of the young child, especially with his mother, condition their formation. However, for purely conceptual reasons, I cannot see how narcissistic disturbances can be lessened by anything other than helping a patient suffering from such disturbances to grow out of his narcissism. What is at issue here is Kohut's conception of narcissism.

I have argued that it embodies three confusions related to each other. The first is the confusion between self and ego in the idea of narcissism as self-love. Kohut takes it to be directed to the self as distinct from the ego and, as such, capable, when transformed, of contributing to its development towards greater wholeness and autonomy. I have argued that it is inherently egocentric and therefore cannot contribute to personal growth.

The second confusion concerns the form which love takes when the ego is both its source and its object and the asymmetry between such love and love of another. Love of another can take different forms. It can be egocentric or narcissistic and it can be mature and respectful of the other in his or her independent existence (see Dilman, 1998). Self-love cannot take a mature form because it is inherently egocentric.

Thirdly, self-esteem, referred to as *amour propre* in French, is thought to be an expression of self-love, that is narcissism, and so identified as having a good opinion of oneself. For what is loved is highly valued. I argued that self-esteem is a form of being which involves personal dignity. It has its source in a person's moral convictions. It can only be attained, therefore, by shedding one's narcissism. Far from being the having of a good opinion of oneself, self-esteem involves humility. Let me add that it is pure psychologism to think of self-renunciation and humility as forms of masochism (*vide* White, 1986, p. 145). The asymmetry I have mentioned between self-love and love of another is relevant here. For while respect is an integral part of a mature love of another, self-love does not involve self-respect or self-esteem.

Finally, in all this both Kohut and I have spoken of coming to oneself, finding oneself, being oneself. This has to do with finding inner cohesion or coming together and being honest with oneself. Kohut (1986) speaks of the self as an 'independent centre of initiative'. We are 'independent', in the sense in which he means it, when we do not copy others, when what we do comes from us, when we have made our own all that makes us who we are – when, in the active sense, we 'own' ourselves. The self is thus each one of us *when this is true of us*, so that we can say 'he is himself'.

This does not mean, however, that a person of whom this is not true cannot speak of something he has done as something he has done *himself* – in the appropriate circumstances. What is in question in such cases is the reflexiveness of personal pronouns. Expressions such as 'he is himself', 'he has found himself', and so on, which are in question in 'self-psychology', are *extensions* of this use in certain special contexts. Such expressions as 'he is not himself today', of course, belong to our everyday use of language and form a half-way house between the use of reflexive pronouns in everyday common-or-garden contexts and their use in the special cases which interest us here. But this latter use does not belong to the language of the markets, if I may put it that way, and calls for clarity which takes philosophical work to achieve.

One thing I emphasised is that the self, in this use of the word, is each one of us in our most intimate struggles: what we search for, what we fail to find, and so on. But it is not something which already exists before a person finds it – if he does – in the course of his life. It is something to the formation of which he contributes in his engagements with others, if honesty means anything to him.

References

Cooper, A. M. (1986). Narcissism. In A. P. Morrison (Ed.) Essential *Papers on Narcissism*. New York: New York University Press.

Dilman, İ. (1998). *Love: Its Forms, Dimensions and Paradoxes*. London: Macmillan.

Dilman, İ. (2000a). Psychology and human behaviour: is there a limit to psychological explanation? *Philosophy*, 75(292), 183–201.

Dilman, İ. (2000b). *Raskolnikov's Rebirth, Psychology and the Understanding of Good and Evil*. Chicago: Open Court.

Eliot, G. (1956). *Middlemarch*. Boston: Houghton Mifflin.

Kafka, F. (1948). *The Diaries, 1910–1913*. London: Secker & Warburg.

Kohut, H. (1986). Forms and transformations of narcissism. In A. P. Morrison (Ed.) *Essential Papers on Narcissism*. New York: New York University Press.

Kohut, H. and Wolf, E. S. (1986). The disorders of the self and their treatment: An outline. In A. P. Morrison (Ed.) *Essential Papers on Narcissism*. New York: New York University Press.

Miller, A. (1986). Depression and grandiosity as related forms of narcissistic disturbances. In A. P. Morrison (Ed.) *Essential Papers on Narcissism*. New York: New York University Press.

Morrison, A. P. (Ed.) (1986). *Essential Papers on Narcissism*. New York: New York University Press.

Plato (1973). *The Last Days of Socrates*. Harmondsworth: Penguin Books.

Proust, M. (1954). *A la Recherche du Temps Perdu*. Vols i–iii. Paris: NRF, Bibliothèque de la Pléide.

Pulver, S. E. (1986). Narcissism: the term and the concept. In A. P. Morrison (Ed.) *Essential Papers on Narcissism*. New York: New York University Press.

Reich, A. (1986). Pathologic forms of self-esteem regulation. In A. P. Morrison (Ed.) *Essential Papers on Narcissism*. New York: New York University Press.

Sartre, J. (1943). *L'Etre et le néant*. Paris: Gallimard.

Stolorow, R. D. (1986). Toward a functional definition of narcissism. In A. P. Morrison (Ed.) *Essential Papers on Narcissism*. New York: New York University Press.

Weil, S. (1948). *La Pesanteur et la grâce*. Paris: Librarie Plon.

White, M. T. (1986). Self relations, object relations, and pathological narcissism. In A. P. Morrison (Ed.) *Essential Papers on Narcissism*. New York: New York University Press.

12
Challenges to Psychoanalytic Methodology

Malcolm Macmillan

What is psychoanalytic knowledge about? Is it about calming the worried well or curing the mentally ill? Actually, we know it isn't about therapy of any kind because there are simply no data that distinguish psychoanalysis as therapy from its competitors. There is also a great deal of data showing that whatever changes its therapy does bring about are not due to its supposedly essential ingredients of 'psychoanalytic process'. In any case, no one, including Freud, values psychoanalysis because it is a therapy.

Is psychoanalytic knowledge about the big questions of the sources and development of human behaviour? Does it constitute a general psychology that helps us to understand human behaviour in the widest sense? I do not think it can be that because psychoanalysis is not one theory or even a core theory around which various extensions can be grouped, like a chorus of theorettes around the prima ballerina. Psychoanalysis gives us a multitude of theories, each striving for the limelight and all dancing to different tunes very few of which harmonise with Freud's original. How does one choose among them? If theories are more or less adequate guides to what is actually the case, and in this instance what is actually the case about people, how do we decide from which we should draw real intellectual sustenance? Some dismiss this question as irrelevant, but I shall argue in my concluding remarks that it is the most important question that can be asked about psychoanalytic knowledge.

That there is no clear answer to the question of what psychoanalytic knowledge is about is a consequence of basic and irremediable defects in the technique for gathering data and interpreting it common to all the schools of psychoanalysis. On my view, psychoanalysis cannot be taken seriously as a way of inquiring into mental processes until analysts from the variant schools meet a three-part challenge. Each needs to show how they overcome the factor of 'suggestion' in gathering data; to convince us that they have resolved the fundamental indeterminism in interpreting those data; and indicate how rational choice might be made between theirs and the other schools. Until that can be done, I believe it likely that what passes for 'psychoanalytic knowledge' is actually only knowledge about those who engage in its clinical craft and who formulate theories based on that practice.

1. Free association and its aims

Free association is the basic method by which psychoanalytic data are gathered. It was central to Freud's primary clinical aim of building up 'a picture of the patient's forgotten years' that was to be 'trustworthy and in all essential respects complete' (Freud, 1937/1964a, p. 258). It was used for gathering the raw material from which this picture was built up, the material itself consisting of allusions to events in the patient's past contained in the ideas emerging in treatment or the fragments of similar memories contained in dreams.

What then was the method? Note first that the term 'free association' is a not very adequate translation into English of the German *freier Einfall*. The German term refers to the ideas of most interest, those that force their way or irrupt into consciousness (Freud 1910/1957a, p. 29. n. 1; 1916–1917/1963, p. 47, n. 1). As a precondition of analytic treatment, Freud required a basic candour from his patients. As they attended to what was being analysed, they had to suspend their judgement on what came to mind and report everything that did. The candour constituted the fundamental rule of psychoanalysis, and the patient's attending to and reporting what came to mind was the method of free association (Freud, 1925/1959, p. 40).

Freud developed free association in his search for the causes of symptoms, dreams, or parapraxes. When patients reported what came to mind, trains of thought emerged that were important to understanding the phenomenon being investigated (Freud, 1901/1958, pp. 635–6). However, these thoughts were not continuous and orderly: the order of recall was chaotic, sequences contained gaps, and patients gave inadequate explanations of those thoughts that did seem to be complete. The gaps indicated the presence of unconscious psychological processes that were just as unknowable in their nature as unobservable physical processes in sciences like chemistry and physics. Free association was one method used by analysts for identifying these analytic unknowables and was used in the same way as the experimental methods of the physicist. Inferring the 'unknowable' processes and then interpolating them among those that were conscious filled the gaps (Freud, 1940/1964b, pp. 196–7). Freud's final and unfinished sentence on the last page of his last work read, 'In consequence of the special character of our discoveries, our scientific work in psychology will consist in translating unconscious processes into conscious ones, and thus filling the gaps in conscious perception' (Freud, 1940/1964b, p. 286).

Free association and the inferences following from it made psychoanalysis, Freud claimed, a natural science. Clearly, the reliability and validity of free association is crucial to this claim.

2. The reliability and validity of free association

Freud claimed that within limits like those of experimental error, free association retrieved data that were valid and reliable. The claim for validity was explicit and strong; in contrast, that for reliability, although equally strong, was slightly less explicit. None the less, free association allowed different analysts to gather essentially the same kinds of data, and those data would be true of the patient, and not about the analyst.

Freud made the validity claim repeatedly. Even as free association was still emerging as a technique he remarked, 'we are not in a position to force anything on the patient . . . or to influence the products of the analysis' (Breuer and Freud, 1895/1955, p. 295). After free association had become his staple, he said that it substantially guaranteed that 'nothing' would be introduced into the structure of the neurosis 'by the expectations of the analyst' (Freud, 1925/1959, p. 41). And again, shortly before his death, the danger of patients being led astray by suggestion 'has certainly been enormously exaggerated' (Freud, 1937/1964a, p. 262).

As to reliability, Freud dismissed the differences between analysts over what they obtained with the method. Those differences resulted either from inadequate training or the inability to maintain a scientific attitude but, like the disagreements between microscopists when the technique of using the instrument was new, they were of 'no great importance in the long run' (Freud, 1940/1964b, p. 197). The psychoanalytic method yielded data that were as reliable as those found with the microscope.

The assumptions on which Freud based these claims can only be summarised here. First, he adopted the same view as Meynert that the determinants of trains of associations were internal and physiological. Apart from helping the patient overcome resistance from such unpleasant affects as might derail a train, neither direct nor indirect suggestion from Freud could direct it to other than its physiologically determined end point (Macmillan, 1997, pp. 107–9). Second, Freud had absorbed Charcot's quite mistaken conclusion that the phenomena of hysteria and hypnosis had a physiological basis and could not be due to suggestion (Macmillan, 1997, pp. 37–47, 64–8). Third, Freud believed that nothing came into the patient's mind that was irrelevant or unconnected with the symptom, dream or parapraxis being investigated, and drew on a set of what I have called *connecting assumptions* to propose relationships even when they were not really there (Macmillan, 1997, pp. 100–5). Fourth, Freud shared Meynert's view that there was, in the logical sense of 'identity', an identity between associations, logical relations and causal connections. A train of associations beginning at a conscious starting point was logically related to the unconscious causes found at the end point (Macmillan, 1997, pp. 106–7). Finally, Freud made explicit a conclusion from Charcot's experiments on artificial trauma that the sensory content of the cause had to be reflected in the symptom and he named this property the *determining quality* of the cause. He then sought it just as deliberately as he disregarded those recollections of his patients that did not possess it (Macmillan, 1997, pp. 55–62, 208–10, 218–22, 284–5).

All the modern versions of psychoanalysis claim to be based on free association and to use the method in much the same way as Freud. Although there are actually differences in its use, the assumptions are the same as Freud's. They are also not questioned.

3. The charge of suggestion

The charge that psychoanalysis is too open to suggestion takes two forms that are sometimes confused. First, it is claimed that whatever results are achieved by psychoanalytic therapy are due to the general effect of suggestion; the second is that the data collected by free association, the typical psychoanalytic method, are massively influenced by suggestions transmitted unconsciously from psychoanalyst to patient. Although I will discuss the first charge briefly, my main concern is with the second.

The use of 'suggestion' to explain therapeutic effects has a very long history. One with an oblique connection with psychoanalysis occurs in the report of the French Royal Commission into the animal magnetism practised by Franz Anton Mesmer. Their experiments had shown that whether Mesmeric phenomena were manifested or not depended only on the subject's belief that magnetic fluid was being applied, and they attributed the effects to *imagination*, that is, to what we now call suggestion. Although they did not investigate mesmeric therapy, their conclusion would have applied to it: 'The animal magnetism may indeed exist without being useful, but it cannot be useful if it does not exist' (Bailly, 1784, p. 126; Tinterow, 1970).

'Suggestion' as direct hypnotic verbal suggestion also has an immediate connection to psychoanalysis. When Freud and Breuer defended themselves against the charge that Breuer's allegedly successful treatment of Anna O. (Bertha Pappenheim) was due to suggestion, it is this meaning of suggestion that they had in mind: Anna O. had been treated before suggestion cures came into existence (Breuer and Freud, 1893/1955, p. 7). It is also this meaning with which Freud later defended himself against the charge that the therapeutic effectiveness of psychoanalytic therapy was due to suggestion (Collins, 1980), but we should note that he added a protective coating: suggestion cures were due to the transference on to the analyst of the positive feelings the patient once had for his or her parents. This explanation replaces one mystery with three. First, it is a covert claim that only psychoanalysis produces genuine cures. Second, accepting it requires one to accept all of Freud's theoretical propositions about libido and symptoms. Mystery three is that although analysts cannot agree on the manifestations of transference, we have to accept its therapeutic role (Macmillan, 1997, pp. 575, 622, 654. See also Macmillan, 1999, 2001a, 2001b).

4. The indeterminacy of interpretation and construction

Freud made sense of the data gathered by free association by what he variously called deciphering, translating, and interpreting single elements of the material (Freud, 1937/1964a, p. 261). However, a fundamental indeterminism plagues both interpretation and the identification of the factors that shape the patient. Between the two it is impossible to judge the trustworthiness of the final picture.

The language analogy

As early as *Studies on Hysteria* Freud used a linguistic analogy to convey the essence of the psychoanalytic interpretation of symptoms (Breuer and Freud, 1895/1955, p. 129). Years later he claimed that the interpretation of dreams was completely analogous to deciphering ancient scripts (Freud 1913/1953, p. 177). The Royal Asiatic Society had made the 'decisive experiment' in 1857 when the agreement it obtained between four independent translators of a newly discovered cuneiform inscription justified what had been already done and gave confidence for future work. Freud claimed that the interpretations of dreams by 'correctly trained analysts' were equally valid and reliable (Freud, 1916–1917/1963, pp. 229–32).

However, there is no significant agreement between interpretations of the same dreams by different psychoanalysts. Formal studies fail to yield even minimal agreement, a result that matches the extraordinary disagreement about the meanings of the dreams of Freud's patients, like Dora (see Macmillan, 1997, pp. 256–3, 278–80, 575, 659–63 for specific studies and instances). Are current psychoanalysts not as clever as Freud thought, and is the technique of interpretation too complex to learn? This seems unlikely: the analysis of even the most complex clinical data shows that agreement is possible provided there are well-defined concepts and well-defined rules for categorising the phenomena (for example, the studies of transference by Luborsky and Crits-Christoph, 1998; Berk and Andersen, 2000). Perhaps, then, it is that Freud left no rules? That is actually the case but when others have subsequently formulated his rules, as did Grinstein (1983), one finds that there is little or no agreement that they are Freud's. The same holds for the aforementioned studies of transference: the rules are agreed on but what the rules are about is not. Is there something about interpretation itself that makes agreement impossible?

Consider what allowed the cuneiform translators to agree. Cuneiform deciphering began from conjectures that some inscriptions would make reference to kings from the geographical area where the inscriptions were found and that the messages would open and close with salutations that followed the linguistic conventions of the area. By such substitution some groups of cuneiform characters had already been assigned meanings before the test.

Freud's analogy breaks down precisely at this point. For the apparently meaningless manifest dream elements to be analogous to the cuneiform characters, analysts would have to have something that corresponds to the known names and salutations. They do not. In using the analogy elsewhere Freud did not always insist on the advantage of a bilingual inscription (Freud, 1896/1962, p. 192; 1913/1953, p. 177; 1937/1964a, pp. 259–60). Commentators sympathetic to Freud have noted, however, that without the second script the latent dream is only an interpretive construction and that interpreting without it is like trying to solve an equation with two unknowns (Foulkes, 1978, p. 45; Spence, 1986. See also Weiss, 1974).

Allow that the manifest content of the dream is actually a language that can be translated. Now, call the manifest content the first script, and the 'language' of the unconscious, or latent content, the second. Despite the Lacanistes, as Timpanaro (1974/1976) notes, the grammar, syntax, lexicon, or rules of this second script are quite unknown. Nothing in the manifest elements corresponds to the already known names and salutations. It is this quite fundamental ignorance that results in the equally fundamental indeterminism of using the data from free association. Psychoanalytic 'translation' actually constructs the meaning of the manifest or first script rather than discovering it in the latent or second script.

Constructions and narratives

The indeterminism of psychoanalytic interpretation also applies to the suppositional pieces of the patient's forgotten early history that Freud called 'constructions' (Freud, 1937/1964a, p. 261). When put to patients, true constructions were supposed to force the recall of real events that patients had repressed. Whereas an interpretation was of a single or limited number of associations, a construction was usually of a complete event. The problem is that constructions are inherently indeterminate. We have no standards against which to judge the trustworthiness of either single constructions or the connected sets of them used to build narrative histories of patients.

Indeterminism can be illustrated in the famous construction Freud put to his patient known as the Rat Man. Freud supposed that when the patient was under six years of age, his father had either 'soundly castigated' him for a misdemeanour to do with masturbation or that he had forbidden his son's masturbation, and threatened him by saying it would be the death of him, possibly also threatening to cut off his penis.[1] Whichever of the constructions was really put to him, the patient is supposed to have suddenly remembered that his mother had often told him about an incident, of which he had no memory of his own, in which his father had beaten him, but not for masturbating or anything sexual. Notice first that neither what the patient did recall was repressed nor was it his own knowledge and that Freud took the mother's story as confirming the construction of the son's history. More important, its content did not resemble either of the constructed events. One must ask how much similarity between a construction and a recollection counts toward trustworthiness or truth.

There are other questions raised by Cioffi and Spence. As put originally by Cioffi, in his 1961 seminar 'Why are We Still Arguing about Freud?' (1998) it is that while we all have a sense of what constitutes an improbable interpretation, neither that sense, nor formal canons of interpretation, helps us decide which among many different, more or less plausible interpretations is true. Nor can any be formulated.[2] Similarly, Spence (1980, 1982) made the related point that narrative explanations – essentially constructed histories – were flexible enough for anything to be fitted to them.

A good illustration of Spence's point is provided by Farrell's comments on Freud's study of Leonardo da Vinci. Despite Freud's well-known massive errors of fact about Leonardo and his work, Farrell concluded 'we must be grateful to him for giving us a simplified case history of Leonardo' (Freud, 1910/1957b; Farrell, 1963. See also Macmillan, 1997, pp. 582–3). Errors of fact did not trouble Farrell any more than they would affect analytical narrators.

Cioffi's argument is nicely illustrated by Bremer's (1976) re-analysis of Freud's study of Michelangelo's statue of Moses (Freud, 1914/1953, 1927/1953), which as Ricoeur insists, illustrates Freud's methods of interpretation very clearly even though it is not a 'case'. Bremer argues that Freud's construction was based 'on several fundamental misconceptions', the most important of which was his use of the account of Moses' *first* ascent of Mount Sinai, after which he broke the Tables, rather than the *second*, during which he received a second set (Exodus: 31–32 vs. 33–34). Bremer notes that no aspects of the statue are inconsistent with the second ascent but that many are inconsistent with the first. In the same year, Bergmann (1976/1982) noted, almost in passing, that it was unfortunate for Freud's interpretation that Michelangelo's Moses had horns because according to Exodus, Moses could have acquired them only on the second ascent after the Lord appears (Exodus 33–34).[3] They indicate, as do the blank stones *Moses* holds, that Michelangelo has shown him during the second ascent (Macmillan and Swales, 2003).

The biblical story of Moses and the facts about Leonardo da Vinci are external referents or criteria that allow choice among interpretations. It is therefore not a question of whether one finds Bremer's interpretation of Moses more plausible or convincing than Freud's, but that his is truer to the facts. The position is similar with psychoanalytic constructions proper. Without external criteria there is no way of judging whether they give the truthful and complete account of the patient's history that Freud set as the goal of analysis. Logically, this problem is identical with that of deciding on the correctness of a translation: in neither case is there a second script or its equivalent. It is not that psychoanalysts cannot be trained to interpret or use rules to analyse complex behaviours. It is rather that no criteria exist against which they can hone their skills as translators, interpreters, or painters of hidden pasts.

5. Free association and the variant schools

If all analysts have access to the same data, and if Freud's methods of data-gathering and interpretation are as reliable and valid as he claimed, why are there variant schools of psychoanalysis? Does free association allow different analysts to gather essentially the same data? Do the schools come about merely because psychoanalysts attend to or select from different parts of the data set, weigh or interpret the components differently, and so make different constructions? Or is the method so unable to prevent suggestions from the analyst that it actually acts as a conduit for transmitting them?

Interpretation: Freud vs. Jung

Perhaps the clearest example of variant schools arising from different interpretations of the same observations is in the emergence of Jung's analytical psychology around 1912. Among the important points of disagreement was Jung's denying the exclusively sexual nature of Freud's concept of libido, which he replaced with a generalised psychic energy, and his questioning the explanatory generality of the repression of libido.

On my reading, there are no facts that could have distinguished between Jung's concept of psychic energy and Freud's of libido. Take, for example, Jung's description of a spring ceremony reportedly once performed by an indigenous Australian people from north of Geraldton in Western Australia, the Watjanti [Wachandi], as part of their ritual to renew the fertility of the earth:

> They dig a hole in the ground, so shaping it and setting it about with bushes so that it looks like a woman's genitals. Then they dance round this hole all night, holding their spears in front of them in imitation of an erect penis. As they dance round, they thrust their spears into the hole, shouting: 'Pulli nira, pulli nira, wataka!' (not a pit, not a pit, but a c[unt]!).
> (Jung, 1952/1956, p. 150)[4]

Jung claimed that the dancers suggest to themselves that the hole is really a vulva, an illusion maintained by not looking at the real object possessed by a woman. The hole is therefore not a *sign* for the female genitalia but a *symbol* of the real earth woman who is to be fertilised. Jung later adduced this behaviour as an example of what he called the canalisation or direction of a non-specific psychic energy into a mode of expression that has making the earth fertile as its real purpose (Jung, 1928/1969, pp. 42–3).

Can Jung's interpretation be differentiated from Freud's? Freud, I believe, would have interpreted the ritual as an instance of sexually motivated sympathetic magic in which, by imitating the sexual act, the dancing, spear thrusting and shouting would magically influence the fertility of the earth (for example, Freud, 1912/1953, pp. 79–81). Behaviour motivated directly by a sexual drive or by a general energy canalised or directed into sexual-like activity? What could differentiate the two?

Nor can one readily see how to choose between Freud's explanation of the consequences of repression in schizophrenia and Jung's alternative. In his study of Daniel Schreber's symptoms of paranoid schizophrenia, Freud (1911/1958) said that Schreber had repressed his homosexual wish toward his psychiatrist by withdrawing or detaching his libido from him. The wish had returned in the form of a delusion that the psychiatrist had sexual designs on him and Schreber's libido, now detached from external reality, also caused him to lose contact with reality and build up a sexually powered fantasy world of his own. As Jung saw it, Freud was saying that it was Schreber's repression/detachment of his libido that brought about his loss of the sense of reality. He wrote to Freud that that loss could not 'be reduced to repression of libido (defined as sexual hunger)' and said he had had difficulties 'throughout the years' in attempting to apply this aspect of libido theory to schizophrenia (McGuire, 1974, Letters 282J of 14 November 1911, and 287J of 11 December 1911).

At the time Jung did not indicate in more detail the basis of his dissatisfaction. He subsequently made the logical point that the withdrawal of libido explained only the loss of erotic interest and not the loss of interest in general. Freud himself, Jung noted, had raised the problem of whether it was through libidinal energy alone that individuals were related to the world about them or whether it was through the energy of the ego instinctual drive – the 'interest' of the instinct of self-preservation – but had finally decided that Schreber's symptoms were mainly or entirely explicable as libidinal withdrawal (Freud, 1911/1958, pp. 73–4). Jung opted for an explanation based on a theory that would take into account the forms of energy that had split off from the original during its development. His psychic energy was first directed to the satisfaction of basic needs, like nutrition, before being canalised into a variety of autonomous activities, such as sex or relating the individual to reality, any one of which could be affected by regression without affecting the other (Jung, 1952/1956, pp. 132–7; 1955/1970, pp. 119–22).

What facts, clinical or otherwise, would have allowed a choice between the two explanations? Did Freud's later alteration of his theory of the instinctual drives that attributed the sense of reality to the energy of the ego-instinctual drive make the decision any easier? The issue is logically identical with that of Abraham's reconstructing an infantile oral-sadistic sub-stage from nothing more than his schizophrenic patient's complex oral symptoms. There the developmental processes he hypothesised were 'hardly accessible to direct observation' (Abraham, 1916/1927. See also Macmillan, 1997, pp. 339–52, 357–8, 529–31).

An identical question can also be asked about the basis for choosing between current variants of Jung's analytical psychology, for example, those discussed in chapters 9, 10, and 11 of the compilation by Young-Eisendrath and Dawson (1997). All are based mainly on different interpretations although one can see that some also involve purely personal preferences, for example, in Young-Eisendrath's choice about anima and animus (pp. 228–9). Neither there nor elsewhere is clinical or observational evidence adduced relevant to choice.

Clinical facts I: Anna Freud vs. Melanie Klein

Differences in the interpretation of simple clinical facts also played the main role in the dispute between Anna Freud and Melanie Klein in the emergence of the latter's version of psychoanalytic theory, although differences in technique did contribute. Between 1941 and 1945 *Discussions of Scientific Controversies* took place within the British Psycho-Analytic Society over the ways Anna Freud and Melanie Klein viewed child psychoanalysis (King and Steiner, 1991). The basic theoretical difference was clear enough: Sigmund Freud had held that the superego formed out of the dissolution of the Oedipus complex at the end of the phallic stage of development (about five years), a position also adopted by his daughter, Anna, whereas Melanie Klein placed its development in the first twelve months.

Klein, who had come to Britain in 1926, based her analyses of adults and children on the direct interpretation of behaviours she took to indicate the transference on to her of the patient's very early hostility toward its mother. In Vienna, Anna Freud had based her technique on the proposition that the child could not form a transference relationship and made interpretations consistent with that limitation. She came to Britain in 1938 after the Nazis forced the Freud family into exile and tension soon became more evident between her followers and Klein's. They had reached a high point by 1940 and the British society undertook a series of discussions designed to resolve the differences.

Everyone agreed that the *Discussions* were to be of a scientific kind although it was obvious that the tensions mainly reflected disagreements over the training of analysts (King and Steiner, 1991, pp. 87–9, 90, 99–100, 216, 925–6). Despite the avowal of the importance of facts and objectivity, the most striking thing about the debates is the almost total absence of agreed on facts, even simple ones being almost impossible to differentiate from interpretation. A good example is provided by the exchange between

Anna Freud and Sylvia Payne. Anna Freud had put her view that the autoerotic and narcissistic state of the child in the first half-year of life meant that it did not regard the mother as an object: the child had then only 'the crudest rudiments of an object relationship'. Payne adduced as contra-evidence the child's refusal to feed from bottles offered by other than their mothers or from the breast of a wet nurse. To her the child was differentiating between objects (King and Steiner, 1991, pp. 417–25, 434–5).

Anna Freud agreed there was a difference in behaviour but attributed it to the form in which the satisfaction was offered rather than to a difference in object. The following exchange then took place:

Dr Payne: It seems to me the difference is one of degree.
Miss Freud: It seems so absolutely different in kind when one watches closely.
Dr Payne: But I have watched it too.
Dr Glover: . . . Alterations of behaviour do not imply that an object relationship in the full sense exists.
Dr Payne: In embryo, if you like –
Miss Freud: To me the difference seems qualitative and not quantitative.
(King and Steiner, 1991, pp. 435–6)

That discussion ended without this relatively simple factual issue being resolved.

Almost immediately it was revived in a discussion of the more complex issue of whether phantasies existed in the first year of life and what their contents were. As Glover summarised that equally inconclusive debate: 'there is controversy about the existence of phantasies up to roughly speaking the first 12 months, and that, as regards phantasies that occur afterwards, the existence of these is not disputed. But that there is controversy about the content ascribed to them' (King and Steiner, 1991, pp. 437–8).

Subsequent to the *Discussions*, few analysts who have made observations of children have confirmed any of the developmental pathways constructed on the basis of inferences drawn from clinical observations made on adults or children. The reasons? Re-evaluating the *Discussions*, Baudry (1994) noticed a lack of understanding of the ways data bear on theory, a point congruent with the failure of a recent clinically oriented history of child psychoanalysis to mention any facts that might clarify or confirm modern psychoanalytic theories of child development (Geissmann and Geissmann, 1992/1998). Consistent with this neglect are Bowlby's (1981) observations on psychoanalysis as a developmental discipline: psychoanalysis was 'nowhere weaker' than in its developmental concepts, a weakness he attributed to the 'pride of place' given construction over developmental observation. Brody (1982) also charged that the failure to confirm developmental theories was because analysts relied on 'verbal and associative' techniques, that is, on free association. The later judgements of Pine (1985) and Wolff (1996), and the peer discussion of Wolff, are consistent with these views. Nor does that part of Westen's (1998) more recent evaluation of Freud's legacy dealing with development require it to be altered (Macmillan, 2001a, 2001b; Weinberger and Westen, 2001).

Clinical facts II: Freud vs. femininity

What purport to be clinical observations are also at the basis of the varying views on female sexuality that emerged in the 1920s and 1930s. By the mid-1920s Freud had settled on the theses that all libido was masculine, that the female was essentially a male who entered the Oedipus complex in the same way as the male, and emerged as a castrated male. However, her emergence was only partial with the result that her superego was weak, her libido lacked control, her capacity for sublimation was lower than that of the male, and her psychological life dominated by a wish for the penis that had been taken from her. A number of psychoanalysts raised problems with Freud's developmental theses and by the early 1930s, although they disagreed on its basis and consequences, many of them had reported cases in which the little girl supposedly had a hostile attitude towards her mother before entering the Oedipal phase. Freud himself eventually agreed and attributed the hostility to the daughter believing the mother had deprived her of her penis (Macmillan, 1997, pp. 504–5).

However, once again, the most striking feature of the various views from the period (recently sampled by Grigg et al., 1999) is the lack of agreement on relatively simple facts about female behaviour and psychological characteristics. No facts were adduced, for example, on whether little girls masturbated by other than rubbing the clitoris, whether the female superego was more or less rigid than the male's, whether women had a lower sense of morality, and whether females had a lower capacity for sublimation than males. On more complex matters such as the starting point of development and the developmental process itself, there is now more disagreement than then.

No solution to these problems is proposed even by those psychoanalysts and sympathisers who recognise Freud's theory of female sexuality as 'problematic' and blame his male viewpoint for confusions in his original formulations, including those who praise Freud's clinical insights into women. But, of course, they never criticise his methods (for example, Chodorow, 1991). Nor do any commence by observing that Freud's original theses were not based on clinical facts but on a stereotypical view of women that he set as the goal for psychoanalysis to explain. Given this stereotypical end point, Freud's 'masculine' starting point practically demanded a tortuous developmental process on which analysts would be unlikely to agree, especially because free association is so open to therapist influence (Macmillan, 1997, 1991, pp. 504–8, 531–3. See also Nagera, 1991; Simon, 1991; Green, 1996).

Clinical facts III: Freud vs. Oedipus

Freud frequently described the Oedipus complex as the nucleus of the neuroses; it was the shibboleth that distinguished real from false analysts (for example, Freud, 1916–1917/1963, p. 337). How then could Basch (in Modell and Sacks, 1985) say at a panel of the American Psychoanalytic Association devoted to re-evaluating the complex that its role as shibboleth now 'limited what it was permissible to discover with the clinical method of psychoanalysis'? A clue is found in one of Freud's remarks on the castration complex that terminated the boy's Oedipus complex and initiated the girl's entry into it. Freud bowed his head in recognition of the great achievement of those virtuosi in 'the art of overlooking' – those analysts who had worked 'for dozens of years' without finding 'a sign' of the existence of a castration complex (Freud, 1925/1961, p. 253, n. 4).

We do not know how the analysts whose perspicacity Freud acknowledged had missed seeing castration and Oedipus. It would be consistent with recent discussions of the complex if their theoretical preconceptions prevented Oedipal data from being generated. According to Simon (in Modell and Sacks, 1985), the theory of the Oedipus complex sensitised the analyst and created such a possibility for prejudiced listening that it made the question of how clinical data could validate the theory so difficult that he was pessimistic that they ever would. Basch had also asked if it was not time to bring psychoanalytic theories about the Oedipus complex in line with 'actual clinical experience'. Almost all the criticisms and qualifications made in the Panel Discussion were developed six years later by Simon (1991) who, after pointing to the problem of defining the Oedipus complex, remarked on the epistemological difficulty arising from the interplay of theoretical expectations and clinical observations. It made it 'difficult, perhaps even impossible, to specify what constitutes the data relevant to whether or not the Oedipus complex is central' (see also Simon and Blass, 1991).

Clinical facts IV: Freud vs. Rank, Ferenczi

Perhaps the clearest *prima facie* case of how facts gathered by free association are created by variations in technique and theoretical orientation is provided by Freud's dispute with Rank over the latter's birth trauma thesis. Rank and Ferenczi had decided to 'experiment' with limiting the length of their psychoanalyses. At a specifiable point during the transference reaction, each told his patients how much more time they had in order to get well. As the limit was approached, Rank observed that the patient repeated 'his own birth for the most part quite faithfully in all its details' and that cures then followed (Rank, 1924/1973, p. 5. See also Rank, 1927). Using the same technique of time-limitation, Ferenczi made similar observations and had similar therapeutic successes (Ferenczi, 1925/1980a, 1925/1980b).

Freud seems never to have had patients who recalled their births and his critique of Rank's thesis drew on no clinical evidence (Freud, 1926/1959). Freud believed that the reminiscences were phantasies, just as eventually did Ferenczi (1927, 1928). How could one choose between these two clinically based conclusions? Was suggestion involved? Rank claimed he had been led to his by the use of Freud's 'technique of [free] association and interpretation' (Rank, 1924/1973, p. 214). On the other hand, when Glover discussed the role of suggestion in therapy, he remarked on 'the rapidity with which some analysts were able to discover "birth traumas" in all their patients for some time after Rank first published his book . . . and before it was officially exploded' (Glover, 1931. See also King and Steiner, 1991, p. 855). That explosion was Freud's critique.

Clinical facts V: Freud vs. Guntrip, Kohut, and others

It would be nice were there to have been a patient seen by two or more analysts of differing theoretical orientations. That ought to provide the basic data for testing whether Freud's method of free association creates its facts but, despite Guntrip and Kohut, that event seems to exist only as a thought analysis. We have to look to therapies other than psychoanalyses for what we need.

Guntrip was analysed by Fairbairn in the 1950s and by Winnicott between 1960 and 1968 (Guntrip, 1975). While the content of the two analyses differed, and did so in accord with the theoretical preoccupations of two analysts, the data are sparse and complicated by the influence of Guntrip's own preconceptions. In reporting his analyses, Guntrip did not appear to find any problem in the variation of clinical content between the two and seems to have attributed it to the subtleties of his problem and their interaction with the personal characteristics of the analysts. Of some interest to part of my argument about constructions is that at least one commentator twice describes the central trauma at the core of Guntrip's 'pathology,' and which he retrieved long after the second analysis had ended, as a 'supposed' event (Eigen, 1981).

Kohut's (1979) data are of even less use than Guntrip's. Apparently coming from his two analyses of the patient he called Mr Z, it turns out that Mr Z was actually Kohut himself, and that the second 'analysis' is some of Kohut's autobiographical material dressed up as a real psychoanalysis (Strozier, 1999, 2001; Barglow, 1999). According to Kohut, the first was conducted according to classical principles and focussed on pre-Oedipal and Oedipal themes; the second began when Kohut was developing his theory of the development of an independent self and focused on the lack of empathy provided by Z's parents.

What can be retrieved from Kohut's semi-fictional account is the frankness with which he accepts that analysts influence clinical data. In the first analysis, which was actually with Ruth Eissler, he describes 'Z' as complying with Kohut's (and Eissler's) beliefs about the importance of psychosexual and Oedipal development by generating Oedipal material. 'Z' also, fictionally of course, accedes to these expectations by suppressing his self-symptoms and allowing them to emerge only in the second analysis. Kohut describes 'Z' producing two different sets of associations to the same dream about his father and, perhaps, as retrieving different memories – Oedipal and self – in the two analyses.

The degree of influence Kohut allows is identical with Gedo's (1980) observation that patients treated within the framework of Kohut's theory did have self-defects but that similar patients treated within a 'classical' framework had only conventional Oedipal problems. These disturbing discrepancies, as Gedo called them, are also congruent with Marmor's (1962) much earlier opinion that free association produced data that validated the theory of the analyst. In addition to what can be learned from psychoanalytic opinion, there is also a huge amount of hard evidence clearly showing that what patients or clients produce in other therapeutic situations is quite definitely a function of the therapist's orientation. Finally, there is what to me is the even stronger evidence from various fringe psychological procedures of the readiness with which pre-birth memories can be produced, including memories from life on galaxies other than our own (Macmillan, 1997, pp. 210–16, 584–5. See also Hassin and Bargh, 2001).

6. Conclusion

At least until very recently, neither the defenders of Freud's psychoanalysis nor its psychoanalytic critics doubted the objectivity of the psychoanalytic method. Both believed it established certain basic facts reasonably securely. The few who did have doubts did not question the method in any depth and never asked whether it created its own data (for example, Brenner, 1968; Arlow and Brenner, 1988. See also Macmillan, 1997, pp. 624–6, 659–63). At most they made claims that the extent to which suggestion creeps in can be carefully monitored but none of these assertions is backed with evidence (for example, Holt, 1997, 1999; Macmillan, 1998).

If psychoanalytic knowledge is being made available primarily for patients or clients to find meaning in their lives, the question of whether what they find is true is of no particular relevance. Even the most bizarre belief system brings that kind of satisfaction to some of the people some of the time. But if psychoanalysis is a general psychology with the primary aim of answering the big questions about behaviour and its development, possibly even allowing us to influence development positively, whether what it tells us is true or not is rather more crucial.

In this regard the confirmation of psychoanalysis through external criteria would, as Cioffi (2001) has argued so cogently, put paid completely to debates about the validity of free association, interpretation and construction. However, even where it might be possible most psychoanalysts do not look for that kind of confirmation. Consequently, without external referents not only will the usefulness of psychoanalysis continue to be limited, but the effects of suggestion and indeterminism on gathering and interpreting clinical data will continue. Precisely because psychoanalysis has no rules for interpreting and constructing – and this is part of its appeal – the amateur can interpret just as convincingly as the professional (Macmillan, 1997, pp. 618–19). External referents are the only things capable of transforming the gathering of psychoanalytic knowledge from what it is now, a vapid parlour game in which (almost) everyone wins and gets prizes for their stories, into something intellectually interesting, perhaps even of practical importance.

Notes

1. The two different constructions come from Freud's published and original case reports (Freud, 1909/1955, pp. 205, 263–5. See also Cioffi, 1985; Esterson, 1993, pp. 62–7).
2. The arguments from Cioffi's 1961 seminar are now included in Cioffi (1998, pp. 1–92, 281–2, 292–5).
3. Michelangelo probably gave Moses horns because that was what Jerome's Latin translation from the Hebrew of *Exodus* said how Moses was glorified. Jerome's rendering is certainly not the mistranslation it is sometimes said to be. Years before, Aquila had made the same choice in his Greek translation, and both he and Jerome had excellent Hebraic authority for their work. The fact is that the Hebrew is so unusual and ambiguous that there is not even certainty of the literal meaning of the phrases in Hebrew let alone in translation (Bowker, 1969/1979; Mellinkoff, 1970; Propp, 1987; Macmillan and Swales, 2003).
4. Presentday transliterations would read 'bulinyida, bulinyida, wardaga!' and sounded as 'buli -nyida, buli -nyida, wardaga!'

References

Abraham, K. (1916/1927). The first pregenital stage of the libido. In K. Abraham, *Selected Papers on Psycho-analysis*. London: Hogarth Press.

Arlow, J. A. and Brenner, C. (1988). The future of psychoanalysis. *Psychoanalytic Quarterly*, 57, 1–14.

Bailly, J. S. (Ed.) (1784). Rapport des commissaires chargés par le Roy de l'examen du magnétisme animal (Report of the commissioners charged by the King to examine animal magnetism). Paris: Imprimerie Royale.

Barglow, P. (1999). Heinzeit on Herr Z: Discussion of Charles Strozier's paper. *Psychoanalytic Review*, 86, 587–93.

Baudry, F. (1994). Revisiting the Freud–Klein controversies fifty years later. *International Journal of Psycho-Analysis*, 75, 367–74.

Bergmann, M. S. (1976/1982). Moses and the evolution of Freud's Jewish identity. In M. Ostow (Ed.) *Judaism and Psychoanalysis*. New York: Ktav Publishing.

Berk, M. S. and Andersen, S. M. (2000). The impact of past relationships on interpersonal behavior: Behavioral confirmation in the social-cognitive process of transference. *Journal of Personal and Social Psychology*, 79, 546–62.

Bernheim, H. (1887/1888). *Suggestive Therapeutics: A Treatise on the Nature and Uses of Hypnotism*. New York: Putnam.

Bowker, J. (1969/1979). *The Targums and Rabbinic Literature: An Introduction to Jewish Interpretations of Scripture* (corrected edn.). Cambridge: Cambridge University Press.

Bowlby, J. (1981). Psychoanalysis as a natural science. *International Review of Psycho-Analysis*, 8, 243–56.

Bremer, R. (1976). Freud and Michelangelo's Moses. *American Imago*, 33, 60–75.

Brenner, C. (1968). Psychoanalysis and science. *Journal of the American Psychoanalytic Association*, 16, 675–96.

Brenner, C. (1982). The concept of the superego: A reformulation. *Psychoanalytic Quarterly*, 51, 501–25.

Breuer, J. and Freud, S. (1893/1955). *On the Psychical Mechanism of Hysterical Phenomena: Preliminary Communication*. The standard edition of the complete psychological works of Sigmund Freud, Vol. 2. London: Hogarth Press.

Breuer, J. and Freud, S. (1895/1955). *Studies on Hysteria*. The standard edition of the complete psychological works of Sigmund Freud, Vol. 2. London: Hogarth Press.

Brody, S. (1982). Psychoanalytic theories of infant development and its disturbances: A critical evaluation. *Psychoanalytic Quarterly*, 51, 526–97.

Burgner, M. (1985). The oedipal experience: Effects on development of an absent father. *International Journal of Psycho-Analysis*, 66, 311–20.

Chodorow, N. (1991). Freud on women. In J. Neu (Ed.) *The Cambridge Companion to Freud*. Cambridge: Cambridge University Press.

Cioffi, F. (1985). Psychoanalysis, pseudo-science, and testability. In G. Currie and A. Musgrave (Eds.) *Popper and the Human Sciences*. Dordrecht: Nijhoff.

Cioffi, F. (1998). *Freud and the Question of Pseudoscience*. Chicago, IL: Open Court.

Cioffi, F. (2001). The rationale for psychoanalytic interpretation [Commentary on Macmillan 2001b]. *Psychological Inquiry*, 12, 161–6.

Collins, S. (1980). Freud and 'The riddle of suggestion'. *International Review of Psycho-Analysis*, 7, 429–37.

Eigen, M. (1981). Guntrip's analysis with Winnicott – A critique of Glatzer and Evans. *Contemporary Psychoanalysis*, 17, 103–11.

Esterson, A (1993). *Seductive Mirage: An Exploration of the Work of Sigmund Freud*. Chicago, IL: Open Court.

Farrell, B. (1963). Introduction to S. Freud's *Leonardo da Vinci and a Memory of His Childhood*. Harmondsworth, Middlesex: Penguin Books.

Ferenczi, S. (1925/1980a). Contra-indications to the 'active' psycho-analytical technique. In S. Ferenczi, *Further Contributions to the Theory and Technique of Psycho-analysis*. 2nd edn. New York: Brunner/Mazel.

Ferenczi, S. (1925/1980b). Psycho-analysis of sexual habits. In S. Ferenczi, *Further Contributions to the Theory and Technique of Psycho-analysis*. 2nd edn. New York: Brunner/Mazel.

Ferenczi, S. (1927). Present-day problems in psycho-analysis. *Archives of Psycho-Analysis*, 1, 522–30.

Ferenczi, S. (1928). Gulliver fantasies. *International Journal of Psycho-Analysis*, 9, 283–300.

Foulkes, D. (1978). *A Grammar of Dreams*. New York: Basic Books.

Freud, S. (1888/1961). *Hysteria*. The standard edition of the complete psychological works of Sigmund Freud, Vol. 1. London: Hogarth Press.

Freud, S. (1891/1961). *Hypnosis*. The standard edition of the complete psychological works of Sigmund Freud, Vol. 1. London: Hogarth Press.

Freud, S. (1896/1962). *The Aetiology of Hysteria*. The standard edition of the complete psychological works of Sigmund Freud, Vol. 3. London: Hogarth Press.
Freud, S. (1901/1958). *On Dreams*. The standard edition of the complete psychological works of Sigmund Freud, Vol. 5. London: Hogarth Press.
Freud, S. (1909/1955). *Notes upon a Case of Obsessional Neurosis*. The standard edition of the complete psychological works of Sigmund Freud, Vol. 10. London: Hogarth Press.
Freud, S. (1910/1957a). *Five Lectures on Psycho-analysis*. The standard edition of the complete psychological works of Sigmund Freud, Vol. 11. London: Hogarth Press.
Freud, S. (1910/1957b). *Leonardo da Vinci and a Memory of his Childhood*. The standard edition of the complete psychological works of Sigmund Freud, Vol. 11. London: Hogarth Press.
Freud, S. (1911/1958). *Psycho-analytic Notes on a Case of paranoia (Dementia paranoides)*. The standard edition of the complete psychological works of Sigmund Freud, Vol. 12. London: Hogarth Press.
Freud, S. (1912/1953). *Totem and Taboo*. The standard edition of the complete psychological works of Sigmund Freud, Vol. 13. London: Hogarth Press.
Freud, S. (1913/1953). *The Claims of Psycho-analysis to Scientific Interest*. The standard edition of the complete psychological works of Sigmund Freud, Vol. 13. London: Hogarth Press.
Freud, S. (1914/1953). *The Moses of Michelangelo*. The standard edition of the complete psychological works of Sigmund Freud, Vol. 13. London: Hogarth Press.
Freud, S. (1916–17/1963). *Introductory Lectures on Psycho-analysis*. The standard edition of the complete psychological works of Sigmund Freud, Vols 15 and 16. London: Hogarth Press.
Freud, S. (1917/1957). *A Metapsychological Supplement to the Theory of Dreams*. The standard edition of the complete psychological works of Sigmund Freud, Vol. 14. London: Hogarth Press.
Freud, S. (1925/1959). *An Autobiographical Study*. The standard edition of the complete psychological works of Sigmund Freud, Vol. 20. London: Hogarth Press.
Freud, S. (1925/1961). *Some Psychical Consequences of the Anatomical Distinction between the Sexes*. The standard edition of the complete psychological works of Sigmund Freud, Vol. 19. London: Hogarth Press.
Freud, S. (1926/1959). *Inhibitions, Symptoms and Anxiety*. The standard edition of the complete psychological works of Sigmund Freud, Vol. 20. London: Hogarth Press.
Freud, S. (1927/1953). Postscript to *The Moses of Michelangelo*. The standard edition of the complete psychological works of Sigmund Freud, Vol. 13. London: Hogarth Press.
Freud, S. (1937/1964a). *Constructions in Analysis*. The standard edition of the complete psychological works of Sigmund Freud, Vol. 23. London: Hogarth Press.
Freud, S. (1940/1964b). *An Outline of Psycho-analysis*. The standard edition of the complete psychological works of Sigmund Freud, Vol. 23. London: Hogarth Press.
Freud, S. (1940/1964c). *Some Elementary Lessons in Psycho-analysis*. The standard edition of the complete psychological works of Sigmund Freud, Vol. 23. London: Hogarth Press.
Gedo, J. E. (1980). Reflections on some current controversies in psychoanalysis. *Journal of the American Psychoanalytic Association*, 28, 363–83.
Geissmann, C. and Geissmann, P. (1992/1998). *A History of Child Psychoanalysis*. Routledge: London.

Glover, E. (1931). The therapeutic effect of inexact interpretation: A contribution to the theory of suggestion. *International Journal of Psycho-Analysis*, 12, 397–411.

Green, A. (1996). Has sexuality anything to do with psychoanalysis? *International Journal of Psycho-Analysis*, 76, 397–411.

Grigg, R., Hecq, D. and Smith, C. (Eds.) (1999). *Female Sexuality: The Early Psychoanalytic Controversies*. New York: Other Press.

Grinstein, A. (1983). *Freud's Rules of Dream Interpretation*. New York: International Universities Press.

Guntrip, H. (1975). My experience of analysis with Fairbairn and Winnicott (How complete a result does psycho-analytic therapy achieve?) *International Review of Psycho-Analysis*, 2, 145–56.

Hassin, R. R. and Bargh, J. A. (2001). It takes two to tango: The therapist, the patient, and automatic aspects of their in-between [Commentary on Macmillan 2001b]. *Psychological Inquiry*, 12, 151–4.

Holt, R. R. (1997). Review of *Freud Evaluated: The Completed Arc*. *Psychoanalytic Books*, 8, 397–410.

Holt, R. R. (1999). The literary critics take on Freud: An assessment of their critiques. In R. M. Prince (Ed.) *The Death of Psychoanalysis: Murder? Suicide? or Rumor Greatly Exaggerated?* Northvale, NJ: Jason Aronson.

Jung, C. G. (1928/1969). On psychic energy. In W. McGuire (Ed.) *The Collected Works of Carl Gustav Jung*. 2nd edn., Vol. 8. London: Routledge and Kegan Paul.

Jung, C. G. (1952/1956). Symbols of transformation: Two. In W. McGuire (Ed.) *The Collected Works of Carl Gustav Jung*. 2nd edn. Vol. 5. London: Routledge and Kegan Paul.

Jung, C. G. (1955/1970). The theory of psychoanalysis. In W. McGuire (Ed.) *The Collected Works of Carl Gustav Jung*. Corrected edn. Vol. 4. London: Routledge and Kegan Paul.

King, P. and Steiner, R. (Eds.) (1991). *The Freud–Klein Controversies 1941–1945*. London: Tavistock.

Kohut, H. (1979). The two analyses of Mr. Z. *International Journal of Psycho-Analysis*, 60, 3–27.

Luborsky, L. and Crits-Christoph, P. (1998). *Understanding Transference: The Core Conflictful Relationship Method*. 2nd edn. Washington, DC: American Psychological Association.

McGuire, W. (Ed.) (1974). *The Freud/Jung Letters: The Correspondence between Sigmund Freud and C. G. Jung*. Princeton, NJ: Princeton University Press.

Macmillan, M. (1997). *Freud Evaluated: The Completed Arc*. Cambridge, MA: MIT Press.

Macmillan, M. [B.] (1998). Letter to the editor. *Psychoanalytic Books*, 9, 133–9.

Macmillan, M. (1999). Partisan reviewing. [On-line]. http://www.hbs.deakin.edu.au/psychology/reviewing.

Macmillan, M. (2001b). [Target article] Limitations to free association and interpretation. *Psychological Inquiry*, 12, 113–28.

Macmillan, M. (2001a). [Author's response] The reliability and validity of Freud's methods of free association and interpretation. *Psychological Inquiry*, 12, 167–75.

Macmillan, M. and Swales, P. J. (2003). Observations from the refuse-heap: Freud, Michelangelo's *Moses*, and psychoanalysis. *American Imago*, 60, 41–104.

Marmor, J. (1962). Psychoanalytic therapy as an educational process. In J. H. Masserman (ed.), *Science and Psychoanalysis*, Vol. 5. New York: Grune and Stratton.

Mellinkoff, R. (1970). *The Horned Moses in Medieval Art and Thought*. Berkeley, CA: University of California Press.

Modell, A. H. and Sacks, M. H. (1985). The Oedipus complex: A reevaluation. Journal of the American Psychoanalytic Association, 33, 201–216.

Nagera, H. (1991). The four-to-six-years stage. In S. I. Greenspan and G. H. Pollack (Eds.) *The Course of Life*. Vol. III. *Middle and Late Childhood*. Madison, CT: International Universities Press.

Pine, F. (1985). *Developmental Theory and Clinical Process*. New Haven, CT: Yale University Press.

Propp, W. H. (1987). The skin of Moses face – transfigured or disfigured? *Catholic Biblical Quarterly*, 49, 375–86.

Rank, O. (1924/1973). *The Trauma of Birth*. New York: Harper Torchbooks.

Rank, O. (1927). [Review of] Inhibitions, symptoms and anxiety. *Mental Hygiene* 11, 181–8.

Robertson, G. M. (1892). Hypnotism at Paris and Nancy. Notes of a visit. *Journal of Mental Science*, 38, 494–531.

Simon, B. (1991). Is the Oedipus complex still the cornerstone of psychoanalysis? Three obstacles to answering the question. *Journal of the American Psychoanalytic Association*, 39, 641–68.

Simon, B. and Blass, R. B. (1991). The development and vicissitudes of Freud's ideas on the Oedipus complex. In J. Neu (Ed.) *The Cambridge Companion to Freud*. Cambridge: Cambridge University Press.

Spence, D. P. (1980). *Narrative Truth and Historical Truth: Meaning and Interpretation in Psychoanalysis*. New York: Norton.

Spence, D. P. (1982). Narrative truth and theoretical truth. *Psychoanalytic Quarterly*, 51, 43–69.

Spence, D. P. (1986). When interpretation masquerades as explanation. *Journal of the American Psychoanalytic Association*, 34, 3–22.

Strozier, C. B. (1999). Heinz Kohut and 'The 2 analyses of Mr. Z': the use (and abuse?) of case material in psychoanalysis. *Psychoanalytic Review*, 86, 569–86.

Strozier, C. B. (2001). *Heinz Kohut: The Making of a Psychoanalyst*. New York: Farrar, Straus and Giroux.

Timpanaro, S. (1974/1976). *The Freudian Slip: Psychoanalysis and Textual Criticism*. London: NLB.

Tinterow, M. M. (1970). *Foundations of Hypnosis: From Mesmer to Freud*. Springfield, IL: Thomas.

Weinberger, J. and Westen, D. (2001). Science and psychodynamics: From arguments about Freud to data [Commentary on Macmillan 2001a]. *Psychological Inquiry*, 12, 129–32.

Weiss, F. (1974). Meaning and dream interpretation. In R. Wollheim (Ed.) *Freud: A Collection of Critical Essays*. New York: Doubleday/Anchor.

Westen, D. (1998). The scientific legacy of Sigmund Freud: Toward a psychodynamically informed psychological science. *Psychological Bulletin*, 124, 333–71.

Wolff, P. H. (1996). The irrelevance of infant observations for psychoanalysis. *Journal of the American Psychoanalytic Association*, 44, 464–74 (with commentaries and reply 392–474).

Young-Eisendrath, P. and Dawson, T. (Eds.) (1997). *The Cambridge Companion to Jung*. Cambridge: Cambridge University Press.

Name Index

Abraham, K. 228
Abrams, M.H. 187, 189, 191, 195n
Achelis, W. 55
Adams, H.E. et al. 153n
Aichhorn, A. 10
Alexander 129
Alexander, Franz 171
Alford, F. 3, 40ff, 51, 52n, 158
Amacher, P. 4, 36n, 57
Anderson, O. 57
Anna O. (Breuer's patient) 222
Anscombe, G.E.M. 177n
Aquinas 190
Aristotle 36n, 64
Arlow, J.A. and Brenner, C. 233
St Augustine 45–6, 189
Augustus 129

Babbage, C. 58
Badcock, C.B. 152n
Bailly, J.S. 222
Baldwin, J.M. 59
Barglow, P. 232
Baudry, F. 229
Beck, L.W. 36n
Bell, S.M. 150
Bellah, R. et al., 181, 188
Benvenuto, B. and Kennedy, R. 47
Benz, E. 189
Bergmann, M.S. 186, 225
Berk, M.S. and Andersen, S.M. 223
Bernfeld, S. 4, 5
Bilder, R.M. and LeFever, F.F. 3
Binet, A. 61
Blake, W. 187
Blakemore C. 95n
Blakemore, S.J. and Decity, J. 153n
Block, N. 65
Bloom, H. 187
Blos, P. 183
Boehme, J. 189
Bollas, C. 8, 178n
Bonaparte, M. 21
Bower, T.G.R. 150
Bowlby, J. 229
Boyd, R. and Richerson, P. 133, 134, 149
Brakel, L.A.W. 4
Brandell, G. 35
Braten, S. 152n, 153n
Braun, H. 57
Bremer, R. 225
Brenner, C. 233
Brentano, F. 2, 16n, 35, 36, 56, 60, 61, 76, 79, 80, 81
Breuer, J. and Freud, S. 222, 223
Brody, S. 229
Brook, A. 3, 4, 20ff, 37n, 88, 158, 159
Brown, R.F. 189

Campos, J.J. 147–8
Campos, J.J. et al. 153n
Cariani, P. 66
Cariani, P. and Delgutte, B. 66
Carnap, R. 56
Carpenter, G. 61, 151
Cavell, M. 2, 177n
Charcot, J.-B. 161, 221
Chodorow, N. 181, 230
Chung, M.C. 1ff
Churchland, P. 67
Churchland, P. and Churchland, P. 80
Cioffi, F. 12, 13, 225, 233
Clark, A. 80
Cohen, A. 56
Cohn, J. and Tronick, E. 151
Coleridge, S.T. 187, 188, 189, 190
Collins, S. 222
Comte, A. 56
Conran, M. 15
Cooper A.M. 205, 213
Copernicus 48
Crick, F. and Kock, C. 64
Cushman, P. 181

Damasio, A.R. 136
Dante 189
Danziger, K. 193

Darwin, C. 20, 132
Davidson, D. 61, 158, 162, 177n
Dawkins, R. 95n
De Sousa, R. 105–10, 116n, 158
Decker, H. 59
Dennett, D. 62, 67, 70, 88, 89
Descartes, R. 2, 88
Dilman, İ. 10, 11, 99ff
Dilthey, W. 15
Doi, T. 181
Dora (Freud's patient) 223
Dostoyevsky, F. 161
Dr Lydgate (*Middlemarch*) 207
Dumont, L. 181
Dürer, A. 128

Echo 203
Edelson, M. 13, 16n
Eigen, M. 232
Eissler, R. 59, 232–3
Eliot, G. 204, 205, 207
Ellenberger, H.F. 35, 56, 57, 59, 160, 161, 166, 177n, 182, 232
Erdelyi, M. 5
Erikson E. 48, 182, 183
Erwin, E. 12, 13, 14, 16n
Esterson, A. 57
Exner, S. 65
Eysenck, H.J. and Wilson, G. 14

Fairbairn, R. 8
Farrell, B. 13, 225
Fechner, G. 59–60, 61
Fenichel, O. 131n, 195n
Ferenczi, S. 231–2
Fichte, J.G. 36n, 56, 187
Flanagan, O. 5, 57
Flügel, J.C. and West, D. 56
Fodor, J. 66, 70
Fonagy, P. 14
Forrester, J. 15
Foucault, M. 51, 52n, 192, 194
Foulkes, D. 224
Fox, G. 189
Frege, F.L.G. 80, 82, 83, 85, 86, 87
Freud, A. 183, 228–30
Freud E.L. 55
Freud, S. 7, 8, 10, 13, 15, 16n, 22, 27, 28, 30, 31, 33, 34, 36, 40–3, 44, 46, 48, 50, 51, 54, 55, 56, 58, 59, 61, 62, 63, 66, 67, 69, 70, 71, 76, 77, 78, 79, 82, 83, 85, 91, 94, 96, 107, 108, 111, 116n, 121–9, 135, 136, 138, 139, 140, 141–2, 147, 151, 152, 157ff, 199, 204, 205, 213, 219, 220, 221, 223, 226
Freud, S. and Breuer, J. 59, 61
Frijda, N.H. et al. 101, 103

Gaines, A.D. 181, 182
Gardiner, P. 259
Gardner, S. 98, 104, 105, 108, 110–15, 118n, 158, 164, 174, 277n
Gedo, J.E. 14, 233
Gedo, J.E. and Wolf, E. 2
Geissman, C. and Geissman, P. 229
Gergen, K.J. 181, 194
Gillett, G. 5, 76ff
Gilligan, C. 181
Gil-White, E. and Richerson, P. 133, 134
Glover, E. 232
Glymour, C. 16n, 54–5, 65
Goethe, J. 128
Goldberg, S. 153n
Goldman, A.I. 177n
Green, E. 230
Greenberg, J. and Mitchell, S. 43, 45
Greenberg, V.D. 55
Grigg, R. et al. 230
Grinstein, A. 223
Grolnick, S. 183
Grünbaum, A. 12, 13, 16n
Guntrip, H. 8, 174, 175
Gupta, R. 57

Habermas, J. 15, 44
Hacking, I. 61
Haig, D. 152n
Hameroff, S. 66
Hamilton, W.D. 152n
Hamilton Sir William 63
Hardcastle, V.G. 66
Hartmann, H. 48, 59, 171, 173, 176n
Hassin, R.R. and Bargh, J.A. 233
Head, H. 82
Hebb, D.O. 65, 79
Hegel, G.W.F. 36, 42, 56, 187
Helmholtz, H. von 20, 34
Herbart, J.F. 20, 32

Hering, E. 63
Hobbes, T. 42
Hölderlin, J.C.F. 187
Holt, R. 4, 159, 184
Hopkins, J. 7, 132ff, 153n, 162, 163, 172, 173, 177n
Horney K. 184, 205
Hrdy, S.B. 135, 152n, 153n
Hume, D. 48, 56, 88
Husserl, E. 79, 80, 82, 83, 85, 86, 95n

Ikhnaton 123, 124

Jackendoff, Ray 67
Jackson, J.H. 4, 58
Jacoby, R. 195n
James W. 10, 61, 65, 194
Janet, P. 61
Jaques, E. 44
Jaspers, K.T. 77, 86, 92
Johnston, M. 158
Jones, E. 4, 21, 36n, 57
Jung, C. 42, 226

Kafka, F. 201
Kant, I. 2, 3, 10, 20ff, 21, 27, 28, 29, 31, 32, 33, 34, 36n, 37n, 56, 64, 76, 80, 82
Kanzer, M. 5
Kernberg, O. 182, 186
King, P. and Steiner, R. 228, 229, 232
Kirschner, R. 9, 10, 181ff
Kitcher, P. 5, 54, 79, 95n, 158, 159
Klein, D. 195n
Klein G. 15
Klein, M. 3, 40, 41, 43–6, 48, 50, 51, 110, 112, 117n, 135, 146, 150, 166, 228–30
Knight, R. 184
Kohut, H. 10, 11, 16n, 47, 182, 184, 186, 199–203, 205, 207, 210, 212, 213, 214–15, 216, 217, 233
Kohut, H. and Wolf, E.S. 210
Kumin, I. 178n
Kurtz, S. 181

La Rochefoucauld, F. 131n
Lacan, J. 3, 40, 46–9, 50, 51, 52, 90, 91, 92
Lashley, K.S. 65, 67
Lear, J. 2, 117n, 277n
Lehrer, R. 57
Levine, M. 6, 103, 159
Lévi-Strauss, C. 91
Libet, B. 66
Lipiner, S. 57
Lipps, T. 20, 36n, 56, 63, 67
Locke, J. 2, 42, 56, 58, 64, 88
Lothane, Z. 13
Louth, A. 196n
Lovejoy, A.O. 196n
Luborsky, L. and Crits-Christoph, P. 223
Lukes, S. 196n

Mach, E. 36n
Mackay, N. 57
Macmillan, M. 12, 13, 219ff
Macmillan, M. and Swales, P.J. 225
Magee, B. 57
Mahler, M. 182, 195n
Mahler, M. et al. 182, 183
Marcuse, H. 40–3, 44, 51
Marmor, J. 233
Marshall, G. 178n
Marx, K. 42
Marx, O. 5
Masson, J.M. 13, 56
Maudsley, H. 61
Mauss, M. 181, 192
McGinn, B. 196n
McGrath, W.J. 57
McGuire, W. 227
Meissner, W.W. 13
Meltzer, D. 44, 46
Meltzoff, A. 139, 153n
Mesmer, F.A. 222
Meyers, D. 140, 153n
Meynert, T. 20, 36n, 221
Michaelangelo 225
Miller, A. 207, 208
Mitchell, S.A. 166
Mock, D. and Parker, G. 152n
Modell, A.H. and Sacks, M.H. 231
Moore, M. 158
Moraitis, G. 4
Morrison, A.P. 211
Moses 123, 124, 225
Mountcastle, V. 66
Muller, J.P. 48

Nagel, E. 12, 14, 115n
Nagera, H. 230
Narcissus 43, 203–4
Natsoulas, T. 55, 57
Nelson, B. 189
Neu, J. 1, 7
Nietzsche, F. 2, 36, 57, 71n
Nunberg, H. and Federn, E. 69

O'Shaugnessy, B. 177n
Oedipus 231
Ogden, T.H. 8, 166
Olinor, M. 182, 185
Orpheus 43
Osiris 123

Panel on the Ideological Wellsprings of Psychoanalysis 20
Paneth, J. 57
Panksepp, J. 136, 152n
Pappenheim, B. 222
Pasteur, L. 21
Pataki, T. 9, 97, 157ff
Payne, S. 229
Pears, D. 158, 164, 166
Perkell, D.H. and Bullock, T.H. 66
Petocz, A. 178n
Pfaff, D.W. 152n
Phillips, A. 195n
Piaget, J. 194
Plato 2, 10, 24, 157, 216
Plotinus 196n
Popper, K. 14
Pribram, K. 66
Prince, H.J. 61
Proust, M. 204, 213
Pulver, S.E. 210

Rachman, S. 14
Rank, O. 57, 195n, 231–2
Rat Man (Freud's patient) 224
Reich, A. 209
Reichenbach, H. 56
Ribot, A. 61
Rice, W.R. and Holland, B. 152n
Richerson, P. and Boyd, R. 133
Ricoeur, P. 15, 225
Rieke, F. et al. 66
Riviere, J. 44
Roazen, P. 14, 15, 195n
Rorty, A. 98–105, 106, 115n, 158
Rosamond (*Middlemarch*) 204, 205, 206, 207
Rousseau, J.-J. 42, 45
Rustin, M. 44
Rycroft, C. 118n

Sachs, D. 96, 111, 112
Sandler, J. 162
Sandler. J. and Sandler, A.M. 162
Sartre, J.-P. 118n, 202
Sass, L. 195n
Saussure, F. de 90
Schaffer, H.R. 147
Schafter R. 15
Scharff, J. 8
Scharff, D. 8
Schelling, F.W. 36n, 56, 187
Schiller, F. 195n
Schopenhauer, A. 2, 20, 34, 35, 36n, 57, 59, 122, 159
Schore, A.N. 152n, 196n
Schreber, D. 227
Schwartz, J. 1, 2, 17n
Searle, J. 88, 94, 153n
Sher, G. 101, 115n
Silverstein, B. 5, 16n, 57
Simon, B. 51, 230
Simon, B. and Blass, R.B. 231
Smith, D.L. 5. 16n, 54, 55, 56, 57, 60, 63, 64, 158, 162
Sober, E. and Wilson, D.S. 132
Socrates 2, 216
Solms, M. 4
Solms, M. and Saling, M. 65
Solms, M. and Turnbull, O. 152n
Solomon, R.C. 57
Spence, D.P. 224, 225
Spiegelberg, H. 56
Spinoza, B. 56
Spitz, R. 178n
Spitzer, M. 65, 79
Stepansky, P. 195n
Sternberg, C.R. et al. 153n
Stevenson R.L. 161
Stolorow, R.D. 207, 209
Strachey, J. 4
Strawson, P. 62
Strozier, C.B. 232
Sullivan, H.S. 184

Sulloway, F. 57
Szasz, T. 10

Taine, H.A. 61
Tallis, R. 49
Taylor, C. 181, 195n, 196n
Thalberg, I. 158
Timpanaro, S. 224
Tinterow, M.M. 222
Trivers, R. 134, 136, 138, 152n, 153n
Trosman, H. and Simmons, R.D. 21, 36n
Turkle, S. 182

Vassalli, G. 2
da Vinci, Leonardo 128, 169, 174, 225
Von Hartmann, E. 35, 36

Wallace, E. 2, 57
Wallis, R.T. 196n
Walsh, D. 189
Weber, M. 181, 196n
Weil, S. 215, 216
Weiss, F. 224
Westen, D. 230
White, M.T. 205, 208
Whyte, L. 59
Will Ladislaw (*Middlemarch*) 207
Williams, L.P. 57
Winnicott, D. 8, 178n, 182, 183, 185, 186, 195n, 232, 266
Wittgenstein, L. 86, 138
Wollheim, R. 16n, 162, 277n
Wordsworth, W. 187
Wundt, W. 79, 82
Young, C. 37n
Young, C. and Brook, A. 2, 20
Young, J. Z. 95n

Young-Eisendrath, P. and Dawson, T. 228

Subject Index

A priori of phantasy 112
Acceptance 11
Achievement 200
Activation vector 66
Adult reproductive success 138
Affective neuroscience 7
Affects 23
Agencies 166
Agencies, quasi-independent 176
Agency 9, 157ff, 162, 163
Aggression 7, 41, 42, 44, 45, 48, 137, 145, 148
Aggressive assertion 183
Akrasia 9, 158
Alienation 47
Altruism 132, 133
Altruistic provider 137
Altruistic reproductive co-operation 137
Amour propre 209, 210, 217
An sich 56
Analytical psychology 226
Anger 9
Anima 228
Animal magnetism 222
Animism 68, 69, 122, 126
Animus 228
Annihilation 121
Anomalous emotion 104
Anthropomorphism 68
Anti-libidinal ego 177n
Anti-naturalism 56
Anti-realism 91
Aphasia 4
Apperception 22, 27
Aristotelianism 196n
Arrogance 208
Assimilation 145
Associationism 80, 84
Associations 221
Associative techniques 229
Athens 40, 46, 51
Atomism 84, 115
Attachment 148–9, 153n
Attachment emotions 108
attachment theory 7
Authentic emotions 109
authenticity 10, 48, 183, 185, 195n, 200, 201, 202, 205
Autoeroticism 229
Automatised cognitive representations 76
Autonomous person/personhood 187, 192
Autonomy 10, 48, 181ff, 199, 205

Bad objects 145
Bad others 139, 140
Bad them 150
Behaviourism 194
Behmenism 190
beliefs 9, 96, 99, 101, 202
Bias 153n
Biblical narrative 191
Bildes 23
Biodicy 191, 192
Biological determinism 90
Biological empiricism 32
Birth trauma thesis 231, 232
Bodily disequilibrium 136
Bodily/motor sensation 31
Borderline personality 9
Brain 4, 58, 65, 79, 89, 91, 94, 136, 159
Brain processes 16n
Buddhism 192
Buddhist morality 46

Care 44
Caritas 44
Cartesian conception of mind 60
Cartesian tradition 2
Cartesianism 63
Castration 126, 129
Castration anxiety 86, 127
Castration complex 231
Categorical imperative 22, 31
Categories 37n

Categorisation 51
Cathect 30
Cathexes 83, 85
Causal concepts 22
Causal connections 221
Causal interaction 83
Censorship 69, 85
Central ego 177n
Central nervous system 79, 160
Change 96–105, 113
Change, difficulty of 98–105
Character 23, 96, 98
Character disorders 114
Chemical conflict 135
Child development 229
Christian martyrs 215–16
Christian mysticism 190, 196n
Christianity 123
Civilisation 158
Classicism 195n
Cognition 59
Cognitive architecture 54
Cognitive processes 56
Cognitive recognition 92
Cognitive science 3, 4, 5, 54, 64
Cognitive structures 77
Cognitive unconscious 76
Coherent self 47
Cohesiveness of self 208
Common-sense psychology 98, 114, 161
Compassion 45
Compensatory daydream 164
Completeness 194
Computational theories of cognition 79
Concepts 29, 30
Concern 44
Condensation 63
Conflict 8, 9, 132ff, 136, 153n, 165, 167, 175, 199
Connecting assumptions 221
Connection 188
Connectionism 65, 79
Connectionist architecture 65
Connectionist model of mind 5
Conscience 126, 133, 145
Conscious 35
Conscious ego 81
Conscious experience 88
Conscious feelings 87
Conscious mental events 64
Conscious self 165
Conscious states 30
Conscious thought 82, 83, 85
Conscious/unconscious interpretations 8
Consciousness 3, 5, 21, 24, 26, 29, 55, 56, 58, 59, 64–7, 80–3, 207, 220
Conservation of emotions 98, 99
Consolidation 148
Constancy 183, 184
Constitutional dispositions 99
Construction 223–6
Constructions, trustworthiness of 224
Continuity 148, 185
Continuity argument 63
Control 41
Co-operation 136–7, 145
Creation 190
Creative work 46
Creativity 213, 214
Crusades 129
Cultural systems 10
Cybernetic associationism 80

Darwinism 77, 78, 92
Death 7, 41, 43, 121, 193, 213
Death drive instinct 41, 42, 166
Death, fear of 120–1, 125–9
Death wish 127
Deceptive procedures 13
Defence mechanisms 8, 121, 164
Defences 48
Defensive functions 108
Deindividuation 153n
Delusion 7
Demonic possession 160, 161
Denial 200
Deontological theory 25
Depression 146, 161, 201, 204
Depressive guilt 46
Depressive position 9, 45, 113, 150
Description 29
Descriptive unconsciousness 26
Destructiveness 193
Detachment 227
Determining quality 222
Developed self 287
Developmental psychology 7, 132, 147

Diagnosis 51
Dignity 210, 217
Dinka 132
Diremption 170, 171, 174
Disappearance 41
Discipline 51
Discursive skills 89
Discursive stream 89
Disillusionment 125
Disorders of the self 11, 200
Displacement 63, 107
Dispositionalism, Dispositionalist theory 60, 61, 63–4
Dissocationism, Dissociationist theory 60, 61, 62–3
Disturbances of self 203, 213
Divided personality 199
Divided self 199
Divine 190
Division 190
Double conscience 22
Doubling 61
Dream elements 224
Dreams 23, 35, 147, 163, 164, 220, 233
Dreams, interpretation of 223
Drive derivations 34
Drive model (Freud) 8
Drive representatives 29
Drives 31, 32
Driving principles 23
Dualism 4, 5, 16n, 56, 59, 61, 63
Dynamic unconscious 76

Ego 3, 21, 24, 26, 28, 30, 31, 35, 48, 49, 52, 85, 96, 145, 167, 199, 211, 215, 217
Ego functions 23, 28, 48
Ego-ideal 168, 170
Ego instinct 166
Ego instinctual drive 227
Ego psychology 10, 20, 173, 176, 181
Ego weakness 170
Egocentricity 11, 216, 217
Ego-protective mechanisms 86
Eliminativism 5, 69
Emotion 6, 15, 132ff
Emotion, etiology of 96ff
Emotion, learning/unlearning 105–10
Emotional change 98, 101
Emotional command systems 136
Emotional conflict 148
Emotional development 136–9
Emotional disposition 98
Emotional repertoire 97
Emotional response 100, 101
Empathy 9, 11, 213, 232
Empirical developmental psychology 147–8
Empiricism 56, 76
Endogenous Q 24
Enlightenment 130
Enlightenment rationalism 195n
Envy 108, 117n
Epiphenomenalism 57
Equanimity 207, 213
Erlebnis 65
Eros 42, 166
Erotic object 168
Evil 191, 193
Evolution 132ff
Evolutionary biology 4
Evolutionary psychology 132
Evolutionary theory 7, 195n
Evolutionary thought 76
Excitation 136
Existential psychology 196n
Existential-humanistic psychology 184
Existentialism 90
Experience 130
Experiential sensitivity 65
Expressive individualist ideal 188
External objects 175
External reality 227
Extinction 130
Extra-conscious forces 94

Facilitation 65
Faith 3, 216
Fall 190
False consensus 153n
False self 176, 207, 208
Falsification 12
Families 136, 143–5
Families, conflict within 134–6
Fantasy world 227
Father/son rivalry 138
Fear 120
Fear of death 125
Feelings, good/bad 9

Femininity 230
Fidelity in the void 216
Final accounting 12
First principle (the One) 190
Fixed ideas 161
Foetus 135
Folk physics 70
Folk psychology 5, 55, 67–71, 114
Fort-da game 41
Free association 13, 220–2, 230, 233
Free association, reliability/validity 221–2
Free will 184
Freedom 184, 185
Functional differentiation 80
Fundamentalism 130

Geisteswissenschaft 20
Genes 132, 133
Genetic interest 135
Genetic programming 102
Genetic relatedness 134
Genome 134
Genomic conflict 152n
Genomic imprinting 152n
God, rejoining with 190
Gods 44, 51
Good mother 183
Good objects 145
Good self 139, 140, 142
Good us 150
Grand L 91
Grandiosity 47
Gratitude 108, 117n
Group conflict 132–4
Group identification 142
Guilt 42, 45, 126

Hate 43, 46, 51
Healthy mindedness 193
Healthy narcissism 203–9
Helplessness 124
Hermeneutics 15
Hinduism 192
Holism 90
Homosexuality 227
Humanism 3
Humility 211, 217
Humour 213, 214
Hyle 81
Hypercathect 29
Hypnosis 35, 59, 221
Hysteria 61, 221

Id 3, 7, 21, 29, 34–5, 48, 49, 52, 200
Ideal self 168
Idealisation 11
Idealism 44, 46
Identification 8, 45, 139–40, 147, 149, 169, 213, 269
Identity 185, 186, 195n, 200, 202, 221
Illusions 7, 47, 129
Images 23, 47
Imagination 160, 161
Immortality 7, 120, 121–5, 129
Immortals 43
Impermanence 213
Inauthenticity 50, 94
Inbreeding 138
Incomplete self 207, 208
Incorrigible knowledge 60
Independence 217
Independent agency 166
Independent self 232
Indeterminism 219
Individuals 143–5
Individuated self 188
Individuation 182, 183, 186
Infancy, Infant 8, 11, 105, 106, 135, 143, 145–6, 149, 151, 182
Infant attachment 162
Infantile aggression 139
Infantile egotism 137
Infantile life 138
Infantile narcissism 205
Infantile phantasy 104, 110, 111
Infantile totemism 123
Infantilisms 159
Ingroup cohesion 7, 139, 140
Ingroup co-operation 136
Inhibition 136
Innate principles of language 133
Innateness 31, 32
Inner 27
Inner conflict 199
Inner self 186
Inner sense 3, 22, 34
Inner worth 210, 211
Inner/outer world 157
Instincts 7, 8, 92, 178n

Instinct of life/destruction 42
Instinctual drives 227
Instinctual fixations 97
Instinctual response 105
Institute for Psychoanalysis, Chicago 10
Intention 204
Intentional descriptions 173
Intentional habits 103
Intentional psychology 161, 162
Intentional sets 99
Intentional wish-fulfilment 165
Intentionality 16n, 81, 98, 99, 104, 115n
Interactionalism 5, 16n
Internal conflict 142–3, 175
Internal mental structure 8
Internal objects 44, 46
Internalisation 47, 160, 183
Interpretation, indeterminacy of 223–6
Introjection 8, 32, 160, 161
Introjects 23
Introspection 21, 59, 60, 61, 68
Intuition 22, 29, 31, 37n
Inverted projection 204
Irrationality 9, 110–15, 165
Islamic morality 46
Islamism 123

Jerusalem 40, 46, 51
Judaism 123
Judeo-Christian morality 46
Judeo-Christian tradition 44, 181, 190

Kabbalism 190
Kant's model of the mind 2–3
Kant's tripartite model of mind 21

Lack 47, 50
Language 3
Latent dream 224
Law of association 89
Libidinal ego 177n
Libidinal relations 167–8
Libidinal withdrawal 227
Libidinised objects 168
Libido 24, 34, 35, 44, 126, 127, 215, 222, 230
Libido, repression of 226
Life after death 124
Linguistic representation 67
Lipstick experiments 47
Localisationism 65
Lockean tradition 2
Logical empiricism 54
Logical relations 221
Los Angeles Psychoanalytic Association 56
Love 43, 44, 46, 51
Love of God 216
Love of self 203
Love of wisdom 216
Luck 207

Magical thinking 118n
Magnetising dispositions 99, 100, 101, 103
Maladaptive emotion 102, 103
Manque 47, 50
Masochism 167, 217
Masturbation 224, 230
Masturbatory phantasy 164
Materialism 4, 5, 56, 58, 59, 64
Materialist metaphysic 191
Maternal deprivation 152n
Maternal identification 178n
Maternal investment 135, 145
Mature narcissism 214
Me/not-me 183
Mechanistic materialism 20
Méconniassance 47
Melancholia 126
Memory 31, 64, 65, 91
Memory trace 30
Mental contents 157
Mental functions 54
Mentalese 66
Merciless violence 145, 151
Mesmerism 59
Metanarratives 52
Metaphysics 55
Metapsychology 4, 50, 67–71, 162, 171, 182
Mind 2, 3, 4, 32, 37n, 40, 41, 56, 58, 64, 69, 81, 84, 93, 136, 159, 191, 220
Mind, Freud's model of 20
Mind, moral model of 46
Mind, theological model 43–6
Mind, partitive 9

Mind, romantic depiction of 10
Mind–body problem 55, 57–9
Mirror neurons 139, 153n
Mirror stage of development 47
Mirror-image misperceptions 139
Mirroring response 47
Misfortune 193
Mnemic images 30
Modernity 49
Moi 47
Monism 5
Monotheism 123
Moral aggression 142
Moral anger 133
Moral categories 44
Moral conflict 142
Moral dignity 212
Moral evil 191
Moral rage 140
Moral reason 3
Morality 22, 31, 32, 44, 45, 120, 132–4, 158
Mother as object 229
Motivation 116n, 132
Motor representations 71n
Motor speech images 30
Multiple personality 22
Myelination 137
Mysticism 189

Narcissism 9, 11, 47, 122, 137, 158, 168, 169, 199ff
Narcissism, higher forms of 212–16
Narcissism, transformation of 214
Narcissistic behaviour disorder 210
Narcissistic delusion 215
Narcissistic disorders 11
Narcissistic disturbances 203, 208, 209, 216
Narcissistic injury 49
Narcissistic personality disorder 10
Narcissistic projection 32
Narratives 224–6
Naturalistic fallacy 44
Nature 191
Naturphilosophie 20
Needs 8
Neo-associationism 79
Neo-Cartesian metaphysics 60
Neocortex 78
Neoplatonism 189, 190, 196n
Nervous system 4, 23, 64, 67
Neural activity 89
Neural networks 93
Neural prototypes 172
Neural pruning 137
Neural stream 89
Neural vectors 65
neuro-anatomy 78
Neurobiology 5, 79, 173
Neurocognitive association 93
Neurocognitive stream 94
Neurocognitive Ucs 92
Neurocognitive vector transformation 89
Neurological unconscious 76ff
Neurology 10, 92, 195n
Neuronal theory 79
Neurophysiological dispositions 60
Neuropsychological system 69
Neuroscience 3, 4, 5, 7, 58, 59, 77, 132
Neurotic emotions 109, 110
Neuroticism 9
Nirvana 41, 123
Noemata 81
Noesis 81
Non-being 41, 42
Non-conscious 26, 59
Non-conscious information processing 54
Non-conscious representations 76
Non-self-regarding love 137
Noumena 26, 57
Noumenal 3, 34
Noumenal psyche 33
Noumenal self 24
Noumenalism 21
Nuer 132

Object cathexes 37n
Object love 205
Object presentation 84
Object relations 97, 157ff, 160, 229
Object relations folk psychology 161
Object relations, internalised 9
Object relations theory 8, 9, 10, 43, 181–2, 266
Object representations 66
Object-catheses 23
Objects 8, 45

Objects of emotion 137
Obliteration 121
Obsessive-compulsive neuroses 6
Occam's razor 62
Occurrent emotion 105
Oedipus complex 25, 86, 126, 138, 200, 213, 228, 230, 231
Omega system 26
Oneness 188
Ontogeny 90
Oral-sadistic sub-stage, infantile 228
Organismic homeostasis 136
Other 149–52
Outbreeding 138
Outer sense 22
Outgroup aggression 7, 139
Outgroup conflict 136, 140
Outgroup violence 143

Pain 7
Paradigm scenario 105, 106, 107, 111
Paradoxes of irrationality 158
Parallelism 5
Paranoia 44
Paranoic traits 146
Paranoid-schizoid position 8, 9, 45, 113, 150
Parapraxes 220
Parental imago 145, 151
Parental investment 7, 134–6, 137–9
Parenting 148
Partition set 171
Partitive conceptions of mind 9, 157, 176
Pathological liar 209
Pathological narcissism 205
Pcpt.-Cs 27, 28, 34
Pcs 85
Penis envy 230
Perception 23, 27, 28, 29, 30, 33, 34, 64, 66, 99, 116n
Percepts 29
Perceptual neurons 64
Persecution 45
Personation 175, 176
Perversions 114
Phallic stage 228
Phantasies 23, 45, 46, 110–15, 136, 148, 153n, 160, 163, 174-5, 229
Phenomena 22, 26, 32
Phenomenal consciousness 65
Phenomenology 77, 80–3, 104
Phi system 27
Philosophical anthropology 16n
Philosophy of mind 3–5, 54ff
Physiological conflict 135
Pietism 196n
Pity 45, 50
Placebo 12
Placenta 135
Placenta genome 138
Platonism 196n
Pleasure 7
Pleasure principle 41, 78, 122
Polypsychic conception 161
Polytheism 123
Positive regard 11
Positivism 20, 56
Postmodern mind 46
Postmodernism 3, 40, 49, 51, 52
Post-romanticism 189
Post-traumatic stress disorder 126
Pre-birth memory 233
Preconceptual content 76
Preconscious, Preconsciousness 24, 26, 27, 69
Pre-reflection 85
Primal wound 87
Primary maternal preoccupation 186
Primary process 28
Principle of association 79, 92
Principle of substitution 41
Processes 23, 85
Project, the 61, 62, 71n
Projection 8, 23, 36n, 107, 139–40, 140–2, 143, 144
Projective identification 8, 153n
Propositional attitudes 172
Protective systems 166
Protestantism, Protestant tradition 191, 198
Proto-content 88, 91
Proto-conversation 149
Pseudoscience 12, 13, 15
Psi system 27
Psyche 3, 20, 21, 22–4, 36, 76, 77, 78, 82, 85, 87, 90, 91, 187
Psyche, Kant's tripartite model 22
Psyche, structure of 31–2
Psyche-neural network 92

Psychiatry 10
Psychic energy 226, 227
Psychic phenomena 4
Psychic reality 160
Psychic states 31
Psychic structure 24, 171
Psychoanalytic autonomy 10
Psychoanalytic developmental psychology 181
Psychoanalytic discourse 181ff
Psychoanalytic interpretation 224
Psychoanalytic knowledge 7–8, 40, 50, 51, 77, 93, 219, 233-4
Psychoanalytic knowledge, post-Freudian 9–11
Psychoanalytic method 221
Psychoanalytic methodology, challenges to 11–16, 219ff
Psychoanalytic thought 79
Psychoanalytic translation 224
Psycho-historical parallelism 191
Psychological birth 182
Psychologism 212
Psychology 57, 58, 76
Psychophysical activity 60
Psycho-physical interactionism 57, 58
Psycho-physical parallelism 57, 58, 93
Psychophysics 195n
Psychosexual development 32
Punishment 133, 140, 145, 267
Punitive mother 176
Pure reason 37n
Puritanism 196n

Qualia 30, 65, 66, 67, 71n
Quantum theory 70

Rage 138
Rapprochement phase 182
Rational choice 219
Rationalism 32, 56
Rationality 10, 183, 184, 186
Reality 122
Reality principle 43, 78
Reason 22, 26, 31, 40, 46, 130, 191
Recapitulation 80
Reconnection 188
Redemption 190, 201
Redemptive reconnection 191
Reductionism 5, 213
Reflection 51, 80–3
Reflective self-scrutiny 94
Regression 124, 186, 209, 212, 227
Regulative principles 26
Reincarnation 123
Relationships 8
Religion 2, 6–7, 61, 121–5, 126, 158
Religious doctrine 189
Religious wars 130
Reparation 3, 40, 43, 45, 46, 50
Reparative morality 45
Representations 22, 23, 24, 35, 37n, 163
Repression 8, 30, 48, 64, 121, 224, 227
Reproductions 107
Reproductive co-operation 136
Reproductive imagination 31
Reproductive rivalry 137
Reproductive thought 31
Resentment 102
Resistance 65, 167, 221
Respect 211
Return 41
Romantic idealism 36n
Romanticism 189, 195n
Ruptures 185, 188

Sadism 167
Salvation 3, 40, 43, 190
Sameness 37n, 185, 227, 228
Schreber case 21
Science 54, 122
Seeking system 136
Selection pressure 133
Self 9, 27, 40, 46, 48, 49, 193, 199ff, 205
Self, cohesive 10
Self, development of 182
Self, images of 139–40
Self, integrated 10
Self, ossification of 96ff
Self, relations 208
Self-abasement 1264
Self-absorption 205
Self-analysis 4, 114
Self-appeasement 264
Self-assertion 10
Self-assertion 183, 185, 187
Self-awareness 31
Self-censure 94

Self-change 114
Self-confidence 11
Self-consciousness 27, 28, 190
Self-consolation 164
Self-control 48, 52
Self-creation 93
Self-deception 9, 13, 96, 116n, 158, 164, 207–8
Self-defects 233
Self-direction 48
Self-esteem 11, 140–2, 144, 200, 201, 205, 209–12, 217
Self-esteem, regulation of 209
Self-esteem, stabilisation of 209
Self-honesty 208
Selfhood 190, 194
Self-image 139
Self-love 11, 169, 203, 206, 211, 212, 215, 217
Self-objects 182
Self-observation 167
Self-personation 170
Self-preservation 126, 127, 227
Self-psychology 8, 10, 11, 182, 199–203, 217
Self-regard 211
Self-reliance 10, 183, 184, 186, 189
Self-respect 210, 217
Self-satisfaction 204
Self-seeking 130
Self-serving biases 139
Self-solicitude 165, 176
Self-sufficiency 169
Self-understanding 49, 59, 162
Self-worth 11
Sense 28, 29, 32, 33
Sensibility 22, 28, 37n
Sentimentality 50
Separate identity 182
Separate selfhood 188
Separateness 185, 186, 194
Separation 190
Separation distress 147
Separation of soul 190
Separation-individuation process 183
Servility 210, 211
Sex 42
Sexual instinct 10, 166
Sexual megalomania 142
Sexual metabolism 142
Shell shock 126
Sibling rivalry 135
Significant cause 99, 100, 101, 103, 105, 116n
Significant immediate cause 100
Significant other 8
Social constructionism 194
Social psychology 7, 132
Social referencing 147
Society for Positivist Philosophy 56
Soma 22, 32
Sorrow 193
Soul 204
Speculative superstructure 70
Spiritual being 130
Spirituality 44
Splits 185
Splitting 8, 9, 30, 61, 175
Stable personality 207
Stoicism 196n
Strange situation 148, 153n
Stranger anxiety 147
Structuralism 90
Structures 166
Subconscious 59, 61
Subconscious forces 77
Subcortical mechanisms of emotion 138
Subcortical mechanisms of motivation 136
Subcortical rage 151
Subcortical systems of motivation 146
Subintentional causation 177n
Subintentionality 163
Sublimation 230
Sublimation of sex 212, 214
Subliminal self 59
Subpersonal entities 174
Subpersonal functional systems 174
Subpersonal neural systems 172
Subpersonal organisation 172
Subpersonal systems 173
Sub-personalities 160
Substitutive satisfaction 163
Success 200
Suffering 181ff, 213
Suggestion 12, 219, 221, 222, 233
Superconscious 59
Superego 3, 21, 24, 26, 32, 40, 42, 126, 145, 159, 167, 200, 214, 228

Supernatural 192
Superstate 42
Supra-individual norms 83
Synaptic growth 137
Syntactic relations 79
Synthesis 21, 22, 28
System Cs 27
Systemic errors 139

Tacit knowledge 76
Talion morality 45
Teche 2
Telos 10
Thanatos 42
Theological model of mind 43, 44
Theory of mind (Freud) 9
Time-limitation 231
Todestrieb 41, 42, 43, 51, 52
Token identity 5
Topographical account of mind 177n
Topographical unconscious 161
Totemism 123
Tragedy 181ff
Tragic limitation 189
Tragic-transcendent vision 194
Transcendence 181ff
Transcendent reconnection 188
Transcendental aesthetic 37n
Transcendental deduction 37n
Transcendental dialectic 37n
Transcendental idealism 56
Transference 105, 107, 160, 222, 223, 228, 231
Transference emotions 106, 108, 109
Transference love 108
Transition 121, 137
Transitional stage 182
Trauma 91
True self 176, 195n, 201, 207

Ucs 83, 85, 86–92
Unconscious 3, 5, 14, 21, 24, 26, 30, 33, 34, 43, 56, 59–62, 79, 92, 125, 128
Unconscious agency 165
Unconscious awareness 87
Unconscious forces 48
Unconscious intentional agency 163, 164, 165
Unconscious knowledge 125–9
Unconscious life 88
Unconscious memory 70
Unconscious pathological processes 220
Unconscious phantasies 114
Unconscious practical reasoning 177n
Unconscious psyche 34
Understanding 22, 26, 27, 28, 31
Unhealthy narcissism 203–9
University of Vienna 10
Unmodified narcissism 214, 215
Unpleasure principle 32
Unselfish concern 44
Unworthiness 211
Us/them representations 149–52
Use–mention confusion 127
Utopia 40, 42

Verbal residues 71n
Verification 12
Vienna 4
Vienna Circle 55, 56
Vorstellung 22, 23

Watjanti fertility rite 226–7
Weltanschauung 32, 55, 57, 58
Wholeness 47
Wiener Kreis 55
Will 35, 159
Wisdom 213, 214, 215, 216
Wish fulfilment 9, 162, 163, 164
Wishful thinking 121, 125, 130
Wish-fulfilment 7, 158
Within-group projection 142
Worthlessness 11, 200

Ø system 28
Ψ neurons 65, 68
Ω system 66, 69
Φ neurons 65